EMPIRE OF ICE
AND STONE

ALSO BY BUDDY LEVY

Labyrinth of Ice: The Triumphant and Tragic Greely Polar Expedition

No Barriers: A Blind Man's Journey to Kayak the Grand Canyon

Geronimo: Leadership Strategies of an American Warrior

River of Darkness: Francisco Orellana's Legendary Voyage of Death and Discovery Down the Amazon

Conquistador: Hernán Cortés, King Montezuma, and the Last Stand of the Aztecs

American Legend: The Real-Life Adventures of David Crockett

Echoes on Rimrock: In Pursuit of the Chukar Partridge

EMPIRE OF ICE AND STONE

THE DISASTROUS AND HEROIC VOYAGE OF THE *KARLUK*

BUDDY LEVY

ST. MARTIN'S
PRESS
NEW YORK

First published in the United States by St. Martin's Press, an imprint of St. Martin's Publishing Group

EMPIRE OF ICE AND STONE. Copyright © 2022 by Buddy Levy. All rights reserved. Printed in the United States of America. For information, address St. Martin's Publishing Group, 120 Broadway, New York, NY 10271.

www.stmartins.com

NOTE TO READER: The images in the included photographic inserts—and particularly their captions—contain spoilers. Some readers may wish to finish the book before viewing the images.

Endpaper credits: Front: Courtesy of Library and Archives Canada.
Back: Courtesy of the Library of Congress

Map by Jeffrey L. Ward

The Library of Congress Cataloging-in-Publication Data is available upon request.

ISBN 978-1-250-27444-1 (hardcover)
ISBN 978-1-250-27445-8 (ebook)

Our books may be purchased in bulk for promotional, educational, or business use. Please contact your local bookseller or the Macmillan Corporate and Premium Sales Department at 1-800-221-7945, extension 5442, or by email at MacmillanSpecialMarkets@macmillan.com.

First Edition: 2022

10 9 8 7 6 5 4 3 2 1

*For my grandson, Luke, who shares with me
a love of the outdoors and wild things*

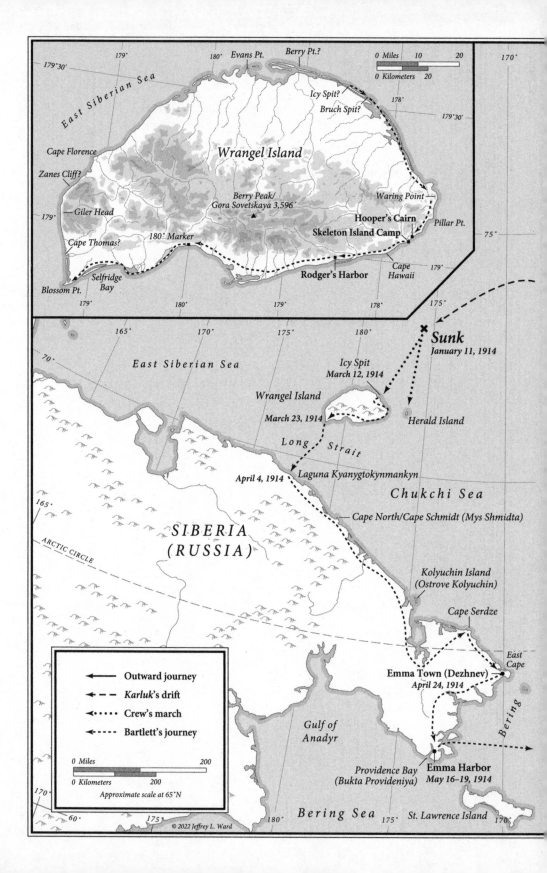

East Siberian Sea

179°30′   179°   180°   Evans Pt.   Berry Pt.?   170°

0 Miles   10   20
0 Kilometers   20

Icy Spit?
Bruch Spit?   178°

179°30′

Wrangel Island

Cape Florence

Zanes Cliff?

Giler Head

Berry Peak/
Gora Sovetskaya 3,596′   Waring Point

Cape Thomas?   180° Marker   Hooper's Cairn   Pillar Pt.

Skeleton Island Camp   75°

Selfridge
Bay   179°

Blossom Pt.   Rodger's Harbor   Cape
Hawaii

179°   180°   179°   178°   175°

× Sunk
January 11, 1914

Icy Spit
March 12, 1914

East Siberian Sea   180°

Wrangel Island

March 23, 1914   0   Herald Island

Long   Strait

April 4, 1914   Laguna Kyanygtokynmankyn

Chukchi Sea

Cape North/Cape Schmidt (Mys Shmidta)

165°

ARCTIC CIRCLE   SIBERIA
(RUSSIA)

Kolyuchin Island
(Ostrove Kolyuchin)

Cape Serdze

East
Cape

Emma Town (Dezhnev)
April 24, 1914

Outward journey

Karluk's drift

Crew's march

Bartlett's journey

Gulf of
Anadyr

Providence Bay
(Bukta Provideniya)   Emma Harbor
May 16–19, 1914

0 Miles   200
0 Kilometers   200
Approximate scale at 65°N

60°   175°   180°   Bering Sea   175°   St. Lawrence Island   170°

© 2022 Jeffrey L. Ward

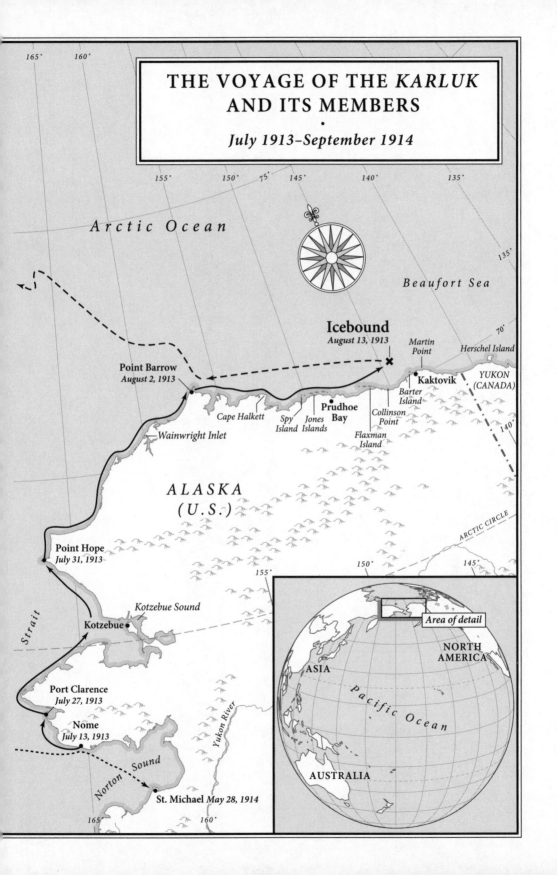

THE VOYAGE OF THE *KARLUK* AND ITS MEMBERS

·

July 1913–September 1914

165°   160°

Arctic Ocean

155°   150°   75°   145°   140°   135°

135°

Beaufort Sea

Icebound
August 13, 1913

Martin
Point

Herschel Island

70°

Point Barrow
August 2, 1913

Kaktovik

Barter
Island

YUKON
(CANADA)

Cape Halkett   Spy   Jones   **Prudhoe**   Collinson
Island Islands   **Bay**   Point

Wainwright Inlet

Flaxman
Island

140°

ALASKA
(U.S.)

ARCTIC CIRCLE

Point Hope
July 31, 1913

155°   150°   145°

Kotzebue Sound

Kotzebue

Strait

Port Clarence
July 27, 1913

Nome
July 13, 1913

Area of detail

NORTH
AMERICA

ASIA

Pacific Ocean

Yukon River

Norton Sound

St. Michael *May 28, 1914*

AUSTRALIA

165°   160°

CONTENTS

THE COMPANY OF
THE *KARLUK*

CREW MEMBERS (AND AGE AT TIME OF
EXPEDITION DEPARTURE IN JUNE 1913)

Robert Abram Bartlett, captain and master mariner (37)

Alexander "Sandy" Anderson, first officer (22)

Charles Barker, second officer (20s)

John Munro, chief engineer (30s)

Robert Williamson, second engineer (36)

John Brady, seaman (20s)

George Breddy, fireman (20s)

Ernest "Charlie" Chafe, messroom boy (19)

Edmund "Ned" Lawrence Golightly (a.k.a. Archie King), seaman (20s)

Fred Maurer, fireman (21)

Stanley Morris, seaman (26)

Robert Templeman, cook and steward (29)

Hugh "Clam" Williams, seaman (20s)

John "Jack" Hadley, carpenter (57)

THE SCIENTIFIC MEMBERS

Vilhjalmur Stefansson, expedition leader (33)

Diamond Jenness, anthropologist (27)

Burt McConnell, secretary (24)

George H. Wilkins, photographer (24)

Henri Beuchat, anthropologist (34)

Alistair Forbes Mackay, surgeon (35)

William Laird McKinlay, magnetician and meteorologist (24)

George Malloch, geologist (33)

Bjarne Mamen, assistant topographer (22)

James Murray, oceanographer (46)

INUIT (ESKIMO) MEMBERS

Pauyuraq "Jerry," hunter (20s)

Asecaq "Jimmy," hunter (20s)

Kataktovik, hunter (19)

Kuraluk, hunter (late 20s)

Kiruk "Auntie," seamstress, wife of Kuraluk (late 20s)

Qagguluk "Helen," daughter of Kuraluk and Kiruk (8)

Mugpi "Ruth," daughter of Kuraluk and Kiruk (3)

Nigeraurak, ship's cat (less than 1 year old)

STEFANSSON'S CARIBOU HUNTING PARTY—
DEPARTED CGS *KARLUK* SEPTEMBER 20, 1913

Vilhjalmur Stefansson, expedition leader (33)

Diamond Jenness, anthropologist (27)

Burt McConnell, secretary (24)

George H. Wilkins, photographer (24)

Pauyuraq "Jerry," hunter (20s)

Asecaq "Jimmy," hunter (20s)

ADVANCE SHORE PARTY—DEPARTED SHIPWRECK CAMP
JANUARY 21, 1914

Bjarne Mamen, assistant topographer (22) (initially led Shore Party
but returned)

Alexander "Sandy" Anderson, first officer (22)

Charles Barker, second officer (20s)

Edmund "Ned" Lawrence Golightly (a.k.a. Archie King), seaman (20s)

John Brady, seaman (20s)

PARTY SEEKING LAND VIA "MAN-HAULING" SLEDS—
DEPARTED SHIPWRECK CAMP FEBRUARY 6, 1914

Alistair Forbes Mackay, surgeon (35)

James Murray, oceanographer (46)

Henri Beuchat, anthropologist (34)

Stanley Morris, seaman (26)

WRANGEL ISLAND PARTY—DEPARTED SHIPWRECK CAMP
FEBRUARY 19–20, 1914

Robert Abram Bartlett, captain and master mariner (37)

William Laird McKinlay, magnetician and meteorologist (24)

Bjarne Mamen, assistant topographer (22)

Kataktovik, hunter (19)

Robert Templeman, cook and steward (29)

Kuraluk, hunter (late 20s)

Kiruk "Auntie," seamstress, wife of Kuraluk (late 20s)

Qagguluk "Helen," daughter of Kuraluk and Kiruk (8)

Mugpi "Ruth," daughter of Kuraluk and Kiruk (3)

John "Jack" Hadley, carpenter (57)

John Munro, chief engineer (30s)

Robert Williamson, second engineer (36)

George Breddy, fireman (20s)

Fred Maurer, fireman (21)

George Malloch, geologist (33)

Hugh "Clam" Williams, seaman (20s)

Ernest "Charlie" Chafe, messroom boy (19)

TIME LINE OF RELEVANT ARCTIC EXPLORATION, EXPEDITIONS, AND DISASTERS*

982   Erik the Red explores Greenland and becomes its first permanent settler.

1497   John Cabot explores the Grand Banks fishing grounds off Labrador and Newfoundland and claims the territory for England.

1594–97   Willem Barents searches for the Northeast Passage, wintering over at Novaya Zemlya in 1596–97.

1610–11   Henry Hudson searches for the Northwest Passage, wintering at Hudson Bay. His crew mutinies, setting Hudson adrift along with his son and seven men. They are never seen again.

1670   Hudson's Bay Company is founded.

1778   Captain James Cook attempts a maritime route through the Arctic to the Pacific Ocean, crossing the Chukchi Sea. The voyage is blocked by sea ice near Icy Cape, Alaska.

1829–33   Captain John Ross explores the Canadian Arctic and becomes the first European to reach the north magnetic pole.

1845–48   Sir John Franklin and Captain Francis Crozier sail HMS

---

* For an even more comprehensive time line, see "The Arctic: Exploration Timeline" at Woods Hole Oceanographic Institution: http://polardiscovery.whoi.edu/arctic/1594.html.

Terror and HMS *Erebus* into the Arctic, searching for the Northwest Passage. The ships are trapped in ice, and 129 expedition members are lost. After many decades and some forty expeditions searching for the lost ships, in 2014 and 2016 the two ships are found, solving a 170-year-old mystery.

1878   Adolf Erik Nordenskiöld successfully completes the first confirmed navigation of the Northeast Passage in SS *Vega*.

1879   Lieutenant Commander George Washington De Long, in USS *Jeannette*, attempts to reach the North Pole. His ship is trapped in ice near Wrangel and Herald Islands in Chukchi Sea and beset for two winters until crushed by the ice. Some twenty members of the crew, including De Long, die of exposure and starvation trying to reach land.

1881–84   First Lieutenant Adolphus Greely of the Fifth United States Cavalry leads Lady Franklin Bay Expedition, setting a record for Farthest North. Eighteen men die on the expedition and rescuers discover signs of cannibalism.

1888   Norwegian Fridtjof Nansen attempts to reach the North Pole on *Fram*. Ship trapped in ice, drifts for thirty-five months, and breaks Greely's Farthest North record.

1903–6   Roald Amundsen navigates the Northwest Passage in his ship *Gjøa*.

1907–9   Dr. Frederick Cook claims to reach the North Pole on April 21, 1908. His claim is disputed.

1907–9   Robert Peary reaches the North Pole on April 6, 1909. Captain Robert Bartlett helms SS *Roosevelt* and makes it within 150 miles of the North Pole, but Peary asks him to return to the *Roosevelt*. Peary's claim, disputed by some, is recognized by the National Geographic Society.

1912   RMS *Titanic* strikes an iceberg and sinks four hundred miles south of Newfoundland, losing more than 1,500 passengers.

1913   The Canadian Arctic Expedition, billed as the most ambitious Arctic scientific expedition in history, departs Canada for undiscovered lands.

Call it love of adventure if you will . . . for as long as there is a square mile of the old earth's surface that is unexplored, man will want to seek out that spot and find out all about it and bring back word of what he finds.

—Captain Robert A. Bartlett

An adventure is a sign of incompetence.

—Vilhjalmur Stefansson

EMPIRE OF ICE
AND STONE

1

BIRTH OF AN EXPLORER

Seattle Daily Times, *September 9, 1912*

AMERICAN EXPLORER DISCOVERS LOST TRIBE OF WHITES,
DESCENDANTS OF LEIF ERICKSSON

The Sun *(New York City), September 10, 1912*

BLOND ESKIMO STORY CONFIRMED!

IN EARLY SEPTEMBER 1912, A SINEWY, SUN-SEARED, ELFISH-LOOKING
man disembarked a steamer at the Port of Seattle with stunning news: He'd
encountered a previously unknown tribe of red-haired, blue-eyed, light-
skinned "Eskimos" of Scandinavian origin who'd never seen another white
person.* He also claimed that he'd met about a thousand Native people with
blond eyebrows and beards, who were taller than other Eskimos, suggesting
a mixture of European and Eskimo blood. The news of the "discovery" was
met with awe and wonder among the global public—and deep curiosity,
excitement, and intrigue among the world's scientific community.

The man telling the story of this spectacular find—one journalist sen-
sationally ranked it "next in importance only to the discovery of the lost

---

* Although I prefer the term Inuit (or other, even more accurate geographically specific and
preferred regional nomenclature), I have in certain instances opted to use the outdated term
Eskimo because it was the expression universally accepted during the period this book covers.

tribes of Israel"—was an Icelandic American named Vilhjalmur Stefansson. He was a daring explorer and ethnologist who had just returned from a four-year odyssey roving about North America's Arctic coastal regions, exploring, mapping, and living off the land and among the Native peoples he encountered around Coronation Gulf and Victoria Island. Stefansson's 1908–12 Arctic Expedition, which had been sponsored by the American Museum of Natural History, was a resounding scientific success. He and his partner, Dr. Rudolph Anderson, had safely returned with a remarkable haul of zoological and ethnological collections, but it was Stefansson's story of the lost tribes—alleged Norse descendants of the legendary Leif Eriksson—that fired the public imagination.

Of his first meeting with these people, Stefansson proclaimed, "That morning . . . I knew I was standing face to face with an important scientific discovery." But there was something else he knew: the story was gaining traction, garnering an audience, and—perhaps most important—the "discovery" was making him famous. Spurred by his initial recounting and a number of highly imaginative journalists' embellishments, the narrative grew: Descendants of the great Erik the Red, who had landed on Greenland in the late tenth century, had managed to make their way to Canada, where they traveled west, intermarried with Indigenous peoples, and survived. Using stone points and local copper for arrows and spearheads, living off seals, walrus, and caribou, they'd flourished in one of the last unexplored and unmapped regions on earth. Their language, Stefansson said, resembled Icelandic, a kind of Scandinavian-Eskimo dialect. It was all astounding.

What Stefansson did not immediately tell anyone as he headed straight for New York to write up his official reports and meet with his patrons at the American Museum of Natural History was that the tale of the Blond Eskimos was neither entirely new nor entirely his own. But he wasn't worried about that just now. The exact details of the Blond Eskimo narrative would work themselves out over time. For now, let the public revel in it and wonder. He would allow the story to resonate and grow, and meanwhile, he would use it to help bolster a grand and ambitious new plan:

to return to the Arctic as soon as possible, with the largest contingent of scientists ever assembled on a polar voyage.

Vilhjalmur Stefansson was in many ways—even after returning from nearly a half decade in the polar north—a rather unlikely looking Arctic explorer. Though blue eyed and of Icelandic descent, at thirty-three he did not possess the stunning Nordic handsomeness of, say, Fridtjof Nansen or the wizened, craggy, leather-skinned appearance of either Roald Amundsen or Robert Peary. Stefansson was slight, even diminutive, with a foppish swale of curly dark hair, but there was a fire in his veins and heart that belied his unimposing stature. He was a knot of sinew and dreams and bravado.

Stefansson was the product of a pioneering family, one accustomed to daily toil outdoors and subsistence living as well as tragedy and disaster. His parents had emigrated from Iceland to Manitoba, Canada, in 1876, settling in a log cabin on the west shore of Lake Winnipeg after two long years of nomadic, hardscrabble existence. But soon after they had cleared forest and begun farming, a great flood swept away most of their cattle and all their hay crop. Spring followed, bringing famine and smallpox and taking two of their young children, a son and a daughter. The infant Vilhjalmur, born William in 1879 just before the flood,* somehow managed to survive, and the bereft Stefanssons left Manitoba, traveling south by ox wagon for the prairies of the Dakota Territory in the United States.

There, in low, timbered country, they built another log cabin, where little Willie—as he was called by his mother and schoolmates—spent the first formative ten years of his life. They farmed the short growing season and spent the long cold winters reading scripture and the Icelanders' sagas by dim tallow candles and fish oil lights. At school Willie Stefansson began reading ravenously in English, though the library offerings at the small schoolhouse were scant. As he put it, "There were never enough

---

* He was born William, nicknamed Willie, and graduated to Bill in his teens. As a junior in college, he legally changed his name, as he put it, "to the Old World Vilhjalmur," as a proud nod to his Icelandic heritage. In later life, intimates called him Stef.

books in our library. This, I feel sure, was largely what made me yearn for more."

Blessed with a clever, active mind and a voracious appetite for learning, Stefansson enrolled at the State University of North Dakota at Grand Forks in his late teens. There, he developed a chameleonlike character he would deploy when needed for the rest of his life, the ability to shape-shift for his own ends. "I am what I want to be," he is quoted as saying. He discovered that being bookish and scholarly impressed his teachers but not his classmates. As a result, because he craved adoration and friendship, he began to "study in secret and loaf in public. As a further refinement, I began to give wrong answers in class even when I knew the correct ones. Immediately, I gained new friends." Even at a young age, he came to understand the power of deception and perception—of what others thought of him—and he manipulated the truth to suit his own purposes. He was learning, as Dale Carnegie later put it, "how to win friends and influence people," whatever the cost.

Stefansson performed well in school, working to pay his way with summer employment like "grubbing"—digging up tree stumps, roots, and rocks to prepare land for plowing—and even hiring on as a cowhand and working cattle drives. On the range, he lived in makeshift haylofts or camped under the stars on the plains and learned to subsist on a diet almost entirely of sowbelly bacon.

Back at college, he dabbled in poetry, even publishing a few poems in the campus magazine. Two events soon altered the trajectory of his life. First, he joined the debate team and won a prize for best individual debater, an achievement that not only earned him a ten-dollar prize but made both the local papers and regional ones from Minneapolis to Winnipeg. His victory confirmed what he'd already sensed: that he had a knack for persuasion. It also garnered him a trip on his first railcar, for he was asked to represent his college at an International Conference of Liberal Religions in Boston. There, he met and apparently impressed a man named William Wallace Fenn, a professor of theology at Harvard.

The second seminal event was expulsion (for excessive absences) from the State University of North Dakota in his junior year. Although he'd excelled in his coursework, Stefansson had missed three consecutive weeks of the term. His explanation was that a high school educator in Grand Forks had needed an emergency operation, and Stefansson, who had done plenty of tutoring in high school and college, offered to fill in since the pay was excellent. But the college president's hands were tied. Rules were rules, and he needed to set an example to all students lest they, too, become habitual truants. The other students admired and looked up to Stefansson; his magnetic personality influenced them greatly, and it simply would not do for them to think that they could miss weeks at a time with no consequences. Of his expulsion Stefansson later said, with a matter-of-factness that underscored his natural ability to instantly adapt to an unexpected situation, "I was given three days to remove myself from the campus." The result was that Stefansson immediately applied to and was accepted at the University of Iowa, where he would finish his bachelor's degree within a year.

Diploma in hand, he began considering the next chapter in his life. Things happened fast for Stefansson; he moved seamlessly through the world, transitioning from one phase to the next with ease, and he was never idle. He had briefly contemplated life as a poet—devouring nearly all the great English poets in numerous languages (including Icelandic and German)—but after reading adventurous tales of explorers, he experienced an epiphany. As he put it, "There is not only the poetry of words but a poetry in deeds. Magellan's voyage rounded out a magnificent conception as fully and finally as ever did a play of Shakespeare's. A law of nature is an imperishable poem." Stefansson had developed a burgeoning interest in the study of anthropology as well. Just before graduating, he had received a letter from William Wallace Fenn asking if he would come to Harvard on a fully paid fellowship. There was one hitch: Fenn wanted him to enroll in the Harvard Divinity School to prepare him for life as a Unitarian clergyman.

Stefansson's mother had wanted him to be a clergyman, too. But then, as now, he had other plans. He sought constant movement, propulsion. In reading about the curriculum at Harvard Divinity School, he noticed that the sciences possessed three main subdivisions: physical anthropology, ethnology, and folklore. Stefansson believed that religion was folklore. He took out his pen and scribed a letter to Fenn, thanking him for the offer but explaining that he did not think he was suited for the ministry. He wondered, however, whether they might allow him to study religion as a branch of anthropology? Would they finance his study of religion as an aspect of folklore?

It was a long shot, and he doubted that they'd go for it. But he received an immediate positive reply, and just two days after graduating from Iowa, he was on his way to enroll at Harvard. His skills of persuasion had worked for him once again.

At Harvard, Stefansson took a position as a doctoral student. He wrote vigorously, even publishing an article on, as he summarized it, "how the Norsemen discovered Greenland about nine hundred years ago, and how they were the first Europeans who ever saw Eskimos." His oratory skills earned him a teaching assistantship, but his time at Harvard was mired in some controversy. He borrowed money from undergraduates and became involved in a scandal for selling exam questions to students. In the end, his mind was too restless for teaching, and he determined to conduct anthropological field research in tropical Africa. For two years he read every book available on Africa, and eventually managed to get himself invited on a British commercial expedition into the heart of East Central Africa. His goals were vague, and he would be poorly funded, but it was better than the doldrums of the classroom.

Everything was set for the Africa expedition when, one day at lunch with colleagues, Stefansson was handed a telegram. He opened it and craned forward, squinting, reading carefully. It was from the American explorer and geologist Ernest de Koven Leffingwell, who was organizing a polar expedition that aimed to chart the Beaufort Sea and "study the Eskimos in Victoria Island who had never seen a white man." Leffingwell, it turned out, had read Stefansson's paper on the Norse discovery of Greenland, and he'd been impressed. He wondered whether Stefansson might want to join him as anthropologist on his upcoming Anglo-American Polar Expedition (1906–8).

Stefansson shelved his books on Africa and began packing warm clothes.

He was headed north.

2

MASTER MARINER

May 1913
Brigus, Newfoundland

CAPTAIN ROBERT "BOB" BARTLETT, STANDING ON THE STEPS OF THE front porch of Hawthorne Cottage, took the telegram from his father. He turned the yellow envelope over and over in his hands. A superstitious mariner, he did not trust telegrams, believing they brought bad news more often than good. They were usually a harbinger of tragedy: the death of a relative, a shipwreck, or some other calamity. He was reluctant to open it.

He'd just returned from a lengthy and unsuccessful sealing voyage, and already he was restless. Their cottage was comfortable, certainly, and it was good to be with family again. His parents were both nearing seventy, and they could use his help. But it didn't do to be idle, to remain landlocked for long. Strong spring winds blew in from the Labrador Sea, raising whitecaps on Conception Bay and rattling the eaves of the cottages in the little fishing village at the far easterly fringe of North America. It was here, just a few miles from St. John's—the last stop and embarkation port of many of the world's great polar voyages—where Bartlett had spent his entire life. Well, where he'd spent those rare, impatient days when he was home at least. Most of his thirty-seven years had been logged—as had the lives of his father and his father before him and his uncles and brothers—at sea.

Bob Bartlett's ancestors had skippered ships in the seal and cod fisheries for generations. The famous Bartletts of Brigus were involved in exploration as well. In 1869, his uncles John and Sam, and his father, William—as captain, first mate, and second mate, respectively—took polar explorer Dr. Isaac Hayes above the Arctic Circle, north as far as the treacherous Melville Bay on the Greenland shores, vainly searching for traces of Sir John Franklin's vanished expedition of 1845. His great-uncle Isaac Bartlett was captain of the *Tigress* in 1874 on the rescue mission searching for Charles Francis Hall's lost USS *Polaris*. He discovered survivors of that shipwreck on a moving raft of ice in the lower reaches of Baffin Bay. They'd been adrift for nearly two hundred days, and yet not one of them had died. Bob Bartlett's great-uncle returned to a hero's welcome.

Seagoing adventure was in Bob Bartlett's blood. Throughout his childhood and teens, on summer vacations from school, he'd joined his father on sealing voyages. At seventeen he commanded his first schooner, the *Osprey*, returning from the rough Labrador waters with his cargo holds bursting with cod. By then he'd been studying for two years at the Methodist College at St. John's, his mother having sent him there with the hope that her eldest son would become a minister. But the thrill of the wind-filled sails, of salt spray washing over the rails, the sight of an open, endless horizon—their draw proved too alluring. He'd tried his best, and though he was an excellent student, he knew the only classroom for him was the next ship, the next sea voyage. He yearned to be, like his father and uncles, a master mariner. But Newfoundland strictly regulated such titles, requiring four years at sea to become second mate, another year to make first mate, and a sixth year, culminating with arduous examination in Halifax, to make master.

Bartlett would later explain his decision to quit school and follow his heart in nautical terms: "I held the tack as long as I could, and then came about, eased off, and ran before the wind of what I was meant to do."

That wind took him, at eighteen, on his first long voyage as a hired seaman aboard the *Corisande*, bound for Brazil carrying a shipment of dried cod. He spent the next six years almost entirely aboard one ship or another:

on cod and sealing vessels in the Labrador waters in spring and summer, on merchant ships every fall and winter. He sailed south to the Caribbean and Latin America on runs for bananas and other tropical fruits scarce in the North; he sailed across the North Atlantic and through the Strait of Gibraltar to the Mediterranean Sea, visiting some of Europe's most vital and vibrant port cities. By 1898, at the age of just twenty-three, he'd passed his written and technical exams and now possessed the right and privilege to command a ship anywhere in the world. His papers also gave him the hard-earned title reserved for those rare men who had the stuff to spend their lives at the ship's wheel or in the crow's nest: captain and master mariner.

Captain Bob Bartlett weighed his options. He could command a fishing or merchant vessel, but he yearned for something new, something different and more challenging. He did not have to wait long. In July of 1898, his uncle John Bartlett came to him with a tantalizing offer. The uncle had been asked to captain the *Windward*, the 320-ton flagship of American Robert Peary's first North Pole expedition. The plan was to sail from New York north clear through the Davis Strait and Smith Sound, aiming as far north between Greenland and Canada's Ellesmere Island as they could go before they were iced in. After that, Peary aimed to strike out with dog-sled teams and go on snowshoes the remaining four or five hundred miles to the North Pole. Uncle John invited his nephew Bob to come along. It promised to be one hell of an adventure.

Bob Bartlett agreed on the spot. This was the beginning of ten years of Arctic service and three attempts at the North Pole alongside the inimitable, complex, and controversial Robert Peary. During the first expedition (1898–1902), Bartlett was first mate aboard the *Windward*; for the next two (1905-6 and 1908–9), he would serve as captain and ice master of the magnificent 1,000-horsepower steel-hulled SS *Roosevelt*.

The 1898 voyage offered enough excitement and drama for an ordinary person's lifetime, but Bob Bartlett—even in his early twenties—was hardly ordinary. The *Windward* became stuck fast in the ice north of Cape Sabine, where, in 1884, Commander Adolphus Greely and his party of twenty-five men had fought starvation and one another during a dark, dreadful, and tragic winter. From the deck of the *Windward*, Bartlett could see the barren, fatal shores of Ellesmere Island and, to the east, twenty-five miles across the Smith Sound, the mountainous Greenland coastline.* He was learning about life above the Arctic Circle, about the capricious mercies of sea ice.

Since Peary knew that the *Windward* would remain icebound until the following spring, he left Bartlett and most of the crew and struck out through December's polar darkness with two dogsled teams to see how far north he could go. They plowed through blizzards and temperatures plunging to -50°F, camping on the ice and sometimes building igloos. He made it as far as Fort Conger, the barracks and base Greely had established at Lady Franklin Bay on northern Ellesmere Island almost twenty years before. But by the time he reached those long-abandoned dwellings, his feet were severely frostbitten, and as they thawed in the warmth of the wooden shelter, they became gangrenous. After a time, he realized his feet would not improve, and he ordered his men to lash him onto a sled and return to the *Windward*, two hundred miles to the south.

When Peary returned in March of 1899, having been gone almost three months, Bartlett helped to lay him out for surgery on the *Windward's* cabin table. Bartlett then assisted the ship's doctor, administering the ether Peary would need for the operation. The skin of his toes had sloughed off almost entirely, the necrotic flesh black and blistered. The doctor amputated eight of his toes. Before long, Peary was up and hobbling around on crutches, eager to start exploring again. Through the whole ordeal, he'd never uttered a word of complaint. Bartlett, deeply impressed by Peary's toughness, asked him how he managed to stand the pain.

Peary just looked up and said stoically, "One can get used to anything, Bartlett."

They spent the next three years far above the Arctic Circle, both aboard

---

* Notably, not far from them, just a couple of days' travel away, Norwegian explorer Fridtjof Nansen was himself held fast by ice, wintering aboard the *Fram* with Otto Sverdrup and studying the Canadian Arctic Archipelago, as it turned out (Putnam, *Mariner of the North*, 62).

the ship and on the ice. Bartlett was deepening his icecraft and navigation skills, spending time with the Greenlandic Inuit of the region. Peary adopted the practice of explorers before him like Roald Amundsen to emulate the survival skills of the Native peoples, and to employ local guides and interpreters. He relied on their superior knowledge of the harsh region and learned how to live in it. Bartlett benefited immensely from this Arctic apprenticeship. He discovered the importance of keeping his feet dry at all costs to avoid the nightmare that Peary had been through. An Eskimo guide showed him how to line the bottoms of his boots with grasses and lichens as insulation to keep the soles of his feet from freezing.

Bartlett came to relish seal meat: cooked, raw, and even decayed. He discovered that mixing seal blubber into his diet allowed him to endure the bitter cold. He learned to relish the rigors of long stints behind a dog team, sometimes up to sixty miles in a day, weaving around open leads in the ice, plowing over hummocks of raftered ice, and keeping his bearings through blinding snowdrifts and polar glare.

Bartlett's third and final North Pole expedition with Peary, in 1908–9, changed everything. By now, Bartlett was Peary's trusted confidant, captain, and navigator, both at sea and on ice. In July of 1908, the *Roosevelt* made port at Oyster Bay, New York, so that President Theodore Roosevelt, the mighty ship's namesake and supporter of the historic endeavor, could inspect her. Bartlett accompanied the president and First Family on a tour of the ship, including the engine room and lower holds, the sailors' berths and captain's quarters. Bartlett, feeling emboldened, addressed the great man directly, confident of their chances to make it all the way this time: "It's ninety or nothing," he said, "the North Pole or bust."

Eight months later, the *Roosevelt* was iced in and wintering near Cape Sheridan, at the northernmost tip of Ellesmere Island, and Bob Bartlett was leading Peary across the Polar Sea toward the North Pole. For many weeks Bartlett drove his dogs at the front, leading "the Pioneer Party": he and his sled team set the course, broke the trail, and determined the distance for each day's march northward. They built igloos along the route and prepared food for Peary and the main party following along. The going was brutal, the jagged sea ice slicing through their mukluks and shredding wooden sled runners.

On the first of April 1909, Peary took Bartlett aside. They stood just shy of latitude 88° north, perhaps a few days of travel, a week at most, from the North Pole. Peary thanked Bartlett for his tireless work; they'd never have come this far without him. But now he wanted Bartlett to return to the *Roosevelt*. Peary had chosen Matthew Henson and four Eskimo men for the remaining few marches to the pole. Henson was the superior dogsled driver, after all. That much was true, Bartlett had to agree. On the other hand, as Bartlett knew—hell, as everyone knew—he was the better navigator. He was the most skilled with a sextant, the best suited to confirm their position, to prove they'd reached the pole. But Peary had made his decision. It was tough on Bartlett to be left out of the final push. It hurt. Yet Bartlett betrayed no emotion then; he only thanked Peary for the honor of taking him this far.

"It's all in the game," Peary said, lowering his eyes northward. "And you've been at it long enough to know how hard a game it is."

Bartlett left his igloo at five o'clock the next morning and walked alone some five miles beyond the encampment. He trekked into a cold, sharp wind, making it to latitude 87°48' north before he stopped. He knew he had to turn around and lead his group south back to the *Roosevelt*. That was his duty now. He was within 150 miles of the vaunted goal that had eluded every explorer who'd ever quested for the pole. His body was sound, his heart and mind strong. But he turned around, bound by oath and duty to Peary, and struck south for the *Roosevelt*.

He had almost touched the farthest end of the earth. He had come ever so close to polar immortality. "Perhaps I cried a little," he said of being forced to turn back. "It was so near."

Now, four years later, he held a telegram and gazed out at the vessels lining the wharf, their rigging clinking in the wind. He turned the ominous cable over a few more times, considering what bad news it might bring. But he had no wife or children to worry about, and no legal troubles. To his recollection, he owed only one person money, and that wasn't enough to warrant a wire. Finally, his weathered hands slowly peeled open the envelope and he read the contents once, then again, noting the last words carefully:

WILL YOU JOIN ME ON THE KARLUK AS MASTER? It was signed, STEFANSSON.

Bartlett's father, looking anxious, leaned on the stairway railing. He asked his son what the telegram said.

Captain Bob smiled. He was going to miss the old man and his mother, but if anyone understood the powerful draw of the Arctic, it was his family.

"I am going back north again."

3

TOWARD THE DISCOVERY OF NEW LANDS

June 1913
Esquimalt, Vancouver Island, British Columbia

CAPTAIN BOB BARTLETT SURVEYED THE CLUTTERED DECKS OF THE CGS *Karluk* as the brigantine sat docked at Canada's west coast naval base. He'd hurried to get here after replying to Stefansson's telegram and then learning that the expedition was set to depart no later than mid-June.

The *Karluk*, on that first inspection, was unimpressive, perhaps even unfit for the proposed journey. Bartlett had ascertained her provenance, as he did for any ship he was going to captain. The 247-ton, 129-foot American-built steam brigantine had served dutifully for twenty-eight years, first as a tender for salmon fishermen in the Aleutian Islands, collecting and transporting fish along the Alaskan coast and delivering them to larger ships, which would take the catch to ports for processing. Her name, he mused, was appropriate for that kind of work, as *karluk* is an Aleutian word for "fish."

The *Karluk* had subsequently been put to whaling work, its sides and bow reinforced with two-inch Australian ironwood. The ship made fourteen voyages to Arctic waters, even wintering over during a handful of them. Stefansson had purchased the vessel for the Canadian Arctic Expedition (CAE) for $10,000, her price enticingly low owing to the whaling industry's decline.

Bartlett scowled at her dilapidated condition. Her holds reeked of whale oil; the cabins belowdecks had soiled, unscrubbed walls; and the floors teemed with cockroaches. The topside decks were a maze of oil drums, tangled line, crates of gear, and large bags of coal. The entrances to the cabins were blocked by bales of ropes and boxes. Bartlett belted out some obscenities, his loud voice reverberating across the cluttered decks and down to the engine room. On his ship, there was never any question of who was in command. "You could hear him on deck before you could see him," an associate recalled.

Bartlett ordered a complete overhaul from stem to stern, including a refurbishing of the weak 150-horsepower steam engine, new sails, new water tanks, and a new sternpost, all at a cost of $6,000—more than half the amount Stefansson had already billed to the Canadian government for the original purchase. But the repairs were necessary. The prow and hull both needed further sheathing and strengthening for the ice that they would encounter, and as this was to be—according to Stefansson and the press—the most ambitious and best-equipped scientific expedition to the Arctic yet, the quarters for the scientists needed refitting to be made more livable.

Bartlett discovered upon his arrival that he had not even been Stefansson's first choice for captain. Stefansson had originally made a verbal commitment to a longtime friend, the Norwegian captain Theodore Pedersen, who quit at the last minute. Pedersen, a noted fur trader and experienced whaler, had clashed with Stefansson over the condition of the *Karluk*. The man had also stumbled across a newspaper article reporting Stefansson's intention to sail the ship as far north as it could go and, if forced to, let her freeze into the ice pack and winter there as a base to go in search of new lands. Wintering in a safe harbor was one thing; surviving a winter bound in ice was something else altogether. So Pedersen bowed out.

In the short time the Norwegian had been involved, he'd only just managed to cobble together a ragtag crew, which Bartlett was now in charge of. Under normal circumstances, Bartlett would have handpicked his own crew. But the CAE, as Bartlett was learning, had hardly been put together under normal circumstances.

Stefansson had been rushed. To secure financial support for his grand scheme, he first met with the heads of the American Museum of Natural History and the National Geographic Society in New York in late 1912. Using his powers of persuasion, he'd convinced them to back his plans for scientific work and discovery, acquiring verbal pledges of $22,500 from each. Once the research funding was settled, in February of 1913, he hurried to Ottawa, where he met with the director of the Geological Survey of Canada and, more important, with Prime Minister Robert Borden.

Borden became entranced by Stefansson's plans and was particularly intrigued by the possibility of gaining sovereignty over a wide swath of Arctic lands and islands. At the time, the area known as the High Arctic was subject to contested sovereignty claims from not only Canada but also Norway and the United States. Borden said that the Canadian government would pay the entire cost of the expedition, with a few stipulations: One was that Stefansson agree to become a naturalized British subject prior to departure. (Canadian-born Stefansson became an American citizen when his family moved to the Dakotas.) The other was that their flagship *Karluk* must fly the Union Jack. The British flag was to be planted on any new lands Stefansson discovered, thus claiming them for Canada.*

Stefansson readily agreed to those terms, but he countered with one of his own: he would serve on the expedition without pay, provided that he retain sole publication rights for the expedition. This stipulation was vitally important to Stefansson, who understood that the financial windfall from articles, books, and lecture tours—should the expedition be

---

* In 1913, the Canadian Confederation and Dominion of Newfoundland were still British Dominions, their residents technically British citizens, with the Union Jack as their official flag. Canadian citizenship was officially recognized when the Canadian Citizenship Act went into effect on January 1, 1947. Newfoundlanders did not become Canadian citizens until 1949, when Newfoundland joined Canada.

successful—was potentially massive. Robert Peary and others had profited handsomely in precisely this way, and Stefansson requested and received written assurances from Borden granting him these rights.

Stefansson knew that time was growing short to pull everything together for a mid-June departure, which was as late as one should set out to safely beat encroaching ice in the northern waters. Stefansson sailed for England on March 1, 1913. At Prime Minister Borden's suggestion, Stefansson met in London with Canada's high commissioner there, the immensely wealthy Lord Strathcona, Donald Smith. Smith used his connections in England's scientific community to help Stefansson obtain specialized equipment and instruments not readily available in Canada, including devices for oceanographic and ethnographic studies. Smith also tapped into his contacts to provide Stefansson with scientists critical for the expedition—an ethnologist, an oceanographer, and a magnetician-meteorologist—as well as a surgeon and, to document the historic events, a cinematographer.

In London, Stefansson also met editors, inking a lucrative agreement for newspaper article, magazine, and book rights with United Newspapers, and he signed deals for image rights—including still and motion pictures—to the Gaumont Company. Stefansson was aware of the value of a good story, both in print and in pictures, and he made every effort to ensure that this expedition would be well documented, and that he would profit from it.

With these contracts in hand, Stefansson hastened to Rome to speak at the International Geographical Conference. He loudly promoted the CAE as a scientific first, even alluding to the potential discoveries as creating a commercial empire in the Canadian North. He spoke of the expedition— due to leave in only a few months—as if it were finalized and had been long in the making, though he was effectively conjuring it right then out of thin air. At the conference, Stefansson consulted with Bartlett's old companion Admiral Robert Peary, who reiterated that Bob Bartlett was the best man to captain the *Karluk*. Peary vouched for Bartlett as the world's greatest living ice navigator.

With the utmost confidence in his choice of Bartlett, Stefansson returned to London. There, he learned via telegram that Dr. Rudolph Anderson, his second-in-command of the expedition, had delayed an order of thousands of pounds of pemmican—a vital polar explorer foodstuff—to perform "purity tests." Anderson reported that one of the US-made brands they were buying might contain trace fragments of metal or glass. Stefansson was incensed, since time was crucial, and the tests might delay the shipment from arriving and being loaded on the *Karluk* before the expedition departed. He'd ordered specific mixtures of canned pemmican for the men (meat and suet with raisins and sugar added for taste) and for the sled dogs (meat and suet only). Stefansson fired back an angry wire to Anderson: DAMN THE PURITY TESTS. ORDER PEMMICAN IMMEDIATELY. WE HAVE NO ALTERNATIVE.*

With those matters taken care of, Stefansson sailed back to New York in late April and hurried to Ottawa, where on May 3, 1913, he officially took the oath of allegiance to His Majesty King George V. He was now formally a British subject, though the formality meant little to him—it was simply a transaction enabling his next moves. Vilhjalmur Stefansson would become whoever they wanted him to be—at least on paper—as long as he got what he wanted.

There remained much to do in a short time. While still in Ottawa, Stefansson finalized the members of the scientific team, hiring them hurriedly and instructing them to make their way as soon as possible to Victoria, where he would meet them at the end of May to outline the details of their duties and responsibilities. (One individual was traveling from Edinburgh, Scotland; one from Norway; and another all the way from New Zealand.) Stefansson remained briefly in Ottawa, dealing with mounds of paperwork and government contracts, but he also spent some days working on a draft of a book he was trying to sell for general audiences, to be called *My Life with the Eskimo*. At least part of his attentions, then, were devoted to his

---

* Dr. Anderson chose to override Stefansson and had the pemmican safety-tested anyway. It was deemed satisfactory and arrived on time for the expedition. Between the Northern and Southern Parties, four different brands of pemmican were used.

previous trip of 1908–12 rather than the impending voyage that loomed only weeks away. He was distracted and scattered.

The scientists arrived sporadically in Victoria between late May and early June, convening at their lodgings in the James Bay Inn. The fourteen members of the international scientific team were a distinguished group, though only two of them had experience in polar travel. From Edinburgh came oceanographer James Murray, who'd recently served as a biologist with Ernest Shackleton aboard the *Nimrod* on the British Antarctic Expedition (1907–9). Fiery, brash, and outspoken, at forty-six Murray was the eldest scientist on the CAE; he was also supremely confident of his abilities, having overseen Shackleton's base camp during the attempt to reach the South Pole. Also signed on was one of Murray's comrades from that *Nimrod* journey, the complicated Alistair Forbes Mackay. Dr. Mackay, a thirty-five-year-old physician and biologist, had made a name for himself on that historic expedition by reaching the south magnetic pole (the world record, at the time, for Farthest South) and achieving the first ascent of the 12,448-foot Mount Erebus. But Dr. Mackay had a reputation of obstinacy and a penchant for alcohol, which Shackleton had cautioned Stefansson about.

A couple of the members were very young and untested but driven and enthusiastic. William McKinlay was a twenty-four-year-old mathematics and science teacher from Glasgow. At just five feet four inches tall, he was affectionately called Wee Mac by his friends, and he'd been recommended to Stefansson by one of McKinlay's professors at the University of Glasgow, himself a polar explorer. McKinlay had received his offer by telegram in late April 1913 and agreed by telephone within the hour to sign on as magnetician and meteorologist. Stefansson told him that he should plan to be gone for up to four years, with a small monthly stipend and all expenses paid. McKinlay did some fast talking with his school board, arranging for a long-term substitute to fill his position.

Fortunately for him, his employer agreed that the opportunity was too exciting to pass up, though McKinlay's emotions were a mixture of thrill and fear: "I remember having heard or read about Arctic exploration, trying to visualize the adventures that lay ahead," he wrote, "and shoving to the back of my mind . . . the reports of death and disaster that were so much a part of Arctic history." From everything he had read, he understood— though he tried his best not to dwell on it—the very real possibility that he would never return to his homeland again. Making him even more apprehensive, during his steamship crossing, they encountered dense fog and massive icebergs in the North Atlantic, very near where the RMS *Titanic* had sunk just a year earlier. With the blaring of the ship's siren echoing off the imposing bergs, he wondered what he'd got himself into.

Younger even than McKinlay, and the last to be hired on, was a strapping twenty-two-year-old Norwegian, Bjarne Mamen. Towering over Wee Mac at six feet two inches, he brimmed with bravado despite his scant Arctic résumé. He had worked as a photographic topographer on the Danish Spitsbergen expedition, and was most recently employed as a forester around Vancouver, where he had learned of Stefansson's plans and practically begged to come along. Of his persistent entreaties, Stefansson remarked: "Poor boy, he wants to go so much I hate to turn him down." Stefansson was impressed that Mamen was a ski champion in Norway, which might prove very useful in ice travel. The Norwegians had modernized skiing as a mode of travel, and Stefansson well knew how Fridtjof Nansen, Mamen's famous countryman, had pioneered the use of skis in Arctic travel during the first crossing of Greenland in 1888. It would be worth having young Mamen along.

On June 7, Stefansson at last arrived in Victoria, spending one night to unwind in the resplendent Empress hotel on the banks of the capital city's Inner Harbour. The next morning, he checked in at the James Bay Inn and immediately called a meeting with all the scientists to discuss the expedition's ambitious if amorphous plans. There was much to deliberate.

All of them had some idea, from various correspondences with Stefansson, about the broad initial goals of the expedition. Stefansson was quick to outline things more specifically: The Northern Party, which he would lead from aboard the flagship *Karluk*, would explore the seas and ice north of Alaska, "taking soundings, looking for signs of animal life, and searching for new land." The scientists would engage in anthropological, biological, geological, oceanographical, and marine and terrestrial study. Those of the Southern Party, under the leadership of Canadian zoologist Dr. Rudolph Anderson, would perform land-based anthropological and geographical study in the Coronation Gulf region and among the many islands off Canada's northern coastline. They should all be proud as well as honored, for they were now a part of "the largest staff of scientific specialists ever carried on a Polar expedition." The plan was to sail from Esquimalt, British Columbia, to Nome, Alaska, where they'd split the two parties, with the Southern Party from that point having access to a schooner Stefansson had recently purchased called the *Alaska*.

A good number of questions arose during that first meeting, and the tone quickly became contentious. Several of the scientists wanted assurances that there would be sufficient food and clothing for the journey. Without offering much in the way of details, Stefansson confirmed that they'd be properly fed, clothed, and sheltered—adding that he'd be hiring a Native seamstress en route. But at any rate, he assured them that the Arctic was—if met on its own terms—a friendly and forgiving place one could learn to live off. He had certainly done so.

Some of the scientists had recently visited the *Karluk*, and they worried that its freshwater tanks were insufficient for their needs. They flatly refused to head north unless the *Karluk* and any other ships involved were either fitted with much larger tanks or brought along some form of distilling apparatus. If not, they feared they would die of thirst. Stefansson scoffed, saying they needn't worry—they'd be able to get fresh water from the top surface of the saltwater sea ice. Murmurs and grunts of doubt filled the tense room. He told them curtly, "The water on top of *all* old sea ice is *always* fresh, the only condition being that it must be far enough from the edge of the floe to be unaffected by salt spray."

There was such general disbelief that in the end, Stefansson had to halt the meeting and send for Captain Bartlett, disrupting his work on the *Karluk* at the docks. Bartlett arrived to confirm that sealers in the Arctic indeed siphoned their water from the top surface of year-old or older ice.

It was common practice—had been for as long as he could remember. It was true, he explained, that new ice or "young ice" had brine trapped in the crystals and was too salty to drink. But as ice ages, the brine leaches out of it, and older, multiyear ice was absolutely fresh and drinkable. He added, grinning at the worried men, that when they reached the ice, he'd pump the tanks to the brim with "the sweetest damn water any scientist ever tasted!"

Stefansson sent Bartlett back to work and handed out the contracts. These were revised and different from those they'd all originally been given when they were enlisted by Stefansson and the Canadian government. A sticking point arose when the men carefully read the language regarding publishing rights: "No public dissemination of news about the expedition during its stay in the Arctic and for a year thereafter; and no magazine articles or popular books were to be written before one year after the return of the expedition." Some of the men balked at these restrictions until Stefansson pointed out that they were being paid and he was not. He was volunteering, so any compensation for him would naturally come from potential publishing and lecture fees.

He conveniently chose not to mention—though the scientists had heard rumors—that he'd recently secured exclusive media rights with United Newspapers, *The New York Times*, and Toronto's *The Globe*. Stefansson then informed them that their personal diaries would need to be turned over to the government at the conclusion of the expedition, and that as expedition leader, he would have access to them for his own literary use, after which they'd be returned to the scientists. Some of the men haggled over these terms.

And there was something else, a newspaper article that had recently appeared. One of the men clutched it angrily in his hands. In it, Stefansson outlined the nature and purpose of this historic scientific venture, but the part that caught everyone's attention was the lengths to which their leader was willing to go in his pursuit of "the unexplored area of a million or so square miles that is represented by white patches on our map, lying between Alaska and the North Pole."

In the article, Stefansson went on to speak for all of them: "The attainment of the purposes of the expedition is more important than the bringing-back safe of the ship in which it sails. This means that while every reasonable precaution will be taken to safeguard the lives of the party, it is realized both by the backers of the expedition and the members of it, that even the lives of the party are secondary to the accomplishment of the work!"

The fiery Scotsman James Murray was particularly incensed, bellowing that he'd never shirked from work a day in his life and never would, but he would not "sell himself, body, mind, and soul" to his leader. Dr. Anderson was so angry that he threatened to resign, until Stefansson assured him that once they sailed from Nome, he'd leave the direction and leadership of the Southern Party entirely in Anderson's hands. Everyone calmed down, and finally, begrudgingly, signed their contracts.

The scientists' treatment as VIPs by Victoria's dignitaries over the next few days momentarily allowed them to forget, or drink away, their concerns. They were feted at the splendid and châteauesque Empress hotel, which was new and catered to wealthy travelers who visited via Canada's transcontinental railway to embark on pleasure cruises departing from the Canadian Pacific Railroad steamship terminal just a block away. There were evening beach picnics with Victoria's high society. Just a day before departure, while Stefansson, Bartlett, and Dr. Anderson enjoyed a lavish hosted luncheon in the dining room at the Empress, two of the dashing younger men—American Burt McConnell (secretary) and Australian George Wilkins (photographer)—sneaked off for an exhilarating afternoon joyride in a touring car with two young society ladies. Later, the press gathered to photograph the entire science staff. Dressed in their finest suits, starched collars, and neckties, their felt fedoras and straw boater hats in hand, they posed before ornate columns. To a man, whatever their reservations, they knew they were poised to embark on a grand and ambitious adventure.

· · ·

On June 17, 1913, remarkably only one week behind schedule, many of the crew and scientific staff stood aboard the cleaned-up decks of the *Karluk*. True to form, Stefansson had managed to alert the press of a formal ceremony on the Canadian Arctic Expedition flagship to be attended by British Columbia's premier, Sir Richard McBride, and Lieutenant Governor T. W. Paterson. Journalists took photographs and scribbled in their notebooks as the dignitaries presented Stefansson and the expedition with Canadian Red and Blue Ensign flags, one to be flown alongside the Royal Union Flag (Union Jack), others to be planted when new lands were found. Waving and cheering crowds lined the wharf at the Esquimalt shipyards, welling with patriotic pride for their country's first official foray into Arctic exploration.

At sunset, Captain Bob Bartlett called for ship's sirens and steamed the *Karluk* away from the docks into Esquimalt Harbour. They were escorted by the Royal Canadian Navy's Pacific Fleet and received resounding cheers from seamen aboard a pair of British naval ships, the HMS *Algerine* and the HMS *Shearwater*. Bartlett waved acknowledgment and respectful thanks to the blaring horns and flag-dipping salutes of the many pleasure boats that had joined the celebratory farewell armada, then gripped the ship's wheel and cast his icy stare—as he had a thousand times before—to the burning sun on the horizon.

4

OMENS

BARTLETT WAS THRILLED TO BE COMMANDING A SHIP INTO NORTH-
ern seas once more, and he spent his time alternately at the helm and up in
the barrel, marveling at the beauty of the jutting fjords and inlets, calving
glaciers, and a snowcapped mountain coastline he'd never seen before. They
journeyed at a modest five knots per hour through the renowned Inside
Passage, entering the Bering Sea on July 2. There they encountered dense
mist that turned to fog, prompting Bartlett to slow to half speed, which, in
the *Karluk*, was very slow indeed. It had not taken long for Bartlett to draw
some conclusions about the ship's performance. Already the engine, which
chief engineer John Munro joked had the power of "an old coffee pot," had
quit several times, as had the steering. Bartlett, prone to outbursts of profanity, huffed and railed at the ship and ordered quick repairs, though he
knew more extensive work would be required once they reached Nome. He
worried that if it was already struggling in open water, it would be no match
for where they were headed, remarking that "she had neither the strength to
sustain ice pressure nor the engine power to force her way through loose ice."

Bartlett would have to wait to voice his concerns to Stefansson. The
expedition leader had disembarked after their ceremonial send-off in Esquimalt, opting to travel by means of the more comfortable steamer SS
Victoria to Nome, where he would meet them. He claimed he had expedition details to finalize, and that was partly true. He'd contracted to pick
up additional supplies in Seattle on the way up. But Stefansson was even

more driven by matters personal and professional, matters he knew had the potential to be very profitable. He'd brought his personal secretary, Gertrude Allen, along on the voyage aboard the *Victoria*, as well as Bella Weitzner, who was an editorial assistant at the American Museum of Natural History. As the ship steamed along, Stefansson dictated revisions and final chapters of his book *My Life with the Eskimo*, which he hoped would be published within a year, while he was gone. He intended to return, whenever that might be, to an infusion of funds and bolstered fame.

As the *Karluk* chugged along, stopping at a few Alaskan ports to take on fresh water, the scientists were mostly idle. A few of them begrudgingly agreed to help haul some of the weighty coal sacks from the upper deck down to the boiler room, but most deemed such manual labor the responsibility of the ship's crew, not theirs. Instead, they lazed on deck when it was warm enough, dazzled by the near-continuous light of the midnight sun. As the ship crept north, cold winds funneled furiously through the Bering Strait, the frigid air cutting through the men's thick woolens and oilskins. They retreated belowdecks to drink coffee and smoke, and even passed the time by engaging in and wagering on friendly boxing matches.

On July 8, after a tedious journey of three thousand miles, Bartlett called to drop anchor offshore at Nome, just a mile from the noted Golden Strand. There, in 1898 at Anvil Creek, gold had been discovered, resulting in a frenzy that caused many fortune seekers to leave the Klondike to stake new claims in Alaska. Within a year, Nome's population had swelled to over ten thousand people, many living in tents along the beach. When Bartlett brought the *Karluk* to dock the next morning, remnant prospectors bent along the beach sands and at the waters of the Snake River mouth where it met the sea, panning for gold.

Stefansson arrived on the *Victoria* early that morning. Nome remained a bustling little coastal village, its economy now supported by the fur trade, fishing, and reindeer herding. A few gold diggers still clung to their dreams, though their pans these days mostly came up empty. For the next few weeks, the expedition members stretched their sea legs ashore while Stefansson attended to final details and organization of the trip. After unloading from the *Victoria* the equipment and provisions obtained in Seattle, as well as much of the *Karluk*'s cargo, Stefansson and Bartlett stood dumbfounded by the vast piles amassing on the dock. It was obvious that they were going to need another ship to transport all the men and gear to Herschel Island, just above the Alaska–Canadian north coast, where Stefansson planned to redistribute everything, split the Northern and Southern Parties, and carry on with their expedition work. By good fortune, one workable ship happened to be for sale: the thirty-ton, twin-screw schooner *Mary Sachs*. Stefansson bought the schooner for $5,000 and immediately hired its previous owner as captain, figuring, who better to pilot the craft?

Bartlett ordered considerable work on the *Karluk* before he'd take it out into the Arctic Ocean. The steering mechanism needed attention. It had been testy and unreliable so far, failing on two occasions on their way to Nome. Bartlett opted for as much of an overhaul as possible before departing, overseeing the blowing out of the boiler, reconditioning the engines again, and filling all the freshwater tanks. With this all taken care of, Bartlett tried to rearrange the stores and equipment, but the task proved difficult. Gear was piled everywhere, and Stefansson wasn't around to help.

According to William McKinlay, there was a great deal of disarray:

> *Tons of additional equipment had arrived on the* Victoria *with Stefansson; tons more were being bought in Nome. All this had to be loaded on our three vessels, and large quantities had to be unloaded from the Karluk and transferred to the other two ships. The perfect method would of course have been to distribute the loads according to the planned destinations and functions of the different ships, but this was not done. . . . In the haste and confusion, when anyone asked where this or that should go, the answer was always the same: "We'll sort that out at Herschel Island."*

Stefansson's absence was the result of yet another meeting that had been called by the scientists. This one lasted over five hours and became combative, mostly pertaining to the Northern Party. Once again, it was

Stefansson's vagueness about their movements and plans that caused deep concern. Some of these, again, were printed in newspaper interviews Stefansson had given—which was certainly news to the scientists. To the scientists, he'd suggested that they'd travel on the *Karluk* until new land was found; if none was discovered, they'd establish a land base on Prince Patrick Island, from which forays would be made into the unknown. But in the newspaper interview, Stefansson had revealed, according to William McKinlay, that the *Karluk* would "probably be frozen in; and in this case, she would certainly be crushed and sink."

The team members were astounded by this revelation, despite Stefansson's assurances that even should this happen, the *Karluk* would be equipped with light skin boats called umiaks, which he said were perfectly suited for travel over sea ice, and they could easily make their way back to shore. Stefansson found the men's repeated questions about a land base, food supply, clothing, and itinerary impertinent and insulting. He'd thought it all through, he told them, and they would be picking up Arctic clothing, dogs for sledging, and Eskimo hunters as they traveled north. He did not feel compelled to explain every detail. They should have unwavering confidence in him as their leader.

But general unease and doubt remained, enough that after the meeting, magnetician-meteorologist McKinlay hastily wrote a letter to one of his closest friends in Scotland, privately addressing "very serious matters" and his deep concerns over the expedition's management, concluding that "Stefansson declared that every member of the scientific staff recognized that his life was a secondary matter compared with the scientific work, which was not only untrue, but in direct opposition to the government's instructions."

Despite the tensions and misgivings, by July 26, two of the ships of their little armada—the *Karluk* and the *Mary Sachs*—were finally ready to sail from Teller, Alaska, about seventy miles northwest of Nome. The *Alaska* was still waiting on some parts to arrive at Teller and would follow shortly after, with Dr. Anderson in charge. Bartlett steamed the heavily laden *Karluk* slowly out to sea, noting how deeply she rode in the water.

He'd run many an overloaded ship during his fishing and sealing days, the holds brimming with catch. Stefansson, not a sea captain himself, joked that the *Karluk* "would never have been allowed to sail had there been at port . . . rigid inspectors." Bartlett was unamused as he steered north into a freshening gale, cutting through the Bering Strait. Later, when they crossed the Arctic Circle, Bartlett did quip to Stefansson and the crew that he'd felt the bump. And at least now they had nearly twenty-four hours of daylight by which to navigate.

They entered the Chukchi Sea between northern Alaska and Russia and were slammed by heavy winds beating down from the northwest, with swirling mists turning to intermittent fog. Once, when the fog lifted for a time, Bartlett scanned everywhere but the *Mary Sachs* was nowhere to be seen. The *Karluk* bucked and rolled into rising waves, sea spray and foam cascading over the rails. Bartlett ordered some of the gear on deck to be taken below, to help redistribute the weight, as the bow of the ship had nosed below the surface a few times. Most of the cabins had taken on water, and the scientists were soaked and seasick, writhing and spewing into buckets from their bunks when Bartlett drew the *Karluk* into shelter at Point Hope, a tiny Eskimo settlement off Alaska's northwestern shore. Here, Stefansson disembarked briefly and returned having hired on two Eskimo hunters and dogsled drivers in their early twenties nicknamed Jerry and Jimmy. Then they were off again.

On August 1, Bartlett spotted iceblink on the horizon ahead. He knew what it meant, and he was both surprised and concerned to see it so soon. He squinted to make sure, but there was no mistake. There it was, a rupturing skein of white light as if torn from the underbelly of the clouds, the glare reflecting off an ice field that must lay just beyond. Bartlett climbed up into the crow's nest and glassed off the starboard bow, his eyes watering from the wind and snow flurries. The pack ice amassed and encroached from the north, a couple of miles away, large floes curling their way toward them. Bartlett had been steaming parallel with the shore, but seeing the ice headed their way, and no available leads to work their way through, he ordered a change of course. He asked young Bjarne Mamen to join him up in the barrel. Mamen's tireless work so far, shoveling coal and even helping to set sails, had impressed the captain. From what Bartlett could see, they'd best sail back to windward for a mile or two and stay in open water, to avoid getting pinched in by the ice that was driving headlong toward land. The snow fell heavily now as the temperature dropped into the twenties, and they crept along almost blindly, hoping to avoid contact with the pack.

The next morning the weather broke slightly, and Bartlett set a northeast course toward Point Barrow, about seventy-five miles away. An offshore wind drove the larger floes from land, providing a lane, and Bartlett pushed the *Karluk* through some loose ice, testing her. Small rafts of cake ice parted easily at the bow, and they nudged along, bashing hard enough into a few larger cakes to topple some of the men. They passed a large pod of walrus, and everyone came out to watch the giant animals, some lazing on floating ice, others swimming along near the ship. Not long afterward, Bartlett elbowed Mamen and pointed to a large white figure moving slowly across the ice. Mamen climbed down and fetched his rifle. Bartlett never took his eyes off the polar bear ambling along on the ice about five hundred yards distant. As a lifelong mariner, Bartlett was superstitious, and the sight of the bear unnerved him. Mamen climbed into one of the whaleboats, and as they got nearer Bartlett barked out to him, "Shoot now."

Mamen's first two shots clearly missed, but his third struck. The great white bear ran a few yards, toppled over, then got up and ran with a speed that astonished everyone, disappearing in the distant white beyond. A little later, Bartlett spotted another bear, this one much closer, just over a hundred yards straight off the bow. Bartlett readied his own rifle and eased his chin down on the stock, exhaling slowly. At thirty yards he fired and struck the bear; then chambered another round and fired again, to make sure. The animal slid from an ice cake, its massive carcass bobbing in the water. Bartlett ordered a whaleboat lowered, and they brought the bear aboard, the photographer Wilkins filming the event. Dr. Mackay measured the bear at just under eight feet long splayed out on the deck. Jimmy and Jerry worked fast, skinning it and cutting it up, slicing through the thick fat and separating the meat, the better cuts for the men and lesser for the dogs.

They stretched the skin out on a frame and placed it up in the rigging to cure in the elements. Bartlett wanted it preserved, telling the men that "the skin of the polar bear makes the best sleeping robe for Arctic use and the skin of a young bear is also the best for trousers, because it will wear the longest." But something about shooting the bear bothered him. In his log, he wrote of the event: "To the average man this would have been a good omen. But to a superstitious Newfoundlander the bear was a beacon toward future disaster. I am more than ever a believer in signs."

5

MIRAGES

FOR THE NEXT FEW DAYS, BARTLETT WOVE THE *KARLUK* THROUGH narrow water leads, zigzagging slowly up the coastline. The ice grew dense, tightly packed around them, the great lumbering cakes moving and shifting with the winds and currents. Bartlett relished the challenge. He had fought the ice of the Kane Basin and the Smith Sound between Ellesmere Island and Greenland, snaking the powerful ironclad SS *Roosevelt* through those diabolical waters much farther north. But the early onset of winter conditions during the first week of August concerned him. In consulting his logbooks and *The American Coast Pilot**—the gold standard guide for navigating the northern waters since the late eighteenth century—the captain could find no records showing snow and ice and low temperatures such as they were encountering this early. How he wished for that glorious ship.

Bartlett stayed constantly in the barrel, belching out orders. Once he called, "Hard a starboard," but the wheelsman misheard him through the wind, and swung them hard to port, bashing them bow-first into a massive floe. Bartlett calmly backed them off and righted them, yet the ice was everywhere he looked, hemming them in from all directions. For the Scotsman William McKinlay, who was witnessing the wonders of a

---

The American Coast Pilot is referred to by Bartlett as either "Coast Pilot book," "Pilot Book," or "Coastal Pilot." I have followed his lead on these varied names for the same guide.

living, moving ice pack for the first time, there was an awesome, dangerous beauty. He scribbled furiously in his journal:

> I was fascinated by the scene. The ice was much broken up and rough, with
> scarcely a level patch of any great extent. The multitude of hummocks of varying
> size and height had weathered throughout the summer so that their surfaces
> were clear of snow and all their edges had been smoothed and rounded. Their
> shapes were infinite in variety and they gleamed and glistened in every conceiv-
> able shade of blue. It was like being in some gigantic sculptor's yard, stacked as
> far as the eye could see with glistening marble blocks cut in a million fantastic
> shapes.

Neither Bartlett nor Stefansson was so enamored with the scene, because by August 3 they were icebound, encased by the pack. Taking observations, they determined that they were at least still moving north, and
were within twenty-five miles of Point Barrow. Intermittently the skies
cleared, and they could see the outline of the Alaskan coast. With the ship
locked by ice and not much to do, Bartlett agreed that the scientists could
disembark onto the floe they'd anchored to and walk about, provided they
were careful and traveled in pairs or small teams, and to watch for polar
bears.

Mamen, accustomed to the snow and ice of Norway, went on a stroll
with the French anthropologist Henri Beuchat, who looked like a child
walking across a skating rink for the first time. "It was amusing," wrote
Mamen in his journal, "to see Beuchat tumbling, running around . . . as
if he had solid ground under his feet." Mamen offered advice and instruction, but Beuchat wouldn't listen: "He took no notice of my advice . . .
and had to pay for it; he fell down between two ice cakes, got wet and
cold, but anyway that was a lesson for him."

Stefansson consulted with Bartlett and said that since it appeared they
weren't going anywhere for a while, he would take the Eskimos Jimmy and
Jerry, and Dr. Mackay, and try to cross the ice by sled to Cape Smyth (now

called Barrow).* Stefansson wanted to negotiate with the villagers and traders at the settlement there for more sled dogs, furs, and a seamstress skilled at sewing skin and fur clothing. Bartlett expressed some misgivings about their leader leaving the ship, but Stefansson insisted, saying the geologist George Malloch had taken readings, and the ship was drifting about five miles a day in that direction anyway, so they'd meet them there.

Several men came from belowdecks to see them off. McKinlay and a few others ran alongside the dogsled, waving and cheering and watching the sled bump and skid across the broken surface of the ice. McKinlay was beginning to love his time on the ice, and he "skipped about like a spring lamb, jumping from pan to pan and floe to floe," excited as a child seeing his first winter snows. Back on board, McKinlay helped Mamen prepare a few pairs of skis, which Mamen was eager to use. They brushed the bottoms with hot pine tar to repel moisture and seal the wooden bases, and Mamen showed McKinlay how boots fit into the leather toe and heel bindings. When the pine tar dried, Mamen mixed up wax to use on the ski bases for glide, combining tar, candle wax, and gasoline. McKinlay was excited by the prospect of skiing, which he'd never tried.

Late that night Jimmy and Jerry returned with the dogs and sled, reporting that the ice terrain had been treacherous, and that Dr. Mackay had plunged once into the water and was near exhaustion by the time they reached land. But he and Stefansson had proceeded on foot, striking for Cape Smyth. They planned to walk all night, their way lit by the continuous light of the midnight sun. McKinlay and the other scientists rummaged through gear and equipment on deck and down belowdecks, trying to make sense of where everything was. Much of it, as they feared, was on the two other ships, wherever they were. When McKinlay pointed this out to Bartlett, the captain just smirked and repeated the refrain, which was now becoming a bad joke to everyone: "We'll sort it out at Herschel Island."

---

* The Inupiaq name for what is now called Barrow, Alaska, is Utqiagvik. Barrow the town lies to the southwest of Point Barrow, the country's northernmost land.

At 2:00 A.M. on August 6, Captain Bartlett woke everyone, calling for full steam. A change in wind and weather had shifted the ice, and he saw an opening. Yelling directions from above, Bartlett managed to steer them clear from the ice and had them moving along again, but after a very short time, the rudder struck submerged ice and the steering broke and they floated between bergs and floes for two frightening hours. McKinlay was shaken by their helplessness, noting that "to be without steering in the middle of an ice pack was a serious business." They managed to fix the steering and get under way again, but not for long. The ice closed in around them, bumping and battering them and halting their progress. Bartlett had a few unsavory things to say about the *Karluk* as they made fast to an ice floe. But by good fortune, they'd come to rest just a mile offshore from Cape Smyth, where they anchored to stable shore ice.

That afternoon, Bartlett and the rest of the men heard dogs barking nearby and looked over the rails to see Dr. Mackay nearing. He was flanked by Eskimos driving large dog teams. He boarded, handing over a letter from Stefansson and explaining to Bartlett—raising his voice over the yelping and snarling of the dogs below—that Stefansson had purchased sleds, some three dozen sled dogs, and had hired a family of Eskimos who would be coming along with them. There was a husband and wife named Kuraluk and Kiruk. Kuraluk, Dr. Mackay said, had a reputation as a fine hunter, and his wife was a skilled seamstress. They'd brought along their two young daughters, eight-year-old Helen and three-year-old Mugpi, who ran playfully around on the ice foot—the ice permanently attached to land and extending out into the sea.

By means of the sleds, Dr. Mackay and the family had brought from Port Smith three umiaks, two single-person skin kayaks for hunting, and piles of pelts and furs and sealskin to be fashioned into proper Arctic garb. The umiaks were like ordinary wooden rowboats but much lighter—their frames were overlaid with stretched sealskins sewn carefully together with tough reindeer sinew. They could hold up to a dozen people and were very durable. Dr. Mackay said they needed to load everything—the gear and dogs and sleds and boats and new members—onto the *Karluk*, and that Stefansson would be arriving later with two more passengers.

Getting everything and everyone on board was difficult and took hours. The umiaks, though light enough, were unwieldy and needed to be tethered alongside the whaleboats. There was the matter of where to put the new arrivals. In the end, Bartlett settled on a compartment next to the ship's laboratory. He had first mate Sandy Anderson direct the project, which required clearing the area of timber, coal, and crates. Mamen, McKinlay, and a couple of the other scientists were enlisted to help. Beuchat complained the entire time, whining—as Mamen described it—like a little puppy. Others wondered openly what in the hell they were doing taking children aboard. Bartlett reminded them that it was not uncommon for a hired Eskimo man to bring his wife and family along, and at any rate they possessed so many skills in Arctic living that they'd undoubtedly be more help than hindrance.

Stefansson arrived later that evening with two men. Kataktovik was just nineteen, and his wife had recently died, leaving him to care for an infant daughter. While visiting the village, Stefansson had inquired about highly skilled hunters, and someone suggested Kataktovik. Stefansson told the young man he would pay him handsomely and provide him with plenty of firearms and ammunition, giving him a rifle on the spot—but explained it was uncertain how long they would be gone. Perhaps a year, maybe two. Kataktovik thought it over and after arranging to leave his tiny daughter with other family members, agreed to come along. He climbed aboard and was told to bunk with Jimmy and Jerry.

The other man with Stefansson was an acquaintance named John "Jack" Hadley, a salty fifty-seven-year-old Englishman who'd spent the last twenty years along the Alaskan north coast, working at various times and places as a trader, trapper, and whaler. His skin was seared brown and leathery from years toiling outside, his bright eyes steely and keen. For the last few years, Hadley had overseen the whaling station at Cape Smyth, but he'd recently lost his Eskimo wife, resigned his post, and intended to go east, to Banks Land, to strike out on his own and establish a trading post there. That was his plan. He needed a change in his life, he said.

Stefansson had agreed to take him along as far as Herschel Island, where he could transfer to either the *Mary Sachs* or the *Alaska*, and one of the two would convey him farther east to Banks Land. Stefansson also thought he might benefit from Hadley's varied skills and knowledge. As the newest and last member boarded the ship, no one knew exactly what his role would be or what he was really doing there, adding another body to the already overcrowded ship. Hadley also brought along his own dog, Molly.

Stefansson valued Hadley's experience in the North: "There were many reasons why I wanted him. For one thing, all my men were new in the Arctic except Bartlett . . . and I felt the need of at least one man I could talk over local conditions with . . . His experience was of all sorts . . . both on board ships and with Eskimos in their skin boats." Stefansson said Hadley could bunk with him in his cabin at the stern.

Bartlett assessed the situation on board and took it in stride. He'd been hired to captain the *Karluk*, and that's what he intended to do. All he needed was the cooperation of the weather and the ice, and they'd be on their way. He knew there'd been some grousing and discontent among the scientists, but they were not his primary concern. A few of them, like the constantly sniping little Beuchat, were technically part of the Southern Party. So were Jenness, Murray, and McKinlay, who were slated to join Dr. Anderson on the *Alaska*—wherever it was.

No, Stefansson would sort the ten scientists out. It was Bartlett's crew who now gave him pause. The men had been hastily assembled before he arrived, and he hadn't time to handpick them, as he would have preferred. Since they'd departed so late in the season, the men who were available hadn't exactly been the cream of the crop either. Of the twelve, nearly all were in their early to mid-twenties, save the chief engineer, John Munro, who was in his thirties, and the second engineer, Robert Williamson, who was thirty-six. The ages of the crew didn't concern Bartlett so much. Rather, it was a rising division, a tension between them and the scientists.

While the crew and scientists bunked separately—the crew's bunks in the bow, the scientists' in the stern—the ship was cramped enough that they were often in close contact while working, eating, and for evening gatherings in the saloon. Sneering comments flew back and forth, some remarks whispered, some intended to be overheard. The crew deemed the scientists haughty because the researchers seemed to behave as if any work that wasn't "science"—of which, so far, there had been very little—was below them. The sailors thought the scientists lazy and snooty. And it was true that all but one of the scientific team (McConnell, technically secretary and responsible for recording events) had university educations, so there was an actual social stratification, and the crew members—whether warranted or not—felt belittled. As a reaction to these slights, some of the crew had also been making degrading comments about the Eskimos, which Bartlett would not allow to continue.

Bartlett pondered the *Karluk* and its bursting numbers, including the thirty snarling sled dogs he now had to accommodate, and wondered whether he hadn't agreed to this venture too hastily. He mentally cataloged some of the other crew members, considering how they'd impressed him so far. He knew they were cramped and uncomfortable in their eight-berth quarters in the ship's bow. The first officer, Alexander "Sandy" Anderson, seemed a good lad, just twenty-two and scrawny, but sinewy strong, always smiling and gregarious. There was a brightness to him. Though Sandy had only recently received his second mate's certificate, Bartlett had been pressed to promote him to first mate back at Esquimalt, when he'd fired the original first mate, finding him incapable and lazy. Sandy was already well liked by the rest of the crew; he whistled and sang songs in his lilting Scottish brogue as he moved effortlessly about the ship.

The cook and steward, Bob Templeman, was one Bartlett would need to keep a close eye on. He was proving only mediocre in the galley, which was unfortunate enough; but there'd been rumors that he was addicted to laudanum, a tincture of morphine that, while common enough for ship's doctors to possess, should under no circumstances be kept for personal consumption. Bartlett had heard that the steward stashed opium vials in his berth and kept some in the kitchen, and he'd noticed that Templeman did appear gaunt and jittery, with a lit cigarette always bobbing on his lower lip as he cooked. Bartlett valued men's actions over rumors and in-nuendo, but he'd watch him closely and take any actions necessary.

Another interesting character whom Bartlett was trying to figure out was the Welsh seaman Hugh Williams. He was a rough-edged, reticent fellow who carried himself like someone you wouldn't want to cross, eye-ing you sidewise with a hint of distrust. He seemed unamused by meal-time banter and mostly stayed to himself, speaking so infrequently that the crew nicknamed him Clam. When he did speak, it was usually to say something wry and sarcastic and worth waiting for, and his quip was accompanied by a delightful smile.

One bright spot, in addition to the tireless Mamen, was the messroom boy, Ernest Chafe, nicknamed "Charlie." The young Canadian—he was just nineteen or twenty—was spirited and cocky, preferring to be off the ship whenever possible, professing a fondness for the outdoors. He claimed to be a crack shot with a rifle, and when some of the older crew loudly doubted his boasts, he produced medals for marksmanship he'd recently won, which for some reason he'd felt compelled to bring along with him. This amused Bartlett, and he hoped the boy was as good a shot as he said he was; he might just prove useful as a hunter.

The job of fireman or stoker was important and dangerous. Aboard the *Karluk* were two men charged with maintaining the fires that supplied steam to the engine room. The hard, long shifts demanded youth and strength as the firemen shoveled coal in the hot, humid bunker, breathing caustic fumes and enduring scalding steam burns. George Breddy was a freckly Welsh kid who talked constantly, and Bartlett sometimes walked away while he was still yammering.

The other fireman, Fred Maurer, intrigued the captain. Bartlett had learned how he ended up on the *Karluk*, overhearing parts of his story in the messroom and other details when he was down checking on their work in the engine room. It turned out that after quitting school in his teens, in 1911, just two years before, he'd headed to San Francisco looking for work and by chance saw a newspaper advertisement wanting deckhands on the whaleship *Belvedere*, which was bound for Arctic waters. Maurer signed on, and during a winter-over at Herschel Island, Maurer had chanced to meet Stefansson, who boarded the *Belvedere* to speak with its captain and ended up telling the crew tales of his exploits among the Eskimos. Maurer had been awed by Stefansson, inspired by the explorer's sense of adventure and daring.

Maurer sailed back south on the *Belvedere* as the whaling ship finished out its seasonal run and was back home in his native Ohio wondering what to do next when he again saw something in a newspaper that caught his eye. It was one of the national stories about Stefansson and the proposed Canadian Arctic Expedition! He managed to find an address and scribbled a note to Stefansson directly, reminding him that they'd met the previous winter at Herschel Island and enthusiastically asking if he might come along. Stefansson consented. As Maurer hastily packed for another adventure, his family—who were glad to have him home and wanted him to stay put—begged him not to go. There were too many risks, too much uncertainty. Why not settle down? The spontaneous youngster took out a coin. "It was heads I go; tails I stay home," he wrote in his diary. "I tossed the coin thrice, and twice the head turned up."

Bartlett found it endearing that the young man now toiling at the boiler in the bowels of the *Karluk* had staked the course of his life on the flip of a coin. It was the kind of thing he himself would do, and for this journey, maybe he had.

With the *Karluk* now fully loaded, Bartlett ascended to the barrel to assess conditions. Some small leads were opening, and he waited and watched, glassing the slow, torturous grind of ice for hours. Much was thick and dense, but here and there rafts splintered and gaped open. But he knew that time was of the essence. The agreed-upon meeting with the *Alaska* and the *Mary Sachs* at Herschel Island was less than a week away, and Bartlett reckoned that in ideal conditions it would take at least three days. What he was staring at—rogue floes, heaving bergs, shifting winds—appeared less than ideal. But they needed to go. At 3:30 A.M. on August 8, he called to weigh anchor and steam ahead, and they pushed out into the pack.

The advance proved slow and cumbersome, but at least they were moving eastward. Before noon they'd managed eight miles, though it was a circuitous battle of route finding, and McKinlay remarked that "at times we appeared to be going around in circles." Whenever Bartlett saw open water, he bellowed for full steam, and their course took them away from the Alaskan coastline.

For a while the going was fair, and the crew and scientists tried to keep busy. McKinlay, one of the only scientists who regularly assisted the crew with their work, even helped heave coal. For the first time in days the sun shone brightly, with temperatures rising to almost 40°F, warm enough that some of the scientists lazed about on the decks in their shirtsleeves. Mamen was spending as much time as he could with Bartlett in the barrel, the captain alternately telling stories and teaching him about ice behavior. Mamen had also offered to help the Eskimos in feeding and watering the dogs in the mornings, and fights erupted over food. One encounter was particularly violent, the huskies snarling and tearing at one another's throats. "I got them separated," wrote Mamen, "but it took some whipping before the ravenous dogs let go of each other."

The midday sun and warmth were short-lived, giving way to more sleet and snow and fog. Land was no longer in sight. Belowdecks, Stefansson began divvying up the Arctic clothing. Some of the scientists and crew, in accord for once, complained that the Eskimos were getting more than their fair share; they had arrived fully dressed in furs and skins and mukluks. Why did they need more? Stefansson tried to quell the discontent, saying that everyone would have enough, but most aboard were now edgy. They'd been idle too long and tempers grew short.

And then they ran aground. Bartlett had taken advantage of a long lead and a break in the skies and driven hard for open water, but about ten miles from the Colville River mouth, running at full power, the *Karluk* hit shallows and struck the muddy river delta extending far offshore. The violent jolt sent men scrambling above to see what was going on. With all hands working furiously and Bartlett calling commands, they managed to ease back off the silty bottom and no serious damage was done to the ship.

By evening they were hemmed in again and drifting in the wrong direction. Stefansson consulted with Bartlett and Hadley, suggesting that he and the scientists of the Southern Party take an umiak and a few tons of equipment and strike across the ice toward land. His rationale was that they might, by chance, meet up with the *Mary Sachs* or the *Alaska* at Point Barrow, where perhaps they'd anchored for fresh water. Bartlett and Hadley conferred with their leader, pointing out the perilous, disordered, and unpredictable nature of the ice, saying flatly that the idea was ludicrous, bordering on suicidal. By way of an illustrative morality tale, Hadley told a story of how once, just off Cape Smyth not far from where they were, he'd been traveling over the ice while hunting, and the floe he was on broke loose and drifted away. At the time, he had two weeks' rations with him. He spent the next fifty-three days alone, drifting through the Beaufort and lower Chukchi Sea, reduced by the end to eating his sealskin coat and a pair of mukluks. He'd floated nearly three hundred miles.

Stefansson seemed impressed enough by Hadley's account to withdraw his suggestion. He said no more about it. But it was becoming clear to Bartlett that his leader would rather be just about anywhere than on this ship.

Snow blew in harder. The scientists whiled away time playing whist and bridge. Wilkins cleaned his cameras and photographic equipment, hoping for something momentous to capture on film. Burt McConnell, Stefansson's secretary, plucked away at his typewriter, the constant clicking of the keys a perpetual annoyance inside the spacious "Cabin De Luxe," which he shared with Mamen, McKinlay, Malloch, and Jenness. Mamen, technically a scientist, was now just as much a crew member, almost never ceasing to work. When not in the barrel with Bartlett or helping with the dogs, he assisted shoveling the coal ash from the burners. His only diversion from work had to do with skiing; he built six pairs of ski poles out of iron tubes, affixing their ends with metal spikes or "tips" that would bite into the ice and help propel them along, should they ever have time to ski.

McKinlay also liked to stay busy, so he helped chief engineer Munro heave tons of coal sacks from the deck down into the starboard bunker, which was nearly empty. The work was hot and backbreaking as they stooped to carry nearly one hundred sacks into the low-ceilinged bunker, and when he finished, McKinlay was black with coal dust clinging to his sweat.

When Maurer wasn't on a shift in the engine room, he rested in his bunk in the foc's'le (forecastle), often teasing or playing with a little black kitten, the honorary ship's cat. It was common to bring cats aboard ships and had been done since ancient times. They were useful for eating rodents, which could gnaw away at ropes or root into food stores and carried disease. Cats were also brought along, superstitiously, to ensure a safe voyage. Back in Esquimalt, someone had suggested to Stefansson that they needed a cat for the *Karluk*, but he balked at the idea, saying that the sled dogs would surely eat it. But just before they set sail, one of the crew slipped onto the dock and snagged a scraggly, stranded kitten and smuggled her aboard, stashing her in the foc's'le. Her chest was splashed with a white splotch and she had a little slash of white running down her nose, but the rest of her was jet black. That was good, as a black cat brought the best luck. They named her Nigeraurak, or Little Black One. Maurer had a soft spot for her and adopted her, feeding her treats when no one was looking.

For a time, they sat motionless in a shallow slick of still water between leads. But then, imperceptibly at first, they started to drift. From the deck, McKinlay was filled with a sense of awe and wonder at all his new experiences, at everything he was witnessing. He'd seen his first polar bear and walrus, his first iceblink, had climbed the rigging to the top of the mainmast and seen a spectacular mirage—the appearance of land towering hundreds of feet in the distance—but learned that it was an optical illusion, the result of temperature inversion and the bending of light. Now, McKinlay stood and watched the skies and surveyed the ice, mesmerized by its character; its power; its spectacular, unsettling sounds—sometimes

cracking like gunfire, sometimes shrieking as it split and cleaved. Sometimes, it seemed almost to have the throaty, guttural sound of an animal
roaring as it came together or parted. As he watched and felt wind stirring,
he sensed the ship begin drifting fast toward the northwest, once again
away from their destination. Once, he believed he could see open water
to the east, and thought that if they could somehow reach it, they might
get clear.

But not yet. Not tonight. What he'd thought was open water was just
another mirage. That evening he felt minuscule and vulnerable, writing in
his journal, "The ice tonight was being crushed everywhere badly, being
reduced in most places to a powder. It is a fascinating sight to watch the
square miles of ice slowly moving together, while the noise of the breaking
and raftering, almost terrifying one with the roar."

6

BESET

FOR TWO MORE DAYS, BARTLETT ATTEMPTED TO PUSH EAST. BOTH HE and Stefansson knew that the window for getting through was about to slam shut. Winter was already upon them, though it was only the second week of August. Bartlett had consulted in his logbooks and the *Coast Pilot* book and determined that, compared with all past records, "The winter of 1913 was unprecedented in the annals of northern Alaska. It came on unusually early . . . and for severity of storm and cold it had no equal on record."

One early morning, Mamen was up in the barrel with Bartlett. It was cold, just 17°F, but Bartlett seemed unaffected by the elements. Mamen was amazed how the experienced navigator saw and ran for openings he himself couldn't see, charging through the cakes. They were constantly ramming ice, and once Mamen was shaken so hard he thought he might fall out, but he clung for his life while Bartlett alternately laughed and cursed. He cursed the ship, mocking its speed and icebreaking abilities. Most surprising to Mamen, the captain had a few unsavory things to say about Stefansson, blurts of venomous diatribe that seemed rather forthcoming, even if Mamen agreed with them.

Bartlett was beginning to confide in Mamen. After all, they were spending hours at a time up there, with no one else to talk to. But after a harsh outburst, Bartlett would just chuckle to himself and cast his glare at the ice horizon once more, almost as if to will them a way forward. Wrote Mamen, impressed by the captain's determination: "He is a man who utilizes all chances to get ahead. . . . But the ice is a bad enemy; it hinders us in all possible ways."

Working this way, still threading and snaking east along the coast, Bartlett navigated constantly. The weather varied even from minute to minute; sometimes snowing, then clearing long enough for the captain to see the shoreline and the mountains beyond on the mainland. From the crow's nest Bartlett spied a sizable lead, but after taking soundings he determined it would be too risky in the overloaded *Karluk*, concluding that they had drawn "too much water to venture into those shallow lanes." Instead, he ordered the crew to make fast to a grounded floe where they could hold what distance they'd gained and wait for the next opportunity, should one come.

The captain and the expedition leader discussed their options, with consultation from Hadley, who knew these waters well. Stefansson trusted Hadley, calling him "a fountain of inexhaustible northern lore." There were two prevailing philosophies for ice navigation: the Atlantic theory and the Alaska or Beaufort Sea theory. The bolder Atlantic theory held that the farther away from land you stayed, the better your chance of finding more open, scattered ice. The downside was that if you were iced in, you were much farther from land. The more cautious Beaufort Sea approach was to hug the coast, staying along the shore if you could, "and if you don't get there this year you may have another chance the next."

Not long after discussing these approaches, Bartlett saw an opening. Strong southwest winds were separating the pack and creating an opening to the north, toward the open sea. It was the bolder course—and diverged from the western Arctic tradition of shore hugging—but after consulting with Stefansson and getting his agreement, Bartlett took his shot. "We steamed along through open water and because the ice near the shore was closely packed, we were driven farther offshore than I would have liked." They steamed north, deliberately away from land, weaving between ice cakes and sometimes ramming violently into them. Watching nervously as they moved away from the shoreline, Hadley offered his opinion: "It may be safe," he said. "But I don't think so."

But now Bartlett was committed, and he followed what lanes there were away from land and out toward the open sea. They made a good many miles until that evening, when they came face-to-face with a giant ice sheet and Bartlett powered down to assess it. To the experienced captain, the scene was eerily familiar: "This was similar to the ice which I have seen in Melville Bay on the west Greenland coast," he wrote in his log. "It was part of the past season's ice. Seldom over a foot thick, it was honey-combed with water holes." He stood there, staring at the sheet of ice, lamenting his little ship's lack of horsepower: "The *Roosevelt* could have plowed her way through it, but the *Karluk* was powerless to do so."

Now halted, they took readings. Bartlett determined that they'd gone some 225 miles from Point Barrow, well more than halfway to Herschel Island, and lay perhaps twenty miles offshore. But he could see the water tightening around them astern, the ice beginning to clasp the *Karluk* in a pincer grip. They made fast to the floe, and first thing the next morning, Bartlett tried forcing his way back south toward land, but they were now floating in a mere hole of water less than two hundred yards wide, with nothing but ice in every direction. After two or three feeble bunts against the ice surrounding them, he ordered the *Karluk* tied up again. There was nowhere else to go.

And there they sat for the next few days. The snow began to fall, lightly at first, then hard and constant, hour after hour. Bartlett came up from a brief nap on August 13 to confirm what he already knew. "The snow formed a blanket on the ice and later on its melting and freezing cemented the ice snugly about the ship so that she was made almost an integral part of the floe itself."

They were beset.

Bartlett took advantage of the downtime to briefly rest—he'd been almost constantly in the barrel for two full days—then roused to check the condition of the *Karluk* after all their recent ice ramming. Examining the stem, he discovered that the ice had shorn off two of the brass stem plates completely and loosened the bolts of others. All needed repair before they moved again, and he set the engineers to the task. He told the rest of the crew, whoever wasn't assigned to specific work detail, "Eat when you feel like it and sleep when you feel like it, for you never know how soon you will have neither."

The oceanographer, Murray, had been taking every opportunity, when they were at a standstill, to employ a cleverly constructed dredge he had brought along. It had a rectangular iron frame welded together, to which he affixed a two-foot-deep mesh cotton bag designed to catch sea creatures. Murray would take the dredge overboard onto the ice along a water lead. He'd fasten a rope to the center of one side of the framework and lower the dredge into the water, playing out the rope until the dredge hit the bottom. In this way, he could also take depth soundings with the marked lead line made for that purpose. Once he'd hit bottom, Murray would put the rope over his shoulder and tromp along the edge of the lead, being careful not to fall in. Using this method, he could manage alone up to a depth of about twenty fathoms (a fathom equals six feet); any deeper, the dredge and rope became too heavy, and he required assistance—sometimes by as many as six others.

Many offered to help, and even though it was cold, wet work, it was exciting to see what the oceanographer might bring up. According to Bartlett, it was novel science: "I don't believe that dredging was ever done in that part of the Arctic before." Murray took the specimens—worms, sea mice, gastropods, long-legged shrimps—and studied them under a microscope in the ship's small laboratory just off the forward hold in the lower deck. Then he took notes and carefully labeled and preserved the specimens.

By now Mamen had several pairs of skis and poles ready, and he took a group of crew and scientists out on the ice for ski instruction. The skies had cleared and the brilliant sunshine, the distant mountains, almost reminded him of home: "We can see the mountains on the mainland; they are splendid with their white covering on top." Some of the men, especially McKinlay and Wilkins, were quick learners, adept and competent as they glided along the smooth, flat cake. Mamen was impressed by how fast they learned, and he showed off a little, expertly illustrating the Telemark and Christiania turns. Others were awkward and clumsy, as stiff as matchsticks, but he knew it would take time: "One cannot expect them to learn all the fine points of skiing at once." He found the anthropologist Beuchat endlessly amusing and comical as he slipped and stumbled and fell, sliding face-first across the ice, his legs splaying out in impossible angles. He wondered if the uncoordinated Frenchman would ever get the hang of it.

They concluded the ski outing with a soccer match. The international contingent had all played since they were boys, and the match got heated. As they raced about, a few fell, cutting up their shins and calves. Mamen, young and highly athletic and in his prime, was also extremely competitive. Going for a ball and desperate to score a goal, he felt his knee pop. He'd injured it years before in a skiing crash, and now he could feel it burning and swelling, but he brushed it off and went back to the match, whose outcome actually meant something to him. In his journal, he made sure to record the following: "It ended with victory for my team . . . but I feel considerably worn out and fatigued."

But Mamen's joy of being out skiing and playing soccer again was tempered by thoughts of home. Back on the *Karluk*, he wrote a letter to his fiancée, Ellen. Tomorrow was her birthday, and the anniversary of their engagement. It seemed as if it were only yesterday that he'd held her fine, delicate hands and slipped the ring onto her finger. But he was worlds away out here. He might as well have been on another planet. He'd tried to keep her out of his mind as much as possible, but he couldn't help conjuring her fine face, her lovely features, and now he was racked by the thought of his beloved's beauty, and a fear that he might never see her again. "I long to go further north and then home," he wrote in his diary, "but the chances are small, yes, infinitely small."

Captain Bartlett's thirty-eighth birthday on August 15 was cause for much celebration. On Arctic voyages, any holiday was a reason to break the monotony, the birthday of a ship's captain even more so. Bartlett surfaced from his quarters freshly shaved and in a fine mood. That evening, the cook ironed and laid out a fine linen tablecloth and dazzled everyone with the meal: roasted beef and beef tongue (tinned); various salads and fruit desserts, and, as McKinlay put it, "The dainties were so numerous that accommodation for them all could not be found on the table." Templeman had clearly outdone himself, for between mouthfuls of the fine fare, members applauded him every time he reappeared with some new delicacy.

Stefansson opened bottles of whiskey and offered unlimited quantities of lime juice and lemonade for the teetotalers, then presented Bartlett with a box of fine cigars, which the captain passed around generously. "We puffed them as if we had been in the most fashionable restaurant in London or New York," wrote McKinlay. Everyone hoisted their cups and toasted Captain Bartlett's health and long life, and the evening's revelry progressed to songs and music. Dr. Mackay, typically acerbic, was loosened by a few whiskeys and broke into a medley of Scottish sing-alongs, accompanied by the other Scotsmen. McKinlay and Wilkins sang a hilarious duet; Hadley played his guitar and sang a solo; and McConnell played a concert on one of the ship's Victrolas, to great cheer and hullabaloo. Wilkins captured a flashlight photograph of the company of men in their merriment, and it was three o'clock before the last of the revelers staggered back to their bunks.

For nearly a week, there they sat, nipped by ice on all sides. The weather had grown calm, with light winds and dull, hazy skies. Bartlett understood that only a dramatic shift in weather, bringing heavy winds, would move the pack enough to change their situation. When the skies cleared briefly, he could see the spectacular Romanzof and Franklin Mountains some thirty miles to the south, snowcapped and gleaming briefly in the distance. Then fog and mist would roll in, shrouding everything.

Stefansson and the rest of the scientists grew restless from inactivity. They played cards and read, and Dr. Mackay challenged all comers to games of chess, wagering tobacco on the outcome. Dr. Mackay was a prodigious smoker, and with his tobacco stock low, he relied on his chess skills to replenish his supplies. No one was able to beat him, and his stockpile of tobacco grew considerably. In the evenings they'd go up to the deck and marvel at the brilliant skies, the air cold and still. The temperatures dipped into the high teens, caking the ship's rigging with a veneer of hoarfrost. McKinlay found beauty in the nights, and how the *Karluk* shone and glimmered, noting the "silvery moon with the halo around her . . . and the frost on the rigging made the ship look like a fairy barque."

And then, almost imperceptibly at first, they began drifting west. They remained imprisoned by ice, trapped within an old floe over a mile wide, but the current was taking them backward over those hard-gained miles. Initially, they were moving just a mile an hour, but when strong winds started blowing from the east, they moved even faster. Bartlett climbed up to the barrel, and his pulse quickened for a moment. He spied "water sky" not far to the east—light glinting off the ocean, confirming open water there. And to the south, between them and the land, lay dark slicks of ice-free sea. Yet there was no way to get there, icebound as they were. He contemplated the distance from the ship to the edge of the floe, and thought of using dynamite to blow lanes ahead of the bow so they might move. He well knew the story of the tragic Greely expedition (1881–84), and how naval commander Winfield Schley had used dynamite to free the rescue ships *Thetis* and *Bear* in a heroic last-ditch effort to save Greely's starving men. But after doing some calculations, Bartlett figured that they'd use all their dynamite to gain even a quarter mile through this ice, so he decided against it.

Stefansson was becoming increasingly impatient and concerned by their westward drift. He called the scientists to his cabin. There was still a chance, he said, to get some of the members of the Southern Party reunited with the *Alaska* and *Mary Sachs*, where they were supposed to be, and where most of their equipment was. They'd have to strike out onto the ice with dogsleds and an umiak and bolt for shore, using the skin boat to cross any open leads they encountered. Once they reached shore, they might be able to determine, by conversing with the coastal inhabitants, the whereabouts of the other ships. If they'd stayed close to shore, they might well have recently passed by. Stefansson even thought it possible—though this seemed absurd to the others—that they could navigate the umiak all the way to Herschel Island if they had to, or if it proved unnavigable, they could abandon the umiak and continue on overland by dogsled, guided by a couple of the Eskimo hunters.

After a lengthy discussion of the men's job descriptions and location of the equipment they'd need to do their work—as well as the equipment's bulk and weight—Stefansson determined that the anthropologists Diamond Jenness and Henri Beuchat should be the ones to go. All along he'd intended that they live and work with various Eskimo groups, learning their languages and studying their lives and habits. Murray was ruled out, as most of his equipment was heavy and already on the *Karluk*; he might just as well do his oceanographic work with her. Wilkins and McKinlay would remain aboard the *Karluk* too.

The frail Beuchat, though he had agreed to go, apparently had misgivings about his decision. On the night before the proposed departure— August 27—snow fell heavily, covering the ice, making it harder to see weak spots where one might break through. Visibility was poor and the Eskimos said they feared the rotten ice. Hearing all of this, Beuchat reported that he was having "palpitations in the heart," and he requested to be examined by Dr. Mackay. After listening carefully with his stethoscope, the doctor was unable to confirm any serious cardiac condition, and Beuchat sheepishly carried on with preparations for departure.

While they waited out the storm, Stefansson provided Jenness with written instructions and traveling expenses. Jenness and Beuchat were to attempt to reach the Southern Party as soon as they could by trying to determine the whereabouts of the *Alaska* and *Mary Sachs*. Should they be unable to locate them, Stefansson authorized the two scientists to perform any work they deemed feasible and "act independently of the expedition if circumstances warranted it . . . as a unit responsible to the Naval Service." Last, Stefansson instructed Jenness to send a telegraph to the *New York Times* providing a news story of their trials and travails thus far.

Around midmorning on August 29, everything was ready and the weather fair enough for the attempt. The fourteen dogs yipped and whined

in the harnesses of the two heavily loaded sleds. Kataktovik had been chosen to accompany them for the entirety of the journey, while the hunters
Jimmy and Jerry, plus several crew members, would serve as escorts at the
beginning, then return to the ship. As the Eskimos and Stefansson had
feared, the snow-covered ice made it hard going in the overloaded sleds.
Just a mile from the ship, the sled carrying the umiak tipped over and
broke through the ice, plunging in clear to the handles. It took all hands
to pull the sled back out, and the umiak's mast snapped off as they yanked
it from the water.

Stefansson had remained aboard the *Karluk*, organizing mail to send
with them, which he encased in a sealed tin. When he was ready, he took
Hadley and another dog team and raced after them, following their trail.
He arrived to find the party soaked and sitting on the poor ice, eating a
cold lunch without tea. Somehow, they had already lost a crucial part of
their Primus stove and were unable to cook anything or even boil water.
The Eskimos told Stefansson that the ice was "no good; very bad." Stefansson could see that they were right. New ice was forming between
the older cakes, so it was going to be impossible to employ the umiak in
water—and it now needed repairs anyway. But neither was the new ice yet
strong enough to support the sleds, which would inevitably keep breaking
through. He called off the mission. They cached some heavy, less necessary
stores there to retrieve later—it was still early afternoon—and ordered
everyone to return to the ship. Heading back, Beuchat broke through the
ice and became so cold and incapacitated that they had to load him into
the umiak and portage him all the way back to the *Karluk*.

The events of the miscarried land attempt weighed on Stefansson. Dr.
Mackay had devised a "drift indicator" and determined that they were
now moving at least twelve miles per day. Stefansson knew as well as Bartlett that drifting along encased in ice, at the mercy of fate, was a dangerous
proposition. He also noticed—again, as did Bartlett—that the ice right
next to the ship was beginning to press against the sides "till she groaned
and quivered with the strain." But for the moment, the ship was holding,
protected from further pressure by the great size of adjacent floes.

With ice amassing in all directions, and the days growing shorter and colder, Stefansson was now resigned. He wrote in his journal: "I had made up my mind that the *Karluk* was not to move under her own power again, and that we were in for a voyage such as that of the *Jeannette* or the *Fram*, drifting for years, if we had the luck to remain unbroken, eventually coming out somewhere towards the Atlantic, either we or our wreckage."

7

THE CARIBOU HUNT

THE *KARLUK* WAS DRIFTING ALONG, FROZEN FAST IN THE CENTER OF an island of ice about a mile and a half wide. By early September nearly everyone aboard knew they might be spending the winter locked in the ice, but not all of them comprehended the danger they were in. Captain Bartlett did, and with the days shortening, he took preparatory measures, rationing the use of kerosene and coal oil. He knew they'd need to conserve both, since much of their intended supply was unfortunately aboard the *Mary Sachs*. He ordered all lamps and stoves extinguished by midnight, and in a gesture that symbolized the official arrival of winter and months of near darkness, the lamp in the saloon was lit for the first time.

Bartlett was also keenly aware of the issue of fresh meat. It was needed to supplement the pemmican rations for the dogs, but there was an added benefit for the men. "Without fresh meat," he logged in his journal, "there was always the danger of scurvy, that blight of so many earlier Arctic explorers."* He sent the Eskimos out hunting for seals and urged any of the crewmen, scientists, and officers not engaged in specific duties to partici-

---

* At the time, though scurvy was known as a dietary deficiency, it was not completely understood. It was known that citrus fruits like lemons and limes appeared to combat the disease, so mariners began taking them on extended voyages (resulting in the British expression "Limeys"). There was also anecdotal evidence that fresh meat worked as well, though it was not understood that it was because nearly all mammals produce their own vitamin C in quantities sufficient to prevent or even treat scurvy.

pate as well, since the expedition would need all the meat they could procure. Seals would be the most prized, as they could be used for food, fuel,
clothing, and to repair the bottoms of damaged umiaks and kayaks once
the skins were stretched and dried. There were other animals in the vicinity
as well: polar bear tracks had been spotted in fresh snow near the ship,
and a scattering of ducks migrating south were using the open water at the
edges of the ice island and in some of the freshwater pools on the surface.
Stefansson had them well supplied with rifles for the seals, bears, and foxes,
and shotguns or "fowling pieces" for the birds.

McKinlay—who had never hunted for seal before—wanted to try.
One day he and anthropologist Diamond Jenness followed the Eskimo
hunters out to a small lead. Just as they arrived, a seal emerged in open water but dipped back under the surface before anyone could fire a shot. The
Eskimos motioned for them to spread out along the lead and wait. After
about thirty minutes the seal resurfaced right in front of McKinlay, who
shouldered his rifle and squeezed off a round, the bullet hitting the surface
just after the seal slipped back under. After what McKinlay thought was
another interminable wait, he and Jenness gave up, unaccustomed to the
patience required. The Eskimos spent eight to ten hours at a time kneeling
or lying silently on the ice, rifles ready, perpetually scanning the water
before them for the telltale blip of a seal coming up for air. Then, moving
as little as possible, they'd shoulder their weapon, aim, exhale, and fire in
one precise, effortless motion. It was impressive to watch their skill, and
they did not miss often.

But McKinlay soon realized that shooting a seal did not guarantee its
procurement. If the seal wasn't dead, it could swim away or slide beneath the
ice; if dead, it might sink quickly or float—but you still had to bring it in.
The Eskimos had devised an ingenious tool for this purpose called a manak.
At the end of a long piece of cod line they attached a five-to-six-pound lead
weight, and a foot or two beyond the weight was tethered a four-clawed
grappling hook. As the seal floated, the hunter would coil the line like a
lasso and, swinging the hook around like a cowpoke roping horses, throw
the hook some feet beyond the seal, then reel in line, snagging the carcass

and dragging it in to the edge of the ice, where they could reach down and grab it.

In early September there were still a few seals in their vicinity. Slowly and painstakingly, the hunters began to bring in two, three, sometimes four a day. Kurulak was the most skilled and successful. McKinlay found the meat—and especially that of younger seals—extremely tasty, noting its dark color and strong, fishy smell. The Eskimos skinned and butchered the animals with remarkable speed, cutting off thick steaks and saving the liver for "seal steak and kidney pie," which Templeman put on the menu once a week.

McKinlay and the other scientists—and Bartlett, too—preferred duck hunting. It was more active and took considerably less patience and expertise. One evening Bartlett, Mamen, and Wilkins took a Peterborough canoe—a wooden Canadian canoe that had been intended for use by the Southern Party in the small creeks and streams of the Mackenzie River—and lashed it to a sled. They dragged the sled to a lead and climbed in the canoe, paddling along in the late light. Bartlett took note of the beauty and tranquility: "The surface of the water was so clear that, although the ship was fully two miles away from us in the ice, her rigging was reflected in our lead. We were getting sunsets now, with the gradual shortening of the daylight; the sunset was red and brilliant . . . giving the white ice the lovely appearance of rose-colored quartz."

When they saw the V-shaped outlines of ducks on the horizon, their wings cupped for landing, they dropped Bartlett off on the ice and he hid behind raised banks of raftered ice that formed a natural blind. When the ducks landed, he blasted a bunch, which Mamen and Wilkins picked up in the canoe. There were a good many ducks landing at the bottom end of the lead, but new ice was forming, and they had to smash it with their paddles to move along, which startled the ducks and made them fly away. So they stashed the canoe for a future hunt and walked back to the *Karluk*, where they found that McKinlay, Jenness, and Beuchat had also had good luck during their outing. Between them they had about fifty ducks to show for the day's hunt.

When not hunting, they were skiing. Bartlett had decided to learn. He knew that Nansen had used skis to reach Farthest North during his 1895 attempt at the North Pole; and Roald Amundsen also used skis to become first to reach the South Pole in 1911. But on his trips with Peary, Bartlett had only ever used snowshoes. Bartlett understood that under the right conditions—with smooth or lightly snow-covered ice—a good skier could travel up to fifty miles a day. Such travel, conserving time and food rations, could be lifesaving. And he had an excellent ski instructor in the champion Mamen, "who had won many prizes for his skill." Bartlett proved a very quick learner, and by his first afternoon he was sidestepping up and then flying down the steep slope of a low-angled iceberg, and even challenging Dr. Mackay to a race.

Mamen—partly to show off but also to practice the technique—showed everyone the Norwegian art of skijoring (literally, "ski-driving"). He harnessed Snap, one of the more compliant dogs, and holding on to the harness straps, gave the dog a flick to the haunches and off they went. Snap learned fast, and soon they were hurtling across the ice, the dog running at full speed and Mamen whooping with joy, his skis bouncing over little bumps as they flew two full miles from the ship in minutes and then returned, Mamen beaming and Snap gobbling up pieces of seal meat he received as a reward.

Mamen was ecstatic to be out skiing, and he managed to get most of the scientists involved in what he called his "ski patrol." They were happy to be doing something, anything to be off the ship and to thwart the inactivity. It was a chance for some levity too. One morning, Dr. Mackay showed up on skis in nothing but "his drawers, sweater, and sporting stockings," and everyone buckled over with laughter at his outfit. Mamen found it hilarious: "The doctor is in his second childhood. . . . Every time he fell, he got his pantaloons full of snow!" Indeed, the cold soon drove him back to the ship for hot tea and warmer clothing. Mamen was impressed by everyone's progress, noting that Bartlett, Dr. Mackay, Wilkins, and Malloch were all coordinated and physically fit. To test them, he organized a cross-country ski competition, "the Karluk Championship Distance Race," and recorded the results in his diary: No. 1 Wilkins 14:46; Dr. Mackay 16:12; McConnell 17:56; Malloch 18:16.

Mamen even built a ski jump very near the ship. Pressure from encroaching ice had created a low-angled rafter about thirty feet high. The men cut ice blocks and stacked them to create a takeoff rise, then smoothed an outrun by covering it with slushy snow and water that froze, making it slick and fast. They'd sidestep up the back side of the jump in softer snow, then, using their poles, propel themselves down the slope and launch off the jump. On his first attempt, Bartlett whooshed down with such speed that he flew fifteen feet in the air before landing, cartwheeling forward and toppling onto his head. He got up, unscathed, and returned for more.

Bartlett clearly understood the importance of diversion. He'd wintered over in the Arctic four times before and knew the dangers that darkness, close quarters, and endless repetition brought. He knew they were now shipbound until next spring—should the ship survive. That meant many months living in tight quarters, in the near-total darkness of winter—the so-called Long Night. Such conditions could produce disastrous effects. Men suffered claustrophobia, anxiety, depression—even insanity—and the history of such expeditions held horror tales of mutiny, suicide, and even murder.* Bartlett had read how Commander Adolphus Greely—who spent three winters in the High Arctic—used physical and mental diversion to maintain order. He organized outdoor games, snowshoe races, shooting competitions—anything to break the monotony and keep his men physically active. Greely also created an indoor lecture series, speaking on various topics ranging from geography to philosophy to history, to keep his men's minds and imaginations occupied. Bartlett would try to provide his own version of Greely's method, in addition to keeping up the regular duties of the ship's routine.

During most of this time, the first two weeks of September, Stefansson was moody and brooding. He seemed distracted and even annoyed,

---

* A compelling read that chronicles onboard insanity is Julian Sancton's *Madhouse at the End of the Earth*, about the first winter-over in Antarctica aboard the *Belgica* in 1898.

noting that the scientists and even the captain "devoted themselves to ski jumping and playing other games around the ship," while he was trying to figure out what, if any, options he might still have to salvage his elaborate and very expensive expedition that wasn't going anywhere. Well, that wasn't exactly true. Using a sextant and confirming the readings with sun and star observations, Murray made a chart that chronicled their drift. After consulting it for many days in a row, Stefansson and Bartlett could see that they were continually moving to the northwest, away from land and headed toward the middle of the Arctic Ocean.

At night, by lamplight, stories went around the saloon in hushed tones about the veritable ship's graveyard where they were headed and the many ships that had been frozen in, crushed, or vanished in this region. McKinlay was spooked by these "ghost stories . . . and one in particular of seventy-five men who left their ship but were all lost."

Dr. Mackay, also deeply affected by the potential consequences of their plight, commented—joking or not, it was hard to tell with him—that he was "reconciled to leaving his bones here, 'never to be seen again.'"

Given their position and their drift, Stefansson privately began considering another attempt to reach land. Not all of them could go, that was certain. There were too many of them, and too much gear, to safely depart en masse, and the previous aborted try showed how fickle the sea ice could be. The leads in the vicinity of the *Karluk* were covered with new ice, which looked beautiful, the top layer coated with a sheen of crystallized triangular ice flowers, but the surface was hardly stable or predictable. Still, Stefansson felt this might be his last chance. On September 17, Stefansson sent Dr. Mackay and Diamond Jenness on a reconnaissance mission to scout for land to the south. Mamen watched the two men from the ship, noting that they were moving in the wrong direction toward the northwest. He strapped on a pair of skis and strode out after them, catching them and turning them due south. Mamen led them along some eight miles, keeping a few large icebergs in view for bearing, but they saw no land and returned to the ship.

By Murray's best estimate, they were now about eighteen miles north of

Beechey Point, approximately sixteen miles east of Oliktok Point, Alaska.*
To try to confirm this, a couple of days later Stefansson sent Mamen and
Dr. Mackay out again. They skiffed along on skis in the cold 8°F morning,
under an intense clear sky that Mamen described as being "as bright as a
mirror." They traveled all day, mostly toward the west, but after twelve
miles they'd sighted no land and turned back, finally straggling onto the
Karluk around dinnertime, with Dr. Mackay exhausted from the effort.

Despite these failed efforts, Stefansson seemed desperate to reach land.
After the evening meal that night, he called a sudden meeting in his cabin
with Bartlett, Mamen, Malloch, and McKinlay. Stefansson declared that
they needed fresh meat for the winter, and he intended to lead a party
ashore on a caribou hunt. This notion raised a few eyebrows. First, because
the Eskimos had been daily bringing in seals, and as McKinlay pointed
out, there was no problem keeping the meat fresh: "The entire pack around
us was a huge natural refrigerator." But even more confusing, Stefansson
had previously said that caribou were nearly extinct in that region of the
northern Alaskan coast, so there must be some other rationale. Stefansson
explained that he needed to go since he was the only one who knew how
to hunt caribou, and because he knew the country and the area's Eskimos
and could potentially buy fish and meat from them. He said he'd be taking along Jimmy and Jerry, since they were experienced hunters, as well as
the photographer Wilkins plus secretary McConnell and anthropologist
Jenness, the latter so that he might begin his study of the Eskimos. Stefansson told Bartlett that he expected to be gone about ten days, "if no
accident happens"—he added rather ominously—and that he would leave
written instructions for the captain to follow during his absence. It was all
very sudden and to most on board seemed spontaneous, unnecessary, and
ill conceived.

All the next morning, under cold, overcast skies, the ship was a bustle of
hurried preparation, with Stefansson yelling out for specific items, directing
the organization of equipment. Mamen cynically remarked, "It was like Je-

---

* Oliktok Point is now the northernmost drivable point in North America.

rusalem's destruction; they didn't know what they had or what they should have." Some of the crew helped, while others, including Bartlett, lined the ship's deck and watched. By noon the caribou-hunting party had assembled on the ice next to the *Karluk*. Twelve of the best dogs, personally selected by Stefansson, yipped and whined, harnessed to two sleds loaded with tents, stoves, fuel alcohol, axes and skinning knives, reindeer-skin sleeping bags and sheepskin sleeping robes, and a few hundred pounds of food, including Underwood pemmican for the men as well as plenty of dog pemmican.

They were well equipped with rifles, shotguns, and ammunition. Mamen had fitted the hunting party out with skis and poles. Wilkins ran about shooting moving pictures as the party got set to leave, and then rather suddenly, on September 20, at around half past one, framed by bands of glinting sunshine, Stefansson strode away from his ship, breaking trail and posing for the movie camera as he headed south.

For some time, those remaining on board watched the men and dogs receding in the distance, growing smaller until they became, according to Fred Maurer, "small black specks against the everlasting white."

And then they vanished.

8
ADRIFT

THE NEXT DAY, A STORM ARRIVED. BARTLETT FELT THE WINDS GAIN-
ing power, and he sent McKinlay up to the barrel to install an anemometer
for accurate readings. McKinlay ran wires from the anemometer down the
length of the mast and along the deck and straight into his cabin, where he
recorded the velocities in his notebook. The captain also dispatched Murray
to set up his tidal gauge and drift indicator. Now remaining on board were
twenty-two men, one woman, two small children, twenty-two sled dogs,
and Nigeraurak, the little kitten. With the expedition leader gone, their lives
were all now solely in Bartlett's hands.

By evening the umiaks and whaleboats, though tethered tight, were
pounding against the sides of the ship, and McKinlay measured the wind
speeds at gale force, upwards of fifty miles per hour.* On the morning of
September 23, the wind was still blowing with ferocity. McKinlay and the
young messroom boy, Charlie Chafe, went for a walk for exercise and to
run a few of the dogs, and snow fell so hard that for a time they could no
longer spot the ship and became disoriented. They managed to stumble
their way back, the snow lashing at their cheeks, and climb into the relative warmth and safety of the *Karluk*.

---

* Interestingly, the wind force scale (known as the Beaufort scale) had been devised in 1805 by
Commander (later Rear Admiral) Francis Beaufort of the Royal Navy. The *Karluk*'s current
location was the Beaufort Sea, named for the same esteemed Irish hydrographer.

Not long afterward, Bartlett returned from the dredge hole with Kataktovik and Kuraluk. The two Eskimos were yammering anxiously and waving their arms. Bartlett took Hadley and Murray, the oceanographer, aside and conversed with them, then reported the news to everyone: they were drifting, and very fast.

Bartlett ordered everything that had been down on the ice—dogs and dogsleds, the duck-hunting canoe, miscellaneous gear—immediately brought on board and secured, fearing that the ice directly around the ship might fracture. He commanded everyone to remain aboard until further notice, suspending all excursions. Murray scribbled furiously in his notebooks, and by evening, he confirmed what Bartlett suspected. The ice floe in which they were trapped was careening out to sea at a speed of thirty miles a day. Between jotting down wind readings, McKinlay wrote in his diary, "We are being carried away from land in the grip of the gale-swept ice pack . . . moving west . . . leaving an ever-widening expanse of Arctic Sea between us and our leader."

For the moment, it was unsafe to leave the ship for any reason, but there remained plenty to do on board. Most important was the matter of proper Arctic clothing. Many of the crew, excluding the Eskimos, were still not suitably fitted out with sufficient winter attire: thick, sheepskin-lined reindeer-skin coats with fur collars; trousers and stockings of sheepskin; mittens and special winter boots for snow and ice, the uppers made from reindeer skin, the soles of tough, durable bearded seal.* The hastily assembled crew members had initially boarded without any of these garments, and the tanned skins and raw woolens needed for them were obtained only when Stefansson had gone ashore at Point Hope, almost two months earlier. Kiruk, the seamstress hired for this duty—whom everyone now called Auntie—had been working tirelessly, sewing outfits for each of the

---

* Members of the expedition refer to the animal variously as ugruk and ugsug. The Inuktitut name for the seal is *ugjuk* (plural, *ugjuit*) or *oogrook* or *oogruk*. So, I'm sticking with "bearded seal."

men. But Bartlett knew she could not get them all attired by herself, so he urged the men to start learning from her and sewing their own clothing. In this Arctic blast, with temperatures dropping and the days shortening, the right clothing was the difference between life and death.

Bartlett enlisted all hands to bring essential provisions—food and stoves and fuel and tents—on deck, and to load the whaleboats with survival supplies for a potential emergency abandonment. "We had to be ready to move at an instant's notice," he wrote in his log. "I had sometimes seen several miles of open water between the pack and the Alaskan coast and we might have to leave the ship and row after the storm was over." He also made sure that the dogs were well fed and ready, and that the best of them had been selected for a team, remarking that "If we had to drive home, they would save our lives."

With everything in order, Bartlett retired to his cabin and read over the letter of instructions that Stefansson had left him. Elements of it were detailed and very specific, with an eye on their scientific purposes. "On days when an onshore wind is blowing, it might be desirable to have Dr. Mackay run lines of soundings out in various directions from the ship," Stefansson wrote, "and if it becomes practicable, send off Malloch and Mamen for surveying purposes. McKinlay should accompany them for the purpose of establishing magnetic stations." Listening to the wind lashing at the rigging, Bartlett frowned. None of that was happening anytime soon.

But another part of the letter caused Bartlett to look up and wonder for a moment. It was eerily prescient. "Should the *Karluk* during our absence be driven from her present position . . . erect one or more beacons, giving information of the ship's location." Well, that had certainly come to pass, and though Bartlett had no idea yet exactly how far they'd drifted or where they now were, it remained too treacherous to send men off the boat and onto the shifting, churning, and crumbling ice.

Other details in the letter outlined Stefansson's proposed itinerary and possible locations, but Bartlett only scoffed at these. Stefansson expected, if the strength of the ice permitted, to make it to Thetis Island, and then to cross over to Beechey Point, but all of this was pure conjecture. Out on the ice, the conditions always dictated one's direction, and very little was certain. Bartlett laughed out loud, then jotted his thoughts in his own log: "You can make all the plans you want in the Far North . . . using all the words in the dictionary. But the finer plan you have the worse it will go to smash when wind and ice and drifting snow take charge."

Such was now the case for those still on the *Karluk*, and certainly for Stefansson and his small contingent plodding along or hunkered down somewhere out there in the ferocious maw of the Arctic storm.

The first night away from the ship, Stefansson had set up tents on the ice as the sun was going down. With their late start, they'd made only about seven miles, picking their way slowly over the thin bands of young, treacherous ice connecting safer, older floes. Stefansson put McConnell, Wilkins, and Jenness in one tent; he'd share the other with Jimmy and Jerry. For Stefansson, ice camping was routine; he'd spent hundreds of such nights out. But his scientists were new to these rigors, and he first illustrated how to pitch the tents, stabilizing them with lines pounded into the ice with metal stakes. Then he showed them how to lay out the "floor skins and sleeping bags in the Eskimo manner," to avoid getting wet.

The next day, they drove the dog teams to a gravelly bar at Spy Island, the westernmost of the Jones Islands, still some four or five miles from the Alaskan coast near the mouth of the Colville River. The ice between the island and the mainland was breakable and rotten, so they made camp, built a driftwood fire, cooked dinner on their sheet-iron stove, and turned in early. That night, finally away from the dreaded *Karluk*, Stefansson's mind had time to wander. The tent snapped in the rising wind, and he could feel a powerful storm blowing up. There was much to ponder: the location of the *Alaska* and the *Mary Sachs*, which he hadn't seen since leaving Nome; the fate of the *Karluk*, for he feared she must have drifted in this storm; the fate of the entire enterprise, for that matter. His grand expedition was now a scattered mess, strewn in disarray across the Arctic.

And in those moments of doubt and thoughts of the unknown, he had time to think about something else: his son. His young son, Alex, just three years old now—whom he'd last seen two years before. And his son's mother, his Inupiat common-law wife, Fanny Pannigabluk: feisty, strong, and tough. When he'd left them they were living at Nunaluk, just a few miles west of Herschel Island. His last words to them were that he'd be back. He had every reason to believe they were still there.

After a fitful night alternately thinking and dreaming of both his expedition and his secret family, Stefansson awoke to find that the skies had cleared enough for him to get a glimpse of his situation. "What I saw," he wrote in his journal, "was very disquieting . . . to seaward the darkness and blotchiness of the clouds showed that the ice was broken where yesterday it had been continuous, with water reflected in the sky, and clouds of dark vapor rising from the leads." From his vantage on the island, all around him was water—nothing but open water between him and the shore, and open water between him and the last place he believed the *Karluk* to be.

Stefansson and the others began collecting the largest pieces of driftwood they could find along the beach. By lashing branches to tree trunks and logs and standing them upright, they constructed a makeshift observation tower about fifteen feet high onto which Stefansson could climb and scan with his binoculars. Gazing to the north, Stefansson caught a glimpse of what appeared to be the *Karluk*'s masts piercing the horizon, but it was hard to be sure in the swirling snow and mist. For a moment he thought that the ship might have broken loose and Bartlett now had her running under steam, but that seemed unlikely. And then he doubted whether what he was seeing was the *Karluk* after all. "The glimpses of her were so fleeting and she was so veiled by fog that I was not even sure that it might not have been a cake of ice that I mistook for her."

The only thing that Stefansson now knew for certain was that he and his small contingent of men and dogs were marooned on the island, at least for a few days. By then, he hoped the temperature would drop enough to harden the lagoon ice between him and land, and once it was safe enough to travel, he'd be able to get ashore to the mainland. When the skies finally cleared, Stefansson climbed up to the top perch of the observation tower and glassed seaward, scanning desperately for the flagship of his Canadian Arctic Expedition. Try as he might, he could not conjure the ship anywhere in the sprawling expanse of sea and ice. "The *Karluk* was gone," he concluded. "We did not know whither, or whether she still survived."

9

"AS LAMBS LEFT
TO THE SLAUGHTER"

FROM HIS PERCH IN THE BARREL, CAPTAIN BARTLETT MOMENTARILY sighted land—or thought he did—until the vista was consumed by snowdrifts and vanished. He climbed down to consult with geologist Malloch, hoping to get at least some indication of their whereabouts. The gale was gathering power, confused bursts of air blasting the ship, the skies torn sheets of blinding snow. Malloch stood on the snow-covered deck at noon on September 25, checking his watch and peering through his sextant, but it was no use; the sun was completely obscured by the squall. Murray's report from his last depth soundings suggested they were still in relatively shallow water, causing Bartlett deep concern. He could hear the terrible roaring and fracturing of the ice near the ship and feared that crushing power. "There was danger," wrote Bartlett, "not only from the great fragments of the floe, which turned and toppled over and over, but also . . . from the heavier floes which occurred here and there and had protruding edges, submerged and hidden, like the long, underwater arm that ripped the side out of the *Titanic*."

Bartlett reiterated to everyone that they mustn't leave the ship under any circumstances without his permission, and they should all sleep fully clothed, prepared to abandon the ship in an instant. Consulting with the scientists, he concluded that they were now drifting at an alarming speed of sixty miles a day to the west, toward the open Chukchi Sea. But it was hardly a smooth, effortless drift. Instead, their hurtling ice floe began to bash into other floes, and they were surrounded by an awful power. McKinlay found their predicament terrifying. Their own floe would crash into another, mashing together and forming huge ridges where the floes collided and piled upward until vertical, some tumbling and crashing down near them, some of the formations as large as buildings. He was worried for their fate, but also dismayed that Stefansson had deserted them, writing, "As the ice pack swept us further and further away from our leader . . . we felt . . . as lambs left to the slaughter."

By now, nearly everyone had harsh words about Stefansson, whom they viewed as having not only abandoned his ship but forsaken them personally. Bartlett pondered their predicament, mulling it over and comparing it to other scrapes and close calls he'd had, including taking the *Roosevelt* through the dangerous, ice-choked gantlet of the Kane Basin and Kennedy Channel to the Arctic Ocean. That trip was harrowing, but then he'd benefited from continuous daylight, allowing him to navigate; plus, he'd known his destination. His present circumstances seemed much worse. Shortening days gave way to coal-black nights, and there was no navigating, since the *Karluk* was not under her own power. Worse still, he had only a vague guess as to their location and believed they "might drift in the ice even to destruction, unable to do anything to save the ship."

Bartlett used wry humor to keep up his spirits and express his displeasure with Stefansson. He wrote in his log: "A nice mess; Stefansson, the leader, ashore and his whole blooming expedition floating around here in the ice out of sight of land. It certainly would have been embarrassing for Stefansson if the Premier of Canada had met him on the beach about that time and said, 'Sir, where's your expedition?'" Bartlett chuckled to himself, amused by his imagined scenario and what Stefansson's feeble answer might have been as he pointed out to the endless polar pack: "They're out there waiting for me, Sir."

But Bartlett's humorous musings were interrupted by the violent power of the pack. By the first of October, a week since their floe had fractured free and begun to drift on its own, he noted that the crashing, rupturing floes were encroaching all around the ship, the "seething masses of ice battling for supremacy" creating so much noise in its shearing that it drowned out the sound of the wailing winds. McKinlay found the noise at times deafening, at times wondrously musical, describing "thunderous rumbles . . . coming from all directions; rending, crashing, tearing noises; grating, screeching; toning down to drumming, booming, murmuring, gurgling, twanging—all the sounds of a gigantic orchestra."

Men stood on the snow-covered deck equally awed and frightened by the oncoming ice, wondering what they would do should it smash their floe and crush the *Karluk*. Anticipating this possibility, Bartlett enlisted Hadley to begin building a Peary-type sled, which they could use along with their other sleds in a potential emergency dash across the ice for land, which now seemed more likely than not.

Admiral Peary had developed his own unique sled design, which evolved over his many years of Arctic exploration. Bartlett was most experienced with this type of sled, having driven them on his trips with Peary. To his mind, it had several improvements over the so-called Eskimo sled or Nome sled, so he wanted at least two of them made. They converted the forward hold into a carpenter's shop for this purpose, needing extra space to work with long pieces of lumber. The sled-making process was elaborate: Hadley fabricated two runners, each made from a long, thirteen-foot piece of hardwood (ash or hickory) about three inches wide. The ends of each runner were turned upward by steaming them, and the entire length of the bottom of each runner was shod with a strip of steel for fast gliding along the ice. The rake of the bow was long and low, with the stern having upturned handles for steering. Hadley did his best with the materials at hand to make exact replicas of the Peary sleds, fashioning the bed, which held the loads, with the most pliable soft wood he could find on board. The entire sled was held together with sealskin lashings rather than nails or bolts, making it flexible and less likely to break apart while moving, heavily laden, over rough sea ice. Bartlett had learned that if you loaded these sleds in the center, they were highly maneuverable and could change direction easily, as he explained to Hadley: "With its long rake fore and aft the sledge will swing as on a pivot, so that when you get in position where you cannot go ahead you can back the sledge or turn it around and even go stern first if necessary, without lifting it."

When Hadley wasn't working on the Peary sleds, he tended to the dogs. Whenever conditions permitted, they were allowed to roam free on the ice, which afforded them exercise. But often, to keep them from fighting and injuring one another, Hadley would have to chain them separately, pounding spikes with a sledgehammer into raftered ice. He fed the dogs a hot mixture of dried fish, cooked rice, and oatmeal, cooked on the galley stove. Templeman often groused about Hadley messing up his kitchen with the dog food—which the cook found absurd—but Bartlett wanted them healthy and fit for service at all times, and this included hot food.

The whaleboats and umiaks had already been loaded with provisions to last twenty days, but Bartlett wanted to be as prepared as possible, so he put McKinlay in charge of organizing large canvas bags stuffed with Jaeger long underwear and whatever fur clothing that Auntie had finished sewing. To these, McKinlay added supplies and food to last them a couple of months out on the ice—pemmican and tins of meat. All was positioned on deck against the rails, where it could easily be thrown overboard.

On the last day of September, Bartlett was up in the barrel when he sighted land. He glassed and recognized the outlines of Eskimo dwellings dotting the shoreline of Cooper Island. It was enticing to think that they remained in striking distance of land. The next morning, still up in the barrel, but now in the teeth of a hearty snowstorm, Bartlett watched as a large fissure emerged in the ice a couple of miles from the ship, running from west to east. The idea of using dynamite crossed his mind once again, but they'd need to be much closer to the open water for that to work. Within a few hours, the heavy winds had closed the ice crack shut, so he scuttled the dynamite option.

The storm did not abate for another two days, pushing them far to the northwest. Then the skies parted and the winds finally calmed, allowing Bartlett to get back up into the crow's nest.* He took Mamen with him, and they could clearly see the tip of Point Barrow just five miles to the south. But the ice island in which they were lodged—which was about two or three miles square—was surrounded by open water on all sides, punctuated by young, unstable ice inshore. Bartlett concluded that it would be too dangerous to attempt either by dogsled or boat; their safest bet was to remain aboard the *Karluk*, where they still had food, shelter, and warmth.

With the improved weather, Bartlett again allowed men to venture off the ship, so long as they stayed nearby and reported their comings and goings to him. He sent the Eskimos off to hunt seals and encouraged the scientists to perform any work they could while the weather was fine, with midday temperatures nearing 20°F. Murray wanted to continue dredging and sounding, and Bartlett applauded his exertions, impressed by the man's efforts at "mapping out the bed of the ocean and outlining the continental shelf. These things and the search for new land in latitudes where man has never set foot before appeal to me."

Mamen had been busy on a project, making a pair of ski boots of the kind Amundsen used in reaching the South Pole—and with clearer weather, he wanted to get out skiing himself again. He convinced Bartlett and Dr. Mackay to join him, and they went again to the jump they'd built near the ship. Bartlett climbed higher than he should have and got too much speed, sailing through the air and landing hard on his side. He got up and shook it off, and though he was in considerable pain, he said nothing of it to either Mamen or the doctor, not wanting them to know how foolish he'd been to risk getting badly hurt. That night, as he struggled to lift his arm to comb his hair, he vowed to himself not to do anything so risky again, at least not intentionally. Everyone's welfare depended on his leadership and strength and soundness; he could ill afford to be injured.

* The storm the men on the *Karluk* were experiencing was at the same time devastating parts of Nome, Alaska.

The evenings in early October brought the first auroral displays. Some on board, like McKinlay, had never seen them before, and they stood on the deck, bundled and buttoned to the neck, awed and captivated by the explosive colors and movement of the phenomenon. At first, just a single streamer appeared, cutting through the obsidian-black sky, but soon the entire sky was illuminated by streamers. McKinlay recorded what he saw, drawing pictures and scribbling descriptions in his diary:

> *A small patch of light shone out near the zenith . . . growing until it was about the size of a full moon. Suddenly from its center there unrolled a huge curtain extending right down to ice level, folding and unfolding with lightning rapidity. In seconds . . . this was repeated until there were seven such curtains waving in the sky, waving and dancing as if blown by a mighty wind. . . . A large stretch of vivid blood-red hung in the west, slowly changing to salmon pink, then yellow and later to green . . . These colors were in vertical bands which chased one another across the curtains in quick succession.*

Though he attempted to sketch what he saw, eventually McKinlay gave up; he was so spellbound by the beauty that he soon set aside his sketchbook and diary and just gazed out into the infinite magnificence, overwhelmed by it. He stayed a long time, the last one still on deck—and yet he had a sense, a feeling, that he was not alone. The awareness was so powerful he could not put it into his own words but jotted down something he remembered from H. G. Wells—a similar experience deep in the night, in fleeting, lonely moments: "I experience a sort of communion of myself with something great that is not myself." The same sense consumed McKinlay for so long that when he finally looked away, he realized that he'd forgotten to put his fur gloves back on when he quit sketching, and he hurried below to find the fingers on both his hands pearl white to the knuckles. He was able to thaw them out near the stove, but they burned with excruciating pain as blood flowed back into them and they returned to life.

As the ship kept drifting, the scientists sought diversions and projects to keep their minds and hands busy. McKinlay, with Bartlett's blessing, worked on a few small construction jobs. In the saloon, he built a series of bookshelves to house much of their extensive polar library, so that everyone could have access to published books, bound logs, ships' journals, and charts. The collection was impressive, including Adolphus Greely's *Three Years of Arctic Service*, which chronicled his triumphant, harrowing, and tragic Lady Franklin Bay Expedition (1881–84); works by Frederick Cook and Robert Peary, Amundsen and Nansen. Of particular interest, and the cause of much discussion and speculation, were the ship journals of George Washington De Long (1879–81). The two-volume, 800-page journal included detailed descriptions of the drift of the *Jeannette* after it had become trapped in the ice near Herald Island in the Chukchi Sea, roughly the direction they were headed.

When McKinlay finished the bookshelves, he built a medicine cabinet for Dr. Mackay. He was pleased with his handiwork, as was the captain. Bartlett liked to rib McKinlay, toward whom he bore a growing affection. Looking at the shelves and medicine chest, he joked, "There are some people who thought they could only teach school until they came on this trip!" Then the old salt gave the young schoolteacher a congratulatory slap on his back, right between the shoulder blades. Such outward praise from Bartlett was rare, and McKinlay blushed a little with pride. Bartlett also had begun giving McKinlay special items that would be useful or make him more comfortable: a knife, a pipe, a warm Jaeger blanket. He even folded two thick lambskins on McKinlay's bunk, all of which convinced McKinlay that his hard work and good attitude were being noticed and appreciated by the skipper.

There were other diversions. McKinlay decided to learn how to speak with the Eskimo family and Kataktovik, the hunter. Auntie had been sewing almost constantly, as well as teaching all the crew and scientists how to sew, and McKinlay felt this process would be more efficient if he could better communicate with her and with her young children, Helen and Mugpi. It would also help him understand the nuances of hunting techniques from Kataktovik and Kuraluk, Auntie's husband. Since Kataktovik knew a little bit of English, he volunteered to hold daily half-hour lessons, which McKinlay, Beuchat, and Dr. Mackay attended.*

Murray's daily dredging and sounding were yielding some interesting results. Between October 8 and 10, he noted that water depth had surpassed twenty fathoms, and readings every few hours showed dramatic increases. With the other scientists, he set up the Kelvin sounding machine, used to take readings from twenty to one hundred fathoms. But after just two days, the water was so deep they had to employ the Lucas automatic sounding machine, which they operated through a hole made in the ice just off the ship's stern. The work was hard and cold, but doing their scientific jobs excited them and kept them going. For protection and some comfort from the wind and snow during the work, they built an igloo above the ice hole. On the third day of continual readings, they reached 1,215 fathoms—or 7,200 feet—well over a mile deep. Everyone was awed by, as McKinlay exclaimed, "the great depths into which our drift has carried us." The work of winding the wire and dredge back up to the surface was so strenuous that they took turns, with teams of two winding up a hundred fathoms at a time before resting. To break up the monotony, they wagered tobacco on who could reel in the fastest. Mamen and Malloch managed to wind in one hundred fathoms of wire in just two minutes, beating McKinlay and Murray's best mark by fifteen seconds.

Based on the depths recorded and the specimens he was bringing up (several starfish, some coral, and especially one peculiar, spherical creature he had never seen before and could find no record of in his encyclopedias), Murray believed that they were performing oceanographic science in a region previously unexplored by man. This notion inspired him, though the work was bitter cold, with temperatures down to –15°F, and he was constantly soaked to the skin from being outside all the time and hauling

---

* The language spoken by Kataktovik, Kuraluk, and his family was probably Inupiaq, spoken throughout much of northern Alaska and closely related to Canadian Inuit and Greenlandic dialects. https://www.uaf.edu/anlc/languages/inupiaq.php.

in the wet wire and dripping dredge. To avoid frostbite, he had to periodically climb back aboard to his quarters to change into dry clothes.

Malloch, while technically a geologist, tried to stay useful and engaged by taking position readings whenever he could, and always relaying these to the captain. He frequently discussed the charts and their drift with Dr. Mackay as well. His work was complicated by the sporadic sunshine, however, and although he was generally very good natured, often singing or whistling while he worked, occasionally he was volatile, losing his temper for no apparent reason. One day after returning to the ship, Malloch entered his cabin to find McKinlay dismantling one of the beds to make the quarters roomier and more comfortable. Malloch snapped, and without warning (according to Mamen, who witnessed the event), "the big fellow went shear berserk on this little innocent man," clasping him from behind with his great bear arms, squeezing him and shaking him about like a child. With Wee Mac—all 140 pounds of him—gasping for air and crying out for help, Malloch eventually released him, dropping him to the floor, then slinking away without explanation or apology. Word of the bizarre incident went round the ship. From then on, others kept a safe distance from him, always eyeing him warily.

The ice conditions around the ship remained unpredictable. One afternoon, Bartlett and Mamen were out for some ski practice, along with Hadley's dog, Molly. They were about a mile and a half from the ship, on a large floe, when the captain heard a loud, rupturing, sickening sound. Between them and the ship, the ice had fractured and was opening fast, separating the captain, Mamen, and Molly. Bartlett and Mamen skied furiously back toward the ship. The crack between them and the ice in which the ship drifted was about ten feet wide, too far to jump. They waited anxiously, with snow beginning to fall and the day's light fading. Molly ran up and down the edge of the lead, barking hysterically, instinctively understanding the trouble they were in. "After a wait of five to ten minutes," Bartlett wrote, "we managed to bridge the gap and get across just in time, but the dog got on another section of ice which broke away and floated off with her." She ran around in circles, and they watched as she floated off, her yelps receding in the twilight.

They climbed safely back on board, saddened by Molly's disappearance but relieved it had not been them. Mamen whistled and called out for Molly, but by dark she had not returned, and they had to report the bad news to Hadley, who took it hard. Wrote Mamen, "Starvation and death are awaiting her now, poor Molly." By amazing fortune, Molly returned to the *Karluk* on her own the next day, hungry but uninjured, evidently coming back over new ice that now covered the lead. But the event served as a reminder of how fickle and ever-changing the ice could be.

In the evenings, by lamplight in the saloon or the Cabin De Luxe, the scientists read Arctic accounts from the library and discussed various subjects. But no matter how far-ranging their conversations forayed into polar history, or talk of their families back home, they always returned to their present plight. They argued about whether Bartlett was doing enough to get them out of their predicament. Dr. Mackay and Murray said they'd been close enough to land to make a run for it more than once. They questioned Bartlett's plans, criticizing him for not laying out detailed options. There was also a good deal of railing about Stefansson. One late night McKinlay confided in the group that right before Stefansson had departed, he saw the expedition leader reading De Long's logs and charts from the *Jeannette*. "He saw that most ships, 99 percent out of 100, in the ice north of Bering Strait are facing certain death, and for fear of losing his life he left the ship."

Hearing this, Beuchat—his face visibly flushed—blurted out, "We are lost. We don't know where we are. Everything is hopeless."

They weren't exactly lost. Malloch's daily observations—using the sun by sextant at noon when possible and navigating by stars on clear nights— gave them a relative idea of their location. The readings were imprecise, but they had enough information, at the very least, to monitor the direction of their drift. Dr. Mackay and Murray spread De Long's charts out on a table, laying handwritten copies of their own longitudes and latitudes next to these for comparison. Sure enough, they were following the path of the *Jeannette*. It didn't help morale that everyone had now read the grim fate of that expedition: the *Jeannette*—a three-masted former British navy gun vessel specially adapted for Arctic conditions—had drifted, locked in the pack as they were, for twenty months. Ice pressure finally crushed the ship, and the crew was forced to abandon it and take to alternately hauling and sailing whaleboats for land. Twenty of the crew of thirty-three, including Captain De Long, died horrible deaths by starvation, scurvy, or exposure to the harsh elements.

Imagining this catastrophe, and the likelihood of their drifting toward the same fate, Dr. Mackay and Murray began scheming. They were bound by their shared experiences in Antarctica with the legendary Ernest Shackleton (*Nimrod* expedition, 1907–9), whose leadership, toughness, and tenacity had gotten his expedition to within one hundred miles of the South Pole. By flickering lamplight, at first in hushed tones, they resolved to abandon the *Karluk* and bolt toward land, taking their chances on their own. After a few nights of discussion, they eventually convinced the impressionable and already fearful Beuchat to go along with them.

McKinlay, who could hear these late-night whisperings through the thin walls, wrote in his diary: "That there are secret conclaves going on is certain." The conspirators quietly approached and invited Mamen to join them. His skill on snow and ice, and his stamina, would be helpful. But the assistant topographer cut them off, sharply responding that it was mutiny, and he'd have none of it. His allegiance was with Captain Bartlett, he told them, "And as long as there are provisions on board and a deck on the *Karluk*, I stay on board." He added, eyeing them with a look of scorn, "Before I leave the *Karluk* I would rather die, for then I will at any rate save my honor." And with that, he stormed out of the room.

Mamen, like McKinlay, was becoming deeply attached to Bartlett. Quitting on him, the ship's captain, as the others were planning to do, not only amounted to mutiny but would also be a stain on his reputation as a Norwegian. He'd been thinking a lot about the heroic exploits of his famous countrymen, reading Amundsen's *Northwest Passage* and *South Pole*, and Nansen's *First Crossing of Greenland* and *Farthest North*. Both men were legends, virtual gods to him. He wanted to become like them. He stayed up late into the night, imagining somehow returning home safely after two or three years on the *Karluk* and cobbling together enough money for a ship of his own. Yes, with that experience, he'd be ready enough. He'd round up some of his adventurous friends—he knew five or six whom he could trust—and lead his own scientific expedition to Franz Josef Land. After a few years away, he and his men would reappear, brave heroes returned from the northlands. Mamen's eyes slowly closed and the book fell shut on his lap as he drifted into dreams and imagined sailing away, the proud red, white, and blue Norwegian flag waving high above his ship in the Arctic wind.

10

A CHANGE OF PLANS

STEFANSSON AND HIS HUNTING PARTY REMAINED STRANDED ON SPY Island for about a week. He had given up looking for the *Karluk*. Stefansson told the others, "There was no sense in searching for her by sled, for there was vastly more water than ice." When he left the ship, Stefansson had planned for a journey of about two weeks at the most, and now food was running short. He knew he needed to get to the mainland as soon as possible. They were low on provisions, and the men were poorly clad, having departed in a hurry. Colder temperatures had thickened the ice and knitted leads together, and, believing it now safe enough to cross, Stefansson called for the men to break camp and harness the dogs. They bolted for the mainland.

Once ashore, they found a suitable camp by the mouth of the Colville River. For the next few days, Stefansson went alone to hunt caribou. The others, and particularly Jimmy and Jerry—who'd been brought along expressly for their hunting skills—found his solitary behavior odd. At the end of each day, Stefansson returned with no meat, though once he claimed to have seen a lone bull in the distance. Setting down his rifle and warming himself by the driftwood fire, he told the other members that he'd failed to get close enough for a shot.

They were hungry, but at least they weren't lost. Stefansson was familiar with the fingered, braided delta of the Colville River, and in fact had camped very near this place back in fall of 1908, when there were still hearty caribou herds. By his reckoning, it was about 150 miles, west along the coast, to Cape Smyth. Stefansson figured that his best bet was to head there. By some miracle, the *Karluk* could reappear along the shoreline. At the very least, he might get some news of his flagship from the Inupiat living along the coast, and he would inquire about any sightings of the *Alaska* and *Mary Sachs* as well.

The conditions remained treacherous. They had to cross numerous ice-covered inlets and bays, sometimes in the dark. The big storm that had blown the *Karluk* away had blanketed everything with a layer of snow that insulated the ice and prevented it from freezing hard. On one occasion, they found themselves on very thin ice that buckled beneath their weight. It began to break and the sled was partway underwater—but the dogs pulled for all they were worth, and they managed to make it safely ashore on the other side. Stefansson thought it was mostly a matter of luck that they lost neither the sled nor any of their lives.

The next day, as they were making their way toward Cape Halkett, one of the Eskimos said that he smelled smoke. Sure enough, about five or six miles farther along, Stefansson sighted a low-slung dwelling. One by one, a family of four emerged from the driftwood house. It was a husband, wife, and two young daughters. Stefansson recognized them from his previous trip here, and the father, Aksiatak, shook hands with everyone and welcomed them into his home, where he hosted them for the next two days.

Aksiatak informed Stefansson that since there were so few caribou, they'd been living primarily off fish caught in nearby Teshekpuk Lake, which was just a couple of miles inland. The fish were plentiful, and Aksiatak generously agreed to supply Stefansson with enough fish to feed his party and the dogs as they traveled on to Cape Smyth. The man also told Stefansson that several families whom Stefansson knew from his previous expedition remained scattered along the coastal region. They would remember him and be able to shelter his party and likely provide them with seal meat too.

Aksiatak was so kind and amenable that Stefansson broached an idea: Perhaps Jenness could winter with Aksiatak and his family. The anthropologist could use that time to study their lifeways, hunting and fishing practices, and their language. The terms were agreed upon, with the plan that after they'd all made it to Cape Smyth and gotten properly outfitted, Jenness would return and live with the family. The photographer, Wilkins, would return as well to document things. Jimmy would accompany them to help with fishing and hunting. Stefansson figured that in this way, at least part of his scientific mission would be fulfilled.

That settled, Stefansson left with the remnant group, stopping at native encampments along the way. One, a small four-house village of related families, took them in and offered them some preserved whale meat from their stores. Through some discussion, Stefansson learned that the whale meat belonged to Kuraluk, Auntie's husband. As he chewed on some of the whale meat, Stefansson had to explain to his hosts, rather sheepishly, that Kuraluk was *somewhere* out there, either on the *Karluk* or on the ice. In truth, he had no idea.

The final push to Cape Smyth was arduous. The men suffered from various complaints. Jenness endured bouts of fever and chills as they plodded along. Burt McConnell and George Wilkins were both limping badly by the end of each long day, describing a different sort of foot or lower leg injury respectively. At a couple of stops along the way, the local inhabitants described having seen a ship that might have been the *Karluk*. They'd spotted it stuck in the ice, three or four miles offshore. They'd wanted to travel across the ice to see if they could help, but were too old and infirm for the journey. They reported seeing ropes in the rigging but no smoke from its stack, so they assumed it had been abandoned. Stefansson filed away this information and pressed on.

By the time they pulled into Cape Smyth on October 12, Stefansson, too, was weak and feverish. He went straight to the local general store, run by a man named Charlie Brower, whom he knew well. Brower was a pioneering sort who'd arrived here at the age of nineteen on a whaler fifty years before and decided to stay. He craved the adventure and wildness of the place. Mostly, he loved the people. Eventually, he got married and had many children. His business—selling furs and Arctic clothing and seal and whale meat and blubber—was very successful. His business acumen and outsize personality had earned him the nickname "the King of the Arctic."

It was from Brower and his store, in fact, that Stefansson had procured the last of the skins and provisions, dogs, and sleds, when he stopped by with the *Karluk* back in August. John Hadley had been working for Brower then, too, when he decided to join the expedition. Auntie, Kurulak, and their children were also from nearby. Now Brower embraced Stefansson and asked him what he was doing back so soon. When they'd said goodbye to each other just two months before, Stefansson's plan was to be gone for at least a few years.

Stefansson explained what had happened and inquired about all his ships. Brower was able to report some good news: both the *Mary Sachs* and the *Alaska* had made it past Point Barrow and were said to be wintering off Collinson Point in Camden Bay, some three hundred miles to the east. To the best of Brower's knowledge, all the crew and scientists of Stefansson's Southern Party were well. As for the *Karluk*, the reports were less certain. A Native living at Point Barrow said he'd seen a ship fitting the *Karluk*'s description about ten miles offshore. When asked which direction it seemed to be going, the man looked to the west. "There," he said, his hand making a sweeping gesture, then pointing toward Siberia.

Stefansson took lodgings at Cape Smyth and contemplated his next moves. First, with the *Alaska* and *Mary Sachs* safe at winter harbor, it made sense that the work of the Southern Party would be able to proceed. At any rate, he determined to personally ensure that it would. He'd lick his wounds here, then reoutfit and regroup, heading to Collinson Point as soon as possible. It would take some time. He admitted—for it was mostly his fault, the result of a late and hasty departure initially from Esquimalt—that his men "on leaving the *Karluk* had been improperly dressed, and this was now remedied through skins and other things supplied us from Mr. Brower's stores and through the assistance of the Eskimo seamstresses of the village."

Jenness and Wilkins needed some time to recover from the injuries they'd sustained during the long trek getting here, so Stefansson decided to let them rest and recuperate for at least a week or two.

And there was the sticky matter of just what to tell the government officials in Ottawa. He had some explaining to do, for sure. Just how, and why, he'd become separated from his flagship would need to be carefully worded, and he anticipated that at least some of the Canadian officials would criticize his judgment. While in his mind the unfortunate series of events made perfect sense and could be logically explained, some people—not just the higher-ups in government but also the public—were bound to see it differently, perhaps going so far as to question his decisions and leadership. Working in his favor was the fact that there was no telegraph or radio capability at Barrow. He knew that the only way to correspond with the outside world from there was through handwritten letters that would leave Barrow on the first of November and be taken south by reindeer-drawn sleds. By the time anyone of importance received his reports, he would already have left for Collinson Point to rejoin the Southern Party and salvage what he could of the expedition and its work.

Additionally, Stefansson planned to use some of this time to draft stories to the *Globe* (Toronto), United Newspapers (London), and the *New York Times*. Enlisting his secretary, Burt McConnell, for the next two weeks Stefansson dictated letters to the newspapers describing the travails the expedition had thus far endured. In these correspondences, Stefansson made certain to skirt any responsibility for their mishaps and the current disarray of the expedition, citing "the worst storm for that season which I have ever seen in the North" as the reason he'd become separated from his ships. The freak storm had certainly contributed to the *Karluk*'s drift, but it was hardly the whole story. He managed to gloss over his dubious decision to leave the ship in the first place, instead claiming that "our expedition was so thoroughly and efficiently organized" that it was only bad luck and unpredictable "Arctic problems" that had caused their present dilemma. He conveniently left out the truth: in his hurry to depart, the wrong men and scientific equipment were on the wrong ships; they'd been ill prepared—as far as clothing was concerned—for winter; and he had not considered the very real possibility that the ships might become separated.

The most important letter, Stefansson knew, was the one he needed to write to the Canadian Department of the Naval Service, which was overseeing the expedition. In particular, he had to appease Deputy Minister G. J. Desbarats, who had the power, should he be so inclined, to order Stefansson to abort the entire endeavor. In his letter to the deputy, Stefansson decided to take a positive and forward-looking tack. As McConnell scribbled furiously to keep up with Stefansson's dictation, the expedition leader outlined his change of plans. First and foremost, he happily reported the safety of the *Alaska* and the *Mary Sachs*. After reoutfitting at Barrow, he strongly believed that the main goals of the expedition could still be achieved: "to explore the ocean north of Alaska and west of the already known Canadian islands to ascertain the presence or absence of new lands."

By meeting up with the *Alaska* and *Mary Sachs* at Collinson Point, he could still direct members to carry out next summer's intended work and primary geographic objectives, "both in the Coronation Gulf where detailed scientific studies would be pursued, and in the Beaufort Sea and Parry archipelago where the main object was geographic discovery—the traversing and study of unexplored seas and the discovery and mapping of unknown lands." He made it all sound very organized and obtainable, omitting the inconvenient truth that all the best sounding equipment and many other instruments needed for the work he described was still on the lost *Karluk*.

As for the fate of the *Karluk*, Stefansson paused and thought long and hard before he spoke the words aloud to McConnell, who waited patiently, then put pen to paper and hung on every word when Stefansson continued his dictation. "I considered it very doubtful whether the *Karluk* as a ship would survive the winter," he said, swallowing before he continued. "Although the *Karluk* was no longer of any use to us and might be in danger of being crushed by the ice . . . the people on board her, being equipped with light skin boats, which were ideal for travel over sea ice, could easily make their way ashore."

Stefansson signed the report and instructed McConnell to seal it and all the other correspondence and prepare it to be taken with the next post departing Barrow by reindeer-drawn sled November 1, 1913. He knew full well that it would be some months until it was received and responded to, and by then he would already be proceeding with his altered plans. And his spirits were lifted by the likelihood that he would soon be reunited with his Inupiat wife, Fanny, and their son, Alex. Sustained by that thought, Stefansson made final preparations to leave Cape Smyth and head east, putting the *Karluk* out of his mind.

11

WINTER IS COMING

CAPTAIN BARTLETT RACED TO THE BOW OF THE SHIP WHEN HE heard the sharp crack, the loud report like the firing of a rifle. But he knew it was no gunshot; it was the ice. All along the sides of the *Karluk*, the ice was heaving and raftering, sharp, jagged shards encroaching. In the low light of the late October evening, it was hard to see clearly, but Bartlett fully understood the sounds and he followed them, craning his head at the shearing and grinding noises fore and aft. Bartlett pulled his fur hat down over his ears and turned his face from the biting, blizzard-driven wind, snow slashing at his cheeks. Using a lantern, he could just make out long, snaking cracks in the ice all around the ship, with a large seam about fifty yards away along the port side, and another rift running just off the bow. He called for Ned Golightly, the seaman who'd been on watch, to get all hands on deck and ready.

Golightly sprinted to the cabins, calling out that the captain needed help. Mamen, who'd been reading De Long's diary of the lost *Jeannette*, tossed the book down and went to help. When he got on deck, he could make out the outline of McKinlay and a few others through sheets of driven snow. Soon, nearly all members were assembled, and Bartlett yelled over the wailing wind that they must go down onto the ice and bring all the supplies, tools, and dogs back on board—and fast.

The men formed a line and began hauling gear back on board, passing items from one to another. Many of the dogs had torn free from their tethers, and they ran about, barking and yowling as the men picked up ice axes and shovels, a couple of sleds, coils of line. They retrieved the sounding apparatus from the igloo above the dredge hole, then struggled to get the umiak hauled back on board and tied down, the high winds catching it and nearly carrying it and the men holding it skittering across the ice.

The dogs proved the most difficult. Some were stranded across a large fissure, separated by a watery gap, and they refused to leap back over. McKinlay and Mamen jumped across the open water and coaxed them back over and to the ship. "Not very safe in the uncertainty of the darkness and the strong blizzard which was raging at the time," recalled McKinlay. After an hour of continuous work and cooperation, everything of value, including all thirty yelping, snarling dogs, was back on the *Karluk*.

Bartlett congratulated everyone on their readiness and hard work, and they returned to their posts or their cabins, safe for the time being. But he told them to remain clothed and "standing by for trouble." Bartlett remained awake all night, periodically going out onto the deck with his lantern to assess the ice and the ship. Two weeks earlier, Bartlett had ordered men using axes and hatchets and saws to cut snow blocks—about two feet thick—and stack them against the ship as high as the poop deck to provide insulation. When this was done, he'd instructed them to cut ice two to three feet around the entire hull and sides of the *Karluk*, freeing her slightly and providing a small buffer between her sides and the ice. For the moment, at least, it seemed to be working.

For the next week, the wind howled incessantly, gusting to sixty miles per hour, and the temperature dropped to –24°F. Bartlett moved about the ship, surveying everything on it and all their surroundings. Huge snowdrifts curled up and onto the bow of the ship like great white waves that had crashed and settled there, frozen in time and place. Hummocks of ice lay in tumbled mounds and blocks like debris strewn at the bottom of an avalanche. Malloch's resumed soundings, which were painfully cold work in the ongoing storm, revealed that they had drifted north for some days and now bore due west again. But what worried Bartlett was that they had moved back into much shallower water—just thirty-six fathoms. This low depth, plus the violence of the storm, explained the fierce upheaval at the surface around the ship.

And now came worse news: the *Karluk* was leaking. Sandy Anderson, the first officer, informed the captain of a slow but steady forward seepage. Bartlett went below to check. He sloshed through ankle-deep water and listened to the sounds of the ship bearing up against the pressing ice: "The poor old *Karluk*," he jotted in his log, "began to suffer worse than ever. She creaked and groaned and, once or twice actually sobbed as the water oozed through her seams. There is nothing more human than a ship in ice pressure." The ship's engine was currently down and under repair, so as there was no steam to run the pumps, Bartlett ordered teams of two men to hand-pump in two-to-three-hour shifts, and eventually they managed to pump the water out.

Bartlett needed to prepare for a few possibilities. The storm had the men penned inside the ship, and they were becoming restless and agitated—and fearful. One night, Mamen confided in him, expressing his concern "as to whether *Karluk* is so strong that she will stand all the pressuring or whether she will follow the *Jeannette* to the bottom."

Bartlett smiled, his sea-weathered face brightening. He lit his pipe and assured him, "Everything that can be done will be done to save her." Then his face turned serious, his piercing blue eyes glinting in the lamplight. "But whether we shall succeed or not, who knows."

Bartlett understood that the ship's fate was not up to him but was in the hands of the ice. Still, he would be good to his word. He determined to lighten her load. When the weather finally eased, he scouted around the ship and located a swath of older ice, thick and consolidated, which he believed could bear immense pressure, and there, he'd have men begin setting up a large deposit of coal, supplies, shelter and food, anything and everything they'd need should the ship go under. The strategy was double-edged: not only would they be ready to abandon ship, but if they took enough material off the *Karluk*, she might rise and reduce the pressure impinging on her sides, saving her.

Some of the men—particularly Mackay, Murray, and the impressionable

Beuchat—grumbled that they'd just recently hauled everything from the ice back up onto the ship. What was the point of taking it all off again? They'd continued to question Bartlett's leadership, and Dr. Mackay demanded a formal meeting to learn of the captain's plans. He wanted specific details and a time line. Bartlett scoffed; there was nothing to discuss. It seemed clear to him that weather and the behavior of the ice would dictate his decisions. To appease Dr. Mackay and the others, Bartlett told them that whatever they needed, if it was on the ship, he'd make sure they had it and that they were taken care of. This assurance, though it was more a deflection than a plan, seemed to pacify the discontents, at least for the time being.

But Bartlett did have a plan. As captain, he simply didn't feel obligated to explain his decisions to these malcontents, these insurrectionists. He'd heard some rumors—very few secrets survived such close confines—that Dr. Mackay had been conspiring with Murray and Beuchat to leave the ship. It seemed beyond foolhardy to Bartlett, bordering on a death wish, to embark onto the ice with the winter darkness upon them. Bartlett chalked it up to bravado on their part, but the discord concerned him.

He also worried about Mackay's general physical and mental condition, his erratic mood swings. During a recent late-night talk, Mamen had confided in him that the doctor had been availing himself of doses of strychnine, which he kept in his medicine stores.* He had apparently been taking it for weeks, in larger and larger doses, as a stimulant to bolster his energy, but it seemed to have the opposite effect. "The day after he has taken it," said Mamen, "he is so weak he has to stay in bed most of the day . . . it ruins him completely." As Dr. Mackay was the ship's surgeon, well versed and in charge of the medicines, Bartlett decided not to confront him about it, but he'd keep a watchful eye on the man.

Bartlett would illustrate his plan through action. He would simultane-

---

* Strychnine, a naturally occurring alkaloid, was first introduced as a rodenticide in 1540. It has been used in subsequent centuries as a digestive, respiratory, and cardiac stimulant, and as an antidote to barbiturate and opioid overdoses. Dr. Mackay may have been using it as either a stimulant or possibly to counteract opiate use.

ously winterize the *Karluk*, making it as comfortable as possible, and have emergency stores and shelter out on the solid ice floe. The hard work would also keep the men occupied. The floe he'd chosen was, as he described it, "about a half an acre in size and thirty feet thick, of blue ice, amply able to stand a good deal of knocking about before breaking up." He had men build a sturdy wooden ramp from the ship down to the ice, flanked for protection by banks of snow blocks on each side, and ordered teams to start transporting things by sled: first the heavy bags of coal and canisters of fuel; then tins of biscuits, pemmican, and cases of canned pork and beef. Working in shifts all day, they also portaged lumber and canvas out onto the ice floe for the construction of a large shelter, should they need it. The work was hard, undertaken during intermittent snow squalls, but most of the men toiled without complaint, happy to be off the ship and at least doing something.

After days of constant trips to and from the big floe, Bartlett was satisfied and called the men to a halt on November 9. From the deck of the ship, interrupting the white horizon, they could see the lumpy outline of their labors, boxes and crates and canvas bags piled high and tied down against bears and the elements. In less than a week, they'd off-loaded many tons. McKinlay, dutiful to his daily diary, recorded the following now stored out on the ice: "250 sacks of coal; 6 cases of codfish; 5 drums of alcohol; 114 cases of biscuit; 19 barrels of molasses; 2000 feet of lumber; 33 cases of gasoline (in ten-gallon drums); 3 cases of cod steaks; 4 cases of dried eggs; 5 casks of beef; 9 sledges; 3 coal stoves with piping; and two wood stoves." Bartlett was so pleased he rewarded the men with the next day, a Sunday, completely off. Everyone took a holiday but Templeman, who still had to cook.

The *Karluk* responded to the lightened load, rising some two feet higher above the waterline, just as Bartlett had hoped. The leak slowed, now requiring just twenty minutes to pump dry instead of three hours. Bartlett next focused on winterizing the ship. All the doors and windows not vital to operations were latched shut and blocked with snow. Men shoveled snow and covered the decks with a layer about two feet deep, providing insulation for the quarters and cabins below. "We're living in a giant igloo," McKinlay joked.

Bartlett was keenly aware of the danger of fire on the ship. There were numerous lamps throughout the cabins, plus quite a few coal stoves: two in the engine room, one in Hadley's carpenter's shop, one in the scientists' workroom, a couple in the kitchen, one in the saloon, and one in the captain's own quarters. Although there were several chemical fire extinguishers on board, Bartlett had men deposit blocks of snow in various places about the ship for putting out fires, plus a hundred-gallon tank of water, kept constantly heated so that it wouldn't freeze.

Bartlett trained the men in a fire drill. Every man had a designated job and set procedures, as he outlined in his log: "If a fire broke out, the ship's bell would be rung and everybody would seize a block of snow or a fire extinguisher or the buckets near the water tank, as his duty required, and help extinguish the fire."

With the emergency provisions on the ice and the ship squared away, Bartlett sent the Eskimo men out hunting seals. They'd need the fresh meat for the long winter. He checked with Hadley and second officer Barker on the progress they'd made with the Peary sleds, and the work was proceeding well: one was finished, the second nearly completed. Bartlett informed the entire crew that Templeman would now serve only two meals a day: breakfast at nine o'clock and dinner at four thirty. Men could get tea at one o'clock and in the evenings before bed, along with coffee or chocolate as they wished, but all lights must be out by midnight, save the watchman's lantern. Whoever drew the unenviable job of night watchman was on duty from six o'clock in the evening until six o'clock the next morning. They made rounds about the ship, tending the fires and keeping the water in the water tank from freezing.

The two daily meals were quite varied and palatable. Templeman served oatmeal with condensed milk at breakfast, usually accompanied by eggs, ham, bacon or salt cod, and coffee. Dinners were hearty, with fresh seal meat or Newfoundland cod, dried potatoes, and some combination of rehydrated vegetables—carrots, asparagus, spinach, parsnips, corn, tomatoes, or beans. Everyone looked forward to dessert, for there was ice cream in multiple flavors, topped with canned fruits, cakes, puddings, and pies.

Bartlett wanted the men busy with a regular routine. Although he was lenient with morning hours, everyone needed to be ready to work by ten o'clock, just after breakfast. He set men to various tasks, including shoveling snow, filling the lockers with coal, hauling in freshwater top ice for melting to drink, putting pemmican up in canvas bags, and sewing clothing. Auntie and the children kept mostly to themselves, with Auntie sewing winter clothes and boots unceasingly.

In the evenings, the men amused themselves with stories and reading, and some of them started a chess league. They all agreed that the winner would receive the box of fifty cigars Stefansson had left on board, which had been intended as a gift for the Royal North-West Mounted Police he knew at Herschel Island. Bartlett even offered a box of twenty-five of his own stock for the runner-up. Mamen joked that since he was just a novice with no chance of winning, the best he could offer was to help the winners smoke their cigars.

And of course, while the men smoked cigarettes and sipped hot tea, talk invariably turned to Stefansson and speculation regarding his whereabouts. It was two months since he'd left them. Had he safely reached land? Had he alerted the Canadian government about their drift? No one on board, not even Bartlett, seemed particularly sorry that he was gone, though some remained bitter that he'd left them. It was suggested that this would no doubt be his last expedition as a leader; how could he possibly be entrusted with another? Some grumbled that there would surely be an official inquiry into his dubious decisions and questionable leadership. In the smoke-filled saloon with the gramophone playing, everyone chuckled at the notion that the newspapers would crucify him. Most hoped he'd become a laughingstock with a ruined reputation.

Mamen, usually outwardly jovial and upbeat, darkened the mood by saying, "If I were in his position under such circumstances, I believe I would spend a bullet on myself."

. . .

Everyone aboard the ship was cheered one afternoon when Kataktovik and Kuraluk returned around four o'clock, holding aloft the skin of a polar bear. They'd shot a young bear along with six seals. And though they now had thirty-four seals—enough, Bartlett figured, to last them until perhaps the end of January—it was the bear everyone was excited about. They took turns petting the soft, snow-white fur of the young animal and eagerly looked forward to the break from seal meat. Two days later, after the carcass had been brought back in and butchered, Templeman served fresh bear steaks, to everyone's delight. McKinlay savored the tender dark-red meat in his mouth, chewing slowly and relishing every delicious bite. He remarked, "It is a near approach to beef! Indeed, I can imagine that it might be mistaken for beef."

On November 11, 1913, around midday, everyone gathered on deck to watch the last sun they would see for a couple of months. The departure of the sun held particular power and ceremony for polar explorers, signaling the onset of "the Long Night." Unfortunately, the day was dull and cloudy, so the sun was too obscured for them to actually see it descend below the horizon, and they returned to their work or to their cabins. But they knew it was gone, not to return until next year. Murray's last observations had located them as far north and west as they'd drifted so far, to latitude 73° north, floating icebound in just twenty-nine fathoms of water somewhere over the continental shelf. They had not seen land in so long, it was impossible to know exactly where they were. "I'd give a thousand dollars to know our position," Bartlett said, only half joking.

With the disappearance of the sun, on clear nights the brightness of the moon and stars, and the dancing auroras, grew more pronounced. Mamen was astounded by the brilliance: "Moonshine . . . a perfectly full moon . . . the snow and ice crystals sparkling like diamonds in the light." McKinlay witnessed it too. Bundled up in his warmest clothes, he walked out onto the ice alone and stared up at the blazing moon, awestruck and homesick: "It is difficult to describe an Arctic moonlight night," he wrote in his journal.

"But the beauty holds one entranced . . . and the same moon will in its own time shine on the dear ones at home. What message could it convey to us if it could? What news of friends and the world at large? It is at such times that one realizes what it means to be this cut off."

And then, two days after the sun had gone down, McKinlay was out on the deck at noon, admiring the full moon, when he noticed a beam of glowing light in the south. There, defying logic, he saw, "just tipping the horizon, the upper limb of the sun." But he doubted what he was seeing. He went below and consulted the library's *Nautical Almanac and Astronomical Ephemeris*, confirming that it could not be the actual sun but rather the sun's light being refracted, like a desert mirage. Still, the appearance even of the distorted illusion of the sun excited him enough to shout for everyone to come look, and soon all had rushed onto the deck—from the foc's'le, from the engine room, from the saloon and the cabin—to see what he was yelling about. Everyone on board, including Captain Bartlett and even Auntie and the children, stood together side by side, staring at the glowing light as it blazed there for a time, offering the remembrance of its warmth, its power, its confirmation of life. Then it faded away.

"Now he is gone," McKinlay said finally. He wrote in his journal, "We would miss him, but we would buoy ourselves up with the knowledge that he still shines on our friends at home and with the hope that he will shine for us again."

12

LONG ARCTIC NIGHTS

The clattering rigging woke bjarne mamen from a nightmare. Wind shrieked as it funneled through the masts above him, and as he wiped his eyes awake, he wondered if doomsday had finally come. At first he thought the sound was ice shattering, and he sat up and listened carefully, but it was only wind gusts tossing boxes and crates about the deck above, the battering of the whaleboats against the hull.

Mamen had not been sleeping well. For the last few weeks, he'd been racked with deep dread, though he didn't tell anyone about it. Not even the captain. In front of his skipper, Mamen did his best to appear strong, even stalwart, impervious to the cold, the wind, the uncertainty. But at night, after he thought of Ellen and said a few prayers for her, he'd been struck with fear, and committed his true feelings only to his journal. "I have gone to bed lately," he wrote, "with a kind of feeling that I shall never wake up again . . . and when the morning comes . . . I feel highly surprised to be among the living." Then he added, with some consolation, "As long as there is life, there is hope."

Sometimes his nightmares involved the dogs. Lately, it had been a full-time job to keep them from killing one another. After the ice broke near the ship, the sled dogs had all been moved onto the deck, but now they were too close together. Once, a terrible fight erupted and a pack of dogs turned on one of the smallest members, a bobtailed dog they'd nicknamed, predictably, Bob. The mass of gnashing teeth and flying fur was too dangerous to break up, so the men who arrived had to watch helplessly as the poor animal was "horribly mutilated . . . his organs completely ruined."

When it was over, the men laid Bob down on some dry canvas bags, making him as comfortable as they could. Mamen watched the dog wheezing and coughing and groaning, his body shaking against the cold. But what most affected Mamen was that as Bob lay dying, Mosse, one of the other dogs, trotted over and lay down next to him. She nuzzled at his head, his chest, then curled in next to him as Bob drew his last breath and expired. Mamen went down to try to get some sleep, but he was kept awake all night by Mosse's wailing and howling.

The dogs were too important to lose, so when the weather quieted down, Bartlett had Kataktovik and Kuraluk build some igloo-style snow kennels in a large snowbank close to the starboard side of the ship. They shoveled coal ashes onto the ice for a kind of floor and there chained up most of the known fighters, separating them from the others as best they could. But Mamen struggled to erase the scenes of that deadly fight and to get the horrible wolflike howling out of his mind.

Another morning, Mamen was ripped from half sleep by loud voices and commotion in the cabin. He sat up, coughing, and through a haze of smoke, he barely made out Barker, the second mate, and Chafe, the mess-room steward, yanking at the stovepipe that led to the messroom. The stove in the messroom had almost gone out, and its smoke was filtering through the stovepipes and into the cabins. Bartlett arrived to help Chafe carry the smoking stove outside onto the deck long enough to clear the smoke. Then he ordered that the stovepipe be rerouted straight up from the messroom onto the deck to avoid further incidents, as this one could have proved fatal to the men inhaling sulfurous fumes. When the smoke finally cleared and the cooled-down stove was returned to the messroom, Bartlett realized that it was November 27—Thanksgiving Day back in the States. He imagined the feasts his good friends in Boston would be enjoying—the drinks and laughter and reveling—and grew nostalgic, but as this was a Canadian expedition, there'd be no observance of the American holiday.

There were strange phenomena occurring outside the ship too. One day McKinlay was out doing his daily jog around the *Karluk*. He'd developed a unique fitness routine to break up the monotony. But also, he wanted to remain strong, ready for whatever rigors might await him. He would jog throughout all the passages of the *Karluk*, sometimes breaking into a sprint across the deck, then trotting double time through every single passage of the *Karluk*, again and again, like, as he put it, "a prisoner exercising in the prison yard." He'd measured it: ten complete laps over and through the ship equaled one mile.

On this afternoon, as he charged along the rail, McKinlay was brought to a halt by something that caught his eye on the northwest horizon. It was dark and funnel shaped, like a weird smoke cloud coming from a steamer's smokestack. A steamship was impossible, he knew. And yet, there was the smoke, rising off the surface and hovering, coiling up from the horizon to about eighty degrees. He went and got the other scientists, and the captain, and showed them. Then another formation appeared, this one to the south-southwest, hovering there for a long time like an inverted tornado. None of the men of science could offer a reasonable explanation for what they were witnessing, with Bartlett saying only that it certainly was not another ship. It was probably clouds above newly open water, funneling in some localized wind event, though he had to admit it was curious indeed. He'd never seen anything quite like it on any of his polar voyages.

After the captain had left, Mamen scrambled up into the barrel to get a better perspective. The smokestack funnels, or whatever they were, had disappeared. But the view from the crow's nest was clear—"ice and more ice as far as the eye could see"—and here and there the horizon was pierced by long, dark masses rising up like mountain ranges. He scanned and scanned, turning his face and shoulders from the wind, his eyes watering as he tried to cipher the dimensions of the blue-black forms. "There were two immensely big patches," he said, "stretching northwest to south-east. They were about ten miles long and one mile wide." When he told Bartlett about them and suggested, with excitement, that they might be land, islands maybe, the captain just spat off the rail and said, "Pressure ridges."

Conditions in some of the cabins were becoming intolerable. One morning, McKinlay awoke in the Cabin De Luxe to find "gleaming icicles hanging from above." They looked like ice stalactites dangling down at him. The walls of his bunk were crystallized from frozen condensation. The room was, he said, "a miniature ice palace, crystals sparkling in the light. All along the outer side of my bunk was a sheet of ice." Then the ice on the walls and ceiling would thaw with the heat of the warming cook-stoves, wetting blankets and clothing and even pooling on the floors. It was happening in other cabins, too, so that everyone was sodden and cold and uncomfortable. About the situation, McKinlay lamented, "Never could there have been found a more dispirited and demoralized group of human beings." The men of Cabin De Luxe showed the problem to Captain Bartlett, and he agreed to move one of the coal stoves in there to maintain a more consistent temperature and reduce the freeze-thaw effect.

Bartlett's best estimate put them now perhaps 150 to 175 miles east of Wrangel Island, a small uninhabited island that lay about 100 miles off the coast of northern Siberia. In the last two months, they'd drifted about 300 miles westward, which, if his assumptions were correct, situated them about halfway between Point Barrow and Wrangel Island. Bartlett and the scientists discussed their likely location and the general direction of their drift, and everyone seemed to agree that they might possibly end up somewhere in the vicinity of Wrangel Island, but it certainly wasn't guaranteed. And Bartlett knew that they might as easily slip north of it and into the East Siberian Sea, exactly as had happened to Captain De Long and the crew of the *Jeannette*. He and everyone else knew how that grim tale ended: almost two years of icebound drifting, then the destruction of the ship in 1881, followed by the slow, excruciating death of twenty of the men.*

Bartlett remained task driven, keeping everyone busy either on the ship or on the ice, whatever the fates had in store for them. He enlisted men to construct wooden boxes to protect their Primus stoves, which would be essential should they be forced to take to the ice. The portable kerosene-burning stoves were an ingenious invention from Sweden and had served many an Arctic explorer well. Bartlett valued them highly and wanted them carefully housed and protected in the special boxes, which they'd be able to load onto sleds, allowing quick access to the stoves to heat food or boil water for tea or coffee. When finished, these boxes were stacked out on the ice floe with the other emergency gear and provisions.

James Murray continued to impress everyone with his tireless seafloor dredging. One day he surfaced from the igloo over the dredge hole, a smile beaming under his frozen beard and mustache. When he got his haul up to the laboratory, the other scientists got to see what he was so excited about. He had an octopus, but more than that: he had eleven specimens of previously unknown animal life. He shook off his frozen clothes and immediately started studying the creatures, drawing them, and recording their shapes and measurements in his notebooks.†

Everyone had begun to look forward to Christmas. On Arctic voyages, celebrations brought a crew together and offered a break from the confinement and tedium. The constant cold of the last month—with a recorded low of –32°F—had kept all but the heartiest, like McKinlay and Murray

---

* There was something else that Bartlett found remarkable, and rather ominous, about the *Jeannette*: three years after she sank, some of her wreckage was discovered by Inuit on the southwest coast of Greenland—nearly three thousand nautical miles from where it had sunk. Based on this finding, Norwegian Fridtjof Nansen intentionally froze his specially built, round-hulled *Fram*—so designed in order to have the ice lift the *Fram* up onto it rather than crush the vessel—into Arctic sea ice, where it drifted across the Arctic Ocean for three years, confirming his theory of transpolar drift. But Bartlett had neither the *Fram* nor food to last three years.

† Unfortunately, all of Murray's notebooks and specimens were lost.

and Mamen, shipbound. Talk of Christmas and the coming New Year was constant, with much speculation about the dinner feast they were sure to have, as they were all tiring of the seal meat. Templeman did mix things up by serving seal liver—meant to be a delicacy—every third day, but it had lost all its former charm. The four foxes Kataktovik and Kuraluk had recently trapped made only one stew. Men fantasized and even wagered on what Templeman might come up with, though he wasn't a particularly imaginative cook. And some of the men, with Bartlett's blessing, discussed a sports tournament to celebrate Christmas Day, weather and ice conditions permitting.

The mood on board felt less contentious than it had been, with a few exceptions. Dr. Mackay confided in Mamen that he would not attempt to embark for land with Beuchat and anyone else who would go with him until the sun returned. It would simply be suicide, he conceded, to try it in darkness. He tried once more to convince Mamen to commit to joining them, but Mamen remained unmoved and utterly devoted to the captain. He told Dr. Mackay, in no uncertain terms, not to bring it up again. At any rate, it was absurd, thought Mamen, to put faith of any kind in Dr. Mackay. His behavior—both Mamen and McKinlay had noticed it and discussed it—was wildly uneven. At dinner he would not say a word to anyone and would fail to even make eye contact with Captain Bartlett. He'd wolf down his food, finishing first, then return immediately to his bunk and sing songs in such a loud and raucous voice that everyone could hear him just next door in the messroom. Then he'd stop singing and blurt out challenges through the walls for any takers to play him in chess. Bartlett worried that the man was becoming unhinged.

George Malloch, too, was acting oddly. He hadn't succumbed to any violent outbursts lately, but one night, for no apparent reason, he dressed in his warmest furs and said he was going to sleep in the chart room. He took a sleeping bag and a few personal belongings and tromped off, leaving the others in Cabin De Luxe perplexed. The next morning at breakfast, everyone had a quiet chuckle when Malloch arrived, as McKinlay put it, "clad in all his furs and looking pinched and blue in the face," from the cold.

McKinlay made sure to keep his distance and not tease the man publicly, remembering the unprovoked great bear hug and choking he'd received not so long ago. Most thought that Malloch would give it up and come in after a night or two, but he was so stubborn he remained in the chart room, bundled in his furs and eiderdown sleeping bag, for weeks. No one quite understood what he was trying to prove, or whether it presaged even more bizarre behavior to come. The Long Night affected some more than others.

The need to constantly burn coal in the stoves was creating another smoke problem. The ship's engines had been shut down for some time and were still being taken apart and overhauled by the engineers, in case of eventual use when the ice broke up in the summer and they were once again free. As a result, to keep everything from freezing completely solid and the cabins survivable, several coal stoves were kept burning continuously, and most were now smoking badly. Constant use resulted in soot buildup in the stovepipes, and that caused poor draft and smoke leaking into cabins, the galley, and the messroom. Because of the bends and turns in the pipes, members tried various innovative attempts to extricate the soot, to mixed and sometimes nearly catastrophic results.

First, McKinlay thought that burning an intensely hot fire might heat the pipes enough to burn the soot out. Mamen watched as McKinlay poured a bunch of alcohol onto the coals and lit a match. But the magnetician used too much alcohol, and the coals burst into flames, leaping out of the stove with a small explosion that knocked him backward onto his hind side. His eyebrows and some of his forehead hair were singed, but after slathering his face and head with Vaseline, he was fine, if a little shaken.

Next, Templeman tried his luck with the constantly smoldering cookstove. He put a trace amount of dynamite powder up in the pipe, hoping that a small explosion would jar some of the soot loose. Fortunately for everyone, he was too timid with the dynamite and there was only a feeble puff, to no effect. To assist the cook, the engineer Williamson and first mate Sandy went above to where the pipe came out on the deck. They fired two blank cartridges down the pipe, which did blow some soot back down. Unfortunately, though the cook fire burned a little better, some of the soot filtered down and into the water tank, so that for the next few days, the men noticed a distinctly sooty taste to their coffee.

Even Captain Bartlett tried to stem the smoke in his cabin. He took some flashlight powder and tossed it into the stove, then started to shut the stove door.* There was a loud boom and Bartlett was rocked backward. He ducked as the stove door came off its hinges and flew right past his head. "If it had hit me it would have killed me," he said. When he got the door back on and the fire going, the smoke problem was indeed improved. "The method . . . was effective but disturbing," he later joked to the men.

The chess tournament ended after much heated competition. One night Dr. Mackay and Munro contested a marathon lasting three and a half hours, with Mackay finally winning. The finals came down to Mackay versus Mamen, who it turns out had sandbagged them all, feigning that he was a novice. At the final tally, the two were tied, and Mamen defeated the doctor in a playoff, winning the coveted box of fifty cigars. Mackay, muttering in disgust, took the smaller box of twenty-five and sulked off to his bunk.

Daytime—primarily from noon to two—afforded a few hours of a kind of twilight by which the men could do some outdoor work. Under Bartlett's instructions, Kataktovik and Kuraluk, with assistance from McKinlay, worked on building a snow house for the dogs to provide more shelter than the small, makeshift igloos they'd previously dug into snowbanks. Bartlett had noticed that the configuration of stacks of coal, biscuit tins, and oil drums stacked on the ice created a natural square between them, which was conveniently enclosed by a large, hardened snowdrift. The square had inside dimensions of about fifteen feet along each wall and was seven feet high. For a roof, Bartlett offered a spare foresail, and this was spread out over the top and tied down, making for a very comfortable shelter.

---

* Used in photography and the first flashlamps, flashlight powder consisted of a mixture of magnesium, potassium chlorate, and antimony sulfide. When ignited, the powder burned quickly, giving off a brilliant white light. It also released a thick cloud of white smoke, which was hazardous to breathe.

December 21—Arctic Midnight—arrived with little onboard fanfare, though it was noteworthy as "the day of days in the Arctic," according to Captain Bartlett. On Arctic expeditions, this day was usually one of much celebration, for now each day would be longer, the sunlight lengthening and improving spirits. Its importance was not lost on McKinlay, who privately observed in his journal, "Today is one of special significance for us, for some time tonight the sun will have reached his southern limit and will begin his return journey to bring us cheer. We should get our first sight of him in about six weeks now. People at home cannot realize the significance of this astronomical fact."

Meanwhile, the winds kicked up again, gusting so hard as to partly blow down the snowbanked wall of the just-finished snow house. Men made repairs as they could, cutting and stacking blocks of ice to shore it up again, shielding their eyes from the driving windswept snow while the dogs huddled inside, whining and whimpering. Hadley removed his own dog, Molly, and took her on board because she was pregnant and close to delivering. He made a bed of wood shavings for her in a corner of the hold, where she would be warm and sheltered when she gave birth, which would be better for the coming pups too.

The Arctic nights were a wonder for those who took the time to step out from their cabins and gaze upward. McKinlay had been giving Kataktovik evening English lessons, at Kataktovik's request. The young Eskimo wanted to learn to communicate verbally and write in English, so McKinlay spent about an hour a night with him, and Kataktovik was an excellent student. It was a good diversion for the Scottish schoolteacher. After the lessons, McKinlay would head up to the deck and treat himself to the nearly full moon beaming through pocked veils of cirrocumulus clouds.

One night after reading the instruments, he looked up to see, just forming, a lunar corona. At first there appeared a glowing circle around the moon, but as he watched, it began to burst with colors: red, then greenish yellow, then whitish blue, the red hues flaring like coal embers at the outermost edges of the ring. After about ten minutes, the corona faded and the clouds parted; the stars glittered like glass fragments, and the moon shone brightly down, illuminating the ice blocks all around into strange shapes and figures, like gargoyles or dinosaurs, their moving silhouettes taking forms beyond his imagination. He returned to his cabin to write in his journal about the wonders he had witnessed: "It was a beautiful spectacle. . . . This certainly is a favored region, so far as heavenly phenomena are concerned."

13

AN ARCTIC CHRISTMAS

MCKINLAY, SANDY, AND WILLIAMSON SAT IN THE GALLEY AT HALF past five on Christmas morning, drinking tea. They'd agreed to rise early and decorate the ship for the day's festivities. After tea they went to the saloon and hung international code flags from the ceilings and draped more across all the walls so that they burst with color. Hadley had given them a bunch of colored ribbon he originally brought along for trading, and they decorated the room and chairs with the red, white, and blue ribbon, which hung like streamers. On a large rectangle of canvas, they wrote Christmas greetings in blue and red paint, hanging the bright sign prominently across from the captain's end of the table. Just behind Bartlett's chair they hung the Canadian Blue Ensign. Pleased with their embellishments, they crept back to their bunks for a little shut-eye ahead of the day's sports festival, set to commence at eleven.

At breakfast, everyone was groggy from a jovial Christmas Eve. Bartlett had produced a few bottles of whiskey for the boys fore and aft, enough to render some hangovers. They'd played the gramophone for hours and sang songs, the aroma of Templeman's baking cakes wafting through the saloon. As a special treat, Templeman served tasty fruit jam along with their usual marmalade, which was much appreciated among the men.

Bartlett didn't want the Eskimos to feel left out, even though Christmas was not a traditional holiday for them. He gave beautiful hunting knives and watches to Kataktovik and Kuraluk and handed Auntie a lovely cotton dress, plus "talcum powder, soap, a looking glass, and comb and a brush," with a cotton dress each for Helen and little Mugpi. Bartlett knew there weren't likely to be many events—besides this evening and maybe New Year's—for the women and girls to use the cotton dresses, but it was a sweet gesture all the same.

McKinlay, Sandy, and Williamson had spent most of the previous day cleverly designing and laying out the various courses for the competitions, and McKinlay had even typed up a sports program, which was posted for all to see:

D.G.S. *KARLUK*. XMAS DAY, 1913

THE EVENTS OF THE SPORTS PROGRAMME

ARRANGED FOR THE DAY

WILL TAKE PLACE IN THE FOLLOWING ORDER:

1. 100 yards sprint
2. Long jump (standing)
3. Long jump (running)
4. Sack race
5. High jump
6. Interval for refreshments
7. Three-legged race
8. Putting the weight
9. 50-yard burst
10. Hop, step, and leap
11. Tug of war
12. Obstacle race
13. Wrestling

Proceedings will commence at 11 A.M. (*Karluk* time); dogs and bookmakers are not allowed on the field.

For the last few days, yet another storm had raged, bringing the usual high winds. Luckily, Christmas Day was calm, and the recent winds had scoured the ice near the ship smooth, giving it the appearance of having been prepared just for the games. The temperature was –23°F, but the air was so still it felt almost pleasant, and everyone dressed in warm clothes and assembled down on the ice at the designated time. Bartlett wanted everyone involved in some way to bolster ship camaraderie and spirit. Typically, there was a built-in segregation on board: the staff and sailors stayed mostly to their forward quarters; the Eskimos spent most of their time in the laboratory, which was also up front; and the officers and scientific staff inhabited the saloon, Cabin De Luxe, and messroom aft. Bartlett encouraged total group participation. He even convinced the irascible Dr. Mackay to act as umpire, pinning a paper rosette on the curmudgeon's coat designating him an official.

Before the events commenced, Bartlett took Mamen aside. A former ski champion in Norway, the assistant topographer was used to high-level competitions and had already proved himself as the best athlete among them. Bartlett quietly asked him to compete in only two events; it wouldn't do for him to go out and win them all. It might demoralize the others, and there would be no prizes for anyone else. Mamen agreed, and inside he brimmed with pride at the captain's acknowledgment of his athletic prowess.

Ten competitors lined up for the hundred-yard sprint, and George Breddy, the fireman, crossed the line first, with three or four of the racers slipping in their mukluks and falling hard onto the ice. As predicted, Mamen easily won both the standing and running long jumps, with chief engineer Munro coming in second in each, impressing everyone.

The sack race had to be modified because the sacks were too frozen to open and get one's leg in. So, after consultation with umpire Mackay, they instead tied each contestant with rope to simulate them being inside a sack, providing great humor as each was bound tight. Sandy turned out to be very springy and an excellent hopper, winning both the sack race and the hop, step, and leap event that followed.

In good spirits, everyone adjourned to the ship to warm up; smoke cigarettes, cigars, and pipes; and sip hot coffee and tea. During the break, Munro pulled off one of his mukluks to reveal a nasty gash in the sole of his foot. While competing in the hundred-yard sprint, he had stepped on a discarded sharp-edged tin just protruding from the ice. The tin edge had sliced clear through the heavy mukluk bottom, and Dr. Mackay cleaned and treated the wound with iodine and bandages. Then everyone was back out onto the field for more.

Breddy won the fifty-yard dash, making it two-for-two in the sprint races, and someone joked that it was fitting to have a fast fireman who could arrive to put out flames in a hurry. Munro, though limping on his cut foot, triumphed in the shot put, garnering loud applause.

The highlight of games by far was the elaborate obstacle course set up by McKinlay, Sandy, and Williamson. It took some time for Mackay to explain the course. The starting line was on the ice about midships and followed a "track" that had been dug running at right angles to the ship. "The track," recorded Bartlett, "was just wide enough for a man to put both feet in and they had to go up the track and back down again; this was no easy task and it was a cause for hilarious mirth to watch them trying to pass each other on the narrow path." Then things got interesting. They had to negotiate a giant snowbank obstacle, which had been shorn slick by the winds; at least half the competitors struggled, slipping back down just as they reached the top. This was followed by a rope maze hung from the jib boom. They had to crawl through the loops of rope and then crawl beneath some sledges that had been turned upside down. Everyone was cheering and yelling encouragement and laughing as the lead constantly changed. Munro, still limping but competing hard, got hung up in the bowlines, his feet caught above him until he was suspended, hanging there upside down. Spectators had to go over and disentangle him. Amid all the chaos, Chafe had steadily plodded along, remarkably coming from dead last to crossing the finish in first place, with practically everyone buckled over in laughter.

With the games concluded, everyone hurried back on board, rubbing themselves warm and giddy from the delightful day. Dinner had been set for half past four, so there was just time to change into slightly better clothes, some of the men donning sweaters. McKinlay had typed up special menu cards, placing one at each table setting. Templeman even brought from the galley a new set of china. The table, adorned with a small artificial Christmas tree, had room for ten, with two chairs and eight stools, so, perhaps as a kind of joke, a big box of dynamite was dragged in as an extended bench to make room for the entire contingent of twelve officers and staff.

Bartlett opened a bottle of whiskey and poured each man a glass. Then he asked all to stand; he wanted to make a toast. It grew quiet and everyone held their glasses high. Bartlett closed his eyes for a moment, growing serious, even solemn. "To the loved ones back home," he offered, and everyone belted back the whiskey and sat back down. "For a spell no one moved or spoke," wrote McKinlay. "We were too full for words. . . . In spirit we were, each of us, thousands of miles away." Privately, they each conjured their loved ones, hoping they were in good health.

Now they turned their attention to the meal. Templeman had outdone himself. He hurried back and forth from the galley, bringing mixed pickles and oyster soup, followed by generous entrées of lobster, bear steak, and ox tongue, with side dishes of potatoes, green peas, and asparagus in a thick cream sauce. The men savored the meal, indulging in multiple servings, though Templeman warned them to save room for dessert. Shortly he returned with plum pudding, mince pies, mixed nuts, and strawberries. Just when everyone thought they might be finished, Murray produced a big Christmas box that had been given to the expedition in Esquimalt by the "Ladies of Victoria, B.C.," for this very occasion. The men leaned forward in anticipation as Murray opened it, revealing a lovely Christmas cake, shortbread, various chocolates, as well as cigars and cigarettes. Oddly, the box also contained a harmonica, with a note that it was designated for the "baby" of the expedition. Perhaps it was meant for little Mugpi, but the men laughed and handed it to Mamen, since he was the youngest among them.

Bartlett got out the Victrola, which had been presented to him by British Columbia premier Sir Richard McBride, and, enjoying their new stock of fresh cigars and cigarettes, they had a concert. Bartlett played a range of records—popular and classical, instrumental and vocal—and Mamen tried his best to accompany with his new harmonica while others sang. But everyone was exhausted from the day's sports events and stuffed from the great feast, so most turned in rather early, feeling absolutely content.

A crack like a lightning strike roused everyone just after breakfast the next morning. The captain, McKinlay, and Mamen were among the first to sprint up on deck to look around. They stared at a large fracture in the ice, "running the whole starboard length of the ship, hard against her side." As they stood listening to the ice creaking and grinding, others arrived, and just then a tremor like a small earthquake shook the ship. Men gasped and grasped for the rails, holding on to anything they could until it passed. A second quaver sent vibrations through the deck boards; they could feel the rumblings through the bottoms of their mukluks. Mamen overheard Beuchat whisper to Murray that he thought "it would be the last of us."

Bartlett hustled to investigate the ship. Ice pressed against the entire length of the starboard side—crushing the lower portion of the gangway—but so far, it hadn't pierced the hull. Down below, in the engine room, there remained a slight leak, but after watching it carefully for some time, Bartlett decided that it wasn't considerably worse than before. Even so, when he got back topside, he ordered that all members "get things ready to leave the ship at once, in case we should have to get out in a hurry."

It was an ominous order, and most everyone was terrified. But Bartlett had been planning for this eventuality. Already there were stockpiles of food and shelter materials out on the big floe, and fuel. Now the men worked to stack extra boxed pemmican out on the deck, as well as cartons of tea tablets. Below, everyone toiled to finish their outfits of fur clothing, double-stitching the overcoats, shirts, and trousers. The process of preparing the skins was tedious and difficult, involving hours of scraping, heating them to make them pliable, then washing to soften them. As they worked, men cussed Stefansson aloud for sending them into the Arctic unprepared;

it seemed insane that they were still making clothes they might need at any moment, but that was the reality. Auntie and the girls worked double time on various-sized pairs of bearded seal boots.

Mamen, usually one of the hardest and quickest workers among them, limped around, wincing with every step and yelping out in pain. During the jumping competitions on Christmas Day, he'd landed awkwardly and aggravated his old knee injury. The day was so joyous that he hadn't complained, but now he was worried. The kneecap was so loose he could move it all around; it looked grotesque floating freely about, and when he straightened his leg to put weight on it, the joint responded with electric bolts of pain. He went to Dr. Mackay, who examined it and confirmed that it was dislocated. He administered some medications and told Mamen to go easy on it, and by the next morning the kneecap had slipped back into place and the swelling subsided, but it still concerned him. He prided himself on his physical abilities and knew that Bartlett needed him at full strength.

During all the hustle and emergency preparations, Molly gave birth to eleven puppies, though a few of them did not survive. A fresh storm was blowing across the expanse, and the presence of new life in this hard place lifted the men's moods. Mamen went with Hadley to look at them, and he was moved: "They are in the best of health considering the circumstances, as well as Molly herself. It was touching to see her love for them, she licked them, gathered them around her so that they should lie comfortable and warm, and . . . we touched them."

To reward the hard work that most everyone was engaged in, Bartlett distributed the prizes for the Christmas Day competitions. There were some very useful items, like snow goggles and heavy wool sweaters and long-sleeved shirts. Others got Gillette safety razors with extra blades or shaving soap and hair clippers. Someone joked that the captain seemed to want better grooming aboard his ship. He was right—washing and hair cutting had been reduced to once a week because heating enough water was such a laborious task.

Then, around midday on December 29, a cry went up from the deck. McKinlay had been taking reading when he spotted a long, low blue cloud. At first, he thought it was only a cloud looming above open water, or one of the great raised pressure ridges that Mamen had shown him, sections of colliding ice upthrust. He could see Sandy up in the barrel, also scanning in the same direction, off to the south-southwest. "Is that land ahead?" McKinlay called out. Sandy scrambled down and stood next to McKinlay. They could both see, through the muted midday twilight, a high mountain peak rising in the distance, piercing the mist. Other lower hills lay like rounded knuckles on either side, but in the center thrust a mountain, rising perhaps two or three thousand feet above the plain. Sandy ran to tell the captain, and McKinlay began shouting, "Land, land ho!"

Soon everyone milled about on deck, looking hopefully across the barren icescape as the ice creaked and ground all around them. A deep haze surrounded the ship, and for a time no one believed McKinlay. Then the haze dispersed and lifted, and there, for all of them to see, was the outline of a large black peak.

It was land.

14

REUNIONS

VILHJALMUR STEFANSSON AND RUDOLPH ANDERSON, THE LEADER OF the Southern Party, stood face-to-face in a cabin twenty-four miles east of Collinson Point, yelling at each other. Their reunion had been civil at first, even cordial. Dr. Anderson was shocked to see Stefansson, and he inquired anxiously about the *Karluk*, for he'd heard only speculation and rumors. Stefansson told Anderson about the unfortunate disappearance of the *Karluk*, though he skirted any responsibility for it and gave no clear explanation for why he'd left the ship other than to say he'd gone caribou hunting. But when Stefansson started to explain his revised plans for the expedition, which included the full cooperation of Dr. Anderson, things quickly deteriorated and became heated, and now the two men were shouting over each other, their hands slamming down on the crude wooden table, their faces puffed and red with anger.

Stefansson told Dr. Anderson that with the *Karluk* gone, he was forming "a New Northern Party," and would need some of the Southern Party's men and resources for his revised expedition plans. Dr. Anderson was still trying to process how in the world the leader of the grand Canadian Arctic Expedition had managed to lose his flagship. He shook his head and stated flatly that he needed all his resources to perform his contracted work.

It was December 18, 1913, and the cabin they were arguing in was a winter shelter between Collinson Point and Herschel Island. Meeting there was a chance accident. Stefansson had made it from Barrow to Collinson Point, where he'd checked in on the wintering *Alaska* and *Mary Sachs* and apprised team members of what had happened since they last saw one another. He was unimpressed by what he saw and learned, writing in his report, "The Southern Party had no intention of attempting any serious work during the winter. They had made a picnic-like attempt at hunting, with no success, and had notified Ottawa that there was no game in the area and that they could do nothing until summer." Stefansson seemed to have conveniently forgotten, or chosen to ignore, the fact that a spontaneous and fruitless caribou hunting trip was what had led him here.

Miffed and privately fuming at Dr. Anderson, he'd pressed on toward Herschel Island, hoping to catch the outgoing mail, which was to leave the Royal North-West Mounted Police station at Herschel Island by the first of the year. Stefansson learned at Collinson Point that Anderson had gone there to dispatch updates on the progress and condition of the Southern Party, and Stefansson hoped to reach him at Herschel Island before the last mail of the year departed on its long, slow, and circuitous journey by sled from the northern Yukon all the way back to Nome, and then by ship to Ottawa.

But when Stefansson arrived at the cabin en route, he found Dr. Anderson there. His second-in-command had already made it to Herschel Island; he was now returning to his base at Collinson Point. When Stefansson told Dr. Anderson about his new plans to appropriate members, equipment, and even the use of the ships originally assigned to the Southern Party, the zoologist grew incensed. Back in June, at one of their contentious meetings in British Columbia, Anderson had bluntly threatened to resign on the spot unless Stefansson agreed to leave the leadership of the Southern Party entirely to him. Now, here was Stefansson, having lost his own ship, again imposing himself on the organization of the Southern Party.

After their tempers settled, Stefansson tried to explain that with the loss of the *Karluk*, his plans had dramatically changed, and he was simply adapting to the new situation. He had no intention of abandoning his original exploration goals; they'd just need to be carried out differently.

But the problem was he required resources that were aboard the *Karluk*, wherever it was. When Dr. Anderson inquired what Stefansson intended to do about the *Karluk* and its complement, Stefansson said coldly, "For good or ill, we're evidently unable to affect the destiny of the *Karluk* in any way and so she was, in a sense, off our minds." It was a cavalier, even cruel attitude, but coming from Stefansson, hardly surprising. He'd moved on, and his own present needs were all that mattered to him.

Dr. Anderson held firm. He told Stefansson that because of his choices, he was now "a leader without anything to lead," and he "had no right to take supplies or equipment." Not only that, but he also said that he thought this new plan to journey north over the ice was just another stunt to gain more notoriety. He said that Stefansson must either assume full control of the Southern Party or absolutely none. There could be no half steps, no meddling whenever he happened to show up, no dropping in unannounced to intervene. It was simply too disruptive. He vehemently reminded Stefansson of the promise he'd made in Esquimalt, and then again in Nome, to leave him to the details of leading the Southern Party. He argued that Stefansson's new plan to explore the Beaufort Sea was more than impractical, it was likely impossible, and that "any attempts to do so would be abortive, resulting in the expenditure of money, the waste of supplies, and probably the loss of lives." It was quite likely, given his abandonment of the *Karluk* and its unknown fate, that lives had already been lost, or would be.

For a few minutes, it was quiet in the cabin. Finally, Stefansson cleared his throat and said that he would not assume control of the Southern Party. He would go on to Herschel Island and proceed with his plans for the New Northern Party. He was adamant, fully determined to go through with the Arctic exploration he'd come here to do, even if that meant "living by forage on the ice of the Polar Sea" with what few resources he already had, plus those he could obtain. Stefansson told Dr. Anderson to return to Collinson Point immediately and "remain in local charge of the base there," adding that he should feel free to put any grievances or objections he had in writing and send those complaints to the government in Ottawa.

Stefansson left the next day for Herschel Island, Dr. Anderson for Collinson Point—both disgruntled, having reached no formal agreement. Of the encounter, Stefansson wrote, "This clash was by no means encouraging, but I felt sure that Dr. Anderson on mature consideration would see the advisability of following instructions."

Stefansson bolted into action. He'd get what he needed, with or without Dr. Anderson's cooperation. First, he made his way east to the *Belvedere*, a well-built three-masted steam whaler locked in the ice just offshore. Stefansson knew that the ship carried some seventy-five tons of the original expedition's equipment and supplies, which had been destined for Herschel Island. Back in Nome in August, he'd contracted with Captain Cottle—a good friend—to convey the equipment there, where, along with everything else aboard the *Alaska*, *Mary Sachs*, and the *Karluk*, it was to be divided between the Northern and Southern Parties.

Stefansson made it aboard the *Belvedere* in time to spend a lovely Christmas with Captain and Mrs. Cottle. Over fine wine and a sumptuous meal, Stefansson convinced the captain to send by ship a good portion of the expedition's supplies from the *Belvedere* to Martin Point, not far to the west, from which Stefansson planned to embark on his first exploratory ice journey. Much of the haul that Stefansson was commandeering had been earmarked for the Southern Party, including large portions of pemmican. But Stefansson thought nothing of it—and Captain Cottle, plied with wine and spirits, happily agreed.

The next day Stefansson left, stopping in to visit another old friend, a trader named Duffy O'Connor. Stefansson knew that O'Connor should have plenty of supplies he could purchase; he'd been in the area for some time. After greetings and handshakes, Stefansson learned—to his surprise and delight—that O'Connor had decided to sell everything and leave the Arctic. He'd had enough of the long, cold winters. Stefansson reached into his bags and pulled out one of the blank checks that the Canadian government had given him for "emergency use." Stefansson reasoned that if this wasn't an emergency, what was? He purchased O'Connor's entire inventory for $6,000. The men shook hands and Stefansson told the trader to pack everything up; he'd be back for the lot of it after conducting some more business at Herschel Island.

Stefansson was thrilled by his good fortune. He left the trading post in the same frame of mind he'd adopted when originally planning and outfitting the Canadian Arctic Expedition: bent on action, doing whatever it took to achieve his goals. Only ten miles east, he visited yet another friend, Captain Martin "Matt" Andreasen, who ran a small trading camp and wintered his fifty-foot schooner, the *Northstar*, there. The two men exchanged greetings, then stories, with Stefansson relating his situation and needs. After considerable persuasion by Stefansson, which included another blank check, Andreasen agreed to sell him all the supplies he had on hand. That was excellent, but Stefansson then started talking about the *Northstar*. It was a nifty, able craft. Though light at fifty tons and able to carry only about twenty tons of freight, it was nimble, fast turning, and most important, especially constructed for ice, with a flat bottom and a bow shaped so that, instead of ramming bluntly into a floe, it would slide right up onto it.

It was the perfect support vessel for exploration in these waters. Stefansson held out the check and asked whether Andreasen would be willing to sell the *Northstar* too. They discussed the price for everything, and in no time, Stefansson was writing a check for $13,000. With a stroke of Stefansson's pen, the government of Canada was now the owner of a small schooner.

Stefansson packed up and headed for Herschel Island. Remarkably, in only a week he'd managed to purchase everything he would need to go north into the unknown and carry out "the entire program reported to the Government from Point Barrow." Perhaps only Stefansson, with his dogged, even maniacal persistence and persuasive powers, could have pulled it off. Now all he needed was a few good men and an Eskimo seamstress and cook, and as he slung his rucksack on his back and strode toward Herschel Island, he was supremely confident he'd soon have both.

. . .

Sometime around the first of the year, Stefansson, now traveling with photographer George Wilkins, arrived at long last at Herschel Island. As they came up the rugged shoreline, he was met by a stout, round-faced, stern-looking Inupiat woman about thirty years old. Beside her stood a handsome little boy of five, dressed in furs, his eyes bright and intelligent, his complexion the color of copper. It was Fanny and Alex. Stefansson reached out to embrace them, but Fanny lurched forward and took hold of his collar and shook him, scolding him for being away so long and for not sending money as he'd promised. He reached into his pockets and feebly handed her a wad of crumpled bills, and then they walked on together toward the village, Fanny still berating him, her arms flailing, and the little fellow trotting along beside them.

However awkwardly, they were reunited, and Stefansson planned to take them with him on his next journey.

15

"FUNERAL MARCH"

THE SIGHTING OF LAND, THOUGH BRIEF AND ILLUSORY, HAD EVERY-
one hopeful about their improved chances. McKinlay drew a picture of
the island in his diary, including the high peak in the center. After consulting with Captain Bartlett and looking closely at the *Coast Pilot* and
comparing their current depth to their charts, they decided it must be
Wrangel Island and the peak probably Berry Peak, whose elevation was
listed at 2,500 feet.*

Seeing land inspired Dr. Mackay, Murray, and Beuchat to resume their
plans to take to the ice on their own. During late-night meetings they
whispered, mulling over when might be the best time to depart. It would
be another few weeks before the sun's full return, so they bided their time
and discussed how best to broach the topic with the captain in a way that
would be the least disruptive. Relations with Dr. Mackay and the captain
had improved since the Christmas festivities, and now the doctor decided
that if he could not get Bartlett's enthusiastic support, he might at least
get his permission.

---

* The peak they were looking at was indeed Berry Peak, named for Lieutenant Robert M.
Berry, commander of the USS *Rodgers*. Berry had led a group that landed on the island in
1881 to search for survivors of the lost USS *Jeannette*. At the time of the rescue mission, their
approximate survey (completed by the U.S. Coast and Geodetic Survey), tabulated the peak
elevation at 2,500 feet. Later, more accurate surveys found the peak to be 3,596 feet tall and
renamed it Gora Sovetskaya.

The New Year was upon them. On December 31, many were thinking of their homes and loved ones and of grand festivities happening far away. Late in the afternoon, Bartlett sat in his cabin, musing: "I realized that it was midnight on Tremont Street and Broadway and thought of the friends who would now be seeing the old year out and the new year in. I wondered what they thought had become of us on the *Karluk*, and whether the news of our unforeseen drift had yet reached them from Stefansson. I could picture the carefree throngs in the hotels waiting for the lights to go out for the moment of midnight and greeting 1914 with a cheer and a song."

Bjarne Mamen grew similarly nostalgic, and anxious when contemplating what the next year had in store for them. He confided in his diary:

> *1913 is gone and will never return. New Year's Eve is quiet for us. How vastly different . . . to be in civilization, and especially at home in my beloved Fatherland, with all my dear ones. But I have chosen this life for myself and will have to be content with it. Well, I am content although it looks dark many a time. The perils threaten one continuously and one has to be wide awake and vigilant, but I hope everything will be well and to the best for all of us on board. I hope that the new year of 1914 will bring better luck than the last one did.*

It was indeed a quiet evening, at least until the Scots got involved. When they realized it was Hogmanay—the Scots word for the last day of the year and a cause for much revelry—they roused at around half past eleven and gathered in the saloon to begin draining a bottle of whiskey Bartlett had provided them for the occasion. They fired up the gramophone as loud as it could play and sang songs and danced jigs, and at midnight, observing the ancient ship practice, they rang out sixteen bells. McKinlay went up onto the deck and paraded "fore and aft, raising the devil with the dinner bell." The rowdy contingent of Scotsmen—of which there were six—had managed to wake everyone aboard.

Munro and Murray were appointed to take whiskey and candied fruit as New Year's greetings to the captain. Bartlett was pleased to see them, and he reciprocated with more whiskey and some special cake he had, and they laughed and told stories for a while. When Munro and Murray returned to the saloon, the Scottish revelers "made the Arctic sing with strains of Auld Lang Syne," and delighted everyone assembled with loud, drunken, and slurred renditions of Robert Burns's poems. Even the dogs got involved, barking into the Arctic night from all the commotion.

On New Year's Day, just after breakfast, McKinlay, Murray, and Breddy were down on the young ice, lining out a soccer field. In response to some bragging by the drunken Scots, a challenge had been issued the night before, and now there would be held, according to the flyer created by McKinlay, the Grand International Football Match—SCOTLAND VS. ALL NATIONS. FIELD OF PLAY: ARCTIC OCEAN.

Bartlett agreed to referee, and the All Nations team installed Auntie as their goalie, clad in a dress and bloomers. The ball was ingeniously made from seal gut, which had been cut into pieces and sewn together; Dr. Mackay added surgeon's plaster over the seams to make it smooth, then encased it in sealskin and inflated it using a pipe stem as a valve. It worked better than expected.

Under cold, clear, brilliant skies, the game was fun for everyone and provided much-needed exercise, though there were quite a few spills and tumbles on the ice. McKinlay collided hard with Chafe, taking a knee to the stomach, which knocked the wind out of him. Bartlett tried to officiate using a whistle, but the metal froze to his lips on his first trilling, tearing off hunks of skin as he pulled it away. For the rest of the game, he resorted to yelling out signals and calls through bloody lips. All Nations won 8–3, a triumph that humbled the Scotsmen, but everyone enjoyed the game so much they planned to hold one every week, ice and weather conditions permitting.

Sometime in the early morning hours of January 2, McKinlay awakened to a strange noise, a kind of humming vibration, like that of a plucked banjo string. He lifted himself from the bed on one elbow and strained to listen, pressing his ear next to the wall, trying to comprehend the peculiar sound. "At times," he wrote, "it was a distinctly musical note, then it became a mere loud noise, and then silence. . . . Until six, I lay awake, listening, at times fascinated at the extreme delicacy of the note."

Captain Bartlett was roused by the noise too. He described it as "a rumbling noise not unlike that which one often hears singing along the telegraph wires on a country road." After breakfast, men went out onto the deck and the sound could still be heard, somewhere in the distance, yet they could see nothing through the gloamy twilight. Bartlett peered intently all around the ship—no significant change directly near the hull. He explained to the men that they were hearing wind over pressure ridges coupled with tremendous ice compression somewhere not far off. He said that the ice was crushing and raftering, and while they were apparently stationary—at least for the moment—the large floe in which they'd been drifting all these months must have been brought to a halt in the shallow waters off the shores of Wrangel Island, and even larger masses of ice were moving and pushing against them, the grinding of floe on floe creating a humming and buzzing noise, punctuated by what sounded like distant drumming or the rumblings of an angry volcano. Vibrations thrummed through the ship.

"I pray it not come any nearer," said McKinlay.

Bartlett understood, from the land he'd seen, that they weren't that close—maybe seventy-five or a hundred miles away. Not close enough to bolt for shore in these light conditions, certainly. And a storm was blowing in; it was already starting to snow. Best to ride it out as long as possible on the *Karluk* and continue preparing fur clothing, sleeping bags, and emergency food and sleds. He had the engineers store kerosene in one-pound tins for sledging and instructed them to trim down all the pick-axes so they weighed less than three pounds each. He worried about the group's ability to move safely across the ice, especially given how much food they'd need to carry for everyone, as well as for the dogs. The Eskimos would be fine, he figured: they were hardened people, accustomed to such rigors. But when it came to the others, he harbored concerns. Only Hadley had extensive polar ice travel experience. The captain would need to count on Mamen, strongest of them all, and McKinlay, whose daily training regimen impressed him. He grinned, picturing the dutiful Scottish schoolteacher running laps around the ship. And Sandy, the first mate, also showed considerable pluck. The seaman would require it before long; of that, Bartlett felt sure.

But there were members who gave him pause. Lately, fireman Breddy had been acting strangely, mumbling to himself as he went about the ship or holding conversations with the dogs, talking to them as if he expected a reply. He'd lost his appetite and had even turned down shots of whiskey—which was quite unusual. Bartlett knew how polar darkness and monotony could wear on a man—he'd seen it many times and it was a serious business. It could lead to madness. He'd need to watch Breddy and hope that the return of the sun helped his mood. Templeman, too, appeared more nervous than usual, chain-smoking at such a rate that he sometimes had two smokes going at once, and just the other day, he'd served Bartlett his midday coffee with a cigarette butt floating in it, which incensed the skipper. He'd had to berate the cook and later asked McKinlay to keep an eye on Templeman and report back if he became any more agitated or erratic.

A snowstorm and easterly gale now hammered across the pack, pounding the ship with gusts and bursts, coating the deck with drifts, and keeping everyone shipbound for days. And then, almost imperceptibly at first, they started moving again, now to the northwest. With the floe's movement came a dreadful ice racket, ever nearer. The noise grew incessant, sometimes sounding like a distant drumbeat, sometimes like weird shrieks and wails. The sounds were particularly unsettling to Beuchat, Murray, and Dr. Mackay. Each, in turn, went to Bartlett's cabin and asked for a sleeping bag, which he gave them. The three worked together in the evenings, preparing for themselves, fabricating man-harnesses for pulling sleds, the technique Dr. Mackay and Murray had used in the Antarctic. They stuffed their rucksacks with personal valuables, food, and even tobacco. Beuchat, his eyes twitching and hands shaking, advised Mamen to "get ready to turn out and go to Wrangel Island any moment." Mamen just went about his business, scraping furs with McKinlay. But he remarked after Beuchat left, "I'm sure of one thing: none of those three will reach land if left to their own resources."

Bartlett sometimes invited McKinlay into his cabin in the evenings. He enjoyed the mathematician's company and conversation. McKinlay was awed by the skipper's tales of travel and his wide-ranging knowledge, his ability to converse at length about topics as diverse as the poetic verses of Omar Khayyám's eleventh-century *Rubáiyát* to American upper-class society to the political mind of Winston Churchill. One evening, while Bartlett was telling him about an Arctic hunting trip he'd guided some wealthy Americans on, McKinlay noticed on the desk a thin book titled *A Book About Roses* by Samuel Reynolds Hole. It was surprising to see such a volume, especially here and now, where it was dark and -25°F outside. McKinlay thought of his mother's rose garden back home, could almost feel the flowers' velvety petals. He imagined their brilliant reds and yellows this coming spring. He picked up the book.

"Do you grow roses?" he asked the captain. Bartlett, then, was brought back home too. He told McKinlay that when he was home in Brigus, though the growing season was short, he loved cultivating roses and other flowers. So the two sat in the cabin of the frozen ship and talked about roses and petunias and tulips, about pruning and watering, and about land and soil, the feeling of rich dark earth running through their fingers.

Later that night, reflecting on their pleasant conversation, McKinlay wrote of how much he loved these discussions with his captain: "They took our minds off our present problems . . . kept us from looking in on ourselves, reminded us that there was still a familiar world that we would return to if we just kept our heads and took things calmly."

After a week of near-constant gale, the storm calmed enough to allow for some off-ship activity. Mamen took full advantage and got out on skis, overjoyed to have them underfoot again. Skiing came as naturally as walking or running to him, and he glided along the wind-polished surface, conscious of fresh cracks all around the ship and sastrugi—raised ridges of windblown snow. He eased into a rhythm, kick-glide, kick-glide, then moved into his double-pole technique, reaching out ahead with both poles, planting them, and, bending at the torso, thrusting himself forward again and again. He thrilled to the sound of the skis sliding across the ice, the improving light of the forenoon, and the freedom of being alone with his thoughts. It was like skiing across a frozen fjord back home in Christiania. Rupturing ice in the distance shook him from his daydreams. He realized that tonight was a full moon and recalled from Captain De Long's *Jeannette* logs that violent ice disturbances coincided with the full moon, so he turned back and skied for the ship as fast as he could.

Late that evening McKinlay went out to take in the skies and the air. Though it was –30°F, he did not feel cold. The glow of the full moon bathed everything in a lustrous light. He walked about a hundred yards beyond the ship, the dry ice crunching beneath his boots, then turned around. Large hummocks of ice cast long, disfigured shadows, and the mounds themselves had been polished to a glassy sheen so that they shimmered like giant gemstones. Stars, muted by the flaming moon, flecked the cloudless sky and auroral streamers hung down like shimmering curtains. He turned and took in the *Karluk*, which rose above the scene like an ice ghost, her rails and deck and rigging sheathed in glittering rime. All at once, McKinlay grew aware of that presence again, a sense that he was not alone. It was something otherworldly, "an exaltation beyond all earthly feeling." The feeling slowly faded away, but the memory was emblazoned in him. When he got back in his bunk, he wrote in his journal, "Whatever hardships the future might hold, whatever fate the North had in store for me, I felt supremely glad I had come."

At 5:00 A.M. on January 10, a violent shudder rumbled through the ship, followed by crashing ice and the terrible grating sound of ice against wood. Men, some only half-clothed, raced about, some to the engine room, some to the deck. McKinlay sprinted topside and found Bartlett, Hadley, and Breddy—who'd been night watchman—already there, shielding their eyes against a howling wind to assess the damage. They could just discern, at the stern of the ship, that the ice had fractured, splitting the dredge-house in two. The ice appeared to be shearing all sides of the ship, and the *Karluk* was rising on the starboard side, listing to port about twenty-five degrees. The deck, which before had been just a few inches above the gangway, was now more than a foot higher.

Hoping to perhaps raise the ship above the ice pressure, Captain Bartlett ordered men to begin throwing all the ice blocks, used as insulation, from the deck and skylights and the outer walls. They shoveled and tossed in shifts, working hour after hour heaving the heavy blocks, while Bartlett sent Kataktovik and Kuraluk and Chafe down onto the ice to release the dogs from the box house and prepare it as living quarters, lining the ice floor with boards and filling the stove so it could be quickly lit.

Working in teams as in a fire drill, all hands toiled through the day, ferrying everything they could from the ship down to the box house and large igloo on the big floe, next to the crates and barrels and cans already piled there. Men collided with one another in the dim light and blinding snow, but there was no panic. Bartlett ordered all lamps and stoves put out, except the galley stove. The last thing they needed was a ship fire on top of everything else. Auntie and Helen worked furiously, sewing skin clothes.

All day long everyone pitched in, unburdening the *Karluk* of everything heavy and that might be of use: tools and the remaining pemmican and packages of paraffin. Tents and bundles of skins and heavy coils of line. Boxes from the galley: dried milk and vegetables, butter and bacon and eggs. All heaved overboard. Once that was done, they turned to their cabins to pack personal effects, while outside the ice churned and ground with the sound of thunder. And all day long, as Bartlett put it, "the poor old *Karluk* struggled in the death grip of the pack." But the strength of the pack ultimately proved too great. At seven o'clock, a burst like a cannon blast shook the ship, and Bartlett raced with Munro toward the engine room. The captain and engineer held a lantern and squinted down into the hold. A great jagged fang of ice had pierced through the hull on the port side, tearing timbers to shreds and destroying the pump. Water rushed in, filling the hold at a frightening speed.

Bartlett went back on deck and shouted, "All hands abandon ship!"

Bartlett sent Auntie and her girls to the box house to start the fire and told Templeman to stay in the galley and serve hot coffee and food as long as possible. Bartlett produced a shot of whiskey to everyone who wanted one, as a bracer against the coming ordeal. The abandonment, while slow and orderly, was a dangerous affair. Outside it was dark, with winds raging at fifty miles per hour and the temperature at –30°F. The shearing ice tore open leads of water ten feet wide, and they had to portage sled loads of everything thrown overboard around these icy depths. Stranded dogs were hurled across the leads, yelping in fear.

During these trials, Dr. Mackay plunged through into the water up to his neck. By great fortune, Sandy was right there next to him, so the first mate hauled Dr. Mackay out, then watched the doctor stumble around aimlessly, his clothes freezing immediately. Sandy and McKinlay managed to get Dr. Mackay back on board and took him to Bartlett's cabin as he alternately raged and babbled for them to leave him alone. As they tore off his frozen clothing and dressed him in dry woolens, they smelled liquor on his breath and realized he was reeling drunk, having availed himself of too much of the whiskey Bartlett had offered.

By 11:00 P.M., the engine room was submerged in eleven feet of water. The *Karluk* remained afloat only because it was being pressured on both sides, held there by giant jaws of ice. Nearly everyone had been working through the night, taking breaks only to warm themselves with hot coffee in the galley. Now all that remained was for everyone to gather the last of their personal belongings and leave the ship for the box house and igloo, where sleeping assignments had been made: in the box house would be all the Eskimos as well as McKinlay, Mamen, Dr. Mackay, Murray, Beuchat, Clam, Golightly, and Chafe; the igloo or snow house Bartlett would share with Munro, Williamson, Breddy, Hadley, Templeman, Maurer, John Brady, Sandy, Barker, Malloch, and Hadley. Captain Bartlett congratulated everyone for their efforts, and at midnight had the Canadian Blue Ensign "hoisted for the last time" to the main topmast. At two in the morning, he ordered everyone to turn in to their respective dwellings on the ice to try to get some sleep, or at least some rest.

Bartlett stayed aboard the ship. He'd packed his personal effects, log-books and journals, and coveted *Rubáiyát* long before, and now he went from his cabin to the galley, where he stoked a huge fire. Men periodically came to visit him during the night. McKinlay had been too wet and cold to sleep, so he went aboard and found Bartlett there in the galley with Hadley, the gramophone blaring as loud as it could go. Bartlett had all 150 records stacked in a pile, and he'd put on a record, play it through, then lift it and toss it into the galley fire and put on another. He did this over and over, one record after the next. After every dozen records or so, the captain walked to the starboard deck and checked the ship's position. He eyed the surroundings, scouting a safe and speedy exit route.

By five o'clock in the morning, the water in the engine room had crested the gratings and was just five feet below the main deck. When he returned to the galley, he found Hadley searching frantically for little Ni-geraurak, the black kitten. Hadley had successfully moved Molly and her newborn puppies over to the ice shelters, but no one had seen the kitten in all the commotion during the night. At last they heard her mewing from a hiding place aft, and Hadley managed to catch her and take her out to the box house, placing her in a basket lined with furs and skins.

Throughout the day, Bartlett remained on the *Karluk*, playing records. Over in the ice houses, everyone was trying to stay warm, dry out clothes, and eat as much as they could get their hands on. They were having something of a feast. "Rummaging among the boxes," wrote McKinlay, "we broke out a tin of ox tongue, tins of roast beef and mutton, several tins of salmon . . . salt pork, cheese, and about a half-dozen old loaves." They stuffed themselves until they could eat no more, then lay back on their sleeping bags, smok-ing cigars. In the afternoon, they took a sounding and found the bottom at thirty-eight fathoms.

At quarter past three, Bartlett felt a lurch beneath his feet and a shudder as the ship settled with a groan. Water cascaded over the decks and ran down the hatches, and Bartlett knew it was finally time. He reached for a record—Chopin's "Funeral March"—placed it on the Victrola, and wound it full, closing his eyes as the first notes rose above the surge of rushing water.

Then he left the galley and went to the railing, holding on tight as the ship was sinking.

"She's going!" he yelled out, and one by one the seamen and crewmen and scientists came from the igloo and snow house and stood on the ice. They came as close as they could, watching Bartlett standing there alone. Then, with the notes of "Funeral March" carried by the Arctic winds, accompanied by the percussive sounds of ship timbers buckling and snapping, Bartlett waited until the rail was just even with the ice and he stepped off his ship.

Everyone stood speechless. They watched as the ship lowered slowly on an even keel. A puff of steam burst upward as water poured in and doused the galley fire. With grace and dignity, the *Karluk* continued downward until only the crow's nest was visible above water, and at last, the Canadian Blue Ensign, flapping in the Arctic wind, submerged into the water and was gone.

16

SHIPWRECK CAMP

FOR SOME TIME, EVERYONE STARED AT THE SURFACE OF THE WATER that had engulfed the *Karluk*. Two umiaks and the whaleboat, all three of which had been on the deck, floated aimlessly, buffeted by the wind. Bartlett pulled down his hood and tried to bite back tears. He'd been shipwrecked twice before—both times on Newfoundland's southern coast—but this time felt different. The *Karluk* had been their home for seven months. And just behind him, marooned on an ice floe in the Arctic Ocean, stood twenty-two men, one woman, two children, twenty-four dogs, six puppies, and a cat. Bartlett took a last look at the glassy surface where the *Karluk* had been. It was already beginning to freeze over at the edges.

"Goodbye, old girl," he said, and turned to face the group.

Bartlett shouted above the wind for all hands to start hauling everything they'd tossed off the *Karluk* and organize it as best they could near the makeshift camp on the floe. He helped, grabbing strewn items, but he could not feel his feet. During the ship's final death throes, he'd been in his light American boots, and now he realized he'd left his best pair of mukluks in his cabin. He hurried to the igloo to warm up and try to sleep; he'd been awake for thirty-six straight hours.

When he got inside, he took off his boots and stood on a fur laid out by the stove. Auntie hovered over him, with blood running down her lips. He asked if she'd fallen on the ice or slammed into a crate or something. "I chew Captain's boots," she said, smiling, and handed them to him.

When he got the full story, with the help of Kuraluk's translation, Bartlett was amazed. As the ship had been sinking, Auntie went to Bartlett's cabin and retrieved his good boots, which needed repairs. She'd gone back to the igloo and "in the Eskimo way had chewed the thick leather into a pliable state and filled the soles with grass. In the cold and snow, and with the hard hide, she had split her lips in twenty places." He just shook his head and thanked her, patting her on her shoulder, humbled by her kindness. Then he passed out, exhausted by the loss of the *Karluk* and the responsibility he bore.

Bartlett awoke after twelve hours. He was now in command of a ship-wrecked party, and he wrote in his journal, "Had we been on a desert island, things might have been brighter. But to be out there on the ever-shifting ice pack, far from land, and faced with the coldest months of the winter night, I could not look ahead without some uneasiness."

The captain was comforted by the hard work of the party, and especially McKinlay, whom he'd put in charge of all stores, which were placed in a large tent right next to the living dwellings. Bartlett issued an order that only he or McKinlay could enter the storehouse. He knew from accounts of the dreadful Greely Expedition what could happen when provisions dwindled and men stole food: that episode ended with the execution of a repeat offender. On inspecting the storehouse, Bartlett was well pleased with McKinlay's organization, and also with the stock of goods they'd managed—through early preparation and last-minute efforts—to lay in.

The inventory, which Bartlett went over item by item with McKinlay, looked like this:

70 suits underwear; 200 pairs Jaeger socks; 6 fleece suits; 100 fawn skins; 20 deerskins; 36 woolen shirts; 3 rolls Burberry gaberdine; 30 Jaeger caps; 2 rolls Jaeger blanketing; 2 large sacks skin boots (100 pairs); 100 pairs Jaeger mitts; 6 Jaeger sweaters; 4 Burberry hunting suits; 12 sealskins; 6 heavy winter skins; 2 large sacks deer legs; 2 bearded seal skins; 20 mattresses; 50 Jaeger blankets.

On the floe outside, ready for quick loading, were the following:

4,056 pounds Underwood pemmican; 5,222 pounds Hudson's Bay pemmican; 3 drums plus 15 cases of coal oil; 250 sacks of coal; 33 cases gasoline; 2000 feet of timber; 1 extra suit sails; matches; 3 coal stoves; 90 feet stove piping; 2 Peterborough canoes; 9 sledges.

Of food . . . 2 boxes tea; 2 boxes butter; 200 tins milk; 250 pounds sugar; 1 box cocoa; 2 boxes chocolate; 1 case codfish; 3 large cases codsteaks; 4 cases dried eggs; 14 cases Pilot bread; 5 barrels beef.

It was an impressive stockpile, but Bartlett was keenly aware of the immense challenges before them. Aboard the *Karluk*, these stores might have been stretched to last a year, perhaps longer. But now, with just nine sledges and eighteen healthy adult dogs, it would be impossible to carry it all at once. They'd need to get to land as soon as possible, and to do so, they'd need to carry sled loads in small teams, and would have to double-haul—taking loads light enough to carry and breaking a trail, then leaving caches and doubling back, returning for more—in a backtracking relay. Moving this way made for backbreaking marches of twelve to fifteen hours. As there remained enough dogs for only a few good teams, the other sleds would need to be man-hauled, pulled by harness ropes lashed across their shoulders like the straps of knapsacks.

Only essentials could be taken when they did make their move: tents, food, fuel, and the lightest, warmest clothing they had. Bartlett contemplated the trials ahead: the polar sea ice, with its ever-shifting pack, left rifts and open leads that would prevent traveling in a straight line; when leads opened, they'd need to either find a narrow nearby crossing, or travel a mile or even farther to find a safe place to cross; to get across young or new ice, they'd need to unload sleds to avoid breaking through, ferrying smaller loads, then reload the sleds on the other side. All of this he and Hadley and Kuraluk were proficient at, but not the others. It would take a toll. And the ice they would encounter was by no means flat. Instead, Bartlett told some of the others, "The ice is continually cracking and shifting and piling up in fantastic ridges from pressure when the fissures close up . . . and its surface is so much rougher than the crystal levels of lakes and ponds on which the landsman goes skating that there can hardly be any comparison."

Route finding would be difficult. In the days before the sinking of the *Karluk*, they'd been drifting north, and had lost sight of Wrangel Island. Based on the information in the *Coast Pilot*, Herald Island lay some forty miles east of Wrangel Island, but it was much smaller, and its shorelines rose in sheer, inaccessible granite cliffs. It was described as "a little island, standing alone out in the Polar Sea." Game would likely be scarcer there than on Wrangel Island, and it would certainly be more difficult for rescue ships—should they come—to land and find them. Bartlett had been fascinated by reading naturalist John Muir's detailed account, *The Cruise of the* Corwin, in which Muir, traveling aboard the USRC *Thomas Corwin* in 1881, went in search of the lost *Jeannette*. They'd somehow managed to land the cutter. Using his considerable mountaineering skills, Muir had scaled the highest point of Herald Island to made observations and collected specimens, but they found no sign of Captain De Long or the *Jeannette*. There were no historical records of any humans ever wintering there. It was not a place where you could survive for long.

Timing was now crucial. They could not leave until the sun returned on January 25, at the earliest. And because their floe was still drifting, there was the possibility that—given what Bartlett knew about the drift of the polar ice pack—they'd skirt beyond Wrangel Island and "slide westward and circle the Pole until, some years hence, we would possibly emerge down through the Greenland Sea." That had happened to Nansen's *Fram* twenty years before. "But by that time," Bartlett committed to his log with a resigned frankness, "we should all be frozen stiff."

They dubbed their camp on the ice floe Shipwreck Camp. Despite their predicament, and their cramped, squalid quarters, the mood remained positive. Most everyone pitched in, sewing skin clothes, sorting rifles and ammunition, repairing Primus stoves, and making the snow house and box house as weatherproof as possible, since the temperature was now averaging about -40°F. The snow house was the smaller of the two dwellings, at fifteen feet long and twelve feet wide, with sturdy wooden rafters and canvas lashed over the top as a roof. The walls were of stacked snow blocks, and though the heat of the stove melted them gradually, they were holding up well. The larger box house was twenty-five feet long and eighteen feet wide, insulated by blocks of snow on the outside. Cleverly, as McKinlay noted in his diary, "The boxes had been placed so that the tops faced inwards, making it possible to withdraw the contents and leave the empty cases as a cupboard."

Templeman was pleased that one end of the box house had been separated into an adjoining kitchen, with its own cooking stove, so he had room to work. Bartlett was proud of the men and encouraged by their high spirits. The upbeat mood was summed up by Mamen, who wrote in his journal, "One might believe that we are a crowd of downhearted and alarmed people after the *Karluk* left us, but no, that is not the case. All look forward to the future with bright eyes and good hope." He added, as if to steel himself for what lay ahead, "I have decided to fight for my life as much as I can."

Even Breddy, who'd been despondent and dark, made a dramatic turn and, as McKinlay put it, "began to behave like a normal human being. As time went on he became the life of the party. So it looked as though it had not been the darkness that had got him down, but the monotony and boredom of life, the inactivity and the helplessness of our situation in the drifting ship. There was plenty to do now."

On January 13, a call came from outside that land could be seen, and members dressed quickly and went out to look. Sure enough, off to the southwest, through dim light, they could make out the rough shape of what must be Wrangel Island. It appeared to be just thirty-five or forty miles away, though distances on the polar plain were deceiving: it might be as far as eighty or even a hundred miles. Still, the sighting caused

general cheer, and when Malloch took a reading, it showed latitude 72°
north—already a full twelve miles south of where the *Karluk* had sunk.
The prevailing winds had shifted and now they were moving toward the
island. This was even better news. Maybe the winds would push them
right to the shore.

Bartlett knew better than to count on that happening, but the sighting
was enough for him to contemplate the most efficient means of getting
everyone safely to land. On Wrangel Island, there might be sufficient driftwood for cooking and warmth. They'd still need to take fuel as insurance,
and it was heavy and would fill up room on the sleds needed to carry food.
There should be game on and around the island: polar bears, foxes, birds,
as well as seals and walrus; but there was no guarantee of their hunting success, so they'd need enough food from Shipwreck Camp to ensure survival
until at least mid- to late summer, when the ice would break up enough to
allow possible rescue by ships. That was their best hope.

Bartlett stood looking at the place where the *Karluk* had been. It was
now just a scar, the watery grave completely iced over. Their survival relied
first on him getting them all safely to Wrangel Island, which would be
hard enough. Then he would have to take one or two of the best and
strongest men—certainly either Kataktovik or Kuraluk—and head south
to the Siberian mainland, where he might encounter villagers who could
help him eventually make it all the way back to Alaska, at which point, he
could wire the Canadian authorities and organize rescue ships. He simply
must somehow get word to the world, because no one knew where they
were.

They could not all go at once. If a bad storm hit, the risk was too great
of having them become separated. Also, since all their food and equipment was at Shipwreck Camp, he couldn't have the whole group away
from it at the same time, lest it drift away. Bartlett decided that, ahead of
the arrival of the sun, he would send an advance shore party—a scouting
team—toward Wrangel Island to establish a trail that would be marked at
intervals by a chain of igloo shelters and food caches. For further marking,
they could flatten out empty pemmican cans and attach these to the food

caches or the igloos so they'd be visible. For safety and insurance, he'd send a small support team of two or three along with the shore party of four men. The shore party would remain on Wrangel Island and establish a base camp there, from which they could explore the island, hunt, and try to find as much driftwood as possible and stockpile it. The support team would then return with empty sleds to Shipwreck Camp. By this time, Bartlett figured, there'd be sufficient sunlight to relay the rest of the people and supplies, in small teams, to Wrangel Island.

While the shore party was away, Bartlett intended to dispatch small parties of two or three of his best remaining men to cache small loads of food and fuel at the igloo campsites along the established route. It was possible that some might drift away on the moving ice pan, but there was enough food and fuel at Shipwreck Camp that this was not a significant concern. His ulterior motive was to give the caching parties needed practice and valuable experience in traveling over the precarious ice.

Bartlett discussed his plan with McKinlay and Mamen, whose leadership had been displayed time and again and whom he trusted. Bartlett puffed at his pipe, then paused and looked serious, the difficulty of the endeavor ahead fixed in his mind. "Now look here," he said. "We are up against it. The Peary trip is going to look like a picnic alongside this, but we are going to see it through." He was counting on them both, but valued them each too much to risk sending them together, should some disaster occur. He'd decided that the shore party would be first and second mates Sandy Anderson and Charles Barker, along with crewman Ned Golightly and geologist Malloch. Mamen would lead them, taking Kataktovik and Kuraluk for their strength and skills at igloo building.

Mamen felt pride in being given the responsibility, but privately, he was racked with doubts and fears. That night he was restless and awoke from fitful dreams, then thought longingly of home, as he recorded in his diary: "My thoughts wandered back to the Fatherland and my home with all its beloved ones, and to our coming journey to save our lives. . . . I hope that with the help of God everything will come out all right, but if not, that we may have a quiet and peaceful death, without much pain or agony."

. . .

Life at Shipwreck Camp settled into a routine similar to the one they'd observed aboard the *Karluk*. Lights out was ten o'clock, and as before, a night watchman was responsible for keeping the fires going and waking up Templeman to prepare the 9:00 A.M. breakfast. The meals were excellent: "Our supper again seemed like a luxury," wrote McKinlay. "Seal meat, pea soup and chunks of bacon . . . the mixture of these with broken hard tack is delicious." Murray, Malloch, and McKinlay kept up with their scientific observations, recording depth soundings, wind speeds, and temperature readings. Mamen oversaw that all the Primus stoves were working properly and tested how long they took to boil water, and how much fuel oil they burned, so that he could estimate the fuel the advance party would need to take with them.

They'd managed to salvage a few books from the *Karluk*'s extensive library and had varied reading to pass around in the evenings: *Jane Eyre*, *Villette*, and *Wuthering Heights*, plus a handful of more recent novels. Bartlett read passages of his beloved *Rubáiyát*, turning the brittle pages slowly and carefully in the smoky lamplight. His treasured volume, which was so worn that he'd repaired numerous well-read pages with surgeon's tape, had been with him on his early sea voyages to South America and Europe during his apprenticeship, and on both his Arctic expeditions with Peary.

He seemed always to be reading it, and when someone asked him what it was that he enjoyed so much about the book, he mused, after consideration, "Perhaps it is because there is something in its philosophy which appeals to my own feeling about life and death. For all my experience and observation leads me to the conclusion that we are to die at the time appointed and not before; this, I suppose, is what is known as fatalism."

A couple of days before the first shore party was set to leave, geologist Malloch approached Bartlett and, stammering as he whispered, asked to be replaced on the journey. He said he was terrified; something didn't feel right. Bartlett tried to reassure him, saying that as one of the fittest and strongest men of the party, he was needed. But Malloch lowered his head

Captain Robert Abram Bartlett,
master mariner and ice navigator.
(Courtesy of the Library of Congress)

Captain Bob in Arctic garb. *(Courtesy of the
Library of Congress)*

Captain Bartlett in repose. *(Courtesy of
the Peary-Macmillan Arctic Museum
and Arctic Studies Center)*

Vilhjalmur Stefansson—Arctic explorer, schemer, and visionary behind the Canadian Arctic Expedition. *(Courtesy of Dartmouth College Library)*

Arctic legends Robert Peary and Robert Bartlett at Battle Harbor, Labrador. Bartlett used the techniques he learned from Peary to navigate the Arctic ice and pressure ridges and keep many of the *Karluk* survivors alive. *(Courtesy of the Library of Congress)*

The Canadian Arctic Expedition scientific staff at Nome prior to final departure, July 1913. Team members: back row (l. to r.): Mamen, McConnell, Chipman, Wilkins, Malloch (wearing cap), Beuchat, O'Neill, Jenness, Cox, and McKinlay; front row (l. to r.): Dr. Mackay, Captain Bartlett, Stefansson, Dr. Anderson, Murray, and Johansen. *(Courtesy of the Library and Archives Canada)*

The H.M.C.S. *Karluk* set to sail from Esquimalt, British Columbia, June 1913.
(Courtesy Library and Archives Canada)

William McKinlay smokes his pipe aboard the *Karluk* after leaving Point Barrow, Alaska, in August of 1913. He is blissfully unaware of the trials and privations he will soon endure.
(*Courtesy of Library and Archives Canada*)

Ethnologist Diamond Jenness (left) and mathematician William
McKinlay aboard the *Karluk*. Jenness would depart the ship with
Stefansson on a caribou hunting trip in September 1913.
(Courtesy of Library and Archives Canada)

Young Bjarne Mamen aboard the *Karluk*, August 1913. Mamen was fittest and strongest among them, full of hopes and dreams for his own future expeditions. *(Courtesy of Dartmouth College Library)*

George Malloch, geologist, en route to Nome aboard the *Karluk*. Malloch was irascible and fiery, with tremendous power and strength. *(Courtesy of Library and Archives Canada)*

George Malloch taking readings during the *Karluk*'s drift. *(Courtesy of Library and Archives Canada)*

John Munro, chief engineer of the *Karluk*, with the *Karluk* beset and drifting in the ice. *(Courtesy of the Library and Archives Canada)*

Fred Maurer with Nigeraurak, the ship's cat, and Hadley's trusty dog Molly. *(Courtesy of Dartmouth College Library)*

Hugh "Clam" Williams, notoriously stoic able seaman, with dog. *(Courtesy of the Peary-Macmillan Arctic museum. In memory of Reginald Wilcox and David C. Nutt)*

Kuraluk and his family were instrumental on the expedition, saving many lives through Kuraluk's tireless hunting, Auntie's expert sewing of Arctic clothing and cooking, and the children's industrious help obtaining game, skinning, and good nature. From l. to r.: Mugpi, Auntie, Kuraluk, and Helen. (*Courtesy of the National Library of Scotland*)

and said he couldn't go. Wind howled outside, blowing snowdrifts into the igloo through holes that had melted in the ice walls. Bartlett thought it a bad idea to send Malloch if he wasn't mentally prepared, so he reluctantly replaced Malloch with the young seaman John Brady, who always took orders well and had shown tenacity and fortitude from the beginning.

On the morning of January 21, the first shore party was ready to leave. McKinlay had drawn two copies of maps of Wrangel Island based on the *Coast Pilot* and Admiralty charts, and he gave one to Mamen and one to Sandy for their trip, in case they got separated. Bartlett had also provided written instructions to both Mamen and Sandy. Early that morning, the men had dug three sleds out from under snowdrifts, and Hadley had separated eighteen of the fittest dogs into the best teams and harnessed them. Kataktovik would drive one sled, Sandy the second, and Kuraluk would follow, driving the third. By half past eight, under cloudy but clearing skies and a light southeast breeze, Bartlett gave the order to go, and the party set off, with Mamen breaking trail on skis.

Mamen felt a heavy weight as he skied ahead, believing that all their fates depended on him. "All are relying on me," he'd written in his diary, "and if I fail now it will mean a great loss to the members of the expedition." Nine of the members who were to remain at Shipwreck Camp accompanied them for the first five miles, helping with bearings and trail-breaking, but at noon turned to head back to Shipwreck Camp. There was much embracing and handshaking, accompanied by *au revoir*s and *good luck*, and then the groups separated and went their own ways.

The winds picked up immediately, making it difficult for Mamen to see more than fifty or sixty yards ahead through swirling snowdrifts. He took out his compass and relied on it to bear southwest. After a couple of hours of tough going, they came to lead-riddled ice that was so thin they had to unload all the sleds and cross with them empty to avoid breaking through, then ferry the gear back over in lighter loads. By late afternoon, everyone was spent, and they built an igloo, roofing it with a canvas tent, and tucked in for the night.

They hunkered into the igloo and tried to stay warm, removing their mukluks and stuffing their feet into special "footbags" made with Burberry cloth on the outside and lined with the fur from a coonskin coat Bartlett had donated for that purpose. The winds gusted hard enough to blow the tent roof off three times, but on each occasion, they managed to grab hold of one flapping end and pull it back down and secure it using Mamen's skis and ski poles and cinching it down with ropes. The storm kept them bound to their snow house for sixteen hours, with the dogs curled outside being buried by drifts.

For the next two days, they slogged over increasingly rough terrain, skirting large hummocks of ice and hauling the sleds over pressure ridges up to twenty feet high. Once, Mamen broke through ice and plunged thigh-deep in water, soaking his feet and legs. There was no shelter for him to stop and change clothing, so he kept going. By the time they made camp after seven difficult miles, his nose, both feet, and middle finger were all frostbitten, but he was finally able to rub them back to life.

Mamen began to worry about their progress and, more important, their direction. They'd yet to glimpse Wrangel Island. Kuraluk started to talk of Auntie and his girls; he hated to be away from them for too long. Mamen and the others tried to cheer him up, but privately, Mamen remained anxious: "I hope that we will reach Wrangel Island tomorrow. . . . It is not the most pleasant time to travel in the Arctic at the end of January . . . but under the circumstances it has to be done."

They slogged eleven miles the next day, but overcast skies still afforded no sighting of Wrangel Island. That night everyone was in slightly better spirits as a result of their progress: "There is no question about land not far away from here; all the ice is young, but it is pressed up in high ridges, and these ridges give us considerable trouble."

Morning brought a few inches of new snow and a slate-gray sky. They broke camp and made good time until around noon, under improving light, when they came to a wide lead. As they were unharnessing the dogs to cross the lead, a vicious fight broke out among the animals. Mamen leaped into a mass of fur and flashing fangs to stop it. He felt a searing pain like a jolt of electricity in his right knee and stumbled, almost tumbling into the middle of the dogfight, but managed to right himself and break it up.

Kataktovik and Kuraluk wrangled the dogs and got them harnessed again, but when Mamen put weight on his leg, it buckled, and he winced in pain. He'd need to camp and rest. Kataktovik went ahead to find a spot, and Mamen eased himself down onto Sandy's sled and rode the half mile, cringing with each bounce over the rough ice. The Eskimos built an igloo and lit Primus stoves, and soon everyone was drinking tea and bolting down biscuits and pemmican.

After the brief warmth of the meal, they all lay wet and shivering, with Sandy and Brady taking turns massaging Mamen's damaged knee. The kneecap had dislocated again. Mamen was despondent: here he was, the leader of the advance shore party, uncertain of where they were and unable to walk. "I don't know how to manage everything now," he scrawled in his diary as the others lay shaking with cold. "If the leg is not all right tomorrow, we must do all we can to reach land and then send Anderson and the two Eskimos back. . . . We must do all that we can to save our lives."

17
THE WRONG ISLAND

INSIDE THE BOX HOUSE AT SHIPWRECK CAMP, EVERYONE GATHERED around the big stove, rejoicing and singing songs. It was January 25, and earlier in the day, the upper rim of the sun, the slightest sliver, had crested the horizon for the first time in seventy-one days. Though its appearance had been faint, all had stood outside to watch the arrival and cheer. "It didn't do much more than stick its nose above the horizon," Bartlett wrote, "but it somehow put new hope in our hearts." It was the fourth time the captain had watched the return of the sun on an Arctic horizon, but this one was the most important, because their very lives depended on better light to travel in.

Buoyed by the glint of illumination, Bartlett remembered something. He led a couple of the others over to some ice rubble at the edge of the *Karluk*'s grave, and with shovels, they started digging around. After much probing, someone's spade struck metal, and Bartlett laughed as he scuffled over and scooped up two cases of oysters he'd grabbed from the galley and tossed overboard as the ship was sinking. That night they enjoyed the delicacy of oyster soup—and a variety of other oyster-based dishes—and now they were smoking pipes and cigarettes and singing songs and reciting poems. By coincidence—or Scot's luck—it was also Robert "Rabbie" Burns's birthday, so the Scots—with Munro taking the lead—took turns reciting their National Bard's most famous poems and songs, including "Tam o' Shanter" and "A Red, Red Rose."

The singing and revelry went on for hours, and nearly everyone got involved. A few songs were accompanied by the rhythmic strumming on a comb. Auntie hummed a few Native songs and was also joined by Helen and Mugpi in a trio rendition of "Twinkle, Twinkle, Little Star." It was the most cheerful, joyous night they'd spent since New Year's Eve. It was –40°F, the night clear and starry and calm. Of the evening, McKinlay recalled, "We had other musical evenings in the box house, but we never quite reached the peak of Sunday, 25 January 1914, when Rabbie Burns was celebrated on an Arctic floe, with oysters instead of haggis."

But a few days later, the euphoria had evaporated, and Bartlett started to worry about Mamen and the advance shore party. They'd been gone more than a week, and the captain was anxious for Mamen, Kataktovik, and Kuraluk to return. They were supposed to have left Sandy and his advance shore party on Wrangel Island, then come straight back to Shipwreck Camp. Where were they?

On the twenty-seventh, the entire sun rose above the horizon, and Bartlett got a good look at land. "In the half light," he wrote, "it varied in size from time to time like a mirage, so we could not tell whether it was Wrangel Island or not." This was confusing and disconcerting. Even more worrisome, the island appeared much farther away than it had before; they were drifting away from it. Bartlett began sending teams of two or three by sled in forays to check the igloo and cache camps that the shore party had set up, and to see if they might meet them on their return. Clam, Breddy, and Hadley returned from one of these and reported finding the first igloo about seven miles away, marked with a flattened pemmican can, but no sign of Mamen. When he got back, Clam's ear was frostbitten and had swollen to twice its normal size, bursting all over with suppurating blisters.

Bartlett ordered a large bonfire lit using a ton of coal, a couple of cases of engine oil, and many gallons of gasoline. He hoped to signal the boys. It was more a smoldering pillar of smoke than a fire, emitting bursts of toxic fumes, but on a clear day he figured the smoke could be seen up to fifteen miles away and might guide them back to camp, which was just a speck in the thousands upon thousands of square miles of constantly moving ice.

Bartlett asked McKinlay to show him their stores. They dug out a dozen seals, frozen solid. These should last a month if they rationed them. They'd salvaged plenty of food from the *Karluk*—more than they'd need for a year—and it was stacked neatly in the storehouse. Bartlett shuffled in the cold and assessed. The problem was that they could carry only so much when they all left Shipwreck Camp, and getting back to it for re-supply was uncertain at best. However he looked at it, food was going to be a problem.

So was shelter. While still on the *Karluk*, Bartlett had directed men to cut and sew heavy canvas into large sheets that could be used as portable bell tents, with straight walls about four feet high and domed tops coming to a point, supported by a single pole in the middle or center, spanning from the ground to the rooftop. Resembling Mongolian huts or yurts that Bartlett knew about, bell tents had been used for thousands of years in Central Asia. They were portable and could be fitted with smokestacks. Bartlett helped men set one up on the ice to test it, and though it was challenging in the wind, they managed to erect it, then take it down and pack it up again. The two tents, Bartlett hoped, would shelter them on the island.

As Bartlett and McKinlay and Hadley were packing and repacking everything, weighing items and deciding how much to put on each sled for their exodus from Shipwreck Camp, Murray approached Bartlett and took him aside. He asked for a sled and provisions for four men for fifty days. He said aloud what Bartlett already knew: he, Dr. Mackay, and Beuchat wished to go it on their own. Bartlett sat with this awhile. On the *Karluk*, he would have considered it mutiny. But now? By ship's law he was still in command, but this was not a military expedition. They were Stefansson's scientists. He wasn't about to hold them here at gunpoint or arrest them. No, it was best to let them go. But he didn't tell Murray that straightaway. He let the man continue.

Murray said that their plan was to try to reach Alaska over the sea ice. Bartlett asked why they wanted to leave, and Murray told him they didn't ascribe to the Peary method. They were Shackleton followers. Bartlett reminded Murray that "Peary's methods largely originated with the Eskimos who have lived in regions of ice and snow for many centuries," and were sound. He said they were taking a great risk, and would be safer staying with him, but he agreed to give them what they'd need: their share of food, sleds, and even dogs. Murray thanked him and said they would not require dogs; they planned to man-haul the sled as they'd done in Antarctica.

The next day, Dr. Mackay approached Bartlett sheepishly and asked for a tent and a pair of canvas pants. Bartlett rooted around the store-house and found a small four-man tent. He had no extra pants but offered his own as well as a full Burberry suit. On the afternoon of January 30, McKinlay watched Dr. Mackay and Beuchat out on the ice, "practicing hauling a sled with 9 cases of pemmican—48 pounds per case—but they could hardly move it."

Bartlett eyed the two men floundering in their harnesses as well, and he was certain their decision was terrible. But they would not be convinced otherwise. They intended to leave within the next few days, weather per-mitting. Later that day, Stanley Morris approached Bartlett and, with his head lowered in shame and his feet shuffling nervously, asked if he could go with Dr. Mackay, Beuchat, and Murray. This was a shock; Morris was one of Bartlett's crew, not one of the scientists, not one of Stefansson's men. But the seaman had been swayed by Dr. Mackay and Murray, whom he looked up to as polar legends. They had, after all, been to Antarctica with the great Sir Ernest Shackleton. And they were fellow Brits. He'd marveled at their storytelling of derring-do and was ultimately drawn to take his chances with these Antarctic heroes and men of science.

Bartlett was hurt by Morris's decision, but as he thought about it, he overcame his feelings and consented. "I felt that he would be of use to them because he was a young man of twenty-six and was handy, so I gave him permission to go." Morris was strong and able, and given Beuchat's feeble physical condition, it would certainly help for them to have him along. Four men were better than three for such work, and they could take turns pulling in pairs.

In the end, Bartlett told Dr. Mackay that McKinlay would parcel out everything they'd need for four men for fifty days, provided they sign a letter releasing their captain of any responsibility for their actions. The next day, Dr. Mackay handed the skipper the following letter:

CANADIAN ARCTIC EXPEDITION

Sunday, Feb. 1st, 1914

Captain Robert Bartlett,

SIR: We, the undersigned, in consideration of the present critical situation, desire to make an attempt to reach land. We ask you to assist us by issuing to us from the general stores all necessary sledging and camping provisions and equipment for the proposed journey as per separate requisition already handed to you. On the understanding that you do so and continue as heretofore to supply us with our proportional share of provisions while we remain in camp, and in the event of our finding it necessary to return to the camp, we declare that we undertake the journey on our own initiative and absolve you from any responsibility whatever in the matter.

    A. Forbes Mackay   H. Beuchat

    James Murray   S.S. Morris

So it was settled. They would leave when they had everything they'd requested and the weather was right.

Out on the ice, Bjarne Mamen and the advance shore party struggled mightily. Mamen remained lashed to a sled, his knee still too unstable to bear weight. All the men's clothing was frozen hard as the ice pan on which they traveled, and open leads had them endlessly zigzagging, rarely able to move for any distance in a straight line. Still, despite their circuitous route, they were getting closer to the island. But the pain in Mamen's leg, jostling along on the sled, was almost unbearable. He was half-frozen from lying each night in makeshift igloos—it had been tough to scrape sufficient snow blocks from the new ice they were on. All of them were suffering.

On the afternoon of January 29, they had run into masses of jumbled ice over sixty feet high, like the icefall at the foot of a glacier. They made camp and, after tea and biscuits, fell asleep, exhausted. They were shaken awake by crashing and cracking ice. The men scurried from their shelter, clutching their belongings. A huge rift had opened just outside the igloo, with water only feet away. The Eskimos harnessed the dogs and loaded the sleds as rubble from the nearby ridges fell near them. After strapping Mamen to a sled, they pulled him from the lead and found safe ice some distance away, where they set up a tent. All night long, Mamen lay in the tent, keeping the Primus stoves going and making tea while the others, in turn, walked back and forth and did short wind sprints to keep their blood flowing and avoid freezing to death.

When Mamen came out of the tent and shakily stood the next morning, two things were certain. There was a massive lead of open water between them and the island they could see—and, worse, the great granite slab before them was the wrong island! "I have come to the conclusion," he wrote in his diary, "that it is not Wrangel Island . . . but Herald Island. It is a shock to us." The small size—about four square miles—made clear it was not Wrangel Island.

It was the last day of January, and they'd been out nine days. Seaman Golightly's foot had suffered frostbite the day before, but he seemed to have improved. The ice they were camped on was slowly drifting away from Herald Island, mere miles off. Mamen stood on his own for the first time in days, and testing his knee, he was able to hop, then limp along by himself. He pondered what to do.

The original plan had been for him to land the shore party at Wrangel Island and then head back to Shipwreck Camp. In their condition and with their diminishing food stores, there was no chance to make it all the way to Wrangel Island now, if they could even find it. "I don't think the boys can manage it much longer and then they also have considerable trouble with me," he wrote, thinking of how his leg was hindering their progress. No, Wrangel Island was out for now. Herald was right there. He had to go back, but surely the others could cross the short distance once the ice knitted together. They'd find a way.

As leader of the shore party, Mamen made a difficult decision. First officer Sandy Anderson, second mate Charles Barker, and seamen Ned Golightly and John Brady would proceed to Herald Island and await contact by the main party at some point; should this fail to occur, they must navigate thirty-eight miles west to Wrangel Island, where the main party would eventually convene. If all went as planned, they'd be there within the next few weeks. Sandy, in charge of the shore party, would take the following provisions: 1 sled, 3½ dozen boxes of matches, 15 candles, 7 gallons of gasoline, 1 stove, 12 boxes of milk and tea, 15 pounds of sugar; 70 pounds of biscuits, 100 pounds of dog pemmican, 300 pounds of Underwood pemmican, 6 boxes of Hudson's Bay pemmican. Though Mamen didn't calculate the shore party's rations down to the day, it was enough food to last at least until they could be retrieved by the main party or, if necessary, make their way to Wrangel Island.

Mamen offered to leave some of the dogs. Unfortunately, one of the best dogs had died from injuries sustained during the big fight that had re-injured Mamen's leg, and Mamen ruefully thought of something Bartlett often said: "If you lose any of those dogs, you'd better not come back yourself." That's how much the dogs meant to survival out here. But in the end, Sandy elected not to take any dogs. The island was close, he said, and a larger team would get Mamen, Kataktovik, and Kuraluk safely back to the main camp faster.

After a short discussion, Mamen relented, agreeing that the dogs would be needed in getting everyone else to Wrangel Island, and he began packing up to leave. With all the dogs and their lightened load, they might get lucky and make good time back to Shipwreck Camp. Of leaving Sandy and the others, Mamen wrote, explaining his decision: "They will now have to manage by themselves and try to get to the island. I could not wait and help them, as there is considerable open water between this camp and the coast, but the distance is not more than five miles at the most, so they can manage and get there alone."

As they said goodbye and parted, first mate Sandy handed Mamen a letter for his skipper:

Ice Pan near Herald Island

Sunday, Feb., 1st, 1914

Cap. R.A. Bartlett,

Dear Sir,

I don't know whether you will altogether approve of my action in sending the dogs back before actually landing but as there is the possibility of having to wait several days before the ice closes again, I thought it best under the circumstance to camp here for the present to endeavor when the opportunity occurs to do the remainder by hand, especially as you will be anxious about the returning party. I don't know if the identity of the island will naturally upset your plans, but I will proceed under the original instructions as if it were Wrangel Island and await developments. . . .

Mamen is taking a list of the stores in our position, so I will refrain from giving one. I regret to report that one of the dogs was killed . . . although we had very little trouble previously.

Hoping Mamen gets back quickly and safely, and all is well in camp. I beg to remain,

Your obedient servant,

A. Anderson

Mamen tucked the letter away, Kataktovik snapped the harness leads, and the dogs lurched forward, speeding out across the ice.

18
ISLANDS OF THE LOST

"THEY'RE HERE! THEY'RE HERE!!" MCKINLAY COULD HEAR BREDDY yelling just outside the box house. McKinlay had been having a hot-water wash and was stripped to the waist, running soaked rags over his chest and arms when he heard the shouting. He quickly threw on a Jaeger shirt and ran outside in time to see the dog teams arriving, their forms just visible in the fading afternoon light. Kataktovik led the first team, with Mamen riding on the sled. Kuraluk pulled up behind, his face beaming when he saw Auntie standing up on an ice rafter; she'd been peering out into the distance, hoping for his arrival, and now she ran down to hug him. The dogs, panting, sent steam plumes into the cold air, then shook, asking to be unharnessed and fed.

Cheers went round the camp. Bartlett trotted forward and slapped Mamen on the back as the others helped him from the sled. "Well done, Norway!" he shouted over the bustle. With excitement but care, they hurried Mamen, Kataktovik, and Kuraluk into the box house and stoked the fire. Bartlett and McKinlay stripped the men of their frozen clothing and dressed them in their own warm garments, handing them their pants and literally giving them the shirts off their backs. Williamson treated Mamen's knee with a massage of alcohol and warm seal oil, then wrapped it in an elastic bandage. "They handled me as if I was a tot," wrote Mamen. Mamen was touched by the warm reception, but hovering over the thrill of their return was the news he had to convey.

Soon everyone crowded into the box house, laughing and shouting and firing off a string of questions: "Did you make it to Wrangel Island?" "What's it like?" "Is there game there?" Bartlett hushed everybody and said that could wait. The men needed tending to, then he'd get their report.

Templeman heated coffee and cocoa, and McKinlay poured mug after mug into them. Next came fried seal steaks, pea soup, scrambled eggs, rice, and hardtack. Everyone enjoyed the big meal, though none so much as the hungry, haggard travelers. After dinner, Bartlett sat with Mamen to hear his report.

He said that their return journey had been fast—just three days— because they had longer days, lighter loads, and most important, they'd been able to camp at the igloos they'd already built on the outward journey. Mamen told of their travails on the ice, of the dogfight and his knee and the death of a dog, of the difficult pressure ridges closer to shore, of almost being swallowed up by leads opening right near their last camp. Mamen reported seeing a lot of bear tracks near Camp 5. Everyone listened quietly, intently. Then, stammering and hedging, Mamen got to the tough part. He described the small island they'd reached and his decision to leave Sandy and the others some miles away, on foot, and their agreement that they'd make it to land when the ice allowed safe passage.

Bartlett said little, but his face showed concern. From the description they gave him, he knew at once it was Herald Island. This posed a few problems. For one, from his readings of Muir and the *Coast Pilot*, he'd learned there was no driftwood on Herald. He hoped they had plenty of fuel. Also, now he'd need to send someone to try to go get them, which complicated his plans of heading directly to Wrangel Island. Bartlett tried not to betray his worries, and simply congratulated Mamen and the Eskimo men on their safe return. They'd discuss what next to do in the morning, and over the coming days.

That night, Mamen luxuriated on one of the mattresses salvaged from the *Karluk*. "Oh, how nice it felt to get into a bed, soft and warm; I lay awake all night just enjoying existence." Although he was exhausted, and infinitely more comfortable than he'd been huddled on the ice in his frozen, wet clothes for nearly two weeks, he barely slept, thinking about

Sandy and the others. He prayed they had made it safely to shore, and tried to imagine them all well, their bellies full. But alternatives—terrible fates of them falling through the ice to their deaths—floated in and out of his thoughts and half dreams, and he trembled through the night.

Dr. Mackay, Murray, Beuchat, and Morris informed the captain they intended to leave early on the morning of February 5. Their plans remained vague. Dr. Mackay said they might use the camps already set up en route (there were now ten), and head initially for Wrangel Island. But if they progressed well enough, they might strike south and make for the Siberian mainland. It would depend on conditions. McKinlay was kind enough to sketch a map of Wrangel Island and give it to Murray; if they ended up there, at least they'd have a lay of the land.

On the morning of the fifth, the abandoning group was up early. They ate a quick breakfast and were assembled with their Nome sled loaded with six hundred pounds of food, shelter, and gear. They also carried letters that some of the members had given them to send to their loved ones once they reached Alaska. Their departure was lurching and slow, burdened as they were. Mamen and McKinlay saw them off, bidding them good luck. Many of the others—including Captain Bartlett—were indifferent, or happy to see them go. They'd all shared some memorable and even joyful times aboard the *Karluk*, but the scientists' discontent was ever present. Now they were finally doing what they'd wanted to do for many months.

Bartlett's objectives were not changed by their departure. He must focus all his energies on reaching Sandy and the others at Herald Island and helping them off; that was essential. He would also continue sending small parties by sled to take food and fuel and supplies to the camps Mamen and Sandy had established. Both Wrangel and Herald Islands lay on the same route south of them, with Herald Island on nearly the exact latitude, though about forty miles due east of Wrangel. Sending Mamen to look for Sandy's party made the most sense, since he'd already been on the route and had the best chance of finding them again.

On February 7, after a few days of rest and recovery, Mamen said his leg felt good enough to embark. He would travel again with Kataktovik and Kuraluk, who by now had the most experience driving dog teams and handling the mercurial animals. Bartlett gave Mamen a sextant and an artificial horizon—a gyroscopic instrument used to provide a horizontal reference plane—to help them find Herald Island and determine, as accurately as possible, its position.

Chafe and Clam set off on a caching run early that morning, driving a team of older and slower but dependable dogs. They hauled a big load on one of the Peary sleds built on the *Karluk*, intending to travel with Mamen's team to where the farthest loads had been cached, about twenty-seven miles south of Shipwreck Camp. From there, Mamen and the Eskimos would load fifty days' food on one of their sleds and go look for Sandy, while Chafe and Clam were to return to Shipwreck Camp for another load.

Mamen's group left just fifteen minutes later, with three sled loads and seventeen dogs, accompanied by McKinlay, Munro, and Maurer. It was still dark, the skies above glowing with lunar corona and an auroral arch hanging down like a veil. Just a mile and a half along the trail, they caught up with Chafe and Clam, who stood shivering, jumping up and down to stay warm. Clam's clothes were entirely encased in a layer of ice. Apparently, while running ahead to confirm the trail in the half light, Clam had broken through young ice, and by the time Chafe got to him, only his head and flailing arms were above water. Chafe dropped the sled handles and dashed to the edge of the crack and managed to pull Clam onto safe ice. But now they were already headed back; Clam needed dry clothes and a fire, and fast. Fireman Maurer volunteered to guide his frozen fellow seaman back to Shipwreck Camp, and they set off at a run, with McKinlay trotting just behind them to make sure they made it.

Munro took over for Clam and they all continued, though they also encountered thin ice. Twice the lead dog, Snooks, broke through, and they stopped to dry him off as best they could, then kept going. But just two miles down the trail, Mamen was struck sideways by a jostling sled, which hit him directly in his injured knee. Once more the searing pain shot down his leg, and he cussed and yelled, biting his lip until it bled.

Within a few hundred yards, it was obvious that he was in no condition to lead the team in what might possibly be a two-to-three-week journey out and back. He did not want to endanger them all. As close as they still were to Shipwreck Camp, the smart choice was to transfer his orders to steward Ernest Chafe.

Mamen could not believe his bad luck, and he felt shame to be letting Bartlett down again so soon. He'd been entrusted to find Sandy, and now here he was relinquishing leadership to the youngest member of the entire party. But Chafe had grit and, like Mamen, was highly competitive. He'd carried his many shooting medals on board the *Karluk* to attest to this. With Kataktovik and Kuraluk along, Mamen felt confident enough to put Chafe in charge of his job. His instructions were simple and clear: "Make the trip to the island and return as quickly as possible."

When Mamen returned to Shipwreck Camp, he was again riding ingloriously on a sled. His worries about Bartlett's disappointment were quickly assuaged. The captain had seen the great Peary returning from Lady Franklin Bay atop a sled, the toes on his feet so frostbitten that eight of them had to be amputated. Rather than show discouragement, Bartlett just patted him paternally on the head and told him to rest it as long as he needed to. "You must keep quiet and get well in your leg," he said. Mamen apologized, they helped him back into bed, and both the skipper and Williamson continued to doctor him. "The Captain, I must say, is indeed nice to me," Mamen wrote in his diary, "I am quite touched at his painstaking care for me, and I hope that in time I may be able to do a little for him in return for what he has done for me and been to me."

For the time being, all Mamen could do to help Bartlett and everyone else was try to recover. He put up a good front and remained outwardly positive, but he battled grave internal doubts. "I have not got my leg back; it hurts badly, and looks quite hopeless for me if I don't get it back soon," he wrote. He privately harbored delusional ideas of remaining at Shipwreck Camp even after everyone had left for Wrangel Island. "I see no other way than stay here until I am all right and go to the coast later, for I do not wish to be a hindrance to the others. I can have it nice and comfortable here, with provisions, clothing and fuel for a year, and in that time I should, I hope, be well." Then the realization that the camp was on a moving ice floe struck him: "But then the question is where will I be a year from now? Perhaps 100–500 miles farther north, and probably the same distance farther west."

The truth was, whatever Mamen's condition, Bartlett would never leave him there alone.

While Mamen lay on a dry mattress in the warm box house at Shipwreck Camp, Chafe, Kataktovik, and Kuraluk clung to an ice floe just fifteen yards long and twenty-five yards wide. They'd managed to make it to within five or six miles of Herald Island, when early in the morning on the second day out, they'd encountered a wall of ice ridges over thirty feet high. They'd ascended the precipitous ice wall to see how they might get over it or through it when a strong blast of wind sent the floe their sleds were on into motion, separating them. The Eskimos and Chafe scampered down, each falling a few times in their hurry. When they reached the sleds, two dogs were already submerged, frantically clawing at the water. The men clasped arms and leaned over and pulled the dogs out, driving both teams to the same side of the large lead. Ice shattered and spat all around them, marooning them on this small chunk of a floe. Since there was no way to get across the water and back over toward the pressure ridges, they built an igloo and waited, trying to stay warm.

All that night and all the next day, they listened to and watched ice fracturing and crumbling around them, sometimes splashing in the water close enough for them to be hit by sea spray. Slabs of their floe were breaking off in the turbulence, shrinking their floating ice island. "The ice," reported Chafe, "that a little while before looked almost impossible to be parted by wind or sea, was now one mass of drifting floes and small bergs, and every now and then one of them would turn turtle, making a big swell that would break off pieces from the floe we were on."

All they could do now was wait. Chafe's thermometer registered –48°F. During the second night on the small ice cake, they heard and then felt the ice splitting directly under their igloo. The rupture smashed one of their sleds into pieces, but they managed, in the darkness, to get all the dogs and their food and gear onto one small flat shelf of their diminishing floe, which was being constantly pummeled to pieces by other, larger floes. They endured a dreadful "night of suffering and waiting," said Chafe, "waiting for some good turn that might free us from that awful prison."

At dawn the next morning they were still alive, huddled together, covered with a few inches of windblown snow. As the light improved, they looked across the water and could clearly see Herald Island; the winds had pushed them to within two miles of its jagged shoreline. There was no question which island it was, because they could also now see Wrangel Island, more than ten times the size, looming up from the southern horizon. For the next few hours, Chafe and the two Eskimo men took turns scanning the rough, nearly vertical shoreline of Herald Island, trying to locate any sign of first mate Sandy Anderson and his lost advance shore party. "With the aid of our powerful glasses," Chafe recorded in his journal, "we were able to see any little object on the land, but could see no moving objects or anything to indicate that the mate or any of his party were or had been on the island." They strained their eyes but saw nothing: No sled, no piles of gear, no tent. No people.

Then, behind them, young ice began knitting together, hardening around their little floe. After several more hours, the Eskimos began testing the ice, at first on foot, poking and prodding with ice axes. They lightened their load, leaving all but five days' food and fuel for themselves, and marked what they were leaving behind with a flag. Then they eased out across the new-formed ice. Almost tiptoeing, with the dogs skittish and whining, they retreated for five full miles until they discovered signs of the main trail again. Wrung out from their ordeal, they quickly built a low igloo and slumped onto the ice floor, fired a Primus stove, and warmed themselves with hot tea. They fed the dogs pemmican and then fell asleep. They'd been awake for sixty consecutive hours.

Chafe woke early, worried sick about Sandy, Barker, Ned, and Brady.

There'd not been a single trace of them: no footprints anywhere, no sled tracks, no strewn pemmican cans. There remained a couple of possibilities that offered hope: Maybe they were on another part of the island. That seemed unlikely, though, since the area they'd scoured with binoculars appeared the only flat place they might have made it ashore. Or, Sandy could have been unable to make the crossing, and had gone instead to Wrangel Island. But Sandy had told Mamen, and written in his letter to Bartlett, that he was going to try to make it to Herald Island. After going over it in his mind and reliving the horrendous nights in the roiling pack ice, Chafe could only draw one conclusion: "I believe the poor fellows met with the same experience as ourselves, and not being as fortunate as we were to escape, they must have perished in the sea." Now he had the grim duty to return to Shipwreck Camp and report the news to Captain Bartlett.

As they made their way north between camps, the going improved and the dogs, fed and rested, ran well. Around midday, after about twenty miles, Chafe saw something up ahead, just visible through a skein of snow blowing across the pan. At first, they were just dark flecks, and he figured they must be blocks of ice, but as he drew closer and shielded his eyes, he could see that they were moving. They were human forms. Could it be them? He snapped his whip, and the dogs loped faster. Chafe pulled up after a mile or so—and they were men, all right, but not Sandy's group. Dr. Mackay and Murray were straining at the harnesses of their sled, barely moving. Morris plodded along behind them. They all looked spent. Their hoods flapped in the wind, and their faces were white with frostbite. "They looked a most pitiful sight," wrote Chafe, "Their clothes were all frozen and stiff as boards."

Chafe, Kataktovik, and Kuraluk greeted them. There was too much wind, so they could not make hot tea for them. Dr. Mackay spoke, his voice a raspy whisper. He said they'd been out nearly ten days, mostly without shelter. They'd had bad luck from the start, with dreadfully slow going. Their load was too heavy, and they'd been discarding things. Some nights ago, they'd left half their load—biscuit and pemmican—on a cake of young ice, but by morning it was submerged in water and inedible. They'd had a hard, hard struggle.

As Morris limped up, one arm dangling useless at his side, Dr. Mackay said that a few days before, Morris had impaled his left hand with a knife while opening a pemmican can, and now he had blood poisoning. He'd had a high fever and he could barely keep up. Morris shook with convulsions, then fell to his knees, dry heaving.

But where was Henri Beuchat? Dr. Mackay turned and pointed behind them. Back a mile or so, he said, with the other half load. Bad, bad shape. Won't survive the night. Chafe told Dr. Mackay that he and the Eskimos must guide them all back to Shipwreck Camp. They needed help. He insisted, but Dr. Mackay refused, saying they'd set out alone and would see it through. Chafe knew he couldn't force the man, a proud, esteemed scientist, but he implored him one more time, now also looking to Murray and Morris, hoping they'd agree to go back. But they were silent, seemingly resigned to their fate. Chafe offered them tins of pemmican to replace what they'd lost, but they said they still had some. Kataktovik presented them with a seal he'd killed the day before, and Chafe convinced them to take a pickax; they'd need it for the pressure ridges they'd encounter.

Chafe warned Dr. Mackay about the open water conditions near Herald Island, urging them to try instead for Wrangel Island, and he pointed southwest. Dr. Mackay and Murray, who'd hardly spoken, leaned into the leather harnesses once more and tottered forward in the direction Chafe had pointed. For a time, Chafe and the Eskimos watched the three figures inch away across the wind-ribbed ice desert; then they mushed the dogs on.

The trail was littered with discarded items; pairs of snow-filled mukluks and mittens, boxes, heavy bundles of fur and fabrics. Soon they came upon Beuchat next to a pile of tins and stores, barely able to stand. He wore no mittens, and his hands were purplish black, swollen and disfigured knobs hanging out of his tattered sleeves. His bare knuckles were mottled with bursting black pustules. He swayed unsteadily, muttering in delirium that his hands and feet had been frozen for two days. When Chafe looked down, he saw that the Frenchman stood on a pair of skin boots that were halfway off his feet. Beuchat coughed and looked at the men, expressionless.

They might still save him if they got him to Shipwreck Camp. He'd almost certainly lose his hands—they'd need to be amputated—and probably his feet. But he might yet live. By now, Beuchat seemed to recognize Chafe and the Eskimos, and he smiled.

"Come back with us," said Chafe. "It's useless for you to try to go any further in your condition. We'll fix you up right."

Beuchat grew clearer in his mind. In a feeble murmur, he said he'd given up hope and would die soon. He'd rather be by himself. It would be best that way. "Go on," he said, wheezing, "leave me alone."

Chafe looked at Kataktovik and Kuraluk, but they remained silent. They knew how this was going to end. Chafe was overwhelmed by guilt and grief. He'd failed to find Sandy, and now he was faced with leaving the refined Frenchman to die on the ice. He tried one last time to convince Beuchat, but it was no use. Instead, Beuchat looked Chafe in the eyes and asked him to convey a message to the captain. He harbored no bad feelings toward him, he said, or any of the others. He wished them all well, and good luck. "Bon chance," he said.

At those last words, Chafe turned away, flicked the harness reins, and the dogs broke into a trot, headed home to Shipwreck Camp.

19

A MOUNTAIN RANGE OF ICE

BARTLETT QUIETLY BROODED OVER THE BLEAK NEWS CHAFE brought him. Eight men were now lost on the ice. He pondered his choices. A heavy gale, with powerful northwest winds and snow, pounded against the box house walls and tattered the canvas roof. It would be too risky and dangerous to send out rescue parties. They'd require all their energies and resources to make their own push toward Wrangel Island when the storm abated. Along the way, they could look for any signs of Sandy's or Dr. Mackay's parties, picking up cache loads left at the camps as they went. That was the only sensible choice now.

Everyone at Shipwreck Camp was anxious and concerned. The stories of the two lost parties circulated in whispers, and now everyone feared their own suffering and possible death on the ice. "I hope we will be able to get over there hale and sound without having suffered too much," Mamen wrote in his diary. "I pity those poor wretches out there. . . . I suppose Beuchat has left this world, poor fellow. . . . If only we could reach land without loss of life." Mamen's leg remained swollen, but with continued seal oil massages by second engineer Williamson, it was finally improving, and he believed he could make the trip.

To bolster morale in camp, Bartlett ordered Templeman to feed the group large breakfasts and let them eat anything else they wanted, and as much of it as they could stomach. They would need their strength for the odyssey ahead, and they'd have to leave tons of food behind anyway. Everyone gorged on bacon, eggs, codfish, seal, hardtack, tea, and coffee for two straight days, finalizing preparations for departure when they weren't eating.

Bartlett's plan was to leave in parties of four over two days, each party with a sled and five dogs. They now had just twenty dogs able to work, so they'd be down to five animals per sled. When Chafe returned, there had been twenty-two, but on assessing all the dogs, two were badly injured and Bartlett ordered them shot and used as dog food. Hadley had the grim job of killing Molly's puppies, which could not be taken along, small and needy as they were. Bartlett did allow Nigeraurak, the ship's cat, to come on the journey. Everyone was fond of her by now. Hadley had even taught her to do a few tricks, and little Mugpi was very attached to her. Maurer sewed a special deerskin bag, lined with fur, for her to travel in, and they could feed her pemmican scraps through an opening at the top. He affixed the opening with a drawstring closure, so one could wear the bag around their neck, or tie it securely to the sled. Bartlett thought she might even bring them good luck.

Bartlett told everyone that Munro would lead the first two teams, departing February 19: Hadley, Williamson, Breddy, and Maurer would be one; Munro, Malloch, Clam, and Chafe the other. Their orders were to go directly toward Wrangel Island. Young Charlie Chafe, who'd just returned from his arduous trip to Herald Island and back, had earned Bartlett's trust and was given responsibility of the dogs.

Captain Bartlett would lead the second two teams on the following day if the weather permitted. They would first try for Herald Island, to see if they might find Sandy's party. They could also use the igloos and any caches Sandy had deposited along the way. Bartlett's team comprised McKinlay, Mamen, and Kataktovik; Templeman was to travel with Kuraluk, Auntie, Helen, and Mugpi. Because of the shortage of dogs on each gang-line, Bartlett instructed everyone to fashion a personal man-line, which they'd no doubt need to help the tired hounds pull the heavy sleds over rough terrain.

Tobacco had almost run out, and on the night before the first teams left, McKinlay filled his pipe with some loose leaf that Templeman, the biggest chain-smoker of them all, had salvaged from piles of butts he ferreted away in an empty soup tin. McKinlay managed to make one pipeful last him all day long, which soothed his nerves until his last puff. Bartlett, too, bemoaned the end of the tobacco, but he did so with a smile, quoting a line from his Newfoundland sealing days: "Narra a bit o' bacca, narra a bit o' comfort!"

Captain Bartlett read over his brief memorandum, signed by McKinlay, Mamen, and Kataktovik. "Canadian Arctic Expedition, Shipwreck Camp, Feb 24th, 1914. Left Camp 10 A.M. Wrangel Island bearing SSW . . . we go with 3 sledges, 12 dogs, and supplies for sixty days." He folded the note and placed it in a copper tank and secured it next to some large boxes, shoring it up with a couple of ice blocks. The note told where the *Karluk* had sunk, and the names of everyone in the various parties as they had departed camp. The written record was a symbolic gesture more than anything, since Bartlett knew that come spring, with the breakup of the ice, the floe and everything they were leaving behind—3,000 pounds of pemmican, 200 sacks of coal, 80 cases of biscuit, a dozen cases of gasoline, the memorandum—would all be obliterated and consumed by the sea, just as the *Karluk* had been. Still, it was an important maritime custom, and often a lifesaving one, to leave records, so he followed the tradition.

Then he, Mamen, McKinlay, and Kataktovik cut strips of the Union Jack to take with them, and Bartlett hoisted the British ensign atop a large mound of snow to fly above the camp. Bartlett was anxious to leave. The first two parties left nearly a week ago, but foul weather had kept Bartlett and the rest bound to camp the entire time. Inside the igloo and box house, they'd all worried dearly about their comrades, who were camped somewhere out there in temperatures that had plunged to −55°F.

Now the skies had finally cleared, and they were ready to go. They took a last look at Shipwreck Camp, which had been their home for a month and a half, a sanctuary on the ice that had sustained them, had been good to them. It had kept them alive.

Bartlett had decided, a few days before, to take three sleds instead of two, each with a four-hundred-pound load. It would mean fewer dogs to pull each sled, but there'd be room for a bit more gear, which he felt they needed. They had loaded hundreds of pounds of pemmican and biscuit, a few thousand tea tablets, rifles and a few hundred rounds of ammunition, Primus stoves, pickaxes, snow knives for building igloos, skins, ropes, spare harnesses, snowshoes and skis, tents and fuel. Bartlett tucked his maritime charts carefully away and gazed south. Looming far in the distance—perhaps forty or fifty miles, he reckoned—he could see Wrangel Island clearly for the first time. "On account of a sudden clearing up of the atmosphere and a temporary cessation of the almost continuous whirling snowdrift, I had a good view . . . the first sure view I had of it."

Now it was his duty to get them all there.

Bartlett drove one dogsled team, with McKinlay at the man-harness, helping to pull. Kataktovik drove the second, with Mamen hobbling along beside it, trying his best to keep up. The extra days in camp had improved his leg, but he wasn't yet strong enough to help haul. Kuraluk was at the lines of the third sled, which got off first. His family had been packed and ready to go for days, and now Auntie trotted along, seemingly unburdened by little toddler Mugpi, who was slung to her back. Helen, just eight years old but sinewy strong and tough, walked easily along, sometimes helping her father with the dogs or righting the sled. McKinlay was awed by these tough children. "The children never seemed to be affected by the cold or any of the hardships which laid low strong white men," he wrote. Templeman traveled with Kuraluk's family.

In the cold, calm weather they moved well, Bartlett's group making fifteen miles by late afternoon. Although they had yet to catch up with Kuraluk's family and Templeman, Bartlett stopped to make camp as the sun was setting and it was getting dark. He pitched a tent instead of taking the time to build an igloo, a decision everyone in his party bemoaned. "We spent a miserable night under canvas," Bartlett wrote. "The tent was not large enough for us, yet all four of us occupied it and our breathing filled it with condensation." McKinlay was too cold to sleep, and he spent much of the night outside the tent, hopping up and down and swinging his arms in circles to stay warm.

It was so cold everyone was up and out of the tent by four, and after a ration of tea, biscuit, and pemmican, they were on their way. Winds had blown over the tracks of the previous sled parties, but many of the flattened pemmican tins remained visible, hammered into pinnacles of ice as markers along the route, and they followed these. They could also still see Wrangel Island hovering on the horizon to the southwest. In this way, sometimes stopping to rest and survey the route ahead, they made it all the way to Camp 4 early on the second day out. The camps were between five and ten miles apart, and it was always uplifting to see an igloo and signs that others had been there. At Camp 4, they discovered the leg of a recently killed polar bear—a very welcome addition to their larder of pemmican and biscuit—and a note from chief engineer Munro, saying that his group had been delayed by the storm and that the trail beyond was rough going. Bartlett was heartened to have news of the advance party.

By late in the afternoon, they arrived at Camp 6 to find Kuraluk's family already resting cozily inside a traditional dome-shaped igloo, the dogs huddled together outside. Bartlett and McKinlay assessed the cache there and were alarmed to find only five gallons of fuel oil. There should have been another twelve gallons. After poking around snowdrifts with picks and failing to find the missing fuel, Bartlett surveyed the ruptured, raftered ice nearby and reasoned that the gallon containers had been swallowed by the ice. Fuel was precious; it ran the stoves that heated their food, and the stoves gave off a modicum of heat inside the igloos. The loss of fuel concerned Bartlett enough to send McKinlay and Kataktovik back to Shipwreck Camp first thing the next morning to retrieve more and bring back as much as he thought he could carry on the sled. He also asked McKinlay to bring back more skins (which could line the igloo bottoms for added warmth), seal meat, and any ammunition they'd left there.

Bartlett estimated they'd made it thirty miles from Shipwreck Camp, twelve on the first day and eighteen the second. The progress pleased him, but he also realized, based on the views he was getting of Wrangel Island, that it was much farther away than he'd estimated. Perhaps twice as far, and that was if they could travel in a straight line. Considering the behavior of ice nearer the shore, he knew that this was unlikely. They were bound to encounter open leads they'd need to work around, adding to the distance. There was no way to accurately know how long it would take, so more fuel would be essential.

Bartlett had learned his lesson during the night in the tent, so with Kataktovik and McKinlay, they started building an igloo. The process involved first finding a relatively level spot and preferably on heavy, sturdy ice that appeared unlikely to fracture, though this proved impossible to predict, and often there wasn't much time at the end of the day in the dying light. They had to work fast. Using long-bladed snow knives as well as handsaws, they cut large blocks of snow and stacked them in a square shape for the lower walls, tapering them in smaller sizes up to the roof. The blocks would vary in size, between a foot and a half to two feet thick, determined by the snow's texture and whether the blocks would break apart.

Building a dome-style igloo took time and required great skill, so Bartlett opted for square walls four to five feet high and used the tent and canvas sled covers as a roof, with snowshoes and a ski lashed together for a tent pole. To ensure an efficient and repeatable system, after the first tier of walls went up, one man was designated to remain inside, leveling the floor and covering it with skins, and also melting ice for water. The other men built the walls, and when it was nearly complete, one man tended to and fed the dogs.

That night, after an hour and a half of work, they crawled in through a small, semicircular opening left in one of the walls. Once in, they filled the hole with a large snow block to make it windproof, punching holes in walls with their fists for ventilation. McKinlay had made tea and warmed some pemmican, and they discussed the taste and merits of the two brands as they chewed languorously, as if it were fine beef from a restaurant. The verdict: the Underwood was too sweet; the Hudson's Bay too fatty. "I do not like either," McKinlay said, laughing, "but I'm glad to have it!"

They huddled together, sleeping fully clothed. Bartlett had instructed everyone to leave their sleeping bags at Shipwreck Camp. They were too heavy and bulky and would take up too much valuable room on the sleds, he said. And anyway, it was dangerous to sleep in the heavy bags while on the ice. If a fracture occurred, one might get stuck in their bag, and they "hobble your arms and legs and you drown," he'd warned. McKinlay removed his stockings and put on a dry pair, placing his boots next to him, where he could quickly get them if needed. Then he slid his feet into his footbag and laid his wet socks across his chest, hoping they might be partly dry by morning, and dozed off.

In the middle of the night, McKinlay sat bolt upright. Kataktovik was shaking him and yelling something and crawling out of the igloo. McKinlay could hear voices in the direction of Kuraluk's igloo, but they were soon drowned out by the awful rupturing of ice, followed by jolts and shocks that rumbled beneath him. "There was an ominous grinding and crushing and our igloo was heaving," he said. He found and pulled on his boots, and then they were all outside in the dark in "a world in torment." Though it was hard to see, the ice was opening up just ten yards from their igloo. They scrambled to get all the sleds and their supplies to a relatively safer floe, but everything was moving all around them, the ice splitting into small pieces everywhere. "The ice was breaking up into small cakes," McKinlay wrote, "if one did not take care to step on just the right spot on a cake, it would sway & tilt & one had to jump for it." The darkness made these leaps terrifying, but they had no choice.

Just as they'd stashed the last of their supplies stashed, they heard another dreadful shatter, and hurried to find that "Kuraluk's igloo split with a roar right through the middle . . . and a lead of water just where they had been sleeping." In the chaos, illuminated by starlight, they saw Mugpi teetering right on the edge, about to fall in, but Auntie grabbed her by the collar and yanked her back just in time. Kuraluk and his family remained calm throughout the ordeal, and when the rupturing subsided, Auntie and the girls crawled into Bartlett's igloo to sleep as if nothing had happened.

For the rest of the night, the men walked back and forth to stay warm, halting in fear whenever the ice fractured and cleaved. "All around us the ice was breaking," remembered Bartlett, "and at times we were on a floating island." It seemed—as they had been in the encased *Karluk* and then at Shipwreck Camp—that they might just be destined for a floating island. Perhaps, thought Bartlett, this was simply their fate.

But by morning the torment had calmed, and already the ice around them was cementing together again, as if healing itself. When he thought it safe, Bartlett sent McKinlay and Kataktovik, with all the dogs and an empty sled, back to Shipwreck Camp for the fuel oil and other essentials. He wanted them to return with one of the Peary sleds they'd left there too. With their light load and a nearly complete dog team, they would be able to travel fast. He said he would wait here for a day, which should give them plenty of time for the round trip.

Later that afternoon, Bartlett took Kuraluk and scouted ahead. The night's upheaval destroyed much of the trail the advance party had made, but there were still traces of sled tracks. As they ascended a high ice ridge, Kuraluk nudged Bartlett and handed him the binoculars, saying he could see something. Bartlett glassed southward, and sure enough, he could make out two human forms "visible against the skyline on a high rafter eight or ten miles away." He wondered what lay beyond.

Late the following afternoon, Bartlett heard dogs barking to the north, and soon McKinlay and Kataktovik pulled up, the dogs panting and foaming at their mouths. The sleds brimmed with goods: 30 gallons of oil, 12 sealskins, and 6,000 tea tablets. Bartlett was elated and thrilled by their speed; they'd made the sixty-mile round trip in under twenty-four hours.

At midday the next day, February 28, Bartlett and his two teams caught up to Munro and Hadley's parties. Oddly, they were coming toward them, as if headed back. Bartlett asked them what was going on. Why were they returning? Munro shook his head. "No way of going through," he said, resigned. Chafe chimed in, confirming Munro's report: "We separated into two different parties," he said, drawing short breaths, "and set out in different directions to try to find a way through . . . after traveling east for two days, we were still not able to see the end."

Bartlett told everyone to set up camp and sit tight. He needed to go ahead and see what in the hell Munro and Chafe were talking about. He mounted the highest raftered ice he could find and squinted to the south, then drew his binoculars up and scanned, almost in disbelief at the absurd monstrosity he saw. Before him, piled up as if giant waves had broken on a shore and frozen in time, was an immense wall of ice, with crenellated ridges jutting over one hundred feet high. It looked like an inland snow-capped mountain range, and as he glassed the horizon running parallel to the land beyond, as far as he could see both east and west, there seemed no end to it.

The boys were right. There was no getting around it. Bartlett took another look through the binoculars, almost to convince himself that this great barrier, this mountain range of ice, was real and not another Arctic optical illusion. Then he turned and headed back to tell the others of his decision. They were going to cut their way through it.

20

THE ICE ROAD

THE ARCTIC NEVER CEASED TO SURPRISE BARTLETT. THAT UNPRE-
dictability was part of its allure, its vicissitudes and moods, its character and personality. And though he thought he'd seen everything in the
North, this mountain range of ice was a new wrinkle. He laughed out
loud, thinking what Peary might say, and he knew what he would do.
They were committed to going forward. There was no other way.

Despite the magnitude of the obstacle, Bartlett could not help but be
impressed by the speed and power of the natural world, and he knew this
wall of ice had only recently formed, thrown up in his way as yet one more
test of his courage and will. The frequent storms—including the one that
had split Kuraluk's igloo in half—"had caused the moving ice to smash
against and slide over the still ice, and the pressure of the 'irresistible force
meeting the immovable body' had thrown the ice into fantastic, mountainous formations as weird as that astounding picture of Chaos before
the Creation that used to ornament the first volume of Ridpath's History
of the World."

There was some good news. The pressure ridge formation here meant
that the moving ice was slamming into stationary, grounded ice, which
must be landlocked ice extending off the shores of Wrangel Island. So, if
they could manage a way through, the island wouldn't be much farther.
And all four of his parties that had left Shipwreck Camp were here, safely
reunited. Bartlett brooded about the fates of Sandy's and Dr. Mackay's

parties, but there was no time to dwell on them now, as their own hercu-
lean task lay ahead.

At their camp—a few igloos and low-slung snow houses with canvas
roofs—Bartlett asked McKinlay to do an assessment of everyone's condition. Malloch's feet—two toes and both heels—were severely frostbitten.
Though he was big and tough and immensely strong (as Wee Mac could attest, having been hoisted in the air and nearly squeezed to death by him on
the *Karluk*), he often let bravado get the best of him, and rather than speak
of pain, he bore it silently. "He had let his feet go," McKinlay reported,
"without telling anyone and they were in very bad shape." Maurer's feet
were also badly frostbitten; he could not feel them at all. Mamen's knee was
fair, but it would be tasked in the days ahead, that he knew. Bartlett knew
it, too, and he ordered Mamen to stay in camp for a few days as the first
parties ascended the pressure ridges. He asked Mamen and Williamson to
attend to Malloch's and Maurer's feet, and they cut away the dead flesh and
bandaged their feet with strips of torn cloth. Everyone else seemed to be
fine. Tired, cold, and hungry, but otherwise in good condition.

Bartlett consulted with McKinlay and Hadley about his plans. He
asked whether they thought they could make it to Shipwreck Camp and
back once more for additional supplies, since it was going to take considerable time—no telling how long—to make it through the ice wall. After
discussing it, McKinlay and Hadley agreed that though the recent storm
and shifting ice would likely have obliterated the trail, they believed they
could get there and back. Bartlett said that they should take Chafe with
them, and while they were gone, he'd begin the assault on the ice barrier.

Bartlett took Kuraluk and Kataktovik and the three, all armed with ice
axes, started hacking a route up and through the jumbled ice. The plan
was to cut a "road" about four feet wide, through which they would relay
sled loads, ferrying them as far as they could, then dumping them and
going back for more. All others who were able would follow behind with
shovels, pickaxes, and snow knives, chopping their way through the ice

that rose in sheer vertical walls on all sides of them. Before he left for Shipwreck Camp, Chafe stood and gaped at the barricade: "The front of it appeared to us like a great prison wall—it was as smooth and perpendicular as if built by a stone mason." There was an eerie, dangerous beauty too. Gargantuan blocks had sheared and fallen and sparkled like great cut gemstones, their sides polished and gleaming tourmaline blue. The tops of many of these enormous blocks were covered with spiky pinnacles, and if any of these slid down or fell off, they'd crush the men.

At the top of the first ridge, Bartlett and the Eskimos could see what they were in for: a continuous series of ridges, each separated by a chasm of between fifty feet and a hundred yards or so. Each ridgetop was so sheer and narrow that one slip, one misstep, and any of them might fall to their deaths. The captain wanted the trail cut and smoothed enough so that the sleds would not be destroyed as they hauled them through the confused ice fall. To do this, when they reached the top of each ridge, they had to use snow knives and saws to cut big chunks of ice and roll them down the other side and use these to "grade a road across" each gorge, again and again, for what appeared at least three miles. "Building a road across," said Bartlett, "was like making the Overland Trail through the Rockies."

Under clear skies, they chipped and hacked and shoveled away at the mountains in temperatures that slid to -55°F. "It was cold, seemingly endless labor," Bartlett said, "for almost every foot of the trail had to be hewn out of the ice . . . to permit our sleds to be drawn over it without being smashed." Man-hauling the partially loaded sleds up each steep incline was exhausting, but the trickiest maneuver was getting the sleds over and down the other side. Bartlett instructed men to tie a long rope salvaged from the *Karluk* to the back of each sled and slowly lower it down the precipitous slope below, taking great care not to let the sled pick up speed and go plummeting and crashing below. At one point, they devised a method of tying a rope to a sled at the top of a ridge to one behind it at the bottom, and by lowering the lead sled down, its weight would pull the other up.

Then they'd cross the next ravine and repeat the process, over and over, yard after hard-won yard.

McKinlay, Hadley, and Chafe—with two sleds and full teams of dogs—had made it back to Shipwreck Camp with little difficulty. The camp was shrouded by snowdrift but was otherwise as they had left it; the box house and igloo still standing, the Blue Ensign snapping in the wind. They got the stove in the box house going and spent a full day drying their clothes and feeding on seal meat, codfish, heated biscuits, and cocoa. Because they could, they cooked for six men instead of three, and ate every bite. They fed the dogs extra rations as well. McKinlay even found an old plug of dried chewing tobacco and ground it up fine and smoked it in his pipe, puffing contentedly. Then they banked up a big fire and slept.

The next morning, following Bartlett's instructions, McKinlay orchestrated the loading of the sleds, piling eight hundred pounds on each, mostly pemmican and fuel. He knew they could not linger long here, though it was comfortable, and they could eat anything they wanted from the remaining stores of the *Karluk*. Fully loaded, there was no telling how long it would take to get back, so they prepared everything and lashed it securely on the sleds. Before they left, McKinlay wrote a note of their recent affairs and the current location of the main party and added it to the copper tank. As the dogs trotted away, McKinlay turned and took a last look at Shipwreck Camp. He wondered what would happen to the written record of their time there, and to the camp itself, and the thousands of articles they were leaving behind: "Would they be devoured in the ice . . . or . . . drift thousands of miles to be washed up on some Atlantic shore?"

McKinlay was right about the weight of their loads. It took them nearly five hours to reach the first camp, and at that rate, he estimated it would take almost a week to make it all the way back to Bartlett and the main outfit. This was no good. Bartlett needed them back as soon as possible. After discussing things with Hadley and Chafe, they decided to dump some of their load, caching about five hundred pounds of pemmican. It helped, and they made much better time, driving the dogs until the sun was low. They stopped to camp, making a poor igloo, as the snow was not consolidated enough for good blocks.

The next day, March 5, they got an early start and reached Camp 4 before noon. About a half mile from Camp 4, they lost the trail and spent an hour hunting around looking for it. They found what appeared to be the trail, but it was "very badly smashed up" and they had to pickax their way through a particularly rough section, with Hadley out front, followed by McKinlay, then Chafe. Late in the afternoon, after a few hours of picking and chopping, they broke through and McKinlay could see sunlight glinting off a flattened pemmican tin stuck to an igloo up ahead. They could camp there. Then he heard the dogs barking hysterically and he whipped around to see Chafe sprinting toward him, waving his ice ax. "Hadley, get the rifle!" he shouted. Right behind Chafe stood a polar bear. The dogs snarled and held the bear off but were getting tangled in their harnesses.

The bear stood still, fixed on the dogs, then dropped to its feet and rushed at them, roaring and skidding to a stop just a few feet from the dogs. Then the bear trotted away, spun around, and charged again, this time coming even closer to the dogs. Clouds of steam came from its open mouth. McKinlay watched, frozen motionless and awestruck, unable to do anything but respect "the to and fro motion of his massive head, the danger from those huge paws." Hadley rushed for the sled and struggled to get his rifle; it was lashed so tightly to the sled he had to pull out his knife and cut it free. He leveled the gun on the bear, which was making another attack at the dogs, and pulled the trigger—but the rifle misfired. Hadley levered the bad cartridge out of the chamber and, as calmly as he could, reloaded. The shot rang out and struck the bear in the head, but it seemed to glance off and "made him more furious than ever, and he rushed viciously at the dogs again." The next shot brought the bear slamming to its knees, and it died right in front of the dogs.

They wanted to skin out and butcher the bear, but it was late and the good skinning tools were up ahead, with Kuraluk and Kataktovik. When they reached the next igloo at Camp 5, the sun was just setting. They pulled up and started putting some skins on the floor and getting out a Primus stove when the dogs set to barking once more. McKinlay came out of the igloo and saw, standing right next to one of the sleds, "another bear, this time a very big fellow," considerably larger than the first. In their frenzy, three dogs broke loose and ran circles around the bear, snarling and gnashing their teeth as the beast lashed its claws at them, raking across the back of one, ripping off a hunk of fur and flesh. Hadley crept on his hands and knees and, with the bear's head now craning across the sled near him, seized the rifle again and rolled and got up, shouldered the rifle and fired. The bear loped off, hit, and Hadley chambered another round and fired. "When the bullet hit him," remembered Chafe, "he jumped in the air, and, turning a complete somersault, landed dead fifteen feet from where he jumped." The bear scoured a deep depression where he landed in the snow-covered ice.

It had been a terrifying, heart-pumping half hour, and it took some time to calm the dogs. The men settled into the igloo, and McKinlay got up to get ice to melt for their tea. He couldn't believe it. There, standing over the second dead bear was a third. This bear did not seem menacing; it just lumbered on all fours, its head low, alternately sniffing the dead bear, then the dogs, which were animated and snarling again. Hadley and Chafe heard the commotion and came out, Hadley clutching his rifle. It was dark, but he could make out the great white form against the skyline and he shot. The bear recoiled and loped away, laboring as it went. It was too dark to go out after a wounded bear, so the men returned to the igloo and tried to get some sleep, but it was nearly impossible with thoughts of the great heads and ferocious jaws of the huge creatures lurking outside. Hadley lay near the igloo doorway, his rifle on his chest all night.

First thing the next morning, the men rose to investigate. They found the third bear lying three hundred yards from the igloo, wheezing and gasping. Hadley quickly shot him to end his pain. Back at the igloo, they fed the dogs as much bear meat as they could eat, and, using a saw, cut off a hindquarter from the second bear and strapped it to the sled to take with them. McKinlay felt terrible. Though he understood that the animals were deadly, and that he and the others were vulnerable and exposed, as he beheld the beautiful creature lying in the snow, its downy white fur matted with blood, a sadness overcame him. "I knew that our lives might depend on being able to kill them, but they were such magnificent animals. I hoped that we would never kill one except for self-protection or food."

McKinlay, Hadley, and Chafe had been gone a week. They knew that Bartlett would be worried about them by now, so they ran the dogs hard for hours, stopping only to examine fresh bear tracks crisscrossing the main trail and keep a keen eye out for more bears. Near midday they saw the first of the great pressure ridges in the distance and two small forms coming their way. When they met up, they were happy to see it was Munro and Clam, each hauling an empty sled. They reported that the captain had sent them out to look for them. The men divided the dogs and loads evenly among the four sleds and started navigating the rough ridges, with Munro leading the way.

As they ascended the winding, narrow path Bartlett and the others had been cutting for days, McKinlay was astonished by what he saw. "Nothing but huge ice cakes and boulders, some as large as houses, which look as if they had been tossed about like pebbles and piled into high ridges" more than one hundred feet high. Night fell and the temperature plunged to –50°F, but they pressed on through dim moonglow, carefully picking their way over the trail that had been worn smooth from day after day of Bartlett and the others ferrying sled loads through. It was bitter cold, but the tough work, the constant climbing and descending, kept them warm enough. "It was laborious . . . and at times, dangerous," wrote McKinlay.

At half past three in the morning, on March 6, they crossed the last of the ridges and, descending, could see the outline of igloos and tents ahead. McKinlay heard shouts below, and when they pulled the dogs up, a cheer went round the camp as people came out to meet them. "The roar of welcome that greeted us," wrote McKinlay, "was only exceeded by the one that went up when we produced the bear meat."

Bartlett clapped the men on their backs and congratulated them on their successful return from Shipwreck Camp. The captain looked weary, his eyes sunken and drawn. It had taken four days to hack a three-mile road through the ice mountain, everyone working constantly, load after load moved forward, unloaded, and returned for yet another cargo load. Bartlett and Kataktovik had done much of the ferrying, the man-harnesses searing into their shoulders with every step. Auntie had carried Mugpi on her back almost the entire way, and now all of them were here, safe. Even Nigeraurak, they said, was purring happily in one of the igloos.

The next morning, in better light, McKinlay and Chafe stood outside with Bartlett. They all gazed at the wall of ice behind them, almost in disbelief that they'd made it through to the landward side. The captain was proud of his achievement. "It was as tough a job as I ever tackled," he said, his voice hoarse from days of calling out commands and encouragement. Later, he would send McKinlay, Hadley, and Kuraluk back for the rest of the bear meat—they could all use the nourishment. But for now, there was time to relish, for a moment, what they had accomplished. "It was with a sense of intense relief," wrote Chafe, "that we looked back at that monster wall, and then gazed over the vast, almost level stretch of ice before us."

Beyond, some thirty miles distant, they could see the dark outline of Wrangel Island rising high up into the sky like a sleeping volcano about to awaken.

21

"NUNA! NUNA!"

WITH EVERYONE SAFE AND ACCOUNTED FOR ON THE LANDWARD side of the ice range, Bartlett ordered that they make their way toward Wrangel Island in the same teams that had originally departed Shipwreck Camp. The groups had traveled well together, and understood one another's personalities, strengths, weaknesses, and pace. They were still not out of danger, for anything could happen in the estimated thirty miles remaining to the island. The recent bear attacks were examples, but the fickle sea ice was still their most formidable foe.

Although the sun was veiled by cloud cover, Bartlett reminded everyone to use their snow goggles to avoid snow or ice blindness. He pointed to Auntie, who was hitching Mugpi onto her back. Auntie was already wearing her Eskimo-style snow goggles, which had wooden eye pieces with small slits in them to reduce the amount of light coming in. McKinlay rooted around in his rucksack and pulled out a pair of his amber-lensed goggles. They worked well except under heavy exertion, when they tended to fog up from condensation and had to be repeatedly wiped clear. The main drawback of the Eskimo-style goggles was that the small slits provided limited vision, but either type was crucial now that they were getting longer days, with the sun blaring down and reflecting off the ice. Intense, prolonged exposure to the ultraviolet light could sear the cornea, causing intense pain initially, then rendering you effectively blind and unable to travel by yourself for a day or two, which, depending on where you were when it happened, could prove fatal.

As the first groups struck south, they could just make out the silhouette of Wrangel Island, its rounded outline like the humped shoulders of a bear. McKinlay, Hadley, and Kuraluk headed back north, the opposite direction, through the carved maze trail to retrieve the bears they'd shot. Picking their way through with empty sleds, Hadley told McKinlay that cutting the path through this frozen range had been harder than anything he'd experienced in over twenty years in the Arctic, which was saying something, since he'd once been marooned on an ice floe for fifty-three days with two weeks' rations, and in the end had been forced to eat his sealskin coat and a pair of mukluks.

Fortunately, they found the bears without much trouble. Kuraluk set to butchering, first venting the animals, as they were bloated with gas, then skinning them, cutting their huge haunches as hindquarters, or hams, and carefully removing the loin or backstraps, a tender delicacy. Kuraluk also took some of the entrails, and the hearts. As McKinlay helped, he noticed something: "Those bears must have been hungry when they called on us, because when we cut up the carcasses all that the three stomachs contained were a few small pebbles." This fact didn't bode well for what food they might themselves be able to harvest, but McKinlay just kept loading the sleds with meat, and then they headed back to meet the main party and continue shoreward.

Bartlett and Kataktovik and Chafe had been taking turns breaking trail, and it was tough going. What had appeared before them as a level plain turned out to be another four miles of lesser pressure ridges that slowed progress. And the light was bad; flat and diffuse, it provided no shadows to alert them to hummocks or snowdrifts, so that they tripped and fell frequently. Also, winds had drifted snow in places two to three feet deep, and they sank up their thighs as they broke trail, each hard-earned step exhausting them. Bartlett decided that lighter loads would allow them to move faster and help ensure that the sleds did not break, but this meant more relaying of loads, which doubled or even tripled the distance a person had to travel, depending on how many shifts one took.

Despite the difficult tramping and hauling, by the end of the day, as they set up camp and built igloos, Bartlett reckoned they'd managed about seven miles. It was bitterly cold, and everyone was drained, but at least they had fresh bear meat to eat. Well, everyone but those in Bartlett's igloo. McKinlay had been fantasizing about it all day but recorded that night in his journal: "Great disappointment in our igloo because Captain would not cook bear meat, being too tired, he said, while all the other houses were enjoying the bear meat!"

Bartlett was determined to get to the island as soon as humanly possible. From reading his *Coast Pilot*, he learned that large sandspits extended great distances into the sea off Wrangel Island's northern shores. This encouraged him, as the ice there would be more stable and grounded, with fewer open leads. He started sending trailbreaking teams at two o'clock each morning, knowing the days would be torturously long but bent on getting them off this cursed ice. In this way, with improving, smoother terrain, over the next three days they made twenty miles, traveling from first light until dark. By the end of each day, everyone was spent and cold and numb, but still the igloos had to be built, the dogs fed. Men chewed their pemmican and bear meat with their eyes closed, sometimes falling asleep while eating.

Bartlett hardly slept, consumed by what he'd need to do next. It would fall on him and at least one other—perhaps two, depending on everyone's condition—to continue to Siberia, and then to Alaska for help. Wrangel Island might sustain them for a time, but who knew how much game was there? Bartlett understood that in these northern waters, the window for a rescue ship was narrow—six weeks at most, during late summer. After that, the ice would close in again, trapping everyone on the island for another year at least. These thoughts raced through Bartlett's mind as he lay shivering on the ice floor of his igloo.

At six o'clock on the morning of March 12, Bartlett was outside the igloo with McKinlay and Mamen, preparing to head out. McKinlay had been up since three, melting ice for tea water and making a meager break-fast of lukewarm pemmican. They organized the dogs and set off, bearing south. The other parties followed the footprints and sled tracks a few hours later. There was no mistaking their destination now. Whenever the clouds parted, the men looked up and surveyed the curve of land ahead, a dark and knobby monolith erupting from the sea.

McKinlay strained at his haul ropes, his throat dry with thirst. He told Mamen, limping along beside him, that he wished they'd stop to make some tea—it had been seven hours since his last sip of water—but Bartlett kept driving forward with Kataktovik. Then, at one o'clock, McKinlay heard yelling up ahead and hurried along to see what was the matter. Perhaps another lead they'd have to find a way to cross, or bears. They'd seen plenty of tracks over the last days. As he got closer, he saw Kataktovik kicking up snow, driving his heel in deep and waving his arms, yelling "*Nuna! Nuna!* Land!"

McKinlay and Mamen sprinted up and knelt at the hole Kataktovik had made with his foot. They took off their mittens and dug through the snow, scooping up pebbles from the hard ground, touching the earth with their fingers. Then they gave a loud cheer and congratulated Captain Bart-lett for getting them here, to the first soil their hands and feet had touched since they'd left Alaska, in July of the previous year, eight months before. Bartlett had Kataktovik start building igloos and sent the others to collect driftwood, which littered the shore. "Here and there on the beach were dead trees which had drifted ashore," he wrote, "with the roots sticking up in the air. We also found planks and other lumber."

Bartlett was relieved. From his readings, he knew that no trees grew on the island, but accounts had mentioned the driftwood, and if there was a great deal of it, his fuel problems would be solved, at least temporarily. They banked up wood and built a huge bonfire, hoping the smoke would spur the trailing parties on and guide them in.

It worked. A few hours later, the remainder of the group arrived, their gaunt faces beaming. "Oh happiness!" exclaimed Chafe as he dropped to the snow-covered ground. "No more open leads. No more midnight alarms!" Everyone was elated, heaving and breathless. Auntie laughed as she took Mugpi down and set the toddler onto the ground. She'd mostly carried the stoic little girl well over one hundred miles from Shipwreck Camp.

Winds were whipping up and it was getting very cold by early afternoon. Bartlett told everyone to hurry with the shelters. They should warm themselves by the big fire, try to dry their wet boots and clothing and otherwise keep moving. Bartlett surveyed the island and the surroundings, an empire of ice and stone. The island extended in length east to west for nearly one hundred miles, with a width of some fifty miles. In the clear light, he could see nearly forty or fifty miles of the northern coast, with Cape Waring lying to the far eastern tip, and Evans Point to the west. He prayed there would be game here. As he surveyed the land, he could see two other large sandspits extending out, and from the maps and descriptions in the *Coast Pilot*, knew they'd landed on Icy Spit, the middle spit of the three that Muir had reported on the northeast side. Between the spits were ice-covered lagoons where, later in spring and early summer, they might find seals and walrus.

Inland, the land rose, steep and valleyed near the shore, hilly and rounded at first, then climbing up to great plateaus. Beyond, crags rose to high peaks. They would scout these lands in the days ahead. Now, as the cold chilled the captain to his marrow, he took stock. Of the twenty-five souls who'd survived Shipwreck Camp, seventeen had made it alive to this desolate, forlorn place at Icy Spit, which they named Shore Camp. He knew in his heart that Dr. Mackay and Beuchat and Murray and Morris were dead. Based on their condition when they were last seen, that was all but certain. But he still held out faint hope for Sandy's party. Perhaps they remained on Herald Island. Or maybe they'd tried—or would try—to make it here. At any rate, there was nothing to do about it now.

His own group of survivors were elated to have reached terra firma, but were physically weary, spent from their constant struggles over the last two weeks. He turned and walked to the roaring driftwood fire, flames and smoke leaping into the air, and warmed his hands. He was struck by the sobering thought that not a single soul in the outside world had any idea that they were here, three hundred miles north of the Arctic Circle, and unless he could tell someone, no one was coming for them.

22

SEARCHING FOR CROCKER LAND

VILHJALMUR STEFANSSON, WELL FED AND RESTED, SAT AT A DESK IN the cozy camp at Collinson Point, Alaska, reading and typing up lists for his upcoming journey north over the Beaufort Sea. The fire from the iron cookstove popped and spat, heating the room to almost unbearably warm, even though he wore only a light woolen shirt and trousers. Outside, members from the remains of his original Northern Party—including the photographer Wilkins, and several members of the Southern Party he'd convinced to remain as a base team for his New Northern Party—were busy loading sleds and getting gear in order. Stefansson wanted a small, nimble team, what he described as "a very few good men rather than a large number of ordinary ones." They boxed up a sextant and other scientific instruments and gear that Dr. Anderson felt belonged to his Southern Party. There remained a good deal of animosity between Stefansson and Dr. Anderson.

It had been nearly three months since his heated argument with Dr. Anderson in the cabin near Collinson Point just before Christmas. In the meantime, Stefansson had gone to Herschel Island, retrieved his wife and son, spent thousands of the Canadian government's money on ships, sleds, food, fuel, and ammunition to reoutfit his program, and now he was ready to leave. It was March 12, 1914—the exact day that Captain Bartlett and the remaining *Karluk* survivors were landing on Wrangel Island.

Stefansson's plan was to embark north with a very small team and search for new lands in the Beaufort Sea. If he was lucky, he might find Crocker Land, the land mass Robert Peary claimed to have seen from a high promontory on the northwestern shore of Ellesmere Island in 1906 after a failed North Pole attempt. No one had yet determined whether Crocker Land existed or not. Stefansson knew that there was already another expedition searching for it, sponsored by the American Museum of Natural History and the American Geographical Society. It was led by an American, Donald Macmillan, and had departed near the time Stefansson's expedition sailed from Alaska on the *Karluk* the previous summer. It would be quite a coup if he could beat them to it, if it existed at all. There were rumors that Peary had fabricated the story about Crocker Land to garner financial backing for his 1909 North Pole attempt. Stefansson intended to see for himself. If Crocker Land existed and he found it first, his fame would rival that of Peary and Nansen and Amundsen.

But beyond the search for new lands and the scientific work he'd be doing, Stefansson had another agenda. He wanted to prove that the Arctic was a friendly place, and that it was quite possible to live off the land (or off the ice) for months or even years without support. He reasoned that with guile and skill, a team of three, adopting the ways of the Eskimo, could catch enough seals and shoot enough walrus, bears, and caribou to survive indefinitely. Dr. Anderson—and perhaps more significant, most of the region's whalers and the local Inupiat along the coast of northern Alaska—believed Stefansson was either suicidal or insane, and maybe both. The risks involved were countless. Ice breakup, which would be happening in the coming months, could easily leave them stranded on a floe, with no escape. Most of the known game was nearer the coast, so starvation was a possibility, as was death by exposure.

Stefansson ignored all the naysayers, and by March 16, 1914, he was at Martin Point, a sandspit peninsula forty miles east of Collinson Point, not far from the Mackenzie River delta. There was a cabin and small community, the remnants of an old trading station. Stefansson decided to leave Fanny and Alex there, hoping to meet back up with them after his return

from his first ice trip. He had settled on Storker Storkerson and Ole Andreason as his traveling companions. The two were hardened Norwegian
sailors who'd been in the area for years, involved in the whaling industry
until its decline in the early 1900s, after which they'd remained and made
a living by trapping and trading. They were both well versed in ice travel.
Traveling light, they'd take provisions for just six to seven weeks, supplementing food with seal meat while on the ice, and with caribou should they
find land. He expected to be back to the Alaskan mainland, either at Point
Barrow or Camden Bay, depending on the behavior of the ice drift, within
a couple of months. If he happened to find land, he'd remain to map it and
explore it for a year or so, heading to Banks Island, or back to Alaska, next
spring. It all depended on what he found.

Dr. Anderson, entirely unsupportive of Stefansson's venture, believed
it to be yet another publicity stunt, a way of garnering newspaper acclaim,
notoriety, and, if he survived, a lucrative lecture tour and book deals. That
Stefansson had instructed George Wilkins to film (both in still and moving photography) his departure, theatrically capturing the team heading
off into the frozen unknown, certainly illustrated his awareness of his image as an intrepid explorer, undaunted and unafraid. But Anderson also
thought Stefansson irresponsible for entirely disregarding the fate of the
members of the *Karluk*, and he'd told him so in sharp words. Rather than
tramping off on a new personal and selfish journey, he should be busy
organizing rescue ships to go search for Bartlett, his crew, and the expedition's scientists, who might be clinging to their lives somewhere out on the
frozen sea or stranded on some island.

Stefansson's reply to Anderson was brusque and direct, with the formality and definitiveness of an order: "No relief expeditions should be
sent out on the grounds that the search for a ship placed like the *Karluk*
has only infinitesimal chances of success and a vessel so sent out would be
likely to be no better situated herself." In Stefansson's mind, either the ship
had been crushed by the ice or it was still drifting. In either case, there was
nothing he could do about it.

Stefansson took Fanny and Alex aside and said a private goodbye. By now he'd spent enough time with little Alex to teach him to read and write. He would see them both again, he promised, hugging them. And then, with Wilkins filming the departure for dramatic cinematic effect, Stefansson, in all his fur garb and with rifle in hand, marched northward onto the icy sea.

23

AN AUDACIOUS PLAN

WRANGEL ISLAND MIGHT EVENTUALLY PROVE THE SANCTUARY THAT saved all their lives, but its first impressions were less than promising. "It is the most desolate looking place I have ever seen," said Chafe their first morning on its shores, "or ever wish to see again."* Bartlett, always planning ahead, immediately sent Kuraluk out to scout for game, and sent Munro and Chafe back to the last ice camp, about nine miles north, to retrieve a cache of supplies left there. He had the others range nearby and collect as much driftwood as they could gather, piling it high. He wanted to keep a big fire going for the time being, not only for warmth and morale but in case the smoke might yet guide Sandy's lost party toward the island. It was a long shot, but he kept the fire burning anyway.

That Bartlett had led them safely here was nothing short of miraculous, and the survivors developed a newfound respect for the tenacious mariner, who had proved he was as adept on moving sea ice as he was at the helm of a ship. Chafe recorded in his journal: "No braver man, nor more loyal to duty than Captain Bartlett, can be found in the world. He shared all the

---

* The remote Wrangel Island is believed to be the last place on earth to support populations of woolly mammoths, until their extinction some six thousand years beyond the extinction of populations on mainland Eurasia and North America. Naturalist John Muir published the first description of the island, referring to it as "severely solitary" land in the "topmost, frost-killed end of creation." Muir, *The Cruise of the* Corwin: *Journal of the Arctic Expedition of 1881 in search of De Long and the* Jeannette (Boston: Houghton Mifflin, 1917).

dangers and hardships, and worked as no man ever before worked, for our safety. . . . I can truly say that if it had not been for Captain Bartlett, not one of us would have ever reached Wrangel Island."

Kuraluk returned that evening to report that he'd traveled about twenty miles round trip to Berry Spit toward the east, but he'd seen only the tracks of a single bear and a single fox. This was foreboding news. To Bartlett it meant that, at least for now, their chances for bears were slim. Bears feed on seals, and the last seal holes they'd seen were between twenty-five and forty miles out on the ice, near the pressure ridges. That explained the bears they'd run into there. As it warmed up later in the spring and early summer, and the ice broke apart closer to the island, the seals would certainly work their way toward shore, bringing the bears with them. But that was a few months away, and food was going to run out. Without fresh meat, they'd have to survive on pemmican.

Bartlett asked McKinlay to do a careful inventory of all the food. McKinlay, meticulous in his task, did a thorough accounting and reported back. All told, there were 390 pounds of Underwood pemmican, 264 pounds of Hudson's Bay pemmican, 2½ cases of biscuits, and 20 gallons of oil. Of dog pemmican, there remained only 120 pounds. Bartlett quickly determined that it was enough pemmican to feed them all full rations for eighty days, though the biscuits would be gone sooner. The rations would get them to early June. By then birds should return, ducks and geese and shorebirds, but they couldn't count on birds sustaining them for long.

Given these rations and scant game, Bartlett thought the best thing to do would be to break the main party into groups, each to settle at camps of their choosing between ten and fifteen miles apart from one another. This would broaden the hunting area, and yet the camps would be close enough that members could check in on one another as well as share any game procured.

But first, everyone needed to rest and recover from their recent journey. They'd been constantly on the move for two weeks, and everyone— remarkably, except for Auntie and her little girls—was hobbling and straggling around slowly, laboring to move. Those who'd spent the most time in the haul lines had aching necks, shoulders, and backs. Maurer's and Malloch's frostbitten feet were slowly improving, but had still not fully healed. Mamen's knee got him here, but the strain had swollen it badly and it would need time to get better.

Time, unfortunately, was something Bartlett knew he did not have. As he looked upon the members and their lot, he reflected: "We were on land but we were a long way from civilization; we need not drown but we might starve or freeze to death if we could not get help within a reasonable time." He knew that with the whaling industry's decline, no ships would be passing anywhere near Wrangel Island come summer. In fact, to Bartlett's knowledge, they were only the second group of humans ever to have set foot on the island. John Muir, aboard the *Corwin*, had been among the first to land, in 1881, looking for any signs of Captain De Long and his lost *Jeannette*.* That was thirty-three years ago, and such intervals of visitation ruled out any chance of someone just happening by. So remote and desolate was the place, Muir had written, "A land more severely solitary could hardly be found anywhere on the face of the globe."†

No. No one was coming here. Their only hope was for Bartlett to go for help. He settled on Kataktovik as the best suited for the journey, and though he knew his decision might raise some objections, he presented his plan to the others. "Kataktovik was sufficiently experienced in ice travel,"

---

* On the day of the *Corwin*'s landing—August 12, 1881—Captain Calvin Hooper had planted a flag and, according to Muir, "took formal possession of it in the name of the United States." He also named the island New Columbia. In fact, in 1911, members of Russia's Arctic Ocean Hydrographic Expedition, aboard the icebreakers *Vaygach* and *Taymyr* under Boris Vilkitsky, landed on the island, though it appears that Bartlett had no knowledge of this. In 1916, the Tsarist government declared that the island belonged to the Russian Empire, a claim that was later disputed, including by Stefansson, the Canadian government, and British Sovereignty ("Wrangel Island": 440–44).

† Despite its remote location and scant resources, Wrangel Island eventually became vigorously contested land, with colonization schemes and numerous claims of sovereignty by the following: Britain, which claimed discovery in 1849; the United States, which planted its flag and later charted, mapped, and explored the island in 1881; Russia, which sent icebreakers there while charting the Arctic Ocean in 1910; and Canada, by virtue of having landed there in 1913 (Webb, *Cold, Cold War*: 1–143).

Bartlett reasoned, "and inured to the hardships of life in the Arctic to know how to take care of himself in the constantly recurring emergencies that menace the traveler on the ever-shifting surface of the sea ice."

As predicted, some took the news badly. Malloch argued that he was the strongest and expressed a desire to go. It was true he was among the strongest physically, but already out on the ice he'd shown repeated disregard for his own personal care, which had resulted in severely frostbitten feet. And on many occasions, he'd exhibited bouts of mental instability. Still, he pressed the issue for hours, telling the captain he was the best choice. When Bartlett calmly but firmly refused him, according to McKinlay, "Malloch nearly went to pieces." He cussed and, in a huff, stormed off to an igloo to sulk.

Mamen was also extremely disappointed. Aboard the *Karluk*, he'd won the captain's favor time and again. He was by far the fittest and fastest of them all, evidenced by Bartlett severely limiting him in the Christmas Day running competitions, knowing he'd win them all. But his damned knee. Bartlett couldn't risk it. Mamen understood, though the decision was tough to come to grips with. He'd begun to regard Captain Bartlett as a father figure, and now he felt like a boy who'd let his father down.

So, it was settled. Bartlett would leave with Kataktovik as soon as possible. The longer he delayed, the greater chance of open leads between Wrangel Island and mainland Siberia, where he must go. He needed to travel light and fast, with a small dog team, and get across before the seasonal southern winds came and set the ice moving. Bartlett sat in his igloo studying the *Coast Pilot*, but its information concerning the northern Siberian coastline was inadequate and many years old. It was hard to say how reliable it was. He looked up from the book and laughed at the absurdity of the endeavor, noting, "I knew as much about Siberia as I knew about Mars!"

But at least he had a plan. He and Kataktovik would speed as fast as they could to the mainland, and then, provided there were Native people living there who could supply them with food, head east along the coast to East Cape, where he believed he could find a ship to take him across the Bering Strait to Alaska. Once there, he could telegraph the Canadian authorities and orchestrate a rescue. He did a rough estimate and, without saying it out loud, realized that his audacious plan involved a trek of at least seven hundred miles, and likely much longer if they were forced to skirt leads or pressure ridges. It appeared absurd. He wasn't in any better condition than the rest of them. But he had no choice.

As Captain Bartlett was finalizing the plans and writing instructions for those remaining on the island, a fierce blizzard struck, bringing heavy snows, hammering winds, and such whiteout conditions that for a few days, everyone remained inside their igloos. Bartlett could not leave in these conditions, so he used the time to keep people busy. Auntie worked at mending clothes, which were tattered and bare from months of heavy use. Men took the canvas bags they'd used to transport the pemmican and repurposed the fabric to make repairs in frayed dog harnesses. Bartlett had planned for a small group to make an attempt back to Shipwreck Camp for more food and fuel, but the weather made it too risky and he called it off for now. Perhaps they could attempt it after he'd left. There remained some fresh bear meat, and everyone relished the savory flesh, knowing they'd be on a strict pemmican diet once the bear meat was gone.

While waiting for the weather to clear, Bartlett carefully considered the divisions of the groups, taking into account various personalities and past interactions. Munro, as most senior officer now that Sandy was gone, must be the overall leader on the island. The four separate parties would live and hunt independently, but they were under Munro's command. As a ship's engineer, he was unaccustomed to such an important role. But Bartlett thought he could handle the pressure, and he privately told him so.

Munro would camp with Breddy and Clam. Maurer, Williamson, and Chafe would be a group, the captain reasoning that it made sense to keep as many of the original ship's crewmen together as possible. The scientists McKinlay, Mamen, and Malloch would camp together, along with Bob Templeman. Bartlett gave McKinlay the larger overall duty of "provision master"—just as he had been at Shipwreck Camp. He was to allocate supplies and food to the various groups and keep—to the extent that he could, given the groups' separation by many miles—a record of their rations from week to week. Bartlett trusted McKinlay implicitly and urged him to check in on each group from time to time, assessing their condition and the mood of their camp, as well as documenting their stores. Kuraluk's family obviously would stay together, with the addition of Hadley. He knew their language better than anyone else and had spent a great deal of time with them at Shipwreck Camp. Besides, he and Kuraluk made an excellent hunting team.

Bartlett impressed upon both Munro and McKinlay—speaking to each privately—the importance of maintaining peaceful dealings and goodwill. Tensions and disagreements were bound to result from the hardships they would endure. He knew that there had been some bad blood between Mamen and Munro while on the *Karluk*, and Munro had, on more than one occasion, been at odds with his fellow crew members Breddy and Williamson. These past disagreements must be swept aside and forgotten, he stressed. They could not allow them to fester or become violent. They had to work together in harmony or things would deteriorate and imperil all the rest. They must work together to survive.

On the morning of March 17, the storm lulled, and Bartlett felt confident enough to send Munro, Breddy, and Clam once again to Shipwreck Camp for food and fuel. The weather was calm enough for him to leave with Kataktovik as well, but he wanted first to see these men off and then make sure that everything in camp at Icy Spit remained in order, and that his instructions for everyone after his departure were clear and would be followed. With the wind settling down to a gentle breeze, Munro led them out with sixteen dogs and one sled. Everyone came out to see them off, shouting, "Good luck!" and "Godspeed!" Bartlett knew it was a risk. The sea had opened and nearly swallowed Kuraluk's entire family on the other side of the ice wall, but given the amount of food that might still be available at Shipwreck Camp, and their finite rations here, it was a risk Bartlett felt was worth taking.

Snows and winds returned, delaying Bartlett's departure. The next morning, the snows continued to flurry under moderate winds, with large drifts piling up around the three igloos at Icy Spit. Bartlett surveyed the skies in every direction and the land to the south, where he was headed; no signs of clearing. No matter. It was time to go, and he reminded himself of his optimistic philosophy: "If you start in the snow you are likely to have fair weather the rest of the way." He bundled up the letters each of them had written to their families and loved ones back home, promising to mail them at the first chance he got. He was taking seven dogs, and dog pemmican for thirty days. He and Kataktovik would have rations of pemmican, sugar, and tea for forty-eight days, plus rifles and ammunition. Before leaving, Bartlett handed McKinlay a letter of instructions, which was to be given to Munro on his return.

Shore Camp, Icy Spit
Wrangel Island, March 18, 1914
My Dear Munro,
I am leaving this morning with seven dogs, one sledge and Kataktovik to get the news of our disaster before the authorities at Ottawa.

During my absence you will be in charge. I have already allocated supplies to the different parties. McKinlay has four men, Hadley is with the Eskimo . . . which makes four people, Mr. Williamson three men, and yourself three men.

McKinlay kindly made out a list for me and I will ask him to give a copy to you, when you get back from your trip to Shipwreck Camp.

You will make a trip to Herald Island to search for traces of the mate's party. On my way I will cover the coast as far as Rodger's Harbor.

The great thing, of course, is the procuring of game. In this Kuraluk will be of great assistance. Let him have the dogs and two others, so he can cover a good deal of ground, and our own parties, scatter them around so that they will be able to hunt . . . give each party enough dogs, if you can spare them, so that they can better cover ground.

As we talked about distributing supplies that you bring, give each on their proportional share. As it stands now there are 80 days pemmican and oil for each person.

Please do all you can to promote good feeling in camp. You will assemble at Rodger's Harbor about the middle of July where I hope to meet you with a ship.

Sincerely yours,
R.A. Bartlett

McKinlay tucked the letter safely away among his few personal belongings inside his igloo, then joined Bartlett and Kataktovik by the sled. The dogs shook in their harnesses and pawed at the snow, rested and eager to work. Captain Bartlett asked McKinlay to walk along for a while so they could talk. Bartlett waved to the others, who tromped around in the cold and waved back, shouting encouragement. As they walked away from Shore Camp, Bartlett slung one arm around McKinlay like a schoolmate and told him to help Munro as much as he could. He was going to need every assistance. They crunched along in the new snow without speaking for a time. After about a half mile, Bartlett stopped and turned and looked McKinlay directly in the eyes. He clapped him hard on the shoulders in his usual way. He said he wished he could put McKinlay in charge overall, but as a scientist with no official position in the ship's company, it wouldn't do. "It would be resented by officers and crew," Bartlett said. But he made it known that McKinlay was his first choice.

McKinlay was touched, and he was tearing up. He knew—though it did no good to think of it—that he might never see the captain again. He paused. Wind blew gusts of biting snow across their faces. Then, to lighten the mood, he said, "I wouldn't have the job for all the tea in China."

Bartlett smiled his big, robust, infectious smile, then laughed, cupping McKinlay across the cheek with his mitten. "Canny Scot," he said.

Then Captain Bartlett turned away, whistled the dogs on, and headed south toward Siberia.

24

HOSPITAL IGLOO

THEIR LEADER WAS GONE. THE INTREPID MASTER MARINER WHO had kept them safe and together aboard the *Karluk*, who'd devised and organized the ingenious and lifesaving Shipwreck Camp on the floe, and who'd led them as they hacked their way through the ice mountains was no longer with them. Already they missed his bellowing laugh, his outbursts of profanity, his constant words of encouragement and approval. A palpable tension and anxiety moved through the members of Shore Camp, a kind of worry that burrowed pit-deep in the stomach. While no one spoke it aloud, all knew that their fates depended on Bartlett and Kataktovik reaching civilization.

Foul weather contributed to the low mood. For days, snows and winds pounded them and drove everyone into their igloos. They went out only when necessary, to fetch ice for melting water or to repair or reinforce their igloos. While building a snowbank wall around the igloo and organizing stores near the door so they'd be easy to get at, McKinlay became sopping wet. "It was bad working with so much drifting snow," he wrote in his diary. "Our skins are all saturated and hopeless for sleeping on. We got inside and lay down for the rest of the day, for nothing could be done outside."

After a sleepless night, McKinlay got up and went outside, still soaked and shivering. He shuffled through a foot of new snow to the big igloo to check on Williamson, Chafe, and Maurer and see how they were faring. All three men were sick, complaining of stomach ailment, joint and limb swelling, and deep fatigue. They assured McKinlay that they only needed more rest and some better weather to get out and about, but he was concerned. "What the trouble is, I don't know," he wrote. "They blame the bear meat, but it has never affected me." He wondered whether, somehow, they'd eaten the bears' livers. He was quite certain that Hadley had taken only hindquarters, backstraps, and hearts but not the livers. He sure hoped so. McKinlay knew from his reading—and the Eskimos understood from long experience—that eating polar bear liver could cause a form of toxic, often fatal, food poisoning. (Polar bear livers contain extremely high levels of vitamin A, because of their seal diet, and consuming it causes sluggishness, irritability, headache, blurred vision, and vomiting. Accounts of early explorers who ate polar bear livers described other horrific symptoms, including the sloughing off of the skin, leaving underlying layers exposed and bloody. The accounts were gruesome, the men suffering terrible agony, finally succumbing to hemorrhage, coma, and then death.*)

With Munro gone temporarily—en route to Shipwreck Camp for more food and fuel—McKinlay felt a keen responsibility to oversee everything at Shore Camp. Bartlett expected that of him, and he bore the duty with pride. He checked in on the other igloos. Kuraluk and his family were in fine shape. But Hadley, though a tough old bugger, looked up from his sodden bedding and said he could hardly walk, blaming his condition on rheumatism. McKinlay spoke with the others and reported in his journal, "Bob [Templeman] and Malloch are so weak that they can hardly do anything for themselves." It was deeply troubling and mysterious. McKinlay felt fine, as did Mamen. Mamen had even been outside a good deal, clearing snow from the entrances of all the igloos and bringing in biscuits and ice.

Late one afternoon, McKinlay could hear, just above the low whistling of the wind, what sounded like animals rooting around outside the igloo. His mind went to bears, and he grabbed his rifle, and he and Ma-

---

* Members of the Dutch explorer-navigator Willem Barents's expedition to Novaya Zemlya, in 1596–97, experienced these horrors (Pitzer, *Icebound*: 203).

men crawled out to investigate. The animals turned out to be sled dogs, shaking snow from their backs and haunches and burrowing into drifts to rest. Unharnessing them were Munro, Breddy, and Clam. Their skin and fur clothing were caked with rime. Munro, slapping his clothes of ice, reported that they'd made it all the way to the other side of the pressure ridges their first day out, with the dogs running well and the trail still easy to follow. But then they'd encountered "an ocean of open water." The three men had camped there and waited for two days, but the water never closed and Clam and Breddy both began to feel sick, lethargic, and complained of pain in their limbs. So they'd been forced to return.

McKinlay moved Clam and Breddy into the igloo with the other sickened men, figuring they could all convalesce in one place, and it would make attending to them easier. In the dim light of the candles and Primus stoves, he noticed that all their faces were swollen, puffy and distended around the eyes, cheeks, and lips. He served them hot tea, followed by a warm soup made with a mixture of bear meat, pemmican, and crumbled-up biscuit. He advised them to drink as much tea as they could; they were all dehydrated, in addition to whatever else was causing their ailments.

That night, just as McKinlay was settling in with a hot cup of his own tea, he heard Breddy shouting from the "hospital igloo."

"Come quick!" he yelled. "Hurry!"

McKinlay and Mamen tossed aside their tea and scrambled to see that the entire roof of the hospital igloo had caved in. Hundreds of pounds of snow blocks covered the sick men lying inside, and they were in danger of suffocating. McKinlay, Mamen, and Kuraluk—who had also hurried at the shouting—dug furiously with their hands, a rifle butt, and a shovel, careful to uncover the men's faces first so they could breathe. After a few tense minutes, all the men were safely unburied, but the igloo needed rebuilding. Kuraluk offered to house the sick men in his igloo while he and the others helped fix the roof, which took a few hours.

As they worked cutting blocks and restacking them, the dogs tore around, snarling and fighting over scraps of harnesses, sled lashings, anything they could find. They were famished. McKinlay watched one run off some distance and lie down, gnawing on someone's mukluk. When they finished the hospital igloo roof and moved the afflicted back inside, McKinlay discovered, in taking an assessment of everyone's conditions, that sometime during the last few days all the toes on one of Chafe's feet had been frozen, and now he was lame too. If they treated and warmed his toes, it looked like he would not lose them, but for now he was also out of commission. That left, at present, only a few of them fit enough to carry out any of Bartlett's instructions.

There remained only about one hundred pounds of dog pemmican, which would last the sixteen dogs one week. McKinlay didn't want to think about what would happen after that. When he went to check on the infirm, he could hear them arguing over food, already complaining about the rations of biscuits.

What a fine mess, thought McKinlay. And Captain Bartlett had been gone for only two days.

25

INTO THE LEADS

BLASTS OF NORTHWEST WINDS POUNDED BARTLETT AND KATAKTO-vik as they bore south across the eastern edge of Wrangel Island. Swirling snow bit at their faces, coating their beards and mustaches in dangling icicles. Through fogging snow goggles in whiteout conditions they could see less than a hundred yards ahead; when big gusts hit, their vision was reduced to ten yards. They moved slowly, following the frozen lagoons, and staying, as best they could, near the shoreline, inside a series of huge, grounded ice floes. Though the visibility was minimal, the footing was good, firm and compacted by the relentless pounding wind.

All day they plodded, passing Cape Waring and arriving near Skeleton Island by early evening, where they stopped to build an igloo. They had made it almost to the bottom of the island, circumnavigating the coastline for some fifty or sixty miles. When they got inside and tried to fire the tea boiler, it was leaking, and Bartlett discovered a small hole in the bottom. He sat and thought about how to fix it, and then it came to him: biscuits! Once, when he was a boy out berry picking with Grandmother Bartlett, the iron boiler they were using to cook their dinner cracked and was leaking water. Grandmother Bartlett soaked a few pounds of biscuit in water and mixed it up like cement, then plastered the wetted biscuit over the crack, sealing it tight. It worked. So now he dug into his bags and found some biscuit and chewed it until it was moist and pasty, then plastered it over the hole in the boiler, pressing it down flat with his thumb. In a few minutes, he and Kataktovik were sipping hot tea with sugar.

Bartlett wanted to scout around near Rodger's Harbor, both to see if either Sandy's or Dr. Mackay's party might by some miracle have made it there, and also to familiarize himself with the place, since it was where he had instructed Munro to convene with everyone by mid-July. The descriptions in the *Coast Pilot* suggested it was the most accessible place to land a ship. On the way down there, Bartlett looked up through pelting snow and saw a pile of rocks perched high on a bluff. He remembered that it was called Hooper's Cairn, built when Captain Hooper and naturalist John Muir had landed in 1881 to search for Captain De Long. Though Bartlett was curious to see what messages they might have left there, it was steep and cliffy and looked like too much effort, and in any case, winds now hurtled down an inland gorge there, slamming them "in terrific squalls that almost lifted us off our feet and whirled the snow down from the mountainside in huge drifts." The snow blowing down the canyon carried fine sand and shards of shale that sliced their faces, and they ducked and winced as they went.

At Rodger's Harbor, though visibility was still terrible, they scouted around and found no traces of human presence. They had seen no tracks or animal life save a lone raven, a dark omen Bartlett tried to dismiss. His intention had been to head directly from Rodger's Harbor across the sea ice of Long Strait in the Chukchi Sea, but on investigating the conditions offshore, they'd found jumbled, broken ice lined up in high ridges, between which were deep piles of soft snow. The dogs would struggle to get through, and Bartlett reckoned they'd have to hack their way across as they had the giant ice wall. Better, he thought, to continue west along the bottom of the island and see if an opening appeared somewhere.

For a couple of days, they advanced along the southern shore with no break in the weather. A few times they tried to work their way through the ice rafters and get out onto the sea ice, but the ice was so rough they snapped a sled runner and spent hours repairing it, then retreated to the coast. The terrain alongshore presented its own problems. Strong winds blew the ground bare in places, making it tough going and hard on the sled. They encountered huge piles of fractured ice they had to pickax through, and drifts so deep they needed snowshoes to cross to avoid floundering crotch-deep in the snow. The dogs did not do well with all the stopping and starting, and a few dogfights erupted that Kataktovik was quick to break up.

On they plodded, and by the night of March 23, they reached Blossom Point, at the far southwest corner of Wrangel Island. As they crawled wearily into their igloo to rest, Bartlett realized that they'd traveled nearly one hundred miles and circumnavigated about half the island. It had been five days, and they still hadn't left the island. Bartlett spent some time consulting his pilot book, which contained scant information, if scant, about the Siberian coast and the people who lived where they were heading. The chart it contained provided a general outline of the coast, but not much more.

Now they had no choice but to strike out onto the ice. From Blossom Point they started south, making about five miles before running into a wall of upthrust ice. Hour after hour they hacked with their axes, carving a road to nudge the sled through. As Bartlett climbed to the top of the rafter, ahead he saw condensed air rising up, indicating the presence of open water "and showing that the ice outside the raftered ice must be moving under the impetus of the high, westerly wind." Bartlett chuckled to himself. This was both a good and a bad sign. Soon they'd be on the open ice, but that meant they'd also be encountering diabolical leads. Bartlett slid on his butt down the slope of the last rafter and called Kataktovik and the dogs onward.

Bartlett was having trouble with his left eye. He'd been wearing his snow goggles for many days now, but sometimes they fogged, and he'd have to take them off to wipe them clear of frost, and even though it had been stormy with no direct sunshine, the glare off the ice was bright enough to have caused some damage. The pain was sharp, then throbbing, and tears ran down his left cheek, solidifying like a tiny frozen waterfall on his face.

The ice was moving, which worried Kataktovik. Bartlett tried to cheer him by saying the open water would bring seals, which in turn would bring bears, and soon they'd be feasting on both. As if on cue, within a few hours Kataktovik spotted a seal and shot it as it swam in an open lead. The ice near the edge of the water was thin and fragile, so Bartlett tied a rope to Kataktovik's waist and stayed back while the Eskimo wriggled on his belly out onto the thin ice, then whirled his manak over his head like a lasso and hurled the hooked ball out past the seal and reeled the line in, snagging the seal with the hooks and dragging it back until he could grab it. Bartlett backed away, pulling Kataktovik and the seal onto firmer ice.

Over the next few days, Bartlett and Kataktovik moved slowly and carefully. The constant motion of the ice presented navigation difficulties as well as grave danger, but they soon developed a system. When they came to a lead, Bartlett would go in one direction along it, Kataktovik the other, both walking parallel to the open water. Whoever found a suitable place to cross first—a sturdy ice bridge or a gap narrow enough to jump across—would fire a revolver into the air; or, if the whirling snows and rising fog abated and it was clear enough, one would climb up onto an ice mound and yell and wave the other over. Often, they had to unharness the dogs and toss them across one at a time. This terrified the dogs, and sometimes they ran off and had to be coaxed back with chunks of pemmican. A few snow bridges between leads looked strong enough to cross with the sled, and they'd make a run at it, whipping and urging the dogs on. Sometimes they broke through, submerging the sled and many of the trailing dogs, and when they made it across, all their gear was soaked and the dogs would huddle and whine, their fur coated with icicles.

Working together, Bartlett and Kataktovik could get a serviceable igloo built in about forty-five minutes. After cutting blocks enough for a few layers, they'd roof the igloo with their tent and weight it down with pemmican tins, snowshoes, and more heavy blocks, then shovel lighter snow on top. Then they would crawl in, with just enough headroom to sit up and boil water for tea and a gruel of pemmican and seal meat. Even though they were exhausted by the end of each day, it was hard to sleep with the wail of the winds, which flapped the tent roof and more than once tore it completely off, so they had to run out onto the ice in the middle of the night and leap on it before it blew away. And there was the constant fear of the ice splitting right beneath them; so they lay fully clothed, curled together for some body heat, shaking and trembling in a half-dozed stupor.

Dealing with the dogs became an ongoing ordeal. They were so hungry that they chewed everything: sled lashings, skin clothing, pemmican tins; they even tried to chew through the canvas sled cover to get at the dead seal. They chewed their densely woven hemp harnesses and got free. One morning, somehow the whole team broke loose and started trotting back in the direction of Wrangel Island. Bartlett hurried to the sled and grabbed a couple of pemmican tins. He jogged after the dogs, calling them by their names and waving the tins. They were now about a half mile from the igloo. If the dogs left them stranded out on the ice, Bartlett knew they were doomed. Using a soothing voice, Bartlett managed to lure them back with the pemmican, and he rewarded them with extra rations, though he feared they'd soon run out. After that incident, each night they'd tie the dogs' snouts shut so they could not chew off their harnesses.

The days blurred into one another. Fog rose from open leads like sea smoke, the ice and snow and skies melding together. Always they were strafed by strong winds. Bartlett occasionally halted, wiped off his snow goggles, and squinted at his compass to ensure they were still bearing south. Then on they trudged. One day they stopped at about five o'clock to build their igloo. Kataktovik was cutting ice blocks and Bartlett was knocking snow and ice off their sleeping robes when suddenly Kataktovik began waving his arms and yelling. Bartlett turned and right next to the sled, just a few feet away, was an enormous polar bear. Bartlett reached for his rifle and chambered a round and fired in one smooth motion. He'd acted so quickly that even at point-blank range, he missed, and the bear rose and stood at the noise, towering above them. Bartlett ratcheted the bolt and fired again, hitting the bear in the front shoulder. The great creature went down with a concussive thud on the ice. Bartlett fired a third time to make sure. He crept near after a few minutes and studied the largest bear he'd seen in twenty years in the Arctic, nearly twelve feet long. Its thick, short hair, white as the snow, waved in the wind. It must have been very old, Bartlett reckoned.

As Kataktovik finished the igloo, Bartlett hacked off a hindquarter, wishing they could carry more but knowing it would make the sled too heavy. They ate some of the meat raw, standing there over the bear, blood running down their chins and freezing, then took some of the fresh meat inside the igloo to boil into a stew. Later, they went outside and cut hunks from the carcass and fed the dogs as much as they could eat. Bartlett could hardly believe that the dogs had not barked, had made no noise at the bear's arrival. Apparently, they'd been too exhausted to even notice or care about it. This gave the captain pause, for he figured the bear must have been tracking them all day, likely following the scent of the seal they'd killed earlier. The next morning, they packed up and bore south with the bloody hindquarter lashed to the sled. Bartlett looked back over his shoulder from time to time, chills running through him: every hummock, every boulder of ice resembled the outline of a bear.

But it was only ice.

26

RATIONING AND DIVISIONS

ON WRANGEL ISLAND, THINGS HAD STARTED TO UNRAVEL THE MO-
ment Bartlett left. McKinlay, understanding the implications of Munro,
Breddy, and Clam's failure to reach Shipwreck Camp, began rationing his
group's food to five biscuits per day and one pound of pemmican. This put
everyone in a foul humor, and since the stormy weather and the mystery
illness kept everyone inside, there was ample time for grousing and petty
arguments.

McKinlay noticed that Templeman, prone to exaggeration in the best
of times, had developed "an unbridled tongue and a capacity for lying."
He was no doubt frayed by narcotic and nicotine withdrawal, having run
out of each at some point—though no one knew exactly when. Now, like
the Eskimos, he was rolling cigarettes out of fresh tea leaves, wasting valuable tea by smoking rather than drinking it. This troubled McKinlay, but
at present he mentioned it only in his diary, not wanting to fuel further
discord. Malloch did not appear to be suffering physically, but, wrote
McKinlay, "he lacked all vitality and had little interest in what went on
around him." Chafe and Williamson remained very ill, and with food
running short already and tempers flaring, McKinlay knew that it would
take all his efforts to keep Shore Camp at Icy Spit from descending into
anarchy. He worried that he would not be up to the task: "A good leader
might have brought out the best in everybody—Captain Bartlett had

proved that. But on our own the misery and desperation of our situation multiplied every weakness, every quirk of personality, every flaw in character a thousandfold."

The best thing to do, the essential thing, was to get the parties separated and set up at their different camps as soon as possible. Munro, wanting to follow Captain Bartlett's instructions, planned to make a trip with McKinlay to Herald Island as soon as the weather broke. They'd promised to look for Sandy's party one last time, and they intended to honor that pledge. It was also agreed that Mamen, Malloch, and Templeman would leave for Rodger's Harbor. McKinlay argued that the distance there—around seventy miles—separated them too much from everyone else, but Mamen and the other two were adamant. Perhaps they wanted to be there because it was the place set forth for their eventual rescue. McKinlay, once again hoping to keep relations amicable, finally agreed, as did Munro, who was at least nominally in charge. A concession was made that Kuraluk would go with them, so he knew exactly where they had camped. Once they'd settled on a spot, he and Mamen would return to Shore Camp to prepare for another attempt to reach Shipwreck Camp and bring back more food. McKinlay and Munro proposed, and all parties agreed, that none of the planned trips should last more than a week, because any longer would stress their food resources—particularly those of the dogs.

On March 21, the weather improved and with it the mood at Shore Camp. They felt the first warm sun in as long as they could remember. Helen and little Mugpi came outside to play, giving Nigeraurak a break from their constant teasing. "The presence of the little children," wrote Chafe in his journal, "created a sort of domestic influence on our frigid quarters. Their play and prattle gave courage to the men, and helped us to forget the dangers that were daily surrounding us."

Williamson and Breddy surfaced from the hospital igloo and walked around; they were still stiff and crampy, they said, but their swollen limbs were improving, to everyone's relief. McKinlay, with calm but stern urging, even managed to roust Malloch and Templeman and get them out into the fresh air. He encouraged them to dry their clothing and skin beddings while the sun was out, and on racks next to the driftwood fire they kept constantly aflame. Wandering around, Templeman stumbled upon a bird feather and brought it back to show everyone. No one could identify the bird, not even Kuraluk or Auntie, but all hoped it was a good sign.

McKinlay and Munro left two days later, taking five dogs and seven days' half rations for the animals, plus man-pemmican and biscuits for eight days. Before they departed to search for Sandy's party, they helped Mamen load his sled and harness nine dogs for his journey south to Rodger's Harbor. Then they said goodbye and headed out in separate directions.

McKinlay and Munro moved well for nearly ten miles, with just a whiff of light easterly breeze in their faces, but then "the light breeze freshened to a moderate gale, and visibility was cut to a few yards in the dense, drifting snow." Then they ran into pressure ridges too high and uneven to get the dogs and sled over. They bore south a few miles and managed to find a route through, then pushed on across rubble ice alternating with thigh-deep snow that slowed them to barely two hundred yards per hour. By the afternoon—traveling solely by compass, as they could see neither the sun nor any island—they'd made an arduous fifteen miles. They were exhausted, and the snow was poor and wouldn't bind together well, so it took them two hours to make their igloo. They had strength enough only to make tea and bolt down some pemmican; then they slept.

For the next two days, they kept on in the same manner, climbing over ridges fifteen to twenty feet high, with deep, blown snow collecting in the valleys between them. At times their vision was reduced to twenty yards, and they tucked their chins and ducked their heads against the biting snow as they stumbled along. By the evening of March 26, they were forced into the lee of a high hummock for shelter, and they spent the night crouched there, hugging one another for warmth until dawn. In the pinkening morning light, the winds subsided enough for them to brew some tea and they agreed to try for a high pressure ridge they could now see in the distance, hoping they'd be able to see something beyond it.

They climbed a pinnacle some twenty-five feet high, and there, perhaps fifteen miles distant, was Herald Island. But between them and the island spread "an impenetrable barrier of pressure ridges" that appeared to extend all the way from Wrangel Island to Herald Island. They recalled the recent backbreaking road cutting, which took many men, and agreed they could go no farther; even with fresh dogs and unlimited food, they could never pick their way through this chaos of ice. From the highest hummock they could ascend, they glassed the northwestern end of Herald Island with powerful binoculars. "We could see the terrible ridges stretching right to the island," McKinlay wrote in his diary, "We could see all along the base of the near vertical cliffs, right up and down the western side. Nowhere could we detect the least sign of anything resembling an encampment, not even on the flattish part of what the chart showed as a sandspit." McKinlay talked it over with Munro and they agreed that if Sandy's party had tried to make it from Herald to Wrangel Island, "they must have been engulfed in the inferno of ice."

By McKinlay's rough reckoning, he and Munro had traveled about thirty-five miles, and now they had to find their way back before they ran out of food. They opened the last tins of pemmican and fed the dogs their measly half rations, then started back. Their trail remained partly visible and intact, so they were able to move faster than they had in coming. Through cloud breaks they sometimes saw Wrangel Island's humpbacked silhouette in the distance, and that drove them onward. The dogs were now slat ribbed and weak, sometimes buckling to their knees. One of them toppled over and they unharnessed it and lifted it onto the sled. Near midnight, they finally dragged themselves into Shore Camp on Icy Spit.

Once they'd warmed by the driftwood fire and had some tea, they learned that Kuraluk had recently shot a bear and its two cubs. The next morning, Kuraluk and Munro went out to bring in the bears. McKinlay could not believe Munro's strength and stamina. After their five-day slog, McKinlay could barely get up. He raised himself to a sitting position, then slumped back down. At first, he thought it was just deep fatigue from their labors, but the aching in his joints felt more like a severe bout of influenza. His feet were so cold he worried he might have frozen them beyond hope, and when he took off his mukluks and stockings to examine them, they weren't frostbitten; instead, they'd swollen grotesquely. Throughout the day, they bloated to twice their normal size as he lay moaning and writhing on damp skins. That night, they feasted on roasted bear meat and bear broth, which McKinlay relished as "a welcome relief from the nauseating pemmican which had been our staple diet since arriving on the island." The meat of the cub was so tender it reminded McKinlay of veal. He sat up and checked his feet again, relieved that the swelling seemed to have stopped, at least for now, at his ankles.

Mamen straggled in alone after dinner. Through short breaths, he said he'd made it as far as Skeleton Island—about three-quarters of the way to Rodger's Harbor—but Malloch had been too weak to go any farther. His illness had returned. Mamen decided to leave Malloch in Templeman's care and come back north to Shore Camp, hoping to go along on the attempt to Shipwreck Camp.

Munro announced that he, Clam, and Chafe would try one last time to get food and fuel from Shipwreck Camp. He told Mamen that it was more important for him to return to Skeleton Island to assist Malloch and Templeman. Mamen was disappointed, but he did not question Munro's decision and he had to admit that the two could barely take care of themselves. They needed his help.

On the morning of April 1, Mamen was packed up and ready to go. He'd wanted to pull one of the Peary sleds, but when he tried, it proved too heavy. Instead, he cleverly fashioned a pair of his skis, some rope, and a few pieces of drifted lumber he'd found into a sleigh big and stable enough to haul but considerably lighter than the Peary sled. He loaded the ski-sleigh with a hefty bear ham, a rucksack, three skins, a footbag, a snow knife, rations of pemmican and tea, and started off. McKinlay wished he could go with him, promising he'd be down to check on Mamen and the others as soon as he was able.

Later in the morning, Munro, Clam, and Chafe also readied to depart. As they lashed provisions and gear on two Peary sleds, the eleven dogs they were taking on the trip started barking and raising their snouts in the air. A large bear was ambling toward camp, but the barking dogs and movement at camp startled the animal, which loped away. Many of the dogs, not yet harnessed, bolted after the bear. Kuraluk grabbed his rifle, and he and Hadley set off in pursuit. About seven miles from camp, Kuraluk spotted the bear and crept close enough to bring it down with one shot. Hoping for success, Breddy, Maurer, and Williamson had followed along with a sled, and later that afternoon, everyone returned, the dogs having been caught, harnessed, and now pulling the sled loaded with the dead bear.

It took some time to swap out the dogs, but Munro, Chafe, and Clam wanted to start for Shipwreck Camp, so they rewarded the dogs with fresh bear scraps and let them rest awhile, then bade farewell to the others and started their journey, hoping the camp would still be standing and would not have drifted away. They'd estimated a trip of at least eighty miles one way, so it was an ambitious and risky undertaking. As they departed, McKinlay lay in the hospital igloo, racked with swollen, aching limbs and joints, the mysterious malaise now coursing through his body.

27

FERRYING

CAPTAIN BARTLETT TOOK OFF HIS SNOW GOGGLES, WIPING THE
condensed ice from the lenses, and squinted at the open lead before him.
The dogs barked and backed away, frightened. Kataktovik was coming
back from a foray to find a better place to cross; he appeared just a dark
fleck against a universe of white. He arrived shaking his head. Nothing
better in that direction. Bartlett had spent an hour scouting in the opposite direction and found no narrower place either. They'd have to cross
here.

It had been like this in the days since shooting the bear: lead after lead,
unloading and crossing and ferrying and reloading again. They'd march
forward for a time, and then come to another lead. It was tedious, tiring,
and slow. And the winds and snow had kept on, so that as Bartlett surveyed
their gear, "everything was white; boxes, bags, sleeping-robes, all the objects, in fact, were blended into the one dead tone." But they had to get it all
across. The present lead was wider than Bartlett would have liked, but there
was some young ice jutting outward toward the other side, with tongues
of drifted snow forming a sort of bridge, and Bartlett had an idea. He
remembered a technique for crossing leads he'd seen as a boy working with
Newfoundland whalers. First, he tied a rope around Kataktovik's waist so
he could pull him out if he fell in. Then he took tent poles from the sled
and, because Kataktovik was lighter, had him walk as far out on the young
ice with the poles as he could. Kataktovik lay the tent poles across, spanning

the open water. Slowly and carefully, Kataktovik got down on his belly and crawled, slithering across the tent poles and snow bridge to the other side.

Bartlett had unloaded most of the sled, leaving just a small load. Two ropes were tied at either end. Kataktovik held a rope tied to the stern, and he eased the partially loaded sled across, unloaded it, and Bartlett hauled it back empty. He placed more items in it and they repeated the process, again and again, until all the stores and gear were safely on Kataktovik's side. All but one dog made it across on their own. The last, Kaiser, had a habit of running off, so Bartlett tethered his collar to the sled, and Kataktovik pulled him over.

Bartlett went last. He lay facedown on the sled and told Kataktovik to sling the rope over his shoulders and run as fast as he could. Kataktovik sprinted and the sled sped over the ice, the runners breaking through, water splashing Bartlett in the face. With the sound of cracking ice and the sled runners submerging, Bartlett feared he might go under, but Kataktovik ran hard, looking over his shoulder until the captain was jostling along on rough ice on the other side.

The procedure, including the time they'd spent looking for a better place to cross, had taken a couple of hours. Bartlett checked the compass, snapped on his snow goggles, whistled the dogs on, and they moved south once more. The drifts ahead appeared level, but in the flat, monochromatic light, they could detect no contours and tumbled into depressions, tripping over raised patches of ice, pitching headlong in light so weird and confusing that, according to Bartlett, "the effect on the eye was as if one were walking in the dark instead of what passed technically for daylight."

Bartlett's eyes burned and ached. He feared becoming completely snow-blind and reminded himself to always keep the snow goggles on now. His throat ached with thirst, but he knew he must wait until evening when they camped. It took too long to stop and melt snow for one drink of water, and the prevalence of leads was increasing, slowing them down. They came to one maw of water about three hundred yards wide. Bartlett shook his head. The lead snaked east to west for a great distance. As they were about to split up in their usual way to find a narrower gap, Bartlett noticed something. Protruding from the northern edge of the lead was a large floe, with a fault line of young ice binding it to the main floe on which they stood. Using ice axes, they chopped away at the weaker young ice, jumping up and down on it to break it loose. They pried the ice island free with tent poles, then boarded the ten-foot-square cake, easing the dogs and sled on and urging them to the center. Bartlett and Kataktovik knelt on either side of the little ice floe and, using their snowshoes as paddles, propelled themselves until they were safe on the southern ice shore.

The days grew longer, the sun breaking through occasionally, making the temperature feel "almost springlike." The warming temperatures worried Bartlett; he feared they'd bring even more open water, but for almost a full day, they had good conditions and made the most consecutive miles since they'd been out on the sea ice, which was nine days. When they finally halted and made their igloo, Bartlett felt confident that they were on a thick and solid floe, with less fear of it splitting beneath them. They slept soundly for the first time in almost two weeks.

The whining and yipping dogs startled them as they sipped their morning tea. Bartlett slammed his fist through the igloo wall; a column of light poured in, blinding him as he tried to look out. But Kataktovik was already belly-crawling out the door, rifle in hand. Bartlett followed. A big bear was cantering away. Kataktovik sprinted after it, then skidded to a stop, leveled the rifle, and fired two shots, dropping him. They took only one hindquarter—it was all they could safely carry—and treated the dogs to some fresh meat as well. In improving light, they struck camp and moved on, chewing on raw bear meat as they went.

Late on the evening of March 30, Captain Bartlett stood on a slight rise of ice, trying to see through his binoculars. It had been the finest day since leaving Wrangel Island twelve days before, the sky cerulean and cloudless, with rose-colored hues at the fringes of his periphery. Bartlett strained to see ahead, but the light sent jabs of pain into his eyes, and he winced, shut them, and looked away.

He waved Kataktovik over and handed him the binoculars, pointing toward the southern horizon. "That land?" he asked.

Kataktovik looked for a few moments, then nodded. "Might be," he said, but he sounded dubious. That night, Bartlett showed Kataktovik the charts in the pilot book again, tracing his finger from Wrangel Island and along the approximate route to where he believed them to be, then showing where they were going. Kataktovik bristled now, a look of worry on his face.

Bartlett asked him what was wrong. In broken English, Kataktovik explained that since he was a boy, he had been told that Alaskan Eskimos were killed if they landed on Siberian shores. He did not want to go there. Bartlett poured him hot tea, assuring him that he had nothing to fear. The people there were kind and would treat them well.

They got up before sunrise, and Bartlett climbed a nearby ridge. His eyes were much improved from the night's sleep, and he looked through the binoculars just as the sun crested the eastern horizon, casting long bands of salmon-colored light across the ice. There, maybe forty miles south, a dark, shadowy mass rose from the frozen plain, its heights capped with snow.

28

LITTLE MOLLY

MUNRO AND CHAFE TURNED AROUND WHEN THEY HEARD CLAM shouting and watched, through blurry tears of snow blindness, as Clam broke through and plunged neck-deep into the water. Clam's dogs pawed furiously, churning up slush at the edge of the young ice, and Clam clung to the sled handles and cried out for help. Munro grabbed a long bamboo pole from his sled, and as fast as they could, he and Chafe maneuvered over the thin ice behind him to try to reach Clam before it was too late. Just as they were about to reach him, the ice cracked and gave way, and they, too, fell through up to their waists, grasping at the ice behind them just in time to keep from going all the way under.

Somehow Munro and Chafe managed to wriggle back onto firm ice. They held out the pole and Clam reached for it and got hold and, pulling together as if in a tug-of-war, they hoisted Clam out of the water. Then all three clutched at the harnesses of the dogs and pulled the soaked, whimpering animals out, followed at last by the waterlogged sled. Clam had been in the water for nearly three minutes, and now he stood, teeth chattering, unable to speak.

Chafe saw that Clam must have lost his fur mittens in the water, for his hands were bare. He quickly gave Clam his own mittens and dug into his gear for a spare pair of wool gloves and put them on. All three men were now wet, and they knew they must move fast to try to get warm again.

They brushed off the dogs, got the sleds squared away, and continued toward Wrangel Island.

All three men, to some degree, were now snow-blind. Munro, Chafe, and Clam staggered slowly forward, forty-five miles from Shore Camp. They were reduced to having one man lead with the dogs while the other two held on to the sled handles and stumbled along with their eyes shut, pulled by the leader and the dogs. It had taken a week of brutal sledding to get here, moving at less than a mile an hour, to the other side of the great ice wall. But in the end, they'd come to an immense expanse of open water and could go no farther. They'd given everything they had— and nearly their lives—but they would not make it to Shipwreck Camp. They'd turned back, and now they were soaked and freezing and low on food and fuel, the dogs famished and hardly able to pull the two sleds. They'd lost a rifle when the sled broke through the ice, along with Chafe's best binoculars, which he'd won in a long-range shooting contest when he was only sixteen. But they had bigger worries now.

Ice floes drifted all around them, leads opening in spidery webs everywhere. Chafe saw a short gap and leaped it, landing on the other side. He reached behind him, grabbed hold of Munro's dogs, and heaved them and the sled across. Munro turned around and helped Clam with his sled, but by the time they got back to the gap, it had widened to over ten feet—too far to jump across. Chafe yelled for them to work around the lead and try to meet him, but the floe he was on had broken free and was drifting farther away from them. Within minutes, they were separated by three hundred yards. He could hear Munro yelling something, but the distance and the sound of roiling ice drowned out his words. Fog and mist settled around Chafe until finally he could not see them anymore.

Chafe tried not to panic. He jumped up and down to stay warm, clapped his hands together, slapped his chest and arms and thighs. Then he assessed the situation. He had five dogs, a sled, and all the remaining food. Munro and Clam had a sled and six dogs, but none of the food. He figured they would try to find him, but as he thought about their condition, he hoped they would hurry on toward Shore Camp. Clam was so wet he'd surely freeze to death if he did not keep moving. Chafe looked around, aghast at his predicament. The five dogs had hunkered into a furry pile. The only thing for him to do was build an igloo and try to survive the night. Weakened, half-starved, and nearly hypothermic, his hands freezing in his spare wool gloves, he set to cutting snow blocks. He had only the strength to stack the wall blocks a couple of feet high; then he draped the canvas sled cover over the top and secured it with more ice blocks.

It looked, he thought, more like a coffin than an igloo. He slid in feet-first, keeping his head by the door opening. The excess canvas of the sled cover flapped around his head in the wind. His hands shook as if palsied, but somehow he succeeded in lighting the Primus stove to melt snow. It took a long time to boil, but the stove offered some warmth as he lay curled next to it. The other boys, he realized, had the tea, so he dropped a chunk of pemmican in the boiling water and watched it congeal into a gruel. But it was food, and it was warm, and he felt better as he drank it, the liquid heat emanating into his core.

His frozen clothes crunched as he shifted and shivered. He feared that if he fell asleep, he would never wake up, so he kept his mind active. He worried about Munro and Clam. Had they stayed to search for him, or kept going? He hoped they had gone on, prayed they wouldn't end up like Dr. Mackay and Murray and Beuchat, succumbing to the Arctic's brutal indifference for life. He almost laughed when he remembered that, when the *Karluk* had been crushed, he went to his bunk and took a handful of his athletic and shooting medals along with him to Shipwreck Camp. It had been vain, but now he thought of those happy days just a few years ago, back on warm, dry land. How easy life had been.

Chafe awoke to the ice beneath him raising him up where he lay. He heard crashing and grinding, and chips from the igloo walls fell around him. He had no idea how long he'd been asleep. But now he had to get out of the igloo, or it *would* prove to be his coffin. He snatched up the Primus stove and pemmican can and wriggled his way out the door. The dogs yipped, tangled in their harnesses. Chafe pulled the sled canvas from the crumbling igloo and fixed it over the sled. As he looked around in the brilliant, early morning light, he could see that the winds in the night had shifted and driven back the floe he was on and slammed it into a much larger floe. He quickly untangled the dogs and coaxed them off, and quite miraculously, he was on his way again.

Under clear bright skies and light winds, he searched around in the direction he thought he'd last seen Munro and Clam, but after an hour or so, he found no trace of them. There was no telling how far he'd drifted during the night. He kept his snow goggles on all the time as his eyes still burned and ached. Chafe reckoned that he was still fifteen miles or so from the big pressure ridges; he could see the glinting outline of the first of them out in the distance. He'd head there, and if he was lucky, he might find the old trail they'd carved out in coming from Shipwreck Camp.

The dogs foundered, pulling so listlessly that he advanced only about five miles that day. The next day he worked for eighteen hours, progressing, to his best estimate, another seven miles. Right at sunset, he saw—though it hurt terribly to strain his eyes—what appeared to be one of the pemmican tin markers they'd put up in making the original route. He built another crude igloo and crawled in. He was out of fuel oil, so for fluids, he sucked on bits of ice and handfuls of snow. One of his feet was badly frozen. His hands, too, felt frostbitten, the woolen gloves not nearly so warm as the mittens he'd given to Clam.

He awoke to find the dog Blondie lying dead on the ice. The dogs had not eaten for two days and had been working almost constantly for three months. It was no wonder. Bronco was also gone, having run away, so now he was down to three dogs, which would make pulling the sled through the ridges nearly impossible. Still, he must try. He reached the ridges and found what he thought was the old trail and, using his pickax to pull himself up the sheer faces, worked his way slowly through the hummocky maze. Up and over he trudged, his throat searing with thirst, until late one night—he had lost track of the days—he reached the steep face of the last of the ice ridges. He was too tired to try to get the sled over, so he unhitched the dogs. By some miracle, he found a small cache of dog pemmican they'd left behind on one of the trips before. He fed the dogs twelve pounds between them and hunkered down to rest.

Twilight brought high winds from the southwest. Chafe roused the dogs, harnessed them, and tried to get them to pull up and over the last of the steep walls, but the dogs lay down, turning their heads in defiance. They would pull no more. He'd have to abandon the sled. Reluctantly, he unharnessed the dogs, and taking only a snow knife, a thick woolen blanket, and a pickax, he moved out. He believed that if he did not make it to Wrangel Island in a single march, he would die.

Two of the dogs trotted off ahead. Chafe's eyes were swelling shut with snow blindness, so he got hold of Molly, Hadley's dog, and tied a rope from her collar to his wrist. She was the smallest of all the dogs they'd brought on the *Karluk*, but tough and feisty with a ton of heart. She was also known to be the best trail finder. If Chafe's eyes went completely, maybe she could find the way. She whined at first, trying to run off with the other two dogs, but Chafe spoke softly to her and tugged her back. All through the day and into the evening, Chafe stumbled behind Molly, trusting her nose and instincts. A few times Chafe toppled over, his weak legs buckling beneath him. One fall on sharp ice ripped his pant leg open at the crotch, and the hole filled with snow. After each spill, Molly waited patiently for him to rise from the ice and keep going.

Chafe could no longer feel his hands or feet. It was like walking on wooden stumps. By what appeared to be sunset—he could half detect hues of flaming orange and violet in the periphery of his ice-caked goggles—he realized the dog had been dragging him for the entire day and more, probably fifteen straight hours. It was no use, he thought. At the first shelter from the wind, he would lie down and die. But there was no shelter, and he wrapped the blanket around him, leaned forward, closed his eyes, and followed Molly's tug on his arm.

And then, a few hours later, Chafe felt himself being towed up a gentle incline. He took off his goggles and blinked. There, just ahead, lay what looked like a pile of driftwood. He staggered a few more steps and saw, with his diminished eyesight in the dim light, the outline of a sled. He was on Icy Spit. He fell to his knees and hugged little Molly, thanking her, in a hoarse whisper, for saving his life. In one long, torturous day she'd led Chafe over a rough and serrated snow and ice trail for thirty miles. He untied her from his wrist and patted her on the head, then stood and wobbled toward the Shore Camp.

McKinlay was feeling a good deal improved. That morning he'd been able to get up and leave the hospital igloo and walk around for the first time in over a week. The swelling in his legs had subsided, and he concluded—though he could not be certain—that his improvement was from eating bear meat rather than pemmican for the last week or so. He had a suspicion that there was something wrong with the pemmican that was making them all so sick. It seemed, to his mind, the only common denominator they all shared. What other explanation was there? "I had apparently beaten the mystery malady," he wrote in his diary, "and I felt I would be restored to strength and well-being if we could have other food than pemmican."

McKinlay and Munro—who had just recently returned from an unsuccessful search for Chafe—were sitting in Kuraluk's igloo about to have their evening tea when they heard the dogs barking and saw the canvas door stirring. Then a head poked through, saying, "How about some tea for me?"

It was Chafe! McKinlay and Munro jumped to their feet and went to him. "Is that you, Charlie?" They could hardly believe it. It was April 13—five days since Munro and Clam had watched Chafe float away on the ice cake. He was in terrible shape. Munro quickly embraced him and helped him all the way into the igloo while McKinlay lit a candle and poured a steaming cup of hot tea through Chafe's cracked and bleeding lips. His face was puffy, his eyes swollen shut. His body shuddered and convulsed as they pulled off his skin boots. The socks came off as well, frozen to the boots. They peeled off his fur pants, which were completely packed with snow and had a tear running from the crotch down to the knee.

In the candlelight they looked him over carefully as he gulped down another cup of tea. One toe and the heel of his right foot were badly frostbitten, as was his right hand. McKinlay held the candle while Munro lanced the blisters on Chafe's hands and feet and wrapped them in cloth bandages. They rooted around and found some dry clothes and helped him into them, covering his feet with dry woolen socks. As Chafe sipped his third cup of tea, they began to exchange stories. Chafe lay back onto some skins and listened quietly. After they'd become separated, Munro said, he and Clam had spent a little time looking for him, but because Clam had been soaked to the neck, and since they had none of the food, they knew their only chance was to hurry back to Shore Camp as quickly as possible. To move faster, they'd abandoned their sled as well as the dogs and traveled south, spending that entire first night walking up and down a short hill, jogging back and forth, doing wind sprints—anything to keep from freezing.

The next morning they'd continued south, plowing through deep snow and across the ridges for forty-eight hours until, by sheer luck, they'd lurched onto the shore at Icy Spit and nearly fell into the hospital igloo. "The soles of Clam's boots were worn almost through," McKinlay said, "and his feet were in extremely bad shape. For hours we took turns at rubbing them and nursing them against our stomachs to try and restore circulation."

After that, Chafe told of his ordeal alone on the ice: how Providence had landed his fractured floe back where he could get off; and how little Molly had led him home. They remained awake for hours, joyous to be reunited, chatting back and forth, recalling details of their trials and asking questions, until one by one, as the candle flickered out, they drifted off to sleep.

29

SMOKE FROM A DISTANT FIRE

CAPTAIN BARTLETT SAT UP WHEN HE HEARD THE ICE CRACKING just outside the igloo. Pain shot through his ribs where he'd fallen on a sharp wedge of ice a couple of days before. Part of the igloo was crumbling, and he and Kataktovik bear-crawled out to have a look, though it was so dark they could see only the outline of a fissure about two feet wide running right next to the igloo. The dogs yelped and whirled around in terrified circles. Working in starlight, they untethered the dogs to let them run loose. Kataktovik fumbled around in the dark, handing items from the igloo that the captain then lashed to the sled. The night was clear and cold, about –50ºF, Bartlett reckoned, though he had no thermometer. But in two decades of Arctic venturing, he'd become pretty accurate in his estimations of temperature. At least there was no wind.

It was too dark to travel yet, so he and Kataktovik and the dogs stood there all night, waiting for daybreak. Periodically, Bartlett hopped up and down, shadowboxed, did calisthenics in place to keep warm. At dawn he fired up the Primus, and they warmed some bear meat and pemmican and drank tea. Bartlett cursed aloud; he'd thought they were through with ice splitting beneath them in the middle of the night, but he'd been wrong. Still, nothing had been lost, and the dogs, other than being haggard and famished, were all right. The last few days of lead-hopping and load-ferrying and pickaxing through rafted ice had been tough. Now, by his best estimate, they were only fifteen miles from land, and he knew that if the ice would cooperate and they stayed cautious and vigilant, they would make it.

But the ice was not cooperating. All around them it ground and heaved and moaned. They had to move. All day long they picked their way south. Bartlett's eyes still hurt, and he wore his spare pair of snow goggles, having shattered the lens of his favorite pair in the fall that had bruised his ribs. Working slowly, winding cautiously, they found some larger floes, and the going was smooth until late afternoon, when offshore condensation diminished their vision to a few yards. The ice was moving too much for Bartlett's liking, so they stopped and built an igloo and, after a restless night of worrying, rose early.

The light and visibility were good, but the captain saw rough terrain ahead. They'd have to pickax through the heaving ridges. Bartlett left Kataktovik and the sled and dogs and went up ahead and climbed a high rafter. Beyond the rafter, an open lead shimmered in the morning light, and just past the lead he saw the ice foot: shore ice permanently attached to the land and protruding some distance into the sea. He went back and told Kataktovik to get ready for some hard work, and by midmorning they were cutting their way, making a road through the rough belts of raised ice that ran east to west, parallel with the mainland shore.

At the last big lead, they found a place where the moving ice they were on came right up to the projecting tongue of the shore ice. It was the best place to cross over, but the dogs were unsettled, afraid to cross. Yelling and snapping at them with the long bamboo pole, Bartlett tried to force them to jump over, but they wouldn't budge. Some lay down on their bellies and whined, and others skittered away. The gap started widening, and Bartlett saw that the floe they were on was drifting—so he quickly pulled out his knife and cut the traces and in one swift move leaped over to the other side, pulling the sled across by himself. He tossed Kataktovik a rope, and the Eskimo ran a few steps and leaped as Bartlett yanked him through the air. The dogs, not wanting to be left behind, came right to the edge, and Bartlett and Kataktovik reached over and got hold of the traces and pulled them to their side.

Bartlett plopped onto his butt in the snow and laughed a deep, guttural laugh. "We were now on land ice," he wrote, "free from open water, and had only rafters, rough ice, and deep snow to contend with." Bartlett sent Kataktovik ahead to find a route through the band of ice ridges while he and the dogs rested. While Kataktovik was gone, Bartlett studied the *Coast Pilot*, trying to determine where they would be making land. He thought back to evenings on the *Karluk* when he'd looked over one of the books in the library, *The Voyage of the* Vega *Round Asia and Europe* by Adolf Erik Nordenskiöld, the Finnish-Swedish aristocrat and explorer. The translation on the *Karluk* had been in German, which Bartlett could not read, but he'd thumbed through the volume many times, looking carefully at the pictures. From what he remembered of the images, "the woods extended in places down to the shore and reindeer lived in the woods." Bartlett could still see only ice and snow, but he hoped there would be reindeer.

He took off his mittens for a minute to thumb through the pages of the pilot book. "The northeast coast of Siberia has been only slightly examined," he read, squinting and blinking at the burning sensation, "and the charts must be taken as sketches and only approximately accurate." Bartlett knew that the coast had first been surveyed by Captain James Cook in 1778; then again by Admiral von Wrangel forty-two years later. Nordenskiöld sailed along the coast near here in 1878, and finally, Lieutenant Hooper, aboard the USRC *Thomas Corwin*, had come here searching for De Long and the lost *Jeannette* in 1881. Bartlett put away the pilot book and stuffed his hands back into his mittens. What the book didn't tell him, and what really interested him, was the nature of the Native people he hoped to meet along the coast. How many were there? How did they live? What did they eat? Were they friendly?

Kataktovik came trotting up, his fur pants covered with fresh snow up to the thighs. He'd found a way through, but they'd need to use their snowshoes. They got out their pickaxes and started hacking a trail through the rough ice. After about four hours, they'd carved a route wide enough for the sled, and Bartlett went back and brought the dogs forward. On the other side of the last high ice ridge, they put on their snowshoes. Kataktovik watched with concern as Bartlett pulled back the canvas sled cover and started tossing heavy items off, leaving enough food for only one day. But the captain felt confident that once on land, they'd find people or game or both, and with the dogs nearly played out, he believed the lighter load necessary.

They clomped along through deep, powdery snow, the snowshoes working brilliantly. By late afternoon, they clomped up the last of the land-fast ice, picked their way through a gap in the ice foot, and stood on the Siberian coast. It was April 4, 1914. Bartlett grinned and shook Kataktovik hard by his shoulders, then sank to his knees. He patted the snow-covered ground with his mittens, breathing thick plumes of condensation into the frigid air. The two had trudged for seventeen days since leaving Icy Spit on Wrangel Island and, by Bartlett's calculations, traveled about two hundred miles. He could not be sure exactly where they had landed,* but he knew for certain, based on his estimates, that they still had many hundreds of miles to go to reach the far eastern coast of Siberia, where he might find a ship to take them to Alaska to seek rescue ships. As difficult as his journey had already been, he knew they were less than a third of the way to their destination. They would need help.

Clouds closed in and snow began to fall, light at first, then heavily. Winds were picking up, so although there was daylight left, Bartlett decided to make camp. As they started cutting snow blocks, Kataktovik pointed to the ground nearby. There, running east along the tundra, were the distinct tracks of a single sled, and dog prints beneath those. Someone had been here recently.

The next morning, their stomachs full from the last of their bear meat, Bartlett and Kataktovik struck camp and started east. Wind had blown the tundra bare in places, but they were able to follow the lone set of sled tracks well enough. The dogs were in terrible condition; of the four

---

* Based on Bartlett's later descriptions of the place, he seems to have landed on the north Siberian coast near Laguna Kyanygtokynmankyn, about sixty miles northwest of Mys Shmidta (Cape Schmidt), which had been his intended landing point.

remaining, only one really seemed to be pulling. Fortunately, compared with the terrible terrain on the ice, the going was smooth. At one point, Kataktovik halted, put his hand up, and nodded his head upward, nosing the air. He said he smelled woodsmoke. Bartlett couldn't smell anything, but he trusted that Kataktovik was right, and hoped it was smoke from a Native settlement.

They'd been walking for about five hours, with Kataktovik up ahead scouting the trail, when the hunter jogged back toward Bartlett, waving his arms. His face looked worried. "Eskimo igloo!" he said, pointing through a clearing in the trees. Bartlett fixed his eyes and could just make out, against a backdrop of white, a group of small black objects. As he stared, he saw that they were moving. Bartlett started walking again, but Kataktovik lingered behind, reluctant to continue. The captain went back and asked Kataktovik what was the matter.

"Eskimo see me, they kill me," he said. "My father, my mother told me long time ago Eskimo from Point Barrow go to Siberia, never come back. Siberian Eskimo kill him." Bartlett eased up to Kataktovik and told him it would be fine. He assured him that no harm would come to them and that they'd be treated kindly. They might even get tobacco and more dogs. Bartlett said he intended to try to get some of the Native inhabitants to travel with them, showing them the way. He'd brought money for this purpose. It took some convincing, but finally Kataktovik agreed to go on, though he remained well behind Bartlett.

As they drew closer, Bartlett saw that the objects moving about were indeed people: "They were running about, apparently very much excited by our approach," he wrote. Three hide-covered huts stood clustered in the distance. Kataktovik was now very tentative, bringing the dogs to a halt. Bartlett told him to stay there, and he would approach first. When Bartlett came within ten yards of the people, he put out his hand and greeted them in English with a big smile. "How do you do?" he said. After a short pause, more people came forward. They were friendly, and Bartlett waved for Kataktovik to follow on. "They immediately rushed towards us and grasped us warmly by the hand, jabbering away in great excitement." Neither Bartlett nor Kataktovik could understand their language, but through their actions, they welcomed the weary travelers. They unharnessed the ragged dogs and fed them, pulling the sled around to the outside of their small wooden house and lifting it up onto a scaffold and under an awning, where it would be out of the dogs' reach and protected from the weather.

As men attended the dogs and sled, a hunched, wrinkled elderly woman grasped Bartlett by his forearm and led him inside a low-roofed dwelling; Kataktovik followed close behind. Once inside, the woman brushed snow from their clothes with a wooden sickle-shaped implement, then lay a reindeer-skin rug out on a wooden platform and indicated that Bartlett and Kataktovik sit down. Bartlett banged his head on the ceiling as he stepped farther inside, and when he was seated, the woman quickly bent and removed his boots and stockings and hung them on the wall near the fire to dry. Another woman attended to Kataktovik. Each man was stripped of his fur jacket and undershirt and given a pair of dry deerskin stockings.

Within a few minutes, Bartlett and Kataktovik sat shirtless and bare chested inside a warm Chukchi yaranga, the walls framed with hefty pieces of driftwood. Bartlett noticed that the dome-shaped roof was constructed of saplings, over which was stretched thick walrus skins. Three lamps burned in the hut, and he saw that there were a dozen or so people inside the large, square room, huddled around on raised pallets against the walls. The pallets were made of turf cut from the tundra, then covered by tanned walrus skins. In the center was a big wooden bowl, brimming with chunks of reindeer meat. Soon the old woman brought steaming tea and a setting of fine china cups and saucers, which Bartlett assumed the Chukchi had acquired from traders. The tiny cups were wrapped in soiled cloth, and the woman took two cups, spat in them, then wiped them out to clean them.

The old woman poured tea for Bartlett and Kataktovik, which she refilled the moment their cups were empty. Then she motioned for them to eat, pointing at the bowl of reindeer meat. Bartlett picked up a piece, and though it was cold and uncooked, he enjoyed the gamey flavor. Next the woman brought a large bowl of walrus meat, which smelled putrid to Bartlett. He tried some, but the flavor was too potent, and he went back to the reindeer. Kataktovik dug into the walrus, relishing the taste he had not had in so many months.

For hours, as the yaranga grew hotter and hotter, they ate and drank tea. Men came and went, and children hovered around, giggling and whispering and pointing at Kataktovik, which made him nervous. The children were sent into an adjoining room separated by a hanging cloth curtain. A man came in and offered them tobacco, handing them pipes with long stems and small bowls. They formally exchanged their names. Through gestures and intonation, they indicated that they wished to know where Bartlett and Kataktovik had come from. Kataktovik tried to speak with the Chukchi but without success, so different were their languages

Bartlett finally took out his pilot book and charts, a pencil, and a box of matches. First, he pointed to Wrangel Island on the map, and with his finger, traced a line from there down to where he believed they were. Then, using matches and forming them into the shape of a ship, he tried to depict the *Karluk*. This confused the men, so instead Bartlett drew a ship with pencil on the chart, surrounded by lines suggesting ice and icebergs, then clapped his hands loudly and erased the ship outline, trying to convey that the ship had been destroyed by the ice. This worked, and the men nodded and voiced their understanding.

Using inquisitive looks and shoulder shrugs, Bartlett tried to ascertain whether there were more settlements like this one along the way. He drew pictures of reindeer, trees, and yarangas on the chart along the coastline toward the east, and lay matches end to end from west to east, indicating that he wanted to go in that direction. One man nodded and tapped his finger on the chart excitedly at the location of Cape North, suggesting people lived there. He also drew a little line to show that the reindeer and herders traveled great distances inland, into the interior.

From what Bartlett could understand, there were coastal people, who subsisted on seals, bears, and walrus; and there were interior people, reindeer herders who traveled inland to the taiga and kept large herds. Their hosts were coastal and built their yarangas close to rivers, where they could catch salmon and trout and have easy access to fresh water. After hours of food and tea and tobacco and pantomime, Bartlett was exhausted, but he persisted in indicating, as clearly as he could, that he and Kataktovik needed to travel east as soon as possible. It was unclear whether his desire was fully communicated, but he decided, if necessary, tomorrow he would harness the dogs to the sled and point them east, which he assumed would get the message across.

Around midnight, everyone—the men, women, and children—all piled onto a large central platform bed. Bartlett and Kataktovik found room at the edges. Smoke from the oil lanterns, the pipe tobacco, and a small cookstove filled the poorly ventilated hut, burning Bartlett's eyes. Incessant coughing came from all quarters. Although he was bone-weary from the grueling seventeen days it had taken to get here, he struggled to sleep, thinking about the *Karluk* survivors on Wrangel Island. "I thought about them all the time," the captain wrote in his diary. "And I worried about them; I wondered how the storms which had so delayed our progress across Long Strait had affected Munro's chances of retrieving the supplies . . . from Shipwreck Camp and getting safely back to the main party, and how the men would find life on the island as the weeks went by and they separated according to my instructions for the hunting which would sooner or later have to be their main dependence."

With these worries consuming his thoughts, Bartlett determined they must rise early. The sled would need some repairs, as would the harnesses, and he hoped the four dogs would have revived enough for the journey ahead, which he estimated to be at least another five hundred miles. There was no time to waste, for the lives of fifteen shipwrecked people depended on him.

30

SEPARATION AND SURGERIES

AT SHORE CAMP, CLAM'S BIG TOE ON HIS LEFT FOOT WAS GANGRE-
nous, black and necrotic. The infection had yet to spread beyond the toe,
but McKinlay and Williamson looked it over carefully and agreed it must
be amputated. If the infection spread, there was the risk he'd lose his entire
foot; worse, he might develop sepsis and die.

McKinlay rooted around for surgical tools. The best he could find consisted of a skinning knife, a broken piece of an old hacksaw blade, and
a pair of tin shears they'd recently used to cut cook pots out of empty
fuel cans. He settled on the tin shears and then boiled snow to sterilize
them. They had no painkillers or anesthetics because Hadley, who was
the keeper of their meager medical stores (which included a small stock of
morphine), was out hunting with Kuraluk. McKinlay did not know where
Hadley kept his stock and was reluctant to go through his things. Engineer Williamson offered to perform the surgery. With wind screaming
outside the hospital igloo, McKinlay and two others held Clam down, one
on each arm and torso, and a third held his head to the side to keep him
from seeing what was happening.

Williamson knelt by Clam's festering foot, operating by candlelight.
He opened the shears and slid them around the toe just above the joint.
The shears were dull from cutting metal, and as Williamson clamped
them shut, they seized when he first hit bone. He rose up and put one

knee on top of his hands as he held the handle, using his full weight to snap the shears shut. Clam's lips were taut and the muscles in his cheeks twitched, but he uttered not a word or cry of pain. The sound of the metal snipping through bone was nauseating, but Williamson finished the job. He discarded the toe and carefully examined the wound. Just above the crude excision remained some gangrenous tissue, which would need to be removed, but Clam had endured enough for one day. Williamson nodded to the others that he was finished, and they released their hold on Clam.

McKinlay was impressed by Clam's toughness. "I have never known anyone who lived up so well to his nickname," he wrote in his diary. "There was never a murmur . . . for sheer guts it was incomparable." Chafe, who'd been lying nearby convalescing, his own foot also dangerously frostbitten, shared those sentiments. "Clam went through the operation heroically," he wrote. "It was a matter of life and death with him, and he knew it."

The final attempt to reach Shipwreck Camp had been costly. For two days after Chafe's miraculous return with Molly, he lay in the hospital igloo, his eyes swollen shut from snow blindness. Then Clam's toe. But there were other losses resulting from the failed journey: eight dogs, two sleds, several skins, two rifles and ammunition, and precious food—all abandoned on the ice so that Munro, Clam, and Chafe could make it back to Icy Spit. It was tough to reconcile. It's true they had been too weak to pull the sleds any longer, but the loss of dogs and food and weapons, McKinlay knew, would be felt eventually, and probably soon.

A few days later, the weather improved enough for the sick and injured to crawl out of the hospital igloo and sit by the driftwood fire. Chafe's frostbitten heel had dying flesh, which needed to be cut away. Outside, in brilliant sunshine, Williamson used his pocketknife to operate, slicing the dead skin off as Chafe cringed and yowled. "It had to be cut six different times," wrote Chafe. Williamson took the opportunity and better light to finish the job on Clam's toe, too, severing the residual gangrenous tissue with his knife. Again, Clam bore the cutting without a sound. Afterward, Williamson dabbed the open wound with silver nitrate to cauterize it, and

Hadley, who'd returned from an unsuccessful hunt with Kuraluk, administered a small dose of morphine to ease his pain—despite Clam's protest that he didn't need it.

McKinlay wanted to head south and join Mamen, Malloch, and Templeman at Rodger's Harbor. For one thing, some of his portion of food rations was with them, as was his best parka. The one he was wearing had a rip so large he feared it was beyond repair, unless Auntie had some extra skins. But McKinlay didn't feel right leaving Munro and this band of invalids, at least not until they were all improved. And he wasn't yet strong enough for the sixty-mile trek himself. He often thought of Mamen and wondered how he and the others were getting along down south, but there were enough challenges here at Icy Spit to occupy him. The fuel oil was so low that soon they'd need to cook and boil water outside on the wood fire. This presented great difficulty in wind and snowstorms. The bear meat was down to two days' rations. It would be just pemmican and tea unless Hadley and Kuraluk—the only two fit enough to hunt—could find game.

For his part, Munro appreciated having McKinlay at Shore Camp. "The school master," as Captain Bartlett playfully referred to him, was a calming presence and offered honest advice and counsel if asked. "I don't know how we would get along without him," Munro wrote of Wee Mac, whose diminutive size was countered by tremendous physical endurance and, more important, a deep inner fortitude and positive outlook. The two men worked together, collecting and chopping firewood, cutting ice, and repairing the igloos, and when McKinlay finally felt strong enough, taking a three- or four-mile walk from camp.

With the bear meat running out, McKinlay supplemented it with bone, fat, and scraps of meat from the dog food tins to make a pot of broth, but that lasted only a couple of days. When it was gone, they "tried experiments with the revolting, unsavoury pemmican," wrote McKinlay, "to try and make it palatable, but with little success." They began to engage in elaborate food fantasies, imagining and describing the wondrous meals they would eat when they returned to civilization. They went back and forth, recalling the fine fare in their favorite restaurants, their most

memorable home-cooked meals and family feasts. In a way, it seemed per-
verse, even cruel, to remind themselves of what they could not have, but
on it went. "There is no end to the ham and eggs, porridge, pies, and fruit,"
wrote McKinlay. "And although we cover the same ground day after day,
we never tire of it."

A break in the weather allowed Hadley and Kuraluk to attempt another hunt. It was agreed they should head up the spits and out onto the
ice to see if any seal had come to the lagoons, which also might bring
bears. They took with them the remaining three dogs and a personal rifle
each, leaving Shore Camp with only one rifle to use. There was no telling
how long they would be gone, but everyone in camp was counting on
them to bring back fresh meat as soon as possible.

Bjarne Mamen strained in the haul ropes, pain searing into his shoulders.
His trip alone, pulling the sled he'd made with the improvised ski runners,
had sapped of his strength. He came to a stop about eight miles north
of Skeleton Island, unable to haul the sled another step. His eyes burned
and itched—a telltale sign of snow blindness. He'd been trudging for two
straight days, stopping only to make tea and eat a bit of the bear meat he'd
brought along from Shore Camp. He was worried about his own condition,
writing in his journal on April 2, "Whether I shall last long enough to
get this load down to Skeleton Island alone, I don't know. I feel tired and
weak, but perhaps tomorrow will give me new strength." Despite his own
condition, he knew he must get to Malloch and Templeman, who, when
he'd left them to make the solo trip to Shore Camp and back, were in bad
shape themselves.

Mamen decided to leave the sled—he could come back for it later—
and with a knapsack take just his footbag, a skin, his snow shovel, and
rifle and go the rest of the way to their camp at Skeleton Island. Through
worsening vision, Mamen could see what looked like smoke rising in the
distance, and two dark specks shaped like human forms. He hurried on,
tripping and limping on his bum knee, and as he drew closer, he saw Templeman coming forward to greet him.

Templeman and Malloch had suffered during Mamen's absence. Three of Malloch's toes were badly frostbitten, and both men complained of pain and swelling in their legs. Apparently, the mystery illness had affected them too. Their camp at Skeleton Island—which lay just off Wrangel Island's southeast coast—was exposed to wind and weather, and Mamen found the place in disarray. Provisions and tools were covered by drifts of snow six feet deep, and the igloo was crumbling. They told Mamen they'd been too weak to repair it. Their Primus stove had failed, and they had not had warm food in days.

Mamen dropped his gear and got to work building another igloo, and when he was finished, they all crawled in and had some hot tea and warm pemmican—he'd left the bear meat with the abandoned ski-sleigh. Templeman admitted that both he and Malloch had worried they'd die if Mamen didn't return. They simply did not have the strength to care for themselves.

Mamen wrapped his feet in his footbag and lay back, holding his hands over his eyes. He dug around in his knapsack and found some medicine and flushed his eyes out with the solution and some water Templeman gave him, and that eased the pain. For the next three days, Mamen lay in the igloo, unable to go outside into the bright sunlight. Templeman brought him water three times a day and helped give Mamen an eye bath, and finally his eyes began to improve. Mamen managed to repair the Primus stove, and late in the day, he was able to get out and about for four hours; he beat and brushed off their sleeping skin, dug out the snow-covered gear, and tidied the igloo. When Mamen crawled back inside, he realized it was April 5—his twenty-third birthday. "The worst one I ever had," he wrote in his diary.

There was no game—not even tracks—around Skeleton Island. Mamen decided that the best thing to do would be to backtrack the few miles north and retrieve the abandoned ski-sled and bear meat near Pillar Point, and then, when they were strong enough, head twenty miles south to Rodger's Harbor. Maybe they'd have better luck with game there, and that was the agreed-upon rendezvous point where Bartlett had told them to convene by mid-July. Certainly, they could expect no rescue before then;

the ice conditions wouldn't allow ships to make it, but any place, in Mamen's mind, was better than Skeleton Island. He especially didn't like the foreboding sound of its name.

Malloch's right foot was putrefying. Mamen noticed the foul smell of rotting flesh and feared he might need surgery, so he left him in camp and started with Templeman to retrieve the abandoned provisions. Under clear, cold skies they made good progress, though after a few hours, Mamen noticed that Templeman was struggling to keep up. Mamen sent the cook back with instructions to build a bigger, better igloo; theirs was too cramped and uncomfortable. When Mamen reached the sled, he found it in good condition; no bears or foxes had disrupted it, so he turned around and hauled it to Skeleton Island by himself. He arrived to find both Malloch and Templeman sound asleep, with no new igloo built. They'd cut no ice for water either. He woke them up and yelled at them for being lazy, cursing loudly at them, but they just mumbled that they'd been too tired, and it was too cold outside.

Mamen built a new igloo himself. Neither Malloch nor Templeman helped, and Mamen was becoming increasingly exhausted, as well as perturbed, from doing everything, including stitching their skin garments, which were ragged from months of hard use. The work was difficult and cold, sewing barehanded in the dim light of a freezing igloo. "I have to begin tailoring for both myself and Malloch," he wrote, adding, "I could swear at and curse Captain Bartlett who has foisted Malloch and Bob [Templeman] on to me . . . for they are of no help and of no use. Malloch is certainly a peculiar fellow; I begin to get sick and tired of him; He needs a nurse-maid wherever he goes." That night, Malloch fouled himself. The wretched man's hands had been too cold to untie the drawstring of his pants, and rather than ask one of the others for help, he'd quietly soiled himself. Mamen helped clean him up, and Malloch said, with a note of appreciative tenderness, "I have you to thank for my life." He seemed to comprehend that without Mamen's round-the-clock work—he was now doing all the cooking as well—he would not survive for long. At Malloch's words, Mamen's ire turned to pity for the man.

One morning Mamen awoke to the sound of something that "gnawed and tramped around our igloo." He thought it must be a bear, so he scrambled out in just his stockings, grabbing Malloch's rifle by the doorway as he exited. Just outside, tearing at the bag of McKinlay's things they'd brought along for him, was an Arctic fox. Mamen fired a few shots and brought down the fox, their first fresh game at Skeleton Island. Mamen skinned the animal and made a large stew, and all of them were so hungry they agreed that it was the finest fare they'd had since leaving the *Karluk*. Malloch gorged himself on at least two pounds of the fox meat. But the fox lasted only a couple of meals, and they were soon back to pemmican. Mamen noted that Malloch was eating more than his share lately, and this behavior, and their dwindling stores, worried him: "Yesterday he ate two pounds of pemmican and today he ate over a pound of pemmican. . . . We will soon be ruined the way he carries on; he must reef his sails if he wants to be with us."

With their oil nearly gone and the fox meat having piqued a desire for more game, on April 18—one month since Captain Bartlett and Kataktovik departed Wrangel Island—Mamen urged the others that they must leave as soon as possible for Rodger's Harbor. But none of them was fit enough to travel. Mamen's knee had buckled while building the igloo, and now every step was excruciating. Templeman complained of stomach pains during the night and vomited all over the skins while trying to crawl for the door.

On April 24, after nearly a week's rest, Mamen decided they had to make the push for Rodger's Harbor. He reinforced the ski-sleigh, then loaded it with skins, footbags, tools, and the food they had left. While he worked, it occurred to him that it had been one month to the day since they left Icy Spit. He wondered what was happening up there, and how they were faring. "I wonder if another month will pass before we see McKinlay," he wrote with concern, "or what is the matter with the others up there. Has Munro not come back, or is illness raging?" When he finished packing provisions, Mamen estimated his ski-sleigh weighed about 225 pounds, while Malloch and Templeman's sled bore only about

60 pounds. They could not take everything, weak as they were, and would have to leave some food and gear behind.

Before starting out, Mamen wrote a letter to McKinlay, whom he hoped would arrive soon:

Skeleton Island, April 24th, 1914

Dear Mac:

I am leaving this place for Rodger's Harbor, or any other place on the coast suitable. . . . If you should happen to arrive here in the meantime, don't stay here, but get down to the coast as soon as you can, take with you all you can carry. We have had hard times all the time, no game, illness have we all had, and I feel very weak yet. The best regards from Bob and Malloch.

Very truly yours,

Bjarne Mamen

After placing the letter in McKinlay's bag and putting it inside the igloo, the men settled into the haul lines and trudged away. Mamen, drawing on his internal strength, dragged his heavy sled solo about ten miles all the way to Cape Hawaii, about half the distance from Skeleton Island to Rodger's Harbor. They swapped sleds there and continued, but after just a couple of miles, the heavier sled proved too much for the two men to pull, and they began complaining and arguing with each other. Mamen offered to switch back with them, and on they plodded. The day was sparkling clear and so warm that Mamen started perspiring, and he stripped off his skin shirt for the first time since leaving Shipwreck Camp two months before.

At the end of a long, hard day, they stopped and built an igloo. With their fuel nearly gone, Mamen built a driftwood fire and they cooked outside. They turned in to their igloo around midnight and were so spent that they stayed inside for the next twenty-four hours, alternately sleeping and eating pemmican and biscuits. Mamen figured they could make it to Rodger's Harbor in one last push, so he roused the others early in the morning, loaded the sleds, and they started off in a glorious sunrise: "The sun rose and threw marvelous light over the ice with all its large and small blocks, a wonderful sight, not a breath of air, everything quiet and peaceful." As they walked along, Mamen heard through the stillness the chirping of birdsong, and the sounds of spring lifted his spirits. Looking around, he saw the blue-green shoots of an Arctic willow poking out of the tundra where the sun had melted the snow.

In the late afternoon, they pulled in to what Mamen determined to be, based on the charts he'd studied, Rodger's Harbor. They dropped their loads and slumped to the ground. Heaps of driftwood lay scattered about in great piles. It might be enough, Mamen figured, to build a small cabin. For now, they set up a tent, for here along the rocky shore the snow had melted away, exposing bare ground. It was a tight squeeze for the three of them, but they were so tired it hardly mattered.

The next morning, Malloch pulled off his stockings. Mamen gagged at the smell as he assessed the damage. The second toe on the right foot, next to Malloch's big toe, was black and putrefying. Mamen got a kettle boiling and searched in his bags for some antiseptic and a small pair of scissors and a needle. He sterilized the instruments in the boiling water, then told Malloch to look away as he took the scissors and cut off the toe at the knuckle. He snipped away as much dying flesh as he could see above the toe, then patted the wound with antiseptic and wrapped the foot in gauze. During the procedure, Malloch gritted his teeth and exhaled through his nose and gasped, but he never cried out.

They'd left a load of provisions back at Skeleton Island, but Mamen knew it would be several days before any of them would have the strength to make the trip. Instead, he and Templeman hunted along the shoreline for a couple of miles but found no animals or even tracks of any kind. It was discouraging. When they returned, a stiff gale blew in off the ice, pinning them in their cramped tent as they sat drinking tea. The tent flapped so hard they thought it would blow down, but somehow it withstood the pounding.

That night, Mamen lay down, exhausted. His body ached all over. He stripped off his pants and looked at his legs in candlelight. "They are about twice as thick as ordinarily," he wrote with deep concern. "I can hardly walk and I move like an old man." He thought of McKinlay and the others at Shore Camp, then closed his eyes and thought of Captain Bartlett. He prayed he and Kataktovik had made it safely across the strait to Siberia, where perhaps they'd get word to the world of their location. He took up his pencil again. "I don't know how this will end," he wrote. "The prospects are certainly not bright."

31
HEADING EAST

CAPTAIN BARTLETT WAS UP AND OUTSIDE EARLY. HE'D SPENT A REST-
less night in the smoke-filled yaranga, twice rising from the hard pallet to
open the door and ventilate the place. He looked over their sled and asked
Kataktovik to repair the cracked runners. Bartlett spent the morning braid-
ing dog harnesses and making new ones out of some spare leather offered
by the Chukchi. He asked one of the Chukchi men—mostly through sign
language—if he could buy a couple of dogs, but the man shook his head;
they had none to spare.

Bartlett was anxious to leave, but strong northwest winds sent
blinding snowdrifts across the tundra, pinning them there. When the
harnesses and sled were finished, Bartlett and Kataktovik spent time inside the yaranga drying all their soaked clothes. Once the clothes dried,
they stitched up tears the garments had suffered from the sharp ice rafters. The old woman who'd first greeted them continued to ply them with
tea and huge servings of sugar. As thanks for her hospitality, Bartlett gave
her a cake of soap and some sewing needles, and he handed her twelve-
year-old son one of his favorite pocketknives. To her young daughter, he
gave an empty tea tin that had depictions of India on the lid. All of them
grinned with gratitude.

Late in the afternoon, Kataktovik came in from feeding their four dogs
to tell Bartlett that one of the Chukchi men had agreed to lead them as
far as Cape North. Bartlett was pleased and grateful; a guide would speed

their progress. They spent the remainder of the day resting and eating; the winds still raged, and visibility was too poor for travel. Before going to bed, Bartlett wrote in his diary: "April 6. Anniversary of the discovery of the North Pole. No doubt in New York the Explorer's Club is entertaining Peary."

The next morning dawned clear, calm, and numbingly cold. As they packed the sled, an older woman from one of the nearby yarangas asked Bartlett and Kataktovik to come into her house. She offered them chunks of dried reindeer fat and sugar, which they ate, smiling. Then the old woman handed Bartlett a new pair of reindeer-skin mittens, which fit well. He was deeply moved by the gesture, and the kindness shown them during their stay. "Never have I been entertained in a finer spirit of true hospitality," he wrote.

They left at ten o'clock. As he'd promised, a Chukchi man went with them, taking one dog and a small, light sled which he often rode on while Bartlett and Kataktovik mostly walked, not wanting to wear out the dogs. The strong winds had shorn the snow to a hard glaze, and they moved fast toward the east until densely wooded, hilly country slowed the dogs to a trot. Their guide kept easily ahead, weaving through thick stands of larch and birch. Bartlett could hardly believe the cold. Even in his new fur-lined reindeer mittens, his hands hurt with cold, and he had to constantly clap them together and pound them against his thighs to maintain blood flow and keep them from freezing, He reckoned it about $-60°F$, and he felt colder than he ever had in his life, even when he'd been near the North Pole.* He was relieved when, that afternoon, they came to a yaranga where they stopped and were warmed with tea.

Two days of hard, bone-chilling travel along the harsh Siberian shoreline—sometimes narrow and exposed to hurtling winds between the forest and the sea—brought them to Cape North. In the fiery sunset, with orange-pink light reflecting off the smooth ice, Bartlett could see a small harbor ahead, ringed by a dozen yarangas. They navigated the perimeter of

---

* Northern Siberia includes several of the coldest permanently inhabited settlements on earth.

the bay and made their way to the opposite shore and arrived at the settlement. Their Chukchi guide raised his arm and pointed to one of the yarangas. Some men came forward, grabbed Bartlett by the arm, and led him to
the front door, where a very tall man stood. He was bedecked in furs, his
face mostly obscured by a hood. The man's extreme height, and what facial
features Bartlett could discern, suggested he was Russian.

"Do you speak English?" Bartlett asked, shifting on his feet to stay
warm.

"Some little," the tall man replied. He pulled open the furs covering
his face and added, "One man he speak more English." Moments later
another man walked up, his feet crunching against the old, dry snow.
Between the two, Bartlett was able to determine that they were indeed
Russian, and that the newcomer had once been a longshoreman in Seattle.
Bartlett was freezing, and he wished someone would invite them inside.
Kataktovik had found a place to put up the dogs and feed them, and he
arrived with a Native man who invited them into his house nearby. Bartlett shook hands with the Russians and left.

The Native man's yaranga was hot and bustling with people. Bartlett
took off his parka and sat down, talking with his host, who knew some
English and some of Kataktovik's language. Using a combination of the
languages, with Kataktovik helping translate, Bartlett learned about
Cape North and what brought people here. There were some gold mines
operating in the surrounding hills, and a number of the yarangas here
were owned by so-called reindeer men, who ran herds of a few thousand
farther in the interior, to the south. The reindeer men came here with
their skins and meat to trade for walrus and seal meat, and blubber for
their oil lamps. Bartlett took out his *Coast Pilot* and charts and explained
the fate of the *Karluk* and tried to convey that his ship had sunk, and his
people remained stranded on Wrangel Island.

What the man said next dumbfounded Bartlett. "Me know *Karluk*."

Remarkably, years before, the man had lived at East Cape when the
whaling was still good and had sometimes gone aboard whaling ships that
anchored there to trade. He'd actually been aboard the *Karluk* while she was

stopped over on one of her trips. It was hard to believe, but it was true. Bartlett explained that he and Kataktovik had come with dogs over the ice of Long Strait, building igloos along the way, and now were trying to get help for the others. The man seemed doubtful that they could have accomplished this journey, but there was no other explanation, and here they were.

While they were talking, women brought them seal meat and tea. Presently the tall Russian came in and joined the conversation. He introduced himself as Mr. Caraieff and invited Bartlett and Kataktovik to spend the night at his house. Bartlett thanked the man who'd once been aboard the *Karluk* and bade him goodbye, shaking his head at the long odds and coincidence of such a meeting.

Mr. Caraieff treated them to a fine meal of Russian bread, salmon, tea, and milk. He informed Captain Bartlett that he had a brother at East Cape who would host them and could help them. Mr. Caraieff handed Bartlett a letter of introduction to present to his brother and assured him he would be well taken care of. It was the most pleasant, comfortable night that Bartlett had spent since before the *Karluk* sank months ago.

Early the next morning, Bartlett went outside to find "the wind was blowing almost a hurricane from the west and sweeping the snow in heavy drifts." He decided to wait it out for a while. He called in on the other Russian, who treated him to a breakfast of flapjacks, hot cocoa, and bear meat, followed by pipefuls of American tobacco. After breakfast Bartlett decided that since the wind would be at their backs, they should get going. They left Cape North before noon, and after a few hours the winds calmed and skies cleared and they traveled well, making many miles by the time they stopped and built an igloo at sunset.

By noon the next day, April 10, the dogs were again struggling. Bartlett and Kataktovik were both suffering too. Kataktovik—who never complained—mentioned that his hands and feet hurt, and not from cold. It was something else, some alien pain he could not fully describe. Bartlett felt it, too, in his arms—a kind of dull, swelling ache. But there was nothing to do but press on. After a few more miles, one of the dogs, Whitey, tumbled over onto his side and refused to get up. He was played out. Bartlett unharnessed him and lifted him onto the sled, hoping he'd recover with some rest. The dogs had been fed well for the last few days, but the near-constant work hauling from Shipwreck Camp to here had broken them down. Bartlett could hardly believe the miles they'd endured, and how any of them could keep going. He knew that if he had any hope of reaching East Cape—still over three hundred miles away—he had to have fresh dogs.

They stopped for the night at a two-yaranga settlement owned by one of the reindeer men. The man invited them in and offered walrus meat and reindeer meat. Bartlett quickly slid the rank-smelling walrus meat over to Kataktovik, who smiled and chewed with vigor. The reindeer man's skin was dark—leathery and the color of obsidian in the dim seal oil light of the dwelling. Of the reindeer men, Bartlett observed with respect and wonder: "Looking after their herds constantly day and night for thirty-six hours, without shelter of any kind . . . their faces were literally burned black from the frost and wind." After the meal, the man offered them lodging for the night. As they drank tea, Bartlett showed the man his maps and indicated where he needed to go. The man nodded, raising his eyebrows in understanding. Bartlett had seen that the man had seven dogs outside, and, through sign language, asked if he might buy some, or even just one. The man shook his head. He did not wish to sell any of his dogs either, dogs being worth a lot more than money.

At sunrise Bartlett was outside harnessing the dogs when the reindeer man approached, leading one of his dogs. Through sign language, he conveyed that Bartlett could borrow the dog, if he sent the animal back once he reached East Cape. Fur traders came back west all the time, and the dog could come with them. Bartlett thanked the man, then rummaged through his sled and brought out a pickax and a razor, which he handed to his host. Kataktovik harnessed the new dog in Whitey's place, and Whitey rode along happily in the sled as they headed east once more.

By now Bartlett was trying to barter for dogs at every settlement he came to. At one yaranga he saw a healthy pack of dogs running around and pulled to a stop. The day was brilliant, intensely clear and bracingly cold, about -50°F. Bartlett took in the scrubby undulating hinterlands, the mountains rising from the sea ice, the ground flecked with lichens poking through the snow. It reminded him of the northern lobe of Ellesmere Island, where he had been with Peary en route to the North Pole. An old man and a boy came out, and Bartlett—using hand gestures and pointing—offered a pair of binoculars for one of the dogs.

The old man objected with a firm headshake. Bartlett then produced a fine Colt .45 revolver and a packet of cartridges. This piqued the man's interest, and Bartlett handed the loaded pistol to the boy and gestured for him to give it a try, pointing at a branch sticking out of the snow some thirty yards away. The boy raised the pistol to shoulder height, aimed, and fired—the blast echoing in the thin cold air. His shot split the branch in two and sent the dogs skittering. The boy and the man whispered quietly for a minute and finally came over nodding in agreement, leading a well-built little white dog to Bartlett. Old Whitey, now rested and perking up at all the activity, leaped from the sled. Kataktovik harnessed the new dog, which they named Colt in honor of the trade, and with five working dogs, they bore southeast across the tundra once more, with Whitey trotting along behind.

That night they built their igloo, and Bartlett told Kataktovik that they should bring the two newest dogs inside, fearing they might try to escape and run back to their homes in the night. After tea and pemmican—and some remaining reindeer meat given to them by the Chukchi—Bartlett and Kataktovik knotted the traces of the two dogs together and lay down on the long ends, hoping to keep them from getting away. In the middle of the night, Bartlett awoke to a freezing draft and discovered a huge hole in the igloo and the dogs gone, their harnesses lying together in a heap. They'd somehow managed to wriggle free of their harnesses and escap. At first light, Bartlett sent Kataktovik back to the yaranga where they'd traded for Colt. Half a day later, Kataktovik returned with Colt, but he'd seen no sign of the other dog.

It was late afternoon, but by now the light was lasting into the night, so they drove the dogs until nearly midnight before stopping to build an igloo. To guard against another escape, Bartlett muzzled Colt's mouth shut with a leather strap and wrapped a trace around his own body as he fell fast asleep. But Colt was sneaky, and once again Bartlett and Kataktovik woke to frigid gusts and a gaping hole in the side of the igloo and no sign of Colt. Cussing, Bartlett spat good riddance. They'd go on without the damn dog.

Late in the evening, just as they were finishing a paltry meal, Bartlett heard voices and barking outside the igloo. He crawled out to see men leading three dog teams. They came up, and one of them unharnessed Colt and brought him over. Bartlett was astounded and thankful. The dog had apparently run all the way home, but the owner, honoring the trade he'd made for the revolver, sent the dog along with this group, who'd backtracked out of their way to return Colt to Bartlett. Bartlett grinned and bowed his head and thanked the men, who turned and went on their way before Bartlett had a chance to even try bartering for more dogs. But at least he had Colt back.

That evening, when they turned in, Bartlett tied Colt's mouth shut with a tight half hitch, "Then I put three or four turns of the rope crisscross on the harness so he would not extricate himself, and tied the rope to myself. The result was that with his continuous restlessness, I got no sleep all night. It was the last time I tried that device; after that I simply tethered him with the rest of the dogs." It worked, and Colt stuck around this time. Bartlett cussed himself, thinking he should have just done that in the first place.

The days began to blur as the captain and Kataktovik moved east along the coast. Sometimes they crossed frozen bays or lagoons, the sled running fast and smooth; other times they progressed haltingly over bare, windshorn ground that wore down the sled runners and tangled the dogs as they lurched to a stop. After many clear, brilliant days in a row, Bartlett's eyes started burning again, becoming inflamed and encrusted despite his use of snow goggles. At times he simply had to remove the goggles to read the pilot book, or clean the frozen lenses, and the sun's reflective blast against the ice and snow now had him wincing and squinting to see ahead.

They came to Cape Vankarem—a low thumb of land protruding from a sandspit into the Chukchi Sea—on April 15. Nordenskiöld had visited here in 1878, describing in his notes the remnants of ancient dwellings and prolific bone piles of reindeer and bears. The waters here were said to be rife with whales and walrus. Through blurring vision, Bartlett could see four yarangas spread in a semicircle, and he stopped at the largest of them. An old man poked his head outside the door and waved for them to enter. They were whisked inside by an elderly woman who quickly had their boots and stockings off and, before any words were spoken, had turned the four pairs inside out and hung them to dry. As Bartlett's eyes adjusted to the lamplight, he could tell that the owner of this place was prosperous: the house was immaculate, recently swept, devoid of the usual smoke and foul air, and there were thick furs lining the pallets and stacked around, some draping the inside walls. Two young girls, the daughters, brought the weary travelers tea with sugar.

The old man came forward with a box of English-language magazines and spread them out before Bartlett: copies of the *National Geographic*, the *Illustrated London News*, *Literary Digest*. Evidently, word of his journey and story had reached here. Bartlett tried to focus his eyes on the magazine covers, but the long days of biting winds, hour after hour of scanning ahead for the right route, and the blinding sun had rendered his eyes too strained for casual reading. At any rate, the dates on the magazines showed them to be a few years old, so there'd be no significant news of the world. Bartlett politely declined, indicating by shutting his fingers near his eyes that he only wanted to sleep.

When he awoke, his body ached all over but his eyes had somewhat improved. Outside, Kataktovik was ready with the dogs, and the yaranga owner was there, too, also with a small team shaking in their harnesses. The man, recalled Bartlett, "seemed to realize that we had great need for getting along as fast as we could," and he offered to guide them to the next village about ten miles away. By route finding and breaking trail ahead, the man got them to the next small cluster of huts in just a few hours. There, Bartlett encountered four grizzled and well-appointed Russian prospectors on their way to the gold mines at Cape North. Each had his own sled and strong teams of twelve dogs each. Bartlett inquired about dogs, but the men needed them for their work. They did offer Bartlett and Kataktovik coarse dark bread, butter—which they'd not enjoyed in months—and tea and sardines.

A few days later, with their dogs lank and ragged, Bartlett stumbled past Cape Onman. He'd hoped to find shelter and sustenance there, but through drifting snow spirals, all he could make out were the husks of abandoned yarangas; for some reason, everyone had left here. Kataktovik found a well-used trail, and they followed it away from the land and out onto the ice at the wide entrance to Kolyuchin Bay, on the northern shore of the Chukchi Peninsula. The dogs skittered and balked, reluctant to go out onto the ice again, but Kataktovik tested it and found it firm, and he urged the dogs on. They crossed in whiteout conditions, aiming for a high bulbous landmass in the distance, which Bartlett described as looking like "a warship bottom up." It was Kolyuchin Island.

When they came off the ice again and onto the shore, Bartlett found a dozen well-kept yarangas of reindeer men and a young man who spoke some English. The man invited them in—he lived there with another young man and their families—and in broken English told Bartlett that he knew the way to East Cape, knew of the traders there. As Bartlett listened and wolfed down flapjacks and cooked seal meat, the young man said, "I bring you East Cape. How much?" And he held out his hands. These people had also heard about Captain Bartlett and his desire to make East Cape. It was remarkable how word had spread east and west along the coast.

Bartlett chewed on the seal meat and pondered the offer. He had only forty-five dollars, lent to him by Hadley before they'd left Wrangel Island, and he knew he'd need money before they were through. But in their condition, they definitely needed help now. After an hour of haggling, Bartlett agreed to pay the man forty dollars. It was too much, but if it got him quickly to East Cape and helped him spread the word of the *Karluk* survivors, it would be worth it. The young man pressed Bartlett to show him the money, but the cagey Newfoundlander said he had the money and would pay when he got where he was going.

Kataktovik had been working tirelessly for many weeks, and his legs were cramping and swelling, and pained him terribly. He was stoic about it, but Bartlett chose to wait a day in the comfortable yaranga, where they'd be well fed by the reindeer men. The dogs also needed food and rest. The next day, April 19, they set out. Bartlett had decided to abandon his sled there; the runners were busted, and it would take too long to repair, so they loaded their essential gear and some pemmican tins onto the sleds of the reindeer men and transferred the dogs to join their teams.

They struck west, back across the wide Kolyuchin Bay, then south, one man walking and the others riding in each sled. Bartlett was impressed by the sleds, which, though crudely fabricated, were light and sturdy, about sixteen feet long. He noticed that periodically the reindeer men would stop, pull water bottles out of their skin parkas, pour water on strips of bearskin, then rub the wetted bearskins up and down the length of the runners. The water quickly froze, creating an ice coating that reduced friction and made the sleds run fast.

After some miles through sparsely timbered country, they came to a single dwelling and halted there. The younger reindeer man then told Bartlett—to the captain's consternation and dismay—that he was returning home. He said he had much work with many reindeer skins he'd left in the interior at his camp there, some two weeks' travel inland. Now that he thought about it, he could not afford the time to travel to East Cape and back, and his skins were more valuable than forty dollars.

Bartlett was livid. But the young man was already unloading their gear and unhitching his dogs. He had clearly made up his mind. He told Bartlett that the Chukchi man who lived here would take him ahead, and that not far east—some fifteen or twenty miles—was an American trader named Olsen who would help them reach East Cape. Bartlett fumed. A deal was a deal, and now the man had reneged, and worse, he and Kataktovik were being left without a sled. After some cussing and yelling,

Bartlett pulled out his money and showed him the four ten-dollar bills that the man would have received for doing what he'd said. Then he put the tens away and pressed the five-dollar bill into his hand as some compensation for his help and to show him that he was an upright man. The reindeer man turned away, half-skulking, and left for home.

Bartlett cursed some more. He thought about how far they'd come and how far they still had to go. Another 125 to 150 miles to East Cape, and then he must somehow find a ship to take them the 240 miles across the Bering Strait to Nome. Every delay could cost lives. He thought of Wee Mac and young Mamen and Munro and Kuraluk's family, tough, sweet little Helen and Mugpi. He prayed that they'd found game and hoped that Munro and Mac were holding things together on those desperate shores.

As he stood next to his paltry pile of gear and the bedraggled dogs, a Chukchi man came from his yaranga. Bartlett persuaded him—offering a pickax, a snow knife, and a couple of steel drills—to help him get to this Mr. Olsen's place. Just after sunrise, Bartlett harnessed his dogs along with the Chukchi man's team, loaded his remaining stores on his sled, and they started off. Bartlett's dogs lagged, hardly able to keep pace and making it tough on the driver, but by midday they arrived at Mr. Olsen's dwelling. The man, Bartlett learned—quite happy to be speaking fluent English with someone again—was a thirty-eight-year-old naturalized American who traded far and wide in this region. As Bartlett and Kataktovik devoured Olsen's homemade bread, Olsen explained that he worked as an agent for Mr. Olaf Swenson of Seattle and was well connected all up and down the coast and in much of northern Alaska.

In the morning, Olsen informed Bartlett that he'd hired a driver and dog team to guide him part of the way to East Cape. The driver's full dog team was a godsend, for by now, of Bartlett's own, only Colt could do any real work. Bartlett had to laugh: after busting out of two igloos and running away twice, Colt had turned out to be a fine dog. Bartlett shook hands with Olsen, thanking him profusely, and they moved out. At first the hired driver rode while Bartlett and Kataktovik trotted behind, but they traded out every few miles to give each man a rest. They passed Pitlekaj, the place,

Bartlett noted, where Nordenskiöld's ship *Vega* had been frozen in the ice in 1878. The *Vega*, the first ship to navigate through the entire Northeast Passage—the sea route connecting the Atlantic and Pacific Oceans via the Arctic Ocean—had remained frozen in for nearly a year, but by luck (or fate, to Bartlett's way of thinking), she'd not been crushed.

At an island about halfway between Kolyuchin Bay and Cape Serdze, Olsen's hired guide said he must return home, but assured Bartlett that he'd be able to find help from here onward. Bartlett dug into his dwindling belongings and compensated the guide with a small, nearly worn-out spade and two packages of tobacco he'd obtained from Olsen. It was tough to part with the tobacco—he'd been without it for so long, and it was now a great pleasure—but it was about all he had left for barter. He'd traded away everything else of any worth.

Bartlett managed to find two Chukchi with sleds who were traveling in the same direction, and they volunteered to help. The sun shone bright, and Bartlett enjoyed its warmth—he reckoned the temperature had risen to just about freezing—but the glare was such that he had to pull his visored hat down over his goggles to shield against the rays. The fresh dogs pulled hard, and by three o'clock in the afternoon, they came to Cape Serdze. In no time, word of their coming arrival having preceded them once more, they were greeted by a man named Wall, a Norwegian of about forty. Bartlett learned that Wall had lived in the United States and spoke perfect English. Bartlett briefly summarized his situation, explaining that he needed to get to East Cape, from where, he was confident, a contact could help convey him to Alaska. Wall said it was ninety miles to East Cape; then he grinned and laughed and said he knew just the man to take them there.

The man was called Corrigan. When Bartlett first heard the name, he thought he must be an Irishman, but Corrigan turned out to be a Siberian Native and a regional legend: "the best-known hunter in Siberia." Corrigan's yaranga showed the fruits of this season's hunting labors: the skins of some twenty fine polar bears and piles of white fox skins, which were highly valued. "He was by far the most prosperous native I had met," wrote Bartlett. Corrigan's English was poor, but he managed to tell Bartlett that he had sixteen fine dogs and a friend who would come along; he'd be honored to take Bartlett and Kataktovik to East Cape.

The terrain from Cape Serdze toward the east was rimmed by high cliffs, and they traveled over rough sea ice where it crashed and tumbled near the shore. Bartlett rode in the sled Corrigan drove, and Kataktovik rode in the one driven by Corrigan's friend. Bartlett held tight to the sled rails as they descended steep declines, and once he looked up to see a cluster of yarangas, the homes of seal and walrus hunters, "perched on shelves projecting out from the face of cliffs," hundreds of feet above the shore. He couldn't figure out how they climbed up to get to them. "They reminded me of pictures I had seen of the homes of the cliff dwellers," Bartlett recalled.

When the ice was smooth, Corrigan ran his dogs at breakneck speeds. "He was a daring and capable dog driver," wrote Bartlett, "and knew how to steer a sled as well as a man can steer a ship." White-knuckled, Bartlett hung on as Corrigan tore along, the sled bouncing and skidding and jostling the captain, whose back ached from the pounding ride. But it was worth it; they made fifty miles in one day, arriving at a yaranga after twelve hours of near-constant travel.

They started very early the next morning, the going rough once more along the shore ice. Near noon, Corrigan drove the sled close against the cliff's walls, and Bartlett watched in fear as the sun's warming rays released rocks and boulders that had been frozen in during winter; now they dislodged and came crashing down the cliff faces, some boulders smashing at the bottom and rolling right across their path, barely missing the dogs. Once they passed the cliffs, the going got smoother. Corrigan pointed in different directions, sometimes inland and sometimes out to sea, carrying on a long monologue, perhaps about his harpooning days or hunting exploits. Bartlett listened, but he understood only the occasional word. Corrigan got very animated as he yelled above the skidding sled and racing dogs, and Bartlett nodded back, pretending to comprehend. After hours of this, Corrigan realized that Bartlett couldn't understand him, and he clapped his hands to his head and made a gesture of desperation and despair. Bartlett just laughed, deeply amused by his efforts.

After another twelve-hour leg, stopping only a couple of times for tea, they reached a place called Emma Town, a few miles southwest of East Cape, at six in the evening. Bartlett rose stiffly from the sled and stretched his legs and aching back. His hands were nearly frozen into fists from clinging to the sled rails. He shuffled over to Kataktovik and shook him enthusiastically in congratulations. The second stage of their odyssey from Wrangel Island was over. The first stage had been the trip from Icy Spit to Siberia. The next stage would be getting across the Bering Strait to Alaska, but he'd worry about that tomorrow. Bartlett pulled off his snow goggles and squinted as he smiled, the creases near his eyes deep and dark as leads in the ice. It was April 24, and they'd been trekking and sledding and marching for thirty-nine days, traveling over seven hundred miles, nearly all of it on foot.

It was a remarkable achievement, but they weren't done yet. Bartlett pulled out the letter of introduction to Mr. Caraieff's brother, who lived in Emma Town. Then he strode toward the settlement to find the man.

32

"AS LONG AS THERE IS LIFE, THERE IS HOPE"

AT RODGER'S HARBOR, A NORTHEAST GALE HAD BEEN HOWLING FOR three days, keeping Mamen, Malloch, and Templeman tent-bound. The wind was so severe that Mamen couldn't light a driftwood fire to make tea, so they were reduced to eating "dry breakfast, dry supper, a half a pound of pemmican twice a day." It was becoming harder and harder for them to swallow the dry pemmican, and they chewed it slowly, nauseated. But Mamen tried to stay positive: "It will soon be better times for us, as soon as the birds come from the south and the ice breaks up the sun will shine for us day and night."

Mamen was worn thin, frayed from constantly caring for Malloch and Templeman. But mostly Malloch. He'd doctored Malloch's feet daily, wrapping the amputation site with gauze bandages, his weak hands shaking as he wound the strips between and around the stinking, necrotic flesh. What little cooking could be done—mostly boiled pemmican—he'd done by himself, though Templeman was technically the cook. When the winds finally died down, Mamen struggled out of the tent, digging through three-foot-deep snowdrifts, and walked down to the sandspit, hoping the exercise might do him good. But his limbs were so heavy, puffy, and sore that he had to stop many times on his way back to rest. While he rested, he combed the spit, finding the bones of birds bleached white from time and weather. He wondered how long they'd been there, and whether his bones would join them one day soon. Then he saw something sparkling among the bones and stooped to pick it up. "I found a stone containing gold," he wrote in his diary. "I will examine it closer tomorrow."

When he returned to the tent, he found Malloch outside, scuffling around in his stockings, either too tired or too delirious to pull on his mukluks. Mamen was furious. What was the use of constantly attending to the man if he wouldn't do anything to care for himself? Mamen cussed him and shepherded him back inside the tent. He pulled off the stockings to find the left foot white with frostbite and spent the next three hours with Malloch's foot pressed against his bare stomach, tucked under his parka, until some circulation and color returned.

Late that night, Mamen wrote in his diary: "He doesn't think, poor man . . . I suppose he is kind of insane. He became a little sad when I told him tonight in what condition his feet were. But right afterwards, he was merry and content. 'They are not any worse than my fingers,' he said with a wry smile and a maniacal laugh." That was true. One of Malloch's fingers had also been so frostbitten that it looked as though he'd lose it. It was difficult to see the gruff, burly Malloch, once so strong and vital, now alternating between serious talk and infantile giggles, reduced to an almost childlike state.

Mamen dearly wished McKinlay would return. Mac could help him take care of these two, and maybe he'd bring fresh meat. He hoped that Kuraluk and Hadley's hunting had been successful. But for now, his sole purpose was nurturing Malloch. Mamen had, after all, initially been hired to come on the expedition as the geologist's assistant. But that seemed so long ago. Now, nearly a year later, his job description had changed from taking readings to that of a nurse and even physician, and while it taxed his own dwindling physical, mental, and emotional resources, the responsibility provided him with purpose. "I sincerely hope that I may have strength to keep him alive until we are taken from here. It is my only wish . . . but the prospects are not bright."

The weather wasn't helping matters. When the winds abated, it snowed; then the snow turned to freezing rain, wetting everything: the tent, their clothes, the piles of driftwood. The dreadful weather cycle kept them inside the tent so much each day that they were developing bedsores, which burned, and the open wounds smelled rank. At least Templeman helped to doctor Malloch when Mamen was too weak. That was a blessing. And any tensions between the men didn't last long. They'd argue, name-call, blow off some steam, but afterward they'd be laughing and joking around again, telling stories and describing meals they'd eaten, or hoped to eat again. Round and round it went, day after day.

Near the middle of May, the weather improved enough for Mamen to go outside for a few hours at a time. He'd walk up to three miles, and though being upright and ambulatory hurt, his body swollen "from head to heel," the fresh air lifted his spirits. The sun came out, revealing patches of melting snow that bode well for the arrival of birds; he could almost taste their flesh, their eggs. He stood on the spit, gazing out at water skies to the south, praying that the open leads would soon bring seals near shore. Mamen even managed to get Malloch outside the tent for a while, though by now the big man could hardly stand without assistance, and he winced with each halting step on his festering feet. Back inside, Mamen offered him water, but Malloch refused it. That night, Mamen confided in his diary: "Malloch is now beyond hope; I expect he will die at any moment."

On the morning of May 17, the skies cleared at Rodger's Harbor. Strong north winds blew snow through the camp. Malloch would not rise even for hot tea, and at ten o'clock he became uncommunicative and unresponsive. Mamen and Templeman hovered over him all day, each in turn talking to him and trying to awaken him, but it was no use. For hours Malloch lay still and silent, his eyes staring opaque and motionless, as if he were looking out through the walls of the tent and into the heavens. Finally, his breathing slowed to a thin, wheezing rasp until, at half past five that afternoon, "he stretched his legs and drew his last breath."

Mamen and Templeman were quiet for a long time. There was nothing to say or do but remember the man when he was hale and hearty. Malloch the fiery, even violent man, the hard drinker prone to wild mood swings.

Who could forget the time he'd come from behind and hoisted Wee Mac in the air, clutching him around the chest and neck in a crushing bear hug, for no apparent reason? Or the weeks he'd spent sleeping alone, with no explanation, in the chart room of the *Karluk*? He slept bedecked in all his furs, until finally the cold had been too much, and he returned to the Cabin De Luxe, his face blue, his beard and eyebrows frosted with icicles. He was dynamic, opinionated, vain, and brilliant, and had been finishing a postgraduate course at Yale when he received Stefansson's offer to come along as the expedition's geologist. It was to be the adventure of a lifetime. Now he lay lifeless on the windswept southern coast of Wrangel Island, dead at just thirty-three.

McKinlay stumbled into the dilapidated camp at Skeleton Island and collapsed. He'd been traveling overland, alone, through deep snow and rough, boulder-strewn ground for seventeen consecutive hours, making nearly forty miles from Icy Spit. Along the way, he often thought of Captain Bartlett's advice that no one travel alone in the Arctic, yet he'd done so out of necessity: alone, without dogs, and unarmed. Breddy had recently made a trip to Skeleton Island and discovered Mamen's note describing the difficult times he and Templeman and Malloch had endured, that they planned on moving to Rodger's Harbor, and the need for McKinlay to "get down to the coast as soon as you can." Now, in the early morning hours of May 18, McKinlay crawled into the dilapidated igloo, its roof caved in, covering what contents remained with heavy blocks of snow. He wrestled free some buried skins, dusted them off, and lay them down on the snow. Kneeling, he picked a few frozen pieces of old biscuit from the snow and sucked on them like lozenges. Then he rolled onto his back and was almost instantly asleep.

McKinlay had come alone because no one back at Icy Spit was in any condition to travel that far. They'd had plenty of troubles of their own over the last few weeks at Shore Camp. Clam's amputated toe had begun to heal, but he remained ill and could walk only short distances around camp to collect driftwood. Chafe's foot had become gangrenous again and required recent cutting by Williamson—so he was out as well. Most of the others were still crippled from the mysterious swelling sickness or otherwise too weak from short rations to make the trip, and Kuraluk and Hadley were needed, as were the dogs, for hunting.

McKinlay tossed and wriggled for warmth in the roofless igloo. He awoke a few times, imagining bears padding just outside, then dozed again. Near dawn he was in a half slumber, and his mind cast back to the tenuous state of things at Shore Camp. Munro had not wanted him to leave, needing him to help keep peace and order. There'd been much discord. Some of it was petty and harmless, verbal rows that were the result of months on end of proximity, insufficient food, and frayed nerves brought on by the sheer difficulty of their daily existence and its mindless monotony.

Recently the igloo walls at camp had begun dripping and disintegrating, soaking the sleeping skins, so everyone was wet and miserable. Despite the freezing nighttime temperatures, they had to erect the tents they'd brought from Shipwreck Camp since there wasn't enough good snow around to repair the igloos. Williamson and Breddy bickered constantly, always at each other with barbs and complaints. One day they'd nearly come to blows, though no one knew just what the argument had been about.

But some disagreements—particularly centering on food—were deadly serious. Recently Kuraluk had returned from a hunting foray with Hadley after being gone eleven days. At first, everyone remaining in camp thought something bad might have happened to them. Perhaps they were attacked by bears or had fallen through the ice. Whispers and speculation moved through the camp, worrying Auntie and the girls. But on May 8, Kuraluk showed up with one small seal. He said that there were three more seals with Hadley at the pressure ridges, thirty miles out on the ice. Everyone was deflated that their hunt had yielded so little, and then Kuraluk said he planned to take his family away from Icy Spit and out to the ridge, where the chances for more seals were better. Several of the men started shouting, claiming that Kuraluk and Hadley were keeping all the seals for themselves. Amidst the yelling and blaming, someone said that if Hadley and Kuraluk didn't share the seals evenly among the rest, they'd shoot the scoundrels.

As the argument and threats got louder, Auntie was busy skinning and cooking up some of the seal her husband had brought in. She fried the liver in blubber in a pemmican tin and handed out sizzling little tidbits as appetizers, then bigger steaks of seal cooked rare, and as their appetites were temporarily satiated, everyone's tempers cooled.

Hadley came in from the ridge a few days later, but he brought no meat with him. He said only one seal was left out there, but for some reason he could not well explain, he'd left it behind. This news incensed some of the men, who accused Hadley of hoarding the seal meat for himself. A few privately spoke to Munro and told him they wanted to have it out with Hadley and learn just what was going on. Munro agreed, and there was a "round-the-fire discussion at which many problems were given airing and some doubts quieted." Auntie fully understood the importance of fresh meat in maintaining general tranquility, and when the last of the bear flesh was used up, she dug into a frozen store of bear parts—heads, cheeks, brains, hearts, kidneys—and cooked these. But McKinlay and Munro knew they had their hands full keeping order and calm at Shore Camp, especially if there were further disagreements about food.

So that was the situation at Shore Camp when McKinlay decided he must go to Mamen to help him and Malloch and Templeman. He had personal reasons, too: some of his own clothes were with them, as was his personal medical kit. And he had to admit that he missed Mamen's company. He'd bonded deeply with Mamen while aboard the *Karluk*, and he missed their long discussions. He was the last of McKinlay's scientist colleagues, and he longed to discuss theories with Mamen, to exchange ideas of mutual interest. All of these were reasons enough to take a break from the bickering and sickness at Shore Camp.

McKinlay awoke in Mamen's igloo at Skeleton Point, shivering and covered in ice and snow. He rose and started immediately for Rodger's Harbor. He struggled through broken, undulating terrain until he reached

Cape Hawaii, where leg cramps and chafed, bleeding thighs forced him to lie down and rest for a while. His throat burned with violent thirst. Finally, he willed himself back to his feet and stumbled south for many hours, traveling nearly thirty miles. At about nine thirty at night, he saw the faint outline of what looked like a tent perhaps a mile distant. In his fatigue, he wondered if it might only be strewn driftwood. McKinlay quickened his pace, and sure enough, he had arrived at their squalid encampment at Rodger's Harbor.

The tattered canvas tent door flapped in the wind as McKinlay parted it and poked his head inside. There was no stove or candlelight, but midnight sun slanted through the open tent flaps to reveal three forms slumped together side by side. The foul odor of rotting flesh assaulted McKinlay's senses. "What a woeful state of affairs I found," McKinlay wrote.

Mamen and Templeman roused when they heard McKinlay entering. They rejoiced that he had come, then told him of Malloch's passing the day before, and explained that because of terrible weather and their weakened condition, they had yet to remove him from the tent. Mamen seemed in a state of shock, and he explained that the previous day, with Malloch dying right next to him, and them spending the night with the dead man, had been the worst day of his life. "I cannot describe how sorry I feel about his death," Mamen said. "But I thank my Heavenly Almighty Father that he had such a quiet death without too great pain." Mamen said he'd been praying all night, then spoke his fear aloud: "Is it death for all of us?"

McKinlay knelt next to the dead man. He emitted a dreadful stench. Mamen said he didn't think Malloch had died from starvation. They'd been giving him helpings of their own rations to strengthen him. It must have been something else. McKinlay tried to console the two men, saying he knew they'd done all they could. His words of encouragement helped, enough that Mamen appeared buttressed, even optimistic: "As long as there is life, there is hope," he wrote in his diary. "There is something that still keeps me alive; all my beloved ones, and with God's help I hope to be at home, hale and hearty, and spend Christmas with them. It is two months today since Captain Bartlett left Icy Spit. I hope to see him again in two months . . . at the latest."

McKinlay was so exhausted that he lay down next to Malloch's corpse and tried to sleep, but the unpleasant odor, the thought of lying next to a dead man, nauseated him. He crawled from the tent on his elbows and knees and heaved violently, spewing bilious foam on the ground. Back inside, he tossed and turned until morning. He got up and made a fire, boiled water, and made them all some tea to revive them. With great effort, the three of them pulled Malloch's stiff body from the tent and rolled it up in the tent fly. They dragged the body some distance from the tent and stacked logs around and on top of Malloch's remains. It was a crude, temporary burial, but as the ground was frozen, it would have to do for now. McKinlay said a short prayer for Malloch, then they went back inside the tent to discuss their options.

McKinlay looked Mamen over and found him in terrible condition, "his body being very much swollen in every part." They discussed what they'd been eating, and Mamen explained that many weeks ago the bear ham they'd brought had run out, and though he'd shot one fox— which, incidentally, had been rooting around in the bag McKinlay came to retrieve—they'd survived almost entirely on Underwood pemmican. McKinlay struggled to understand this "most curious illness," concluding that it must certainly be the pemmican. If Mamen and Templeman were to survive, they'd need fresh meat and a break from pemmican, which Mamen could no longer stomach. The prospects, he reasoned, were greatest back at Icy Spit, where Kuraluk and Hadley were at least having some success getting seals. If he could somehow summon the strength, he intended to lead them back north to Shore Camp.

Mamen and Templeman agreed to attempt to make it back north with McKinlay. The plan was to rest and try to gather enough strength and leave on May 20. McKinlay had brought some tins of condensed milk, and he fed these to Mamen, who appeared weaker and sicker than Templeman. That morning, though, Templeman wasn't feeling strong enough to travel, and they decided to wait another day. McKinlay went out and added more driftwood, a few logs, and some stones to Malloch's burial mound, hoping to keep animals from molesting the body. He knew it likely wouldn't be enough to protect poor Malloch, but it was all he could do.

A fierce storm blew in, covering everything once again with snow. McKinlay went outside the tent and could hardly see a few yards in front of him. Sky and earth and sea ice congealed into a continuous, pewter-gray haze, and after a few minutes of his face being pelted with sleet, he retreated to the grim comfort of the tent. They'd have to wait until the weather cleared. He kept pouring warm milk down Mamen, pressing the tin cup to his lips and tipping it back, urging him to drink as he would a child. Mamen appreciated the gesture, nodding thanks and sipping the sweet liquid. He wanted badly to leave this place of death and prayed the milk would give him the strength to make it at least to Skeleton Island, if not all the way to Icy Spit. Anywhere but here. The thought of Malloch's dead body so near gave him chills. He could neither eat nor sleep. "I don't get a moment's peace as long as I am here," he wrote in his diary, conjuring the geologist in his death trance. "Malloch and his staring eyes are continuously before me."

The storm finally broke, and on the morning of May 23, McKinlay and Templeman packed up a few essentials, and McKinlay placed more logs on Malloch's body. He called out to Mamen that it was time to leave. Mamen crawled from the tent door and rose unsteadily to his knees, then stood for a moment, teetering, and fell to the ground. McKinlay and Templeman helped Mamen to his feet, and he stepped feebly, his legs buckled beneath him, and collapsed on the hard ground once more. They helped Mamen back inside the tent and lay him down. McKinlay saw it was no use. With dogs, they could transport him north, but they had none at Rodger's Harbor.

The only hope now was to have Templeman remain to look after Mamen, and McKinlay would strike for Skeleton Island to fetch a tin of Hudson's Bay pemmican he'd left there. Mamen had been unable to consume the "nauseating and disagreeable" Underwood pemmican any longer and hadn't eaten any for the last four days. McKinlay prayed that Mamen might at least be able to stomach the Hudson's Bay brand. It would be about a fifty-mile round trip on foot, but under the circumstances, it seemed the last, best chance for Mamen's survival.

That afternoon, McKinlay stuffed a tin of condensed milk, some tea, and matches into his satchel and set off for Skeleton Island. He had to hurry. Mamen would not last long.

33

ANYTHING MIGHT YET HAPPEN

CAPTAIN BARTLETT LAY IN A BED IN THE HOME OF MR. CARAIEFF AT Emma Town. He tried to rise, but his feet, legs, hands, and arms were so swollen and painful he slumped back down, every bit of energy drained from him. His bloodshot eyes burned and itched, and he fought the urge to rub them. The hair on top of his head was worn to the scalp from the perpetual use of his parka hood over the last month and a half, and though his body was bloated with swelling, he'd lost forty pounds getting here. Kataktovik was also bone-thin from the voyage, but he suffered none of the grotesque swelling experienced by the captain.

As soon as they'd arrived, Bartlett found and presented his introductory letter to Mr. Caraieff, who kindly took them into his home. Caraieff was educated, with a university degree from Vladivostok, and his English was excellent. Bartlett immediately explained his predicament and need to get news of the *Karluk* disaster—and the survivors on Wrangel Island—to the world as soon as possible.

Caraieff had understood Bartlett's situation and calmly laid out several possibilities. The sea ice in the Bering Strait remained too unpredictable for safe sled crossing, but if Bartlett were willing to wait until late May or early June, the strait would likely open up enough for crossing in a whaleboat or trading ship. Bartlett could not wait that long. Another option was to travel 275 miles overland south to Anadyr, where there was a wireless station. But they might be stopped by ice breakup in the wide rivers they'd need to cross to get there, and there was the chance that the unpredictable wireless station would be out of commission or unmanned, and he would have wasted precious time. A final solution was to wait until the first week of June, when a schooner was scheduled to depart Emma Harbor for Nome. Caraieff thought that he could get Bartlett on that schooner.

Bartlett had weighed the options and quickly settled on the risky over-land trip to Anadyr, reasoning that even if the wireless station was down, he could catch a ship from there to Nome. With his course of action settled upon, the captain had begun making inquiries for local guides to take him on the journey, but the swelling in his limbs had rendered him first unable to walk more than a few steps and progressed until he was bedridden. In his words, he'd become "a helpless invalid." Now, as he lay suffering, his puffy eyes crusted half-shut, he worried that all his efforts to help the marooned *Karluk* members had been in vain.

Caraieff had a Russian servant named Koshimuroff who attended to Bartlett daily, bathing him in a pork barrel filled with hot water and massaging his aching, distended limbs. Now, on the third day after his arrival, the captain was finally able to sit up and then, with great effort, stand on his legs and limp into the front room of the house, where he found a comfortable chair and English-language magazines on a coffee table. As Bartlett was thumbing through one of the magazines, looking at pictures—his vision remained too blurry to read the small print—in walked a formal Russian man of about forty who thrust out his hand and introduced himself as Baron Kleist, supervisor of northeastern Siberia. He was, as Bartlett would soon discover, a prominent and well-connected man in the region.

Baron Kleist spoke English well, and he told Bartlett that he'd heard about his troubles from the American trader, Mr. Olsen, at Kolyuchin Bay. He wished to help in any way he could. He said that he was leaving May 10 for his home at Emma Harbor, and invited Bartlett to join him. From there, he felt sure he could use his extensive regional connections to get Bartlett to American shores, and it would be preferable to traveling nearly three hundred miles to Anadyr, especially in his diminished condition. Bartlett accepted Baron Kleist's kind offer.

As Bartlett convalesced, he had a long talk with Kataktovik to decide what he wanted to do. Bartlett had hired him on at Point Barrow, but Kataktovik said he now wished to go to Point Hope, Alaska, some three hundred miles south of Barrow. He did not explain his reasons, but Bartlett was so indebted to the young man he was happy to oblige and arranged for Kataktovik to remain here at East Cape until the ice broke up and the navigation season opened, at which time he could travel by ship to Point Hope. Bartlett thanked Kataktovik for his loyal, selfless service and promised to pay him his wages once he reached civilization and could wire the Canadian government for funds. He would also leave Kataktovik with plenty of food and provisions to ensure his comfort.

Corrigan, the so-called daredevil of Siberia who'd brought them here, came to Bartlett and said he needed to return to Cape Serdze. As thanks for his invaluable assistance, Bartlett gave him his best pair of binoculars, with the provision that Corrigan promise not to trade them. Corrigan agreed, smiling as he departed on what Bartlett knew would be a thrilling, hair-raising sled journey.

Bartlett now had everything organized and was nearly strong enough to travel when his throat became so sore that he could barely swallow. His voice grew hoarse. On top of his other malaise, with his diminished immune system he'd contracted acute tonsillitis and developed a high fever. Mr. Caraieff had some medicines on hand, and Bartlett treated himself with peroxide and alum until, after a few days, the infection subsided.

On May 10, as promised, Baron Kleist was ready to head to Emma Harbor. The trip would be about two hundred miles by sled, and though Bartlett was still feeble, the baron said that "the season was advancing, and, at any moment, a thaw might set in which would break up the ice in the rivers and interfere with the journey," so they should be on their way. Bartlett thanked Mr. Caraieff for his many kindnesses, and asked that he care for his dogs—they were pretty used up, and Baron Kleist had fresh dog teams.

Karluk jammed in the ice off of the north coast of Alaska. The men are pumping aboard freshwater that forms in summer as pools on top of sea ice. *(Courtesy of Dartmouth College Library)*

Karluk drifting with umiaks mounted and ready. *(Courtesy Library and Archives Canada)*

Unloading umiaks on the ice. The traditional skin boats were light and strong. (*Courtesy of Library and Archives Canada*)

Men hauling the dredge near *Karluk*'s stern. (*Courtesy Peary-Macmillan Arctic Museum. In Memory of Reginald Wilcox and David C. Nutt.*)

Stefansson leaving the *Karluk* on the caribou hunt, September 20, 1913. His controversial and fateful decision came with disastrous consequences. (*Courtesy of the National Library of Scotland*)

Fanny (Pannigabluk) and Alex Stefansson,
Vilhjalmur Stefansson's "secret" family.
(*Courtesy of Dartmouth College Library*)

Karluk just before she sank in January 1914. The ice blocks beneath had helped raise the
ship out of the ice, protecting the hull from sharp encroaching ice for a time. *(Courtesy*

Shipwreck Camp. Bartlett had ordered tons of gear and food placed on the ice in case the *Karluk* sank. (*Courtesy Peary-Macmillan Arctic Museum. In Memory of Reginald Wilcox and David C. Nutt*)

McKinlay's plan of Shipwreck Camp. (*Courtesy of the Peary-Macmillan Arctic Museum. In Memory of Reginald Wilcox and David C. Nutt*)

Sledging through the brutal pressure ridges between Shipwreck Camp and Wrangel Island. (*Courtesy of Library and Archives Canada*)

Expedition members atop the pressure ridges. (*Courtesy of Library and Archives Canada*)

Member ascending "ice rafters" or pressure ridges. Some they encountered and had to cut their way through reached over one-hundred feet high. (*Courtesy of Dartmouth College Library*)

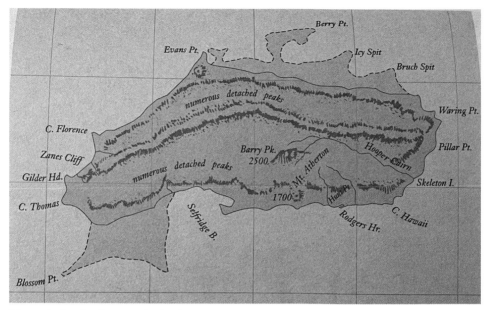

Mamen's sketch of Wrangel Island. (*Courtesy of Bowdoin College Library*)

The "Snowhouse" on Wrangel Island where Breddy, Williamson, and Maurer stayed for a time. Breddy is standing beside the deerskins drying atop the house. (*Courtesy of Library and Archives Canada*)

Fred Maurer with first seal killed on Wrangel Island. (*Courtesy of Dartmouth College Library*)

Right: Fred Maurer ready to hunt. Wrangel Island, spring 1914. (*Courtesy of Dartmouth College Library*)

John Munro skinning a seal on Wrangel Island. (*Courtesy of Library and Archives Canada*)

Kuraluk and his family on Wrangel Island. (*Courtesy of Library and Archives Canada*)

Nigeraurak in the snow. The tough little cat kept up morale and brought good luck. (*Courtesy of the National Library of Scotland*)

Kataktovik prepared to leave Wrangel Island with Captain Bartlett on their dangerous trek across the Long Strait to Siberia. March 1914. (*Courtesy of the National Library of Scotland*)

Setting up camp at Cape Waring after moving south from Icy Spit, Wrangel Island. (*Courtesy of the National Library of Scotland*)

The tents at Cape Waring. The crewmen stayed in the dome or the "bell tent" on left; McKinlay stayed with Hadley, Kuraluk, Auntie, Helen, and Mugpi in the tent on the right. (*Courtesy of the National Library of Scotland*)

William McKinlay (left) and Kuraluk building a wood-framed skin kayak for hunting walrus. The cliffs of Cape Waring are in the background. (*Courtesy of the National Library of Scotland*)

John Hadley dragging in a seal at Cape Waring, Wrangel Island, June 1914. (*Courtesy of Dartmouth College Library*)

Auntie, Helen, and Mugpi at Cape Waring. Auntie is skinning a seal; Helen is standing on sled rail, and Mugpi is playing on the ice. (*Courtesy of the National Library of Scotland*)

Meat-drying rack at Cape Waring. Members were drying meat in preparation for surviving a second winter on Wrangel Island. (*Courtesy of the Peary-Arctic Museum. In Memory of Reginald Wilcox and David C. Nutt*)

Camp at Rodger's Harbor, June 1914. If Captain Bartlett and Kataktovik made it through, it was here that help was to come. (*Courtesy of Dartmouth College Library*)

Camp at Rodger's Harbor. (*Courtesy of the Peary-Macmillan Arctic Museum. In Memory of Reginald Wilcox and David C. Nutt*)

John Munro and Robert Templeman drinking tea and eating seal meat at Rodger's Harbor. (*Courtesy of Library and Archives Canada*)

Fred Maurer and Robert Templeman raising flag to reaffirm British right to Wrangel Island, July 1, 1914. (*Courtesy of Dartmouth College Library*)

Templeman and Munro suffering at Rodger's Harbor. (*Courtesy of Library and Archives Canada*)

George Malloch's and Bjarne Mamen's Grave at Rodger's Harbor, with the flag at half-mast. (*Courtesy of Dartmouth College Library*)

Rescue ships *Bear* and *Corwin* in heavy ice off of Nome, Alaska. Captain Bartlett, aboard the *Bear*, knew that time was running out. (*Courtesy of the Library of Congress*)

The rescue ship *King and Winge*, in search of the *Karluk* survivors, in the pack ice. (*Courtesy Saltwater People Historical Society*)

Rescue party at Cape Waring, September 7, 1914. (*Courtesy of the Peary-Macmillan Arctic Museum. In Memory of Reginald Cox and David C. Nutt*)

Survivors of the *Karluk* disaster aboard the *Bear*, returning to Alaska. (*Courtesy of the Peary-Macmillan Arctic Museum. In Memory of Reginald Cox and David C. Nutt*)

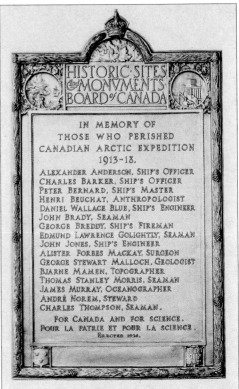

Mugpi, just three years old when the expedition set sail. Her toughness and good humor impressed everyone during the ordeal. (*Courtesy of the Library of Congress*)

Plaque commemorating those who died during the Canadian Arctic Expedition. (*Courtesy of the Canadian Museum of History*)

Kataktovik was there to see them off. Bartlett gripped him by the shoulders and thanked him again for his tireless, faithful assistance. Without his superb navigating through the devious leads, his igloo-building skills, his marksmanship and hunting abilities, Bartlett would never have made it this far. The young Inupiaq man—just nineteen years old when he'd boarded the *Karluk*—had risked his own life countless times, and certainly saved the captain's more than once. Bartlett handed him the rifle they'd brought with them on their journey, which Kataktovik had used so well to shoot the bears and seals that had sustained them. Bartlett looked into the dark eyes of the tough and tenacious man, then shook his hand warmly, promising that they would meet again soon.

Thick fog and heavy snows enveloped the dog teams and sleds. Bartlett could hardly see past the lead dogs, and for three days they drove through alternating mist and snow and freezing rain, through the flat, gray-blue light of the midnight sun. Bartlett rode much of the time; on occasion he hopped off and tried to trot along, but his legs were too weak and wobbly to keep up with the dogs, and he'd jump back in the sled. His fur clothing was tattered and worn thin from abuse, and he got soaked to the skin and so cold while riding that he feared he'd get sick again, but now and then they stopped at yarangas for tea and bear or reindeer meat, which bolstered him. They'd take a short nap, then be on their way again, the visibility so poor they navigated mainly by compass.

They were destined initially for a settlement of reindeer people on the northern side of St. Lawrence Bay. Around midday on May 13, Baron Kleist's drivers pulled the teams to a halt and stood discussing which way to go, pointing in various directions. They finally settled on a route and headed that way, arriving shortly at the steep slope of the bay's shoreline. Then, as if startled by something, the dogs bolted. Bartlett leaped into his sled as it sped off, and he held on in terror as the teams went racing down the grade. "The dogs had scented the reindeer," Bartlett recorded in his journal, and they bolted for the settlement like horses headed for the barn. "How we got along without being flung bodily against the numerous boulders that lined our pathway and killed outright, I never knew." Some-how, they made the bottom of the escarpment unscathed, and there found a well-worn trail leading to the reindeer settlement.

The reindeer men there ran a large herd. Bartlett described the men as "tall, fine fellows, somewhat resembling North American Indians." They spent the entire winter in the interior with the animals—the first reindeer Bartlett had seen since landing on Siberia—and every spring, the men returned to the coast with their herd. The reindeer men knew Baron Kleist and welcomed them all in and fed them freshly cooked reindeer meat. Bartlett enjoyed the comfort of the warm yaranga, and he dried his sodden, tattered fur parka while they ate. Bartlett had devel-oped a fondness for one of Baron Kleist's drivers, a tiny native Siberian of just over four feet tall nicknamed—with a literalness that Bartlett found endearing—Little. Little spoke serviceable English and was proud of it: "Me make baron speak plenty English," he quipped with a grin. He told Bartlett that he owned a motorboat and would take him across to Nome if Bartlett could not find a ship leaving soon. He said he'd do it if Bart-lett, a master mariner, would navigate through the ice. Bartlett agreed to this arrangement as a backup plan, chuckling as Little stood next to the fire by the very tall hosts.

Revitalized by the food and rest, they went on, crossing the ice of St. Lawrence Bay and skirting its eastern shores before bearing overland for several miles. The weather had improved—as had, finally, Bartlett's eyes—and for the first time since leaving Emma Town, he took in sweep-ing panoramic vistas of the wild country. The hills near the bay rose grad-ually, then flattened to immense plateaus, great expanses of ice and snow and stone. Between the flat, fast ice and the rises and descents into and out of the frozen bays, they averaged about five miles an hour. Bartlett rode along, taking it all in, marveling at the skill of the dog drivers as they navigated a severe decline into the mouth of the bay. The dogs ran well on the ice, and they crossed the bay over to the southern shore, where they climbed another steep grade and followed the mainland for some twenty miles until they reached a cluster of yarangas. Here they ate, and afterward Bartlett stripped from his soaked furs and wrapped himself in a warm, dry reindeer-skin robe provided by the hosts and then slept for a few hours.

Because of the near-constant daylight, the only thing that distinguished night and day for Bartlett was the time on his chronometer. They could travel at any time, and often went straight through the night, taking advantage of the cooler temperatures and firmer, faster ice. Their stops at yarangas along the route were usually just long enough to eat and nap for an hour or two. The dogs ran so hard and fast that Bartlett rode constantly now, and though his back ached from sitting and jouncing in the sled, his old strength was returning. As he rode along, Bartlett admired the spectacular, rugged country, much of it resembling the coastline of northern Greenland. Interspersed among his recollections of similar country he'd traveled were thoughts of McKinlay and Mamen and Munro and all the others on Wrangel Island.

They came upon a Chukchi woman who was driving a handsome team of dogs, and the baron's drivers stopped to talk with her, confirming the accuracy of their route toward Emma Harbor. As they waved goodbye, Baron Kleist asked Bartlett what he thought of her. The captain was a little taken aback, even perplexed by the question. Did the baron wish to know his opinion of the woman's appearance? Then Baron Kleist explained, as best he could, and Bartlett was fascinated by what he learned: "This was not really a woman but a man who had, so to speak, turned himself into a woman. It was, it seemed, a custom among these Siberians to do this and a man who thus transformed himself acted like a woman, dressed like a woman, talked like a woman and was looked upon by the other Chukchi as a woman."*

---

* The Chukchi (as well as the neighboring Koryak and Kamchadal) are a nomadic and shamanic people who embrace a third gender. Third-gender Chukchi could accompany men on the hunt as well as provide a caretaking role for the family.

At one yaranga, while being served tea, Baron Kleist was speaking with the host when Captain Bartlett heard a name that caught his attention: Captain Pedersen. He leaned in and asked the baron to explain what they were talking about. Baron Kleist said that apparently there was a whaling ship that had been in the nearby waters of Indian Point, and the ship's master was a man named Captain Pedersen. Bartlett grew interested, since he knew of Captain Pedersen, if it was the same man. Pedersen had been the very man who oversaw the purchase of the *Karluk* and had been Stefansson's first choice to captain the vessel on the Canadian Arctic Expedition. He had originally captained the *Karluk* from San Francisco to Esquimalt but after a falling-out with Stefansson over the dreadful condition of the ship quit at the last minute; that's why Stefansson had sent the telegram to Bartlett asking him to come along. If this was the same captain, perhaps he could get word to him somehow and manage to secure passage to Nome.

After many days of near-constant travel, they reached a steep divide leading to Emma Harbor. A thick curtain of mist and clouds hovered over a line of high mountains that formed a peninsula between Emma Harbor and Providence Bay. Strong gusts occasionally lifted and split the cloud cover, revealing "stern and forbidding" peaks that rose like fortress battlements. The divide was treacherous, severe, and riddled with boulders, but the dogs pulled hard, chuffing and panting, until they reached the top. They stopped to rest the dogs on the high ridge, and Bartlett took in the view: "I could look down to Emma Harbor and see open water out to Providence Bay. The land was white with snow and the ice near the shore was unbroken, so that the open water beyond seemed as black as coal-tar, shining against the white."

Sensing home, the dogs bolted, careening down the other side at terrifying speed. Bartlett hung on as the dogs sprinted. He could hear the sled's brake pole grinding against rock and ice as they plunged downward, the sled jerking from side to side as if on a bobsled run. Bartlett held his breath for the last of the harrowing descent, and they spilled out onto the flats and pulled up in front of Baron Kleist's house at seven in the morning on May 16. The 175-mile trip from East Cape had taken six days.

Captain Bartlett was welcomed into the luxurious timbered home. The interior was warm and cozy and inviting, its appointments of linens, table-cloths, and fine tea settings the handiwork of the baroness, who was away visiting relatives. Baron Kleist said, with pride, that the materials for the house had been brought over from Vladivostok only five years earlier, so the house was sturdy and clean and new. Almost immediately, the baron's chef appeared with a hearty and opulent breakfast, and as Bartlett chewed languorously on the delicious fare, his mind cast to Wrangel Island and he felt a twinge of guilt, worried whether they had enough food. "Two months had gone by since I had parted from the men on Icy Spit," he recorded. "If all went well, I should be back for them in two months more, and I hoped they were holding out all right and would be in good shape when I reached them again."

Baron Kleist's personal physician, Dr. Golovkoff, treated Bartlett's still-swollen limbs and lingering throat infection, and in a few days had him well enough to walk around Emma Harbor and inquire about ships possi-bly heading to Alaska. At one small trading outpost he met the proprietor, a Mr. Thompson, who'd been born in the Baltic Sea region but spoke fluent English. Since he traded with whalers and trading vessels, he made it his business to know about the comings and goings of all ships. He told Bart-lett that a Captain Pedersen had been in the neighboring waters recently on a ship called the *Herman*. Bartlett asked Mr. Thompson for pen and paper, and he wrote a letter to Captain Pedersen briefly explaining his dire predicament and desperate need to get to Alaska, entreating him, if possi-ble, to call on him at Emma Harbor and come to his aid. Thompson took the letter, sealed it in an envelope, and sent a trusted Chukchi man to try, somehow, to get the letter to Captain Pedersen.

Bartlett wasn't the kind of man to leave his success to the chance of just one letter, so he dispatched several Chukchi men with letters to various small harbors in the region. Baron Kleist also helped, using his breadth of influence to spread the word of Bartlett's need for help all along the coast. Now there appeared nothing to do but wait—and hope.

Early on the morning of May 19, three days after his arrival at Emma Harbor, Bartlett was drinking tea on Baron Kleist's porch when he saw the whaleship *Herman* steaming into port. He quickly packed up what little he had with him and headed for the port, where he boarded the *Herman* and was soon shaking hands with stout Captain Theodore Pedersen, the very man who'd sailed the *Karluk* as far as Esquimalt. The Norwegian had heard about Bartlett's plight at one of his trading stops up the coast, and now agreed to convey Bartlett to Alaska immediately.

Many of the townsfolk, including Baron Kleist, had come down to the wharf. Bartlett, still clad in his tattered furs, thanked the baron for his transportation from Emma Town at East Cape and his many other kindnesses and assistance, then he turned and strode up the gangway, relieved to be on a sailing ship once more and yet anxious about what lay ahead. With tenacity, endurance, good luck, and a series of generous guides and hosts, he had almost completed the last leg of his journey, but he wasn't done yet. And Bartlett knew—better than nearly anyone—that in these fickle, dangerous, ice-filled waters, anything might yet happen.

34
SNOW-BLIND

MCKINLAY SHOVED HIS HAND INTO THE BREAST POCKET OF HIS UN-
dershirt, groping for his snow goggles. They were not there. He tried all his
pockets, feeling for the hard case he kept the goggles in, but it was gone; he
must have dropped it along the way, or the case fell out when he'd pulled
his shirt and parka over his head.

He was many miles from Rodger's Harbor, heading for Skeleton Island,
and now his eyes burned as if scratched by sandpaper. McKinlay cursed
himself: He desperately needed the damn goggles. But he'd come too far
to turn back now, and he didn't know exactly where he was anyway. "The
ice scape had changed out of all recognition in the snow and winds of the
past few days," he wrote. "I was on the lookout for Cape Hawaii, but must
have passed it without identifying it."

He wandered onward, unsure of either his location or his direction.
In addition to being unable to identify any landmarks, knee-deep water
on top of ice kept forcing McKinlay to make circuitous detours, further
confusing him. He could make out steep cliffs on his left, so he knew that
he must be somewhere along the eastern coastline, but the cliffs were too
steep to climb. His route had taken him farther east than he wished to go,
somewhere out on the ice. He thought that the water he'd encountered
might be from river runoff where it met the sea near Skeleton Island, but
he could not believe he'd traveled that far yet. He'd lost all sense of time
and direction, and panic overtook him.

"It was the only time in all my experience, on the ship, in the ice pack, on the island, that I felt fear," he wrote. "Not fear of danger, but from the weight of my responsibility to Mamen, the helpless frustration of being lost while he waited for me to bring help." A sickening feeling welled in his belly, a profound dread. He plodded onward, trying always to keep the dark outline of cliffs and shoreline on his left. At least that told him he was heading north. Hours passed and he found himself plowing through deep, wet snow. He squinted through searing eye pain and thought he could see the dim outline of a cape, a dark promontory. Cape Waring? The soles of his feet alternately burned and went numb, and he feared he'd frozen them badly.

He gathered all his strength and kept moving, one sluggish step, then another, trying to slow his breathing and calm himself and ease into a tempered cadence. Dozens of steps became hundreds, then thousands. At some point he stopped and guzzled his tin of condensed milk and went on. After countless hours, he realized he was no longer on the ice but seemed to be close to the big lagoon between spits on the north coast, for he'd come to low, shadowy foothills. Using the vague outline of the headland as a guide, he aimed for it and kept on, closing his eyes as he walked, then opening them to slits just long enough to confirm the cape. He stumbled forward, feeling sharp rocks underfoot, until he opened his eyes to see "dark pebbly patches from which the snow had cleared." He reckoned—though he could hardly believe it—that he must be about ten or fifteen miles from Shore Camp. He conjured words from the psalm that often sustained him: "I to the hills will lift mine eyes, from whence doth come my aid?" He had no choice but to keep going.

McKinlay entered the tent at Shore Camp and shook Munro awake. In a hoarse whisper, he gave brief details: Malloch was dead, Mamen in critical shape. Then McKinlay collapsed onto a dry skin, spent to his core. He assessed his condition: "My boots and stockings and legs were soaked through, well above my knees. The soles of my boots were worn into huge holes. Where the holes were the skin was gone, and my feet were raw and bleeding." He was too tired to do anything about his feet, so he lay there as he was, soaking wet, freezing cold, bleeding, and despondent. He asked Munro the time and date. It was 4:30 A.M., May 25, 1914. He'd walked sixty miles in about forty hours, and in his snow-blind state, completely missed Skeleton Island, where he'd intended to retrieve the Hudson's Bay pemmican for Mamen.

When McKinlay awoke, he stripped out of his wet and tattered boots and stockings and tended to his feet: "There was hardly a piece of skin left on my toes and heels," he wrote in his diary. But fortunately, they were not frozen. Given his state, though, he would need some time to recover. It would now fall on Munro to go to Rodger's Harbor to help Mamen and Templeman. Munro agreed, saying he'd take Maurer, who was fittest among those remaining to attempt the long, hard journey.

Munro left with Maurer around midday on May 26. In addition to helping Mamen, Munro had agreed with McKinlay that he should assess the area around Rodger's Harbor for signs of game, nesting shorebirds, or anything that might prove favorable for a future move down there by the entire party. Per Captain Bartlett's instructions, it was there—sometime after mid-July—that rescue would come. So it made sense to scout the area well, since McKinlay hadn't had time to do so.

Munro and Maurer moved fast, arriving at Skeleton Island the next morning at ten, having traveled all through the night. They found the roofless igloo there nearly disintegrated, the walls caving inward. The interior was a mound of compacted snow, and they dug around, using empty pemmican tins as shovels, finding some skins, some containers of biscuit, and a few tins of the Hudson's Bay pemmican McKinlay had said would be there. They packed it up and continued, hoping to get it to Mamen in time. Munro saw hundreds of birds landing in the high cliffs above the seashore, where they appeared to be nesting, which was a good sign. Soon there might be enough for them to shoot, and perhaps get eggs as well.

As they rounded Cape Hawaii and traversed the south shore of Wrangel Island, Munro and Maurer were encouraged by the sound of ducks and geese, the birds winging in Vs across the skyline. Great piles of driftwood

lay on the shore, good for making fires and for building shelters to supplement their tents. After a few more hours, they saw a single tattered tent
ahead on a sandspit and they hurried there, calling out to Mamen and
Templeman.

Just as they arrived and dropped their gear, Templeman crawled from
the tent. He was shaking all over, babbling in a delirium. His terror-filled
eyes darted wildly about, and he reached out to touch Munro and Maurer
to make sure they were real, then fell to his knees and wept. Both dead, he
told them through fits and cries. Mamen and Malloch, both dead. He was
alone with the dead men, not knowing if anyone would ever come.

Munro managed to calm Templeman and make him some tea. Templeman told them that after McKinlay had left, Mamen grew weaker and
more worried each day. Templeman described feeding Mamen the last of
the condensed milk mixed with some whiskey he still had, which revived
Mamen for a time. He'd talked of home: how he wished to be there, how he
longed for his family, for his dear, lovely fiancée, Ellen. How he'd planned
to somehow make it back to them in Norway. He must make it; he had
expeditions of his own to lead. When he got stronger, he said, if Captain
Bartlett failed to rescue them, he'd help Templeman build a driftwood hut
for winter. When the ice was right and he was strong again, he'd ski across
to Siberia and make his way to a ship and sail home. It was going to be all
right, he said. He still had a good pair of skis, and that was all he needed.

Templeman paused, his voice starting to break. He said that at four in
the morning on May 26, Mamen had asked him to light a fire and make
him some tea. Templeman did so, and the two sipped tea for a time before
they both dozed off again. Templeman woke a half hour later and tried to
stir Mamen, but he was sleeping peacefully, so he let him be. A while after
that, Templeman tried once more to wake Mamen; he shook the young
man, but he was gone.

It was hard to fathom that Bjarne Mamen was dead at just twenty-
three. Without question, he'd been the strongest among them. Watching
him ski was a thing of beauty, his arms and legs in perfect unison as he
kicked and glided along, the sound of the ice slicing under his skis like

music. His tall frame had been lithe and lean, and he possessed a rare combination of speed and endurance. He'd been so fit and strong and fast that Captain Bartlett took him aside before the Christmas Day sports competitions and asked that he compete in only two events so that he would not win them all. And he'd obliged, knowing it was best for the crew, best for everyone aboard the *Karluk*.

Bjarne Mamen had dreamed of leading his own expeditions. He had dreamed of becoming an Arctic legend, like his countrymen Nansen and Amundsen. Now, like George Malloch, Bjarne Mamen lay in a heap beneath a rude pile of driftwood and stones, whipped by wind and snow.

35

NEWS TO THE WORLD

THE FIRST THING CAPTAIN PEDERSEN DID AFTER WELCOMING HIS fellow captain aboard the *Herman* was offer Bartlett a fresh change of woolen and cotton "American clothes," a jacket and trousers. His putrid fur clothing reeked, the elbows and shoulders were tattered, and the sleeves were covered in seal oil and the fat from roasted reindeer and walrus meat. Bartlett happily changed garments in his comfortable quarters, then met Captain Pedersen on deck. Bartlett thanked Pedersen profusely for altering his trading course and coming for him, for he knew that there would be a cost to the captain and his crew, who worked on shares. Captain Pedersen just scoffed and waved Bartlett off, saying it was no worry at all; he'd had terrible weather and dismal trading along the Siberian coast anyway. The change of scenery would do them all good. They could always return when the weather improved.

As they steamed east across the Bering Sea, the captains compared tales. Bartlett provided cursory details about the *Karluk* becoming beset, drifting, and being crushed and sinking, and their survival at Shipwreck Camp and trek over the pressure ridges to Wrangel Island. Captain Pedersen, a wizened and stoic Norwegian seaman, listened and nodded, neither shocked nor surprised by the events that seemed almost commonplace up here. For his part, after he'd left the *Karluk*, he'd gained captainship of the *Elvira*. As Arctic conditions would have it, during the same time the *Karluk* was being driven from shore and encased in ice, the *Elvira* was crushed and sank off Alaska's north coast. With no embellishments, excuses, or explanations, Captain Pedersen said he'd then "made his way overland to Fairbanks, had thence gone to San Francisco and taken command of another ship, the *Herman*."

And now here they both were. It was an altogether remarkable—almost unbelievable—series of events that had brought them together, but neither considered it out of the ordinary, or even noteworthy, for life in the Arctic.

On May 24, they reached a tongue of shore-fast ice extending twelve miles out to sea that prevented them from landing at Nome. "There was nothing to do," Bartlett wrote, "but lie off shore . . . and hope for the ice to break up enough to enable the ship to be worked nearer the town." Bartlett grew impatient, consumed with worry for the survivors at Wrangel Island as the *Herman* sat, day after day, with no improvement in ice conditions. Finally, on the afternoon of the twenty-seventh—a week since leaving Emma Harbor—Captain Pedersen suggested they forget about Nome and instead head southeast to St. Michael, Alaska, where there was a wireless station operated by the United States Army's Signal Corps. Captain Bartlett agreed, and was relieved to be under way again. They steamed along the coastline and then east across Norton Sound, arriving off St. Michael early the next morning. Bartlett stood anxiously on deck, trying to see anything on shore, but thick fog prevented a clear view all day long. That evening the fog finally lifted, and they were able to steam within a mile of the harbor, but ice again prevented them from getting any closer.

Captain Pedersen saw that Bartlett simply had to land, so he ordered some crewmen to lower a dinghy and row the two captains to a thick band of ice nearer the shore, and the two men got out and walked over the ice to shore. It was the first time Bartlett's feet had touched American soil in over a year. They walked together toward the wireless station, but when they arrived at the front steps, to Bartlett's disbelief, the windows were shuttered, and the office was closed for the night. They turned and headed toward the main town to find accommodations for Bartlett, when to Bartlett's great surprise, they encountered US Marshal Hugh J. Lee. Captain Bartlett knew the man. He'd first met him in 1896, at his father's fishing station on the Labrador coast, and they'd met again last summer in Nome, when Bartlett was on the way up in the *Karluk*. Lee wanted to know what in the world Captain Bartlett was doing here, and Bartlett summarily briefed him.

Marshal Lee said not to worry, he'd take it from here. The two captains shook hands, and Captain Pedersen returned to the *Herman* to continue his trading voyage,* as Lee led Bartlett over to the only open hotel, where he booked him a comfortable room. They sat up deep into the night while Bartlett filled in the many details of the *Karluk*'s drift, loss, and their countless trials and misadventures.

Bartlett went to the Signal Corps wireless office first thing in the morning. He'd written a detailed message to the authorities of the Canadian government in Ottawa and handed it to the sergeant behind the desk to dispatch. The bureaucratic sergeant asked for full payment before he would send it. Bartlett was nearly out of money, having spent most of it getting here. He leaned in close, his face reddening, and told the sergeant that the message was important. The sergeant shrugged: rules were rules. Bartlett exhaled, trying to keep his composure at this man's stubbornness. To get here to send this message, he'd traveled—mostly on foot—over seven hundred miles with Kataktovik, then another two hundred riding on a sled. He was frayed, gaunt, and desperately impatient. Lives hung in the balance. Bartlett's short temper exploded, and the two men argued until Marshal Lee, hearing the disagreement from outside, came in. The marshal explained to the situation to the sergeant. Perhaps his badge helped, because in minutes, the man at the desk sent the telegram, and Bartlett had carte blanche to send and receive as many telegrams as he needed to, on credit.

Captain Bartlett tipped his hat to the sergeant and walked out of the office. A wave of relief swept over him. He'd managed to convey the news of

---

* Captain Pedersen's detour assisting Bartlett did not go unremunerated. The owners of H. Liebes & Co., San Francisco, later invoiced the Canadian government in the amount of $5,500 for providing Bartlett passage from Emma Harbor, Russia, to St. Michael, Alaska (Auditor General Report, 1920; Stuart E. Jenness, Stefansson, 73).

the *Karluk*'s fate to the world. He had never wavered in his resolve, though many times he'd believed he might fail, or even die trying. He thought about Wee Mac and the burly, irascible Malloch and tireless Bjarne Mamen and wondered how they were holding up. He remembered how badly Mamen had wanted to come with him—and would have, had he been fit enough to make the trip. He thought of Kuraluk and Hadley: Had they found plentiful game? He wondered whether Munro's leadership was up to the task of holding the marooned band together. Despite all these concerns and fears, Bartlett felt good. He'd done what he had to do. Now he must wait for the response from Ottawa, while at the same time, make inquiries into what able ships might be in the vicinity in the coming months, ships that could be diverted for a rescue mission to Wrangel Island.

For the next few days, Bartlett shuffled from the hotel to the wireless office. The Naval Service Department in Canada responded immediately, expressing relief about the survivors—they had assumed the *Karluk* lost, and all on board perished—and assuring Captain Bartlett full support in rescue operations. But because of Bartlett's location and relative proximity to Wrangel Island, the Naval Service asked for his advice regarding ships and timing of the operation. He would know—or be able to discover— what ships would be best suited, and precisely when ice conditions would permit rescue attempts.

As to ice conditions, Bartlett knew that it would not be until midsummer for ice breakup to allow safe and successful approach to Wrangel Island's frozen shorelines. He could still see Rodger's Harbor in his mind, bleak and barren, among the most remote and least visited places on earth. He pictured the entire party there, all well if a little hungry and worse for wear.

Bartlett immediately made inquiries at St. Michael and learned of a few possibilities. Two Russian icebreakers—*Taimir* and *Vaigatch*—had wintered at Vladivostok.* They were powerful, steel-hulled craft set to embark

---

* Alternative spellings for these two steamers are *Taymyr* and *Vaygach*.

on exploring voyages. One or both might be enticed to help in the relief. A third Russian icebreaker, *Nadjeshny*, was idle and under repairs, but it might also be available in the coming months. And Bartlett was most intrigued to learn that the US revenue cutter *Bear* was in the vicinity, scheduled to deliver mail at Nome. The *Bear*, Bartlett knew, had been instrumental in rescuing Commander Adolphus Greely and a handful of other survivors on the shores of Ellesmere Island in the Smith Sound thirty years before. Perhaps this was a good omen. With all this information in hand, Bartlett hurried back to the wireless office and sent the following dispatch:

St. Michael's, Alaska,

May 30, 1914

Hon. G. J. Desbarats,

Naval Service, Ottowa, Canada

Russian ice breakers *Taimir* and *Vaigatch* soon make annual exploring trip north coast Siberia. Strongly advise you try arrange Russian Government these vessels relieve men. Vessels wintered Vladivostock but may have already left for north. Failing this arrangement another Russian icebreaker *Nadjeshny* lying idle Vladivostock might be obtained. Another chance United States revenue cutter *Bear* now in Bering Sea. Possible arrangements United States Government. If *Bear* goes should seek convoy Russian ice-breakers. No other available vessels these waters. My opinion July or early August before ice breaks up around Wrangell though seasons differ. Plenty bird other animal life island—good Eskimo hunter should not suffer food. I want go relief ships. Russian ships have wireless can get in touch with them if already at sea.

BARTLETT, CAPTAIN.

With that message sent, Captain Bartlett settled into what he knew would be a frustrating, anxious waiting game. But there was nothing else for him to do but maintain frequent correspondence with Canada and alert them to any other developments. Meanwhile, he would try to regain his full strength and stay occupied by reading and writing letters and telegrams to his family in Newfoundland and his close friends in Boston and New York. There was much to catch up on. The very day he'd arrived at St. Michael, the *Empress of Ireland*, a 570-foot ocean liner and the pride of Canadian Pacific Steamships, had struck a Norwegian collier in thick fog near the mouth of the Saint Lawrence River and sank within minutes, losing perhaps a thousand of its nearly fifteen hundred passengers. Details were still coming in. It was astounding and tragic news, just two years after the horrific *Titanic* disaster. It appeared grim indeed and hard to process given everything already weighing on him.

And he had to deal with the press himself. Soon after notifying Ottawa of the *Karluk* story—in cryptic and abbreviated telegraphese—he'd been contacted by the *Nome Daily Nugget* for a story. He provided more details, but when it was published in that paper, and reprinted the same day in the *New York Times*, there were numerous inaccuracies and "assumptions" that rankled him. The article said—referring to Bartlett's journey from Wrangel Island—"It is assumed, also, that as soon as the days became of sufficient length to permit travel, Bartlett, accompanied by the five Eskimos . . . set out for Bering Sea." He'd of course traveled only with Kataktovik, and he'd gone across the Long Strait in the Chukchi Sea to Siberia, so they had that all wrong. The story also claimed that "The *Herman* will go in relief of the *Karluk*'s crew as soon as she can get through the Bering Straits into the arctic," which was not the case. Captain Pedersen had continued his trading and whaling voyage, now more than a week behind schedule.

Such inaccuracies were annoying, and misinformation could potentially worry friends, families, and loved ones of the survivors. He quickly drafted and dispatched his own summary of events from St. Michael, relating their trials from the time Stefansson left the ship until now. The piece was published in the *New York Times* on June 1, 1914.* Writing about Stefansson's departure opened an old wound, and got Bartlett wondering: Where *was*

---

* Ironically, Bartlett's version contains some inaccuracies of its own. Most had to do with dates. In his condition after the long ordeal, he seemed to mix up the months, writing that his departure with Kataktovik from Wrangel Island had been on February 18, when it was in fact March 18, 1914.

Stefansson? Since he'd been at St. Michael, Bartlett had heard only snippets of rumors: that he'd made it back safely to Alaska's northern shore and subsequently reoutfitted to continue his research somewhere north of the Mackenzie River. Bartlett knew better than to put much stock in the scant information; he'd get the full report—or Stefansson's version of it, anyway—eventually.

And one way or another, he'd deal with Stefansson later.

36

EXODUS TO
CAPE WARING

MCKINLAY WAS RECUPERATING AT SHORE CAMP. HE'D BATHED AND
bandaged his bludgeoned feet, and though they stung to walk on, he was
ambulatory, and being up and around did him good. He was worried sick
about Mamen and prayed that any day now Munro and Maurer would return with him and Bob "Cookie" Templeman. McKinlay's debacle getting
lost and failing to return to them bore away at him, and he felt a twinge of
guilty shame—but there was nothing to be done about it now. All he could
do was get himself right enough to help the others here at Shore Camp,
where the "swelling complaint" continued to plague members. Both Clam
and Williamson were afflicted still, and now Breddy and Chafe were succumbing. McKinlay believed that his own decent health was the result of
including milk in his diet, and even more vital, his positive mental state: "I
had long felt that my mental attitude was more important than any physical weakness," he wrote. "I knew I must expect a spell of bodily weakness
until we could get fresh meat, but I also knew that the limit to which my
body could be driven had not yet been reached."

When Munro and Maurer had not returned in the first few days of
June, Kuraluk announced that he intended to take his family south to Skeleton Island; he thought there might be more game there. Hadley wished to
go with them, and as Munro was technically in charge but absent, McKinlay agreed to help them move. McKinlay suggested he go along with them,
and then, once they were situated, he'd take the sled and the last three

remaining dogs back to Shore Camp. He would caretake the infirm for as long as he was needed. McKinlay figured he would eventually make it all the way back down to Rodger's Harbor, now that the needs of the entire group had changed, and he was most useful helping everyone else.

McKinlay's eyes still hurt, but he found a spare pair of snow goggles, and on June 4, with Kuraluk breaking trail, they departed Shore Camp at Icy Spit. Hadley drove the sled and dogs, and McKinlay limped along with Auntie, Helen, and Mugpi, who took turns carrying Nigeraurak in her little bag. McKinlay struggled to keep up, and he watched as the children jogged easily ahead of him until they disappeared in the distance. After about six slow miles, he caught up with the group where they'd stopped for tea, and afterward he was able to keep pace. Around midday they stopped again to rest and drink water, and that afternoon they reached Bruch Spit, having made a dozen miles since morning.

They decided to pitch a tent there and continue the last twenty or so miles to Cape Waring in the morning. Hadley boiled reindeer hair and blubber for the dogs. Their own dinner consisted only of pemmican fried in blubber, but Auntie did at least surprise McKinlay with a chunk of the more palatable Hudson's Bay variety, the last of her stores. As McKinlay slowly chewed the greasy bolus, he watched—both impressed and amused by their industriousness—as Helen and Mugpi plucked and then boiled a dead owl they'd found along the trail. There wasn't much meat on it, but they gnawed it down to the bones and sucked the marrow.

The barking dogs awoke McKinlay around one in the morning. It was Munro and Maurer coming from Rodger's Harbor. They brought the terrible news of Mamen's recent death. Everyone grew somber, but the news hit McKinlay especially hard. When he left him, Mamen had been in grave shape, and the news was not a complete surprise, but he couldn't help feeling some responsibility for getting lost and failing to make it back to him. At the very least, he could have comforted him in his passing. McKinlay choked up remembering Mamen teaching him how to ski, and then had to smile as he recalled that one day near the ship when Captain Bartlett had followed Mamen off the big jump they built and landed hard on his backside, his skis and poles a tangled mess. But now McKinlay mourned the loss of a fellow he'd bonded with over knowledge and ideas: "It gave me a terrible shock," he wrote. "The last of my scientist colleagues had gone."

Munro and Maurer tried to buttress McKinlay's spirits by saying that Templeman had assured them Mamen died peacefully in his sleep. But now they were all quite worried about Templeman. They'd wanted him to come with them, but he was too weak to walk. Now he was alone at Rodger's Harbor in a tent near the rough graves of two dead men, and already his mental state was tenuous. He'd been half-crazed with fright and famine when they arrived, and they'd promised to return as soon as they could. Though they'd moved the tent some distance from the bodies and reinforced it, it was hard to imagine the loneliness and terror he must be enduring. They'd need to return to offer him morale and physical support soon, for he could not hunt or fend for himself, and he was dangerously low on food.

Munro took McKinlay aside and discussed plans. There was, said Munro, some positive news. On the way from Rodger's Harbor, they'd passed Cape Waring, and the beach was strewn with ample driftwood. Even more encouraging, "tens of thousands of crowbills were nesting on the cliffs south of Cape Waring."* As evidence, Munro produced a dozen of the birds, which he'd shot with Malloch's Mauser pistol. Munro thought that the best current action would be for McKinlay to go with Hadley and Kuraluk and his family there, to a prominent sandspit he'd seen near a small bay, and set up the large dome-shaped bell tents that they'd brought from the *Karluk*. Munro and Maurer would help McKinlay make a few trips back north to Shore Camp and guide the others there too. The hunting prospects, and arrival of birds, appeared most promising near Cape Waring. After they were all safely encamped, Munro—and possibly Maurer—would return to

---

* The birds referenced, which Chafe also refers to as the "crowbill duck," were the common murre of the auk family, among the most numerous bird species in the Northern Hemisphere, which have colony populations that sometimes number in the millions and have some of the most densely packed nesting colonies of any bird species in the world. Sitting upright on their cliff dwellings, with their white fronts and black head, neck, and backs, the murre presents the appearance of a penguin.

Templeman at Rodger's Harbor. With this settled, Munro and Maurer departed north to Shore Camp to gather their belongings before moving down to support Templeman at Rodger's Harbor.

Meanwhile, McKinlay, Hadley, and Kuraluk's family headed south to the agreed-upon Cape Waring campsite. Instead of staying inland, Kuraluk took them out onto the sea ice east of the headland, and although the soft ice worried McKinlay, it held. By the morning of June 5, they'd made it to their destination.

They plopped down onto the sandspit and were just boiling tea when a flock of geese flew overhead, and to McKinlay's amazement, Kuraluk shouldered his rifle and fired into the sky, bringing down a fat goose that landed on the gravel right next to them. "No sooner was it dead," wrote McKinlay, "than it was plucked and in the pot and we had a fine feed of stewed goose." The taste of fresh meat revived everyone and inspired Hadley and Kuraluk to go hunting. Kuraluk returned first, dragging a young seal and carrying six seagulls. Auntie and the girls, smiling and laughing, skinned the seal, and Auntie cut slabs and started cooking some of the seal for dinner. Hadley arrived just as the seal was ready to eat, bringing with him ten more seagulls. "So was founded our new home," wrote McKinlay that night, in much better spirits, "and as Genesis has it, 'There was still corn in Egypt . . . that we may live and not die.'"

McKinlay tried to shore himself up for the travails the next few days would bring. It would be a struggle to go north to Shore Camp and transport Clam, Chafe, Breddy, and Williamson the thirty or so hard miles back to Cape Waring, but he had to try. He sat in the tent eating a stew Auntie had made using parts of seagull, seal, and blubber. Then Hadley surprised McKinlay with a cigarette, the first smoke he'd enjoyed in months. It wasn't tobacco; Hadley had scraped the bark off what he thought was a dwarf species of Arctic willow, then ground the bark and rolled cigarettes from pages of paper torn from his freemasonry books, which he'd saved from the *Karluk*. The smoke was sweet and relaxing and soothed McKinlay for the task ahead. Hadley, puffing on a cigarette, then asked McKinlay if he wanted to move in with him and Kuraluk's family when he got back. McKinlay appreciated the gesture, desiring some sense of belonging. He agreed, provided it was okay with Munro.

Auntie handed McKinlay a cooked gull to eat on the trail and packed half a dozen more uncooked birds for him to take to the men still at Shore Camp. He'd have to go alone again despite Captain Bartlett's repeated warnings against solo travel. Kuraluk and his entire family were suffering snow blindness from the recent trip to Cape Waring, and Hadley needed to hunt for food.

McKinlay, strengthened by the seal and seagull meat, made great time, arriving back at Shore Camp by early afternoon. Everyone there was happy to see him but most anxious to know whether he'd come with fresh meat, and when he produced the seagulls, they appeared deflated, having hoped for bear or seal or walrus. "But after I let them have a taste of my cooked gull," recorded McKinlay, "they changed their attitude pretty quickly and could hardly wait to have their birds cooked."

Munro was still at Shore Camp, readying his things, and he'd broken down some of the camp. McKinlay told him of Hadley's invitation, and Munro had no objection to it. Now it was time to start the move. McKinlay's idea was to use the sled and take all the tents and gear halfway to Cape Waring while Breddy and Chafe walked there with Munro and Maurer. Then McKinlay would double back to get Williamson and Clam; both were so sick they would be forced to ride in the sled. Clam's toe amputation wound prevented him from walking, and both he and Williamson remained afflicted by the swelling sickness.

The journey to the halfway point and back was tiring for McKinlay. After a quick cup of black tea, he situated Clam and Williamson in the sled and started off once more. The load burdened the dogs, and McKinlay drove them, lurching along awkwardly at the sled handles. When they arrived at the designated stopping place, McKinlay found everyone sound asleep, splayed on the ground. No tents were erected, and they'd built no cook fire. He called to Munro and the others, but no one got up to help him as he unhitched and fed the dogs rotten chunks of seal parts and blubber, then attended to Clam and Williamson, assisting them one at a time from the sled and leading them to some skins he'd laid out on the ground. McKinlay, too, bedded down on the ground, too tired to do anything more. He'd been going for nearly twenty-four straight hours.

The next morning, Munro suggested that since Maurer knew the way, he should guide Breddy and Chafe to Cape Waring on foot, while McKinlay and Munro transported Clam and essential gear there in the sled, leaving Williamson behind for the time being. They'd come back for him later. The day was dull and foggy, and within an hour, McKinlay and Munro came to a disagreement about the route. Munro had led them in the wrong direction for hours, and finally McKinlay snapped, yelling that they should be staying nearer the lagoon, which led to the headland. Soon the two were shouting at each other as Clam sat silent on the sled.

McKinlay's emotions had finally boiled over, and it had nothing to do with the best route to Cape Waring. The truth was, Munro's decision to go to Rodger's Harbor really bothered him. Munro would be down there, having only Templeman and Maurer to worry about, while McKinlay would be left in charge of everyone else. He felt like he was being forced to do Munro's job, and it was an unfair amount of responsibility. He'd hired on as a magnetician-meteorologist, and now, having lost first Stefansson and then Captain Bartlett, he was in effect inheriting the position of expedition leader. It felt like more pressure than he could bear.

While they were still barking at each other, McKinlay took over trailbreaking. He was still fuming as he walked along, but then he noticed something up ahead, coming from a bare patch of ground in the snowfield: it was a splash of dazzling purple color. He stopped yelling and knelt to look at it. "It was a patch of lovely little wildflower . . . a purple patch striking in its contrast to the surrounding white wilderness. . . . The edge of the snow had been undercut by the wind and the little plants were alive with color for quite a distance under the snow." McKinlay stared in awe at the beauty, the life springing forth from this lifeless place. He stopped arguing with Munro and was overcome with a feeling of profound calm. He thought for a moment of his late-night talks with Bartlett on the *Karluk* about roses and other flowers; he thought about Bjarne Mamen and the adage he'd heard him utter: "As long as there is life, there is hope." McKinlay looked up from the gorgeous little flowers, smiled, and went forward, leading Munro and Clam straight into camp.

That night, he felt renewed by the wildflower he had seen. "My spirit was lifted," he wrote. "My mood transformed, my outlook changed . . . Thoughts of death had been uppermost in our minds these recent days, but here was proof that life could still triumph in this bleak landscape. I arrived in camp with feelings of renewed faith and hope." It helped that while they'd been away, Kuraluk had killed a large seal, and Hadley had bagged ten crowbills. As Auntie prepared the fresh seal meat, Maurer arrived with Breddy and Chafe around nine o'clock, and they all ate together.

All that was left was to go back for Williamson. McKinlay, with re-newed magnanimity—and a full stomach—offered to go. Auntie parceled out some seal meat for him to give Williamson. The dogs were so run-down by now that they strained pulling the sled even though it was empty, forcing McKinlay to walk rather than ride. He arrived to find Williamson asleep on the ground in a heap of gear, and he woke him gently and fed him the seal meat. McKinlay loaded everything on the sled, fed the dogs some seal parts, and they started back for Cape Waring at four in the morning, though by now, in the constant light, time was irrelevant.

McKinlay opted for the lagoon route and for a while they had fast, firm ice, but it didn't last. They began to encounter melting ice, and big pools of water on the surface covered with just a sheen of thin ice. The dogs balked at the pools, halting and shying away even as McKinlay urged them for-ward. At one place, the animals skidded to a stop, and the sled broke through the ice, sliding into the water at a sharp angle, with Williamson clinging to the rails for his life. McKinlay managed to manhandle the sled and wrest it from the water, but the dogs were so skittish they broke from their traces and ran off in the direction of Cape Waring. At least, thought McKinlay, he knew where they were heading.

McKinlay hauled the sled shoreward and off the dangerous ice, but he did not have the strength to go far. Williamson, soaked and cold and feverish, got out of the sled and tried to walk, grasping at the sled handles to keep from pitching forward, but he lurched only a few dozen reeling steps before he stopped and bent over, heaving with fatigue and sickness. They were nearly ten miles from the others at Cape Waring, and without the dogs, Williamson would never get there. McKinlay offered to pitch a tent for him and go on for help, but Williamson declined, saying he'd just lie back down on the sled. McKinlay prepared bedding in the sled bottom of "sealskin, a heavy deerskin and two fawn skins," and wrapped him in wool blankets and the canvas tent fly and went on for help, telling him someone would be back for him soon.

The snow in the low foothills was softening and McKinlay broke through to his thighs as he trudged forward, cursing the dogs. The day was bright now and McKinlay realized that in the food-and sleep-deprived odyssey of the last two days, he'd forgotten to wear his snow goggles. It was an unforgivable mistake, but there was nothing to do about it now except plod on, his eyes afire. He straggled into camp half-blind, shielding his eyes with his forearm, but was relieved to learn that the dogs had come straight here and Kuraluk had taken them to retrieve Williamson.

McKinlay entered the large dome tent—his new home he'd be sharing with Kuraluk's family and Hadley—and tumbled over, spent. He'd been going almost constantly for three days, and needed sleep, but the burning in his eyes kept him awake, and he felt an intense urge to rub them, to "ease the feeling in them of being full of sand and grit." He fought the temptation, knowing it would only make things worse. As he lay in agony, his eyes swelled completely shut. He tried in vain to will himself to sleep, but he kept thinking about Williamson alone on the sled and could only lie awake, his eyes in agony. Sometime in the afternoon he heard the dogs outside the tent, and Williamson's voice, and knew that Kuraluk had gotten him in safely. Everyone except Templeman was now at Waring Point.

The next morning, McKinlay could barely see, so he listened carefully to what was happening around him. Munro came in to tell him he was leaving with Maurer for Rodger's Harbor. Later, Hadley sat beside him and took out his medical kit—which had been retrieved from things left previously at Skeleton Island—and injected McKinlay's eyes with cocaine, then irrigated them with zinc sulfate and wrapped his head and eyes in a cloth bandage. For days, McKinlay was led around the camp by Helen and Mugpi, who seemed to find it an amusing game, and Auntie had to feed him by hand.

The trip from Shore Camp down to Cape Waring had also been tough on Clam. His feet seemed little changed—at least so far requiring no further surgery—but his body was grossly enlarged from the swelling sickness, his limbs and torso engorged to nearly twice their normal size. For days after their arrival, they had to keep Clam propped up in a sitting position, "For when he lay down he would choke and his eyes would roll right around so that you could see the whites of them only," Chafe wrote in his diary. Clam was in such bad shape that Chafe, Breddy, and Williamson—sharing a tent with him—expected him to die at any moment. But he hung on.

One night days later, McKinlay was awakened by moaning and wailing from the other tent, and dire shouts that Williamson could not breathe. He could hear Williamson crying out about chest pains, about a burning in his heart. Hadley rushed out to help, returning to inform McKinlay that he'd found Williamson "sitting on a log, the fear of death on his face." Williamson was convinced that he was having a heart attack, but after examining him and questioning him, Hadley concluded it was just a case of acute heartburn and indigestion. He gave him some medicine from the diminishing stores in the kit, and Williamson calmed down. Hadley discovered that those in the other tent had consumed two crowbills apiece and shared a couple of gulls. Williamson's attack of indigestion was likely from gorging too much, too fast with a severely shrunken stomach.

This was the second incidence of someone overeating or not equitably sharing food with the group, and it concerned McKinlay. Honesty and fairness would be essential to avoid devolving into anarchy. McKinlay took off his eye bandages in the tent long enough to record in his journal, "It was apparent that rationing of food was going to be just as much trouble when we had plenty as when we had practically none."

37

THE *BEAR*

CAPTAIN BARTLETT WAS GETTING AROUND MUCH BETTER, HAVING received further medical treatment during his stay in St. Michael, this time from a US government physician stationed there. Each day, Bartlett would walk from his hotel down to the wireless station, where the workers at the office—now warmed up to the seasoned mariner and fond of his stories— gave him copies and papers to read, as he put it, "So that I could get an idea of what was happening in the world." He got snippets about unrest and violence breaking out in Europe. Tensions were high, and widespread war appeared imminent. But Bartlett flipped through these reports with distracted interest. The news of the *Karluk* survivors, it seemed to him, was much more pressing and important, and he was frustrated by· the waiting. He wanted to act and grew more impatient with each day.

Then, when he least expected it, fortune turned Bartlett's way. The *Bear*, which had been en route to Nome, carrying mail, was unable to land there because of the same ice that had prevented Captain Pedersen from anchoring there in the *Herman*. Instead, the *Bear* kept on going and docked at St. Michael. Bartlett wasted no time in boarding the ship and seeking out its skipper, Captain Cochran. They discussed the dire straits of those marooned on Wrangel Island, and Captain Cochran and his officers expressed their desire to attempt a rescue. Animated, Bartlett said he wished to accompany them. That would be fine. The problem was, said Captain Cochran, that he had yet to receive any official orders to alter his itinerary.

And he had numerous preexisting stops and responsibilities. Among them, he had on board an important dignitary, Lord William Percy, the son of the Duke of Northumberland. Lord Percy had engaged the *Bear* to study the waterfowl—and particularly ducks—of the northern waters. Additionally, the *Bear* was also scheduled to deliver mail along the Siberian shores and serve throughout the region for various other deliveries of goods and passengers.

Out of curiosity—and to get a good look at the ship—Bartlett sought Lord Percy out. "My first meeting with him," he wrote, "was down in the 'tween-decks of the *Bear*, in a corner among boxes and barrels, surrounded by various kinds of knives, scissors, and other gear necessary to mount birds." They had a very sociable chat and Lord Percy passed on well-wishes from some of Bartlett's friends in Boston and New York who had learned of his safe landing in Alaska. Bartlett was impressed by Lord Percy's ornithological knowledge, and the two developed an instant connection.

Captain Bartlett was also impressed by the ship—a dual steam-powered and sailing vessel built in Scotland in 1874 for sealing—which had been reinforced especially for ice-filled waters and was a forerunner of more modern icebreakers. The *Bear* had been involved in not only the dangerous and heroic rescue of Commander Greely and surviving members of the Lady Franklin Bay Expedition in 1884 but more recent relief efforts following the 1906 San Francisco earthquake as well. If any ship could make it through those waters, Bartlett figured it was the *Bear*. After spending time with Cochran, Bartlett was equally confident that "her master . . . was not afraid to put her in the ice." Bartlett felt that Providence might once again have stepped in: "On the whole," he wrote, "it seemed to me that it would be a matter of singular interest for the *Bear* to rescue the *Karluk* survivors as she had rescued the Greely party thirty years before, on the other side of the continent."

Unfortunately, it was time for the *Bear* to head across and into Siberian waters to deliver mail and perform some other obligations. Captain Bartlett bade goodbye to Lord Percy and Captain Cochran, hoping that he'd see them again, and very soon. All he needed was the official orders to come through from the US government, and Cochran would turn around and come for him, either at St. Michael or Nome.

Anxious and not wanting to remain idle in St. Michael any longer, Bartlett secured passage by motorboat to Nome. The smaller craft was able to get him close enough to disembark, despite the thick ice there. Once in Nome, Bartlett continued investigating various rescue options. He spent much of his time at the harbor, talking with captains leaving on walrus-hunting or trading expeditions, imploring them—if they came anywhere in the vicinity of Wrangel Island during their travels—to look for the survivors along the shorelines. They were amenable, but most told him that the reports of the season's ice were not at all encouraging: the ice was densely packed, and "people were saying that the ice conditions were the worst in history."

So Bartlett's excruciating waiting game continued. He now feared, based on the current reports of ice conditions, that it would be early August—and quite probably later—before any ship might reach Wrangel Island. He felt sadness and guilt, thinking about the survivors. In his haste to leave on his journey with Kataktovik, he'd written his instructions to Munro telling him to move to Rodger's Harbor in mid-July, when they should expect rescue. But now, reflecting on it, he knew he'd given them all the impression that help would come much sooner than it actually might, if it came at all.

38

CROWBILL POINT

CLAM REFUSED TO DIE. AFTER SPITTING UP BLOODY FOAM AND having his eyes roll back in his head more than once, he miraculously revived. Then, after a few days, he improved dramatically. Not that he was any more talkative, but he was able to rise and move around the tent, scuffling and dragging his mangled foot. Everyone had been worried that he would succumb to the same fate as Malloch and Mamen, but for the moment, his stoic stubbornness seemed to be keeping him alive.

Their nickname for the cliffy area around Cape Waring was Crowbill Point, because of the large number of birds there. Five main cliffs dotted the cape, the first about two miles from camp and the last of them some five miles away. Initially the hunters were quite productive, though it was a vigorous day's event to hunt the farthest of the cliffs and return—a journey, with detours to jump creeks or avoid water—of a dozen miles. Chafe and Breddy did the hunting for their tent while Clam and Williamson convalesced. Kuraluk and Hadley hunted for their tent until McKinlay was able to remove the bandages from his eyes and contribute.

When the crowbills were nesting and huddled together, a hunter could get between a dozen and twenty-five of the birds in a night. But since the men had no shotguns, they had to use their pistols and rifles, and the haul of birds came at a considerable cost to their ammunition, which was not unlimited. Both tents agreed that all the birds—all game, for that matter—would be divided equally between the tents based on the number of persons, regardless of who shot the game. This, in theory, would ensure equal and fair distribution, since they were all living together in close proximity at Cape Waring and hunting was for their communal survival. Williamson's tent had four people, and Hadley's five, since as they counted young Helen and Mugpi as one adult. Once the kill was divided, each tent was then in charge of storing, cooking, and rationing their own stores. That was the agreement, anyway.

McKinlay was relieved to have his eyesight again, reveling in the simple act of being able to feed himself. "It was a joy," he wrote, "to be able to eat my evening meal without help, picking my bird to the last scrap of meat." And he continued to be impressed by Auntie's skillful rationing, which was having the effect of their portions lasting twice as long as that of Williamson's tent. "The difference," recorded McKinlay, was that Auntie "cooked only one bird per meal and we drank tea with it, saving the juice, which we boiled up later, with seal blubber and some seal blood." The result was that for Auntie, the same number of birds extended to a second meal, a rich blood soup. Williamson, Breddy, Chafe, and Clam were eating two birds each per meal and consuming all their soup. McKinlay observed their excessive consumption, and it worried him.

The crowbills left the cliffs at intervals in great numbers, heading out to open water to feed. Sometimes they were gone a day, sometimes two. When they left, the hunters would try for seagulls. One day Kuraluk and Hadley were off at the cliffs. McKinlay had stayed behind with Auntie and the girls to mend some of his clothes, since he was planning a trip down to Skeleton Island to retrieve some of his things and recover anything else of use to the group. As he sewed, he heard some footsteps outside the tent and peered through a small hole and watched as Chafe and Breddy brazenly helped themselves to Auntie's soup. His tent's soup! "They went about it so freely," McKinlay wrote, "that I was sure that they thought no one else was in camp." Then McKinlay watched as Breddy reached into Auntie's storage tin and handled his tent's birds, and later, when he checked and counted them, they were indeed one short. For the moment

McKinlay said nothing, but Breddy and Chafe were certainly going to need to be watched.

One evening McKinlay decided his eyes were finally well enough for him to make the trip to Skeleton Island. His knapsack was still there, as were many rounds for the Mauser pistol. He poked his head into Williamson's tent and asked for the Mauser, figuring he might encounter game either going or returning. He was also reluctant to travel alone and unarmed, in the event of bears. But Williamson said Munro had instructed him that the Mauser was to remain with this tent. McKinlay found this reasoning odd, and he didn't really believe it, but he chose not to press the issue and struck out at nine o'clock with the sled and the three dogs. Not long into his journey, thick fog settled over the coast and he found himself pushing through deep snowmelt, sometimes wading to his waist. The dogs floundered, and he had to pick his way inland but managed to reach Skeleton Island sometime during the night.

Munro had taken most everything already, but McKinlay loaded what remained onto the sled, and after a brief rest, he returned to Cape Waring at eleven the next morning, soaked and tired. When he arrived, a gale was blowing and Auntie and Hadley were outside their dilapidated tent, securing the pegs with logs and large pieces of driftwood to keep it from being blown completely down. He dropped the sled and hurried to help. Chafe and Breddy were outside, securing their own tent, and the gale wreaked havoc across the camp: cooking pots and tins flew through the air, skittering across the beach; flaming driftwood blew a conflagration, chunks of coals and embers trailing into the sky. Everyone was running around, yelling, calling out directions, and after rolling enough logs and stones on the windward sides of the tents, they managed to get them all righted and standing again.

The wind abated after a few hours, and McKinlay took inventory of the items he'd brought back: 270 rounds of Mauser ammunition; 7 tins of pemmican; 1 empty biscuit tin; 1 empty coal oil tin; and his personal knapsack, which he noted "had been thoroughly ransacked. Many of my belongings were missing, among them two Jaeger caps, a sack of boot packing, a notebook, several pairs of Jaeger socks and my compass." McKinlay was equally saddened and angered by the thievery, as it meant it would now be hard to know whom to trust. Munro and Maurer had most recently been to Skeleton Island and had contact with the bag, but several others had access previously, including Breddy. It might have been any of them. He knew that it was no one in his own tent, since none of them had been down to Skeleton Island.

About one o'clock in the morning on June 18, Munro and Maurer showed up from Rodger's Harbor. They sat down next to Hadley's tent and cooked ten crowbills, and to McKinlay's shock, "they ate every one of them at one sitting." They apparently weren't overly concerned about rationing, saying that there were flocks of ducks around Rodger's Harbor. Neither did they offer to share any of their birds. The biggest issue was ammunition. That's why they had come. As Munro chewed away on a crowbill leg, he told Hadley to give him fifty rounds for his rifle. McKinlay quickly did the math, since from his time way back at Shipwreck Camp, he'd overseen all the inventory. The 50 rounds would give Munro, counting what he claimed he still had left, 170 rounds for him, Maurer, and Templeman. That left only 146 rounds for Kuraluk and Hadley to use in their rifles, and they had to effectively support all ten members at Cape Waring.

Hadley argued that the distribution of ammunition was unfair, and that given how few they'd be left with, they'd no longer be able to shoot birds and would have to save the precious ammo for seals or bears or walrus—anything bigger. But they'd seen no larger game for some time. The two men hollered back and forth at each other until Munro reminded Hadley that Captain Bartlett had left him in charge. Hadley handed over the fifty rounds but did so under protest.

McKinlay took Munro aside, out of earshot of the others. He confided in Munro that there'd been some stealing by members of the other tent and mentioned the items missing from his personal bag. Munro assured McKinlay that he hadn't touched any articles in his bag when he'd left it at Skeleton Point and continued down to Templeman at Rodger's Harbor. McKinlay wasn't sure whether to believe him. At any rate, Munro promised McKinlay that he'd make a note and log the incidents of stealing in his report for the captain.

Munro and Maurer spent most of the day sleeping outside the tents, not once visiting the men in Williamson's tent. It seemed odd behavior to McKinlay—especially for a so-called leader—as if they were now operating on their own, disconnected from the larger group. Breddy noticed it, too, and late in the afternoon he came out and "demanded in very strong language that they visit the other tent." Breddy asked Hadley and McKinlay to come along as witnesses to the meeting. At first it was relatively civil. Breddy and Williamson wanted everyone to be here at Cape Waring so they could all work together and take care of one another and forage for food as one. Munro firmly reminded them of Bartlett's orders that they maintain separate camps and fend for themselves. Someone barked back that no ship was ever coming, and they'd have to survive the winter here.

Voices rose and, according to McKinlay, "All the pent-up ill-feelings of months erupted in an orgy of charges and counter charges. The language was loud and obscene. It was almost impossible to make sense out of the barrage of words." Breddy called McKinlay nothing but a "bloody scientist!" and said that Maurer should remain here at Cape Waring and McKinlay should go to Rodger's Harbor, where he belonged in the first place. Munro retorted that McKinlay no longer wished to be there, which wasn't true—he simply had not been physically able to go before. McKinlay listened to the screaming and blaming, his head aching. He longed to be "away from all the moaning and whining and suspicion" and the stealing, but there was nothing to do about it now. Maurer had taken his place at Rodger's Harbor, and that was that. And per Bartlett's instructions, someone needed to be there in case a ship came. In the end, the yelling and bickering subsided, and Munro and Maurer struck south again to be with Templeman, who was still alone at Rodger's Harbor and needed their help. He could not survive alone.

Hadley and McKinlay now understood they'd need to be incredibly sparing with ammunition. They talked it over with Kuraluk and he agreed. He immediately started fashioning a bow and arrows out of driftwood and willows to hunt birds with. Hadley and McKinlay forayed some distance out onto the lowland bluffs beyond the cliffs to assess prospects for seals in the lagoon. As they looked out to the northeast, they were convinced they could see land beyond Herald Island. They knew it was unlikely, yet there it seemed to loom on the horizon. Two days later they saw it again. McKinlay knew that it was almost certainly an Arctic mirage playing tricks on him. But they continued to see it day after day and felt so certain it was land that they named it Borden Land after Canada's prime minister. Illusion or not, it would be their private discovery for the annals of the Canadian Arctic Expedition. Whatever Stefansson might find— wherever the hell he was—they had found and named Borden Land, real or not, and it proved an amusing distraction as they scoured the horizon for seals.

Privately, McKinlay and Hadley also knew—from the amount of sea ice still surrounding the island—that Bartlett's rescue ship estimate of mid-July was optimistic at best. That date was only a few weeks away. No ship would get here before the middle of August, they concluded, and it could be even later, or not at all should conditions conspire against them. They well remembered the ice that had trapped the *Karluk* last August and held her in its death grip for months. With just 140 rifle rounds and Kuraluk's bow and arrows, they'd somehow have to sustain themselves for at least two months. "We had to face the possibility that a ship might not be able to get through before the ice closed in again," McKinlay recorded in his diary, "or that the Skipper might never have reached civilization. Then we would have another winter ahead of us. But that prospect was too awful to contemplate."

So they focused on the only thing they could: the present. How could they procure food and at the same time conserve precious ammunition? Hadley had an idea: They'd build a tall ladder, with rope rails and driftwood rungs, and carry it to the cliffs. Then they'd use the ladder to climb down the cliff faces onto the flat ledges and raid the crowbill or gull nests of eggs—as well as capturing any birds they could. That night they hiked the few miles to the cliffs and scrambled up to the bottom of one of the ledges where they'd seen birds flying and landing. Together, they propped the ladder up at an angle and McKinlay began a slow, methodical ascent, one slick and rickety rung at a time.

The top of the ledge was a few feet above the last rung of the ladder. McKinlay stood precariously on the top rung while Hadley tried to hold it steady, but the ladder wobbled dangerously. McKinlay reached out for a rock protruding from the cliff face to haul himself over the top, but as he pulled himself up the rock gave way, coming loose in his hand. He plummeted backward, loose rocks flying through the air next to him, and both the rocks and McKinlay sailed past Hadley, who ducked just in time. McKinlay thumped hard in snow and slid several yards before slamming onto ice at the cliff bottom. He got up, brushed himself off, and checked his limbs. Fortunately, he was only badly bruised and shaking with fear. Nothing had broken.

After that accident they moved to some more accessible cliffs and McKinlay reluctantly climbed the ladder again, but the ledges they raided yielded only ten eggs. They figured they were too early, since most of the nests were empty, and hoped for better luck in the weeks ahead. McKinlay's hind end and back ached so badly from the fall that he could not hunt the next day. While McKinlay recovered in camp, Hadley had another idea. They would build a bosun's chair out of a flat piece of drift lumber and some cordage, and using this, they could lower McKinlay from a cliff top down to get eggs. McKinlay agreed to try it once he got over the soreness and fright from the recent fall and regained some strength: "Unfortunately the kind of diet we were getting made me in no condition for such mountaineering exploits," he had to admit.

Everyone at Cape Waring continued to subsist on birds and bird eggs, with occasional supplement from the few tins of pemmican McKinlay had brought back from Skeleton Island, but that was almost gone now. Both Kuraluk and Auntie had been getting a few birds each day with the bow and arrows, and even little Helen had been hunting with some success. She came trotting back to camp one morning carrying a dead seagull.

She'd devised a clever hunting method: "She had fastened a piece of blubber to a feather quill, to which she attached a piece of string, anchored by a stone. When the gull swallowed the blubber, the quill stuck in its gullet." McKinlay smiled as he watched Helen and Mugpi pluck and cook the bird, then share it between themselves, giving a few scraps to little Nigeraurak. But the daily bird kill was merely subsistence, and sometimes the hunters were out for nearly twenty-four hours just to bring back a dozen birds and a handful of eggs.

Chafe and Breddy did all the hunting for the other tent, but they were going through their rations too fast, and it remained a constant worry to McKinlay and Hadley. They needed a seal, and soon. McKinlay saw one on the morning of June 21, on the ice about 250 yards beyond the cliffs to the north of the beach, but the seal proved wary, sliding off the ice and down into his hole when McKinlay tried to creep closer. McKinlay told Hadley about the big seal, and Hadley stalked it for two days, lying in wait stationary on the ice while the seal was basking, then creeping closer every time the seal slept. Hour after hour Hadley stalked and silently slithered along the ice, until at last he got close enough and fired. It was a direct hit, but the seal slipped down the ice and into its hole.

Hadley walked back toward camp, hungry and dejected, when suddenly a seal popped up for air in a tidal crack that ran parallel to the beach. Hadley shouldered his rifle and fired, then ran over and dragged the seal out of the water before it could swim away. As he pulled it onto shore, he noticed two bullet holes—remarkably, it was the same seal he'd shot just minutes before. Everyone in camp was excited as Hadley came in dragging the large seal. Auntie and Kuraluk helped Hadley skin and butcher it, and that night they divided the seal evenly between the two tents and feasted on the first full meal they'd had in two weeks. McKinlay was giddy with the fare: "A good helping of underdone seal meat with fresh blubber, and luscious seal soup, flavored with fish, for the stock had been enriched by boiling the seal's stomach, and it was full of tomcod, a small fish about the size of a sardine."

With Auntie's careful rationing, her tent had enough seal to last at least four days. Breddy, Chafe, Clam, and Williamson were less frugal. That night they fried liver and ate almost all the rest of their share. Hadley barked at them again about their overindulgence, but they hardly listened as they chewed greedily, with liver blood running down their beards. They finished all their seal the next morning at breakfast, and had the gall to complain about Auntie's distribution, which she'd done in their presence.

McKinlay recorded the disagreement in his diary: "They were grumbling about the previous day's share-out. . . . Now they were threatening all kinds of trouble, including keeping to themselves all they shot with the Mauser." McKinlay and Hadley just shook their heads in disgust, for they shared everything equally, without question. True to their threats, in the evening Chafe and Breddy went out for birds and eggs and returned with a couple of eggs and four birds, which they cooked for their tent and did not share.

Things were becoming dangerously tense, and McKinlay lay in his tent worrying silently, unable to sleep. He thought of the horrors that the members of the Greely Expedition endured at Cape Sabine as they awaited rescue. They'd survived eight months on just forty days' rations, supplemented by a single polar bear, the odd seal, and near the end, small crustaceans netted from a tidal pool. But things had devolved into anarchy, with men stealing and hoarding food from one another, and they'd even resorted to cannibalism. That thought sent a shiver through McKinlay's entire body. He remembered that when the food thief got caught, after repeated warnings, Commander Greely had ordered—and his men had carried out—a firing squad execution. McKinlay tossed and turned most of the night, trying desperately to drive such thoughts from his mind.

The sound of a gun blast nearby woke him. He hurried for the tent door and stuck his head out to look around. Was he dreaming? Had someone shot at a duck flying over? Or a bear in camp? But there was no one outside. Then he heard Williamson's voice yelling out in panic:

"Clam! Call Hadley! Breddy has shot himself!"

39

"OUR SUSPICIONS HAVE BEEN RAISED"

MCKINLAY SPRINTED TO THE OTHER TENT, WITH HADLEY AND KU-raluk right behind him. Everyone had heard the gunshot, then Williamson's screams. McKinlay flung open the canvas door and burst into the tent. It smelled of spent gunpowder. In the dim light he could see Breddy, lying motionless on his back. McKinlay knelt, repulsed by what he witnessed. Breddy's right eye was gone, blown apart, "powder burned and blackened" where the bullet had entered. There was a bloody exit wound on the left side of his head, just above his ear, slightly higher than the entry point. The bullet had apparently passed through his brain.

Hadley pressed in close, and together, he and McKinlay surveyed the scene. Breddy's right arm was slung alongside his body, his left arm draped over his chest. The Mauser pistol lay at Breddy's left side. Williamson reached over from where he sat on his bed nearest Breddy and picked up the pistol and handed it to Hadley. Clam sat up in his bed farther off, still covered in his blankets, staring blankly at the scene.

Hadley held the Mauser and eyed the two men warily. "Have you another gun in here?" he asked. "Yes," they said in unison. They were both white with fear.

"Give it to me and I'll look after it," Hadley said flatly. It was not a request. Williamson handed him a rifle, a .401 Winchester, and the only three cartridges they had left. Hadley took it. It was his own rifle that he'd lent to Williamson way back at Shipwreck Camp. He hadn't used it for so long that he'd almost forgotten about it.

McKinlay asked Clam and Williamson to describe what had happened. They said they'd been awakened by the shot blast—that's all they knew. Chafe was gone, out hunting. It had to be suicide, or an accident. There was no other explanation. McKinlay and Hadley lifted Breddy and carried him outside and set him on the ground. McKinlay scanned around for a suitable grave site, noting a little rise just behind camp. Williamson and Clam came out and in the presence of everyone, Williamson went through Breddy's bag, tossing the effects on the hard ground. Amid Breddy's stuff were all the items that had been stolen from McKinlay's bag, including his compass, which was rolled up in a sock. No one said anything as a light wind swept over the beach, tossing grit and gravel into Breddy's blood-matted hair.

McKinlay turned away, shocked and dismayed by what had happened. Down the beach about a half mile from camp, he could see Chafe returning from his hunt. He looked to be laboring. McKinlay walked out to meet him and found him struggling to drag two dozen crowbills behind him, tethered by their necks to some old dog traces.

"There's been more trouble in camp," McKinlay said to Chafe.

"What's the trouble now, Mac?"

McKinlay gave Chafe the grim report. Chafe bent over in anguish and disbelief. Seeing his pain, McKinlay took the traces and dragged the birds for him as they returned to camp. Breddy lay there next to a log, covered with a tattered blanket. Chafe stared at his friend for a long time. He'd spent countless hours with the ship's fireman on the *Karluk*, working together and joking around and telling stories into the night as the ice-locked ship creaked and groaned. They'd been igloo and tent mates for months now, ever since Shipwreck Camp. Since they'd been here at Cape Waring, they'd been hunting partners, and just yesterday, Chafe had asked Breddy to accompany him to Crowbill Point. Now Chafe looked up and spoke, his voice frail and whispery: "Last night, when I was getting ready for my hunt,

Breddy came to me and said he was not going with me, but was going to get up early in the morning and clean his revolver, and was going to go out to one of the seal holes to try and get a seal. The poor fellow . . . cleaning his revolver when it accidentally went off."

In the silence that followed, McKinlay could not help wondering: was it an accident or had Breddy taken his own life? If he had committed suicide, what drove him to it? Lack of food? They were all very hungry, and certainly malnourished. Maybe he simply couldn't bear the thought of another long winter on this forlorn island, the thought of starving to death. He'd exhibited bouts of depression aboard the *Karluk*, erratic behavior they all remembered. But this?

McKinlay went with Kuraluk to the top of the knoll behind the camp, and, using an ax, they chopped away at the frozen ground, then dug out the loosened earth with a flat board that served as a shovel. When they thought it was deep enough, they returned to the body. Together with Hadley, they fashioned a stretcher out of tent poles and canvas and hauled Breddy's body up the hill to the grave. When they slid him into the rude depression, it was clear the hole would need to be enlarged to accommodate Breddy's body, still much bloated by the lingering illness. McKinlay said he'd come back and finish the grave later; it was going to take hours to dig down into the permafrost.

Despite the sudden tragedy, they still desperately needed food. Chafe's haul of twenty-three crowbills would not last long. Hadley and Kuraluk headed back out to hunt. Hadley came back that evening empty-handed, having missed a long shot at a seal. But Kuraluk returned dragging a fat seal, and that night Auntie made her special "blood soup." First, she cooked slabs of seal meat, boiling it in water. Then she removed the meat from the pot and began trickling blood from the seal slowly into the boiling water, stirring constantly. She added enough blood for the soup to thicken, then removed the pot to let the liquid cool. After eating the slabs, they sipped at the dense, rich, tangy blood soup, which—even though one of their fellow crew members lay dead on the ground less than a hundred yards away—was warming and deeply satisfying.

. . .

McKinlay spent much of the next day deepening Breddy's grave. It was strange and unsettling to hack into the hard, frozen ground hour after hour next to a dead man. He had to resist the urge to talk to Breddy, and a few times his mind flashed on the image of seeing him dead in the tent, the odd positioning of his arms and hands, the powder-burned hole in his eye and head.

That evening, with the pall of death hanging over Cape Waring, the two tents ate together. Williamson came over with two birds Chafe had shot and handed them to Auntie like a kind of peace offering. Then, after shuffling nervously and making small talk for a time, Williamson admitted that their tent had been holding back birds and eggs for some time, not reporting all their catch; and that Breddy had been stealing birds from Auntie's stores. After Williamson's confession, Chafe and Clam came out of the tent looking sheepish and contrite, and they all ate Auntie's cooking quietly but with a new sense of unity.

When they were done eating together, McKinlay, Hadley, and Kuraluk walked up the slope to the grave site. They smoothed out the bottom some more, then, working together, they lowered Breddy's body down and covered it with planks and driftwood. There wasn't much wood up there, and they'd need to scour the beach for more—it would take a few trips up and down the hill to pile enough to keep the animals from disturbing Breddy—but for now, this crude burial would have to suffice.

The tragedy was a trauma to everyone, but Williamson seemed most changed by it. He started interacting with the children for the first time, giving them little gifts of trinkets and chunks of his last hoarded pemmican. His behavior seemed remorseful, almost repentant. He was up and around more, helping to collect driftwood and stoke the fire. While his behavior was an improvement over his past contentiousness, something about the dramatic change struck McKinlay as curious, even disconcerting. It was as if he'd been liberated by Breddy's death.

The single seal did not last long between nine people, three dogs, and a cat. Chafe continued his evening hunts at Crowbill Point, and Hadley and McKinlay worked to improve and lengthen the ladder for another try at "egging." The additions to the ladder made it heavier and even more unwieldy, but they managed to haul it to the cliffs and lean it against the rock face as the crowbills flew overhead and landed on the shelves. The guttural, low-pitched calls of the colony rose in a braying din, a deafening *aaaaarrr, ARR-ahh*, so loud and cacophonic that Hadley had to shout directions and encouragement as McKinlay eased up the sagging ladder. After his recent fall, McKinlay climbed slowly and with great care. The higher he went, the more the ladder bowed, but he made it to the plateau, and as the black-and-white birds flew off, he managed to pilfer twenty-one eggs and shoot three crowbills with Hadley's revolver.

Back at camp, they discovered that Kuraluk had caught by hand a big eider duck, which for some reason—probably injury—could not fly. It was a decent day's haul, and they each ate two fried eggs and shared the duck and the crowbills. Some of the eggs were unfortunately too advanced in development to still be considered eggs, but they ate them anyway. Chafe joked about it, quipping, "They would not have been considered marketable under the Pure Food Laws of any country. But there were no Pure Food Laws on Wrangel Island, so we ate anything that would sustain life." By the next day, they were completely out of food again. Kuraluk returned sometime in the middle of the night to report that he'd killed two seals—but they were a long way away and he'd need help bringing them in.

To bring in the seals, McKinlay accompanied Kuraluk and Helen the next morning, taking the dogs and sled. It was fourteen miles round trip over melting ice and rough terrain. Deepwater pools along the shoreline wetted them through to the skin. McKinlay fell over with exhaustion when they got back, and he worried about the severe physical cost that the subsistence hunting was having on him. "I began to be aware of my extreme weakness," he wrote. "And this journey made me acutely conscious of the effect malnutrition was having on me." It was almost the end of June. The seals seemed to be farther and farther away from the campsite, probably scared off by the shooting of crowbills at the cliffs. While

McKinlay sat next to the fire, watching Auntie and the girls skin and hack at the seals, he wondered which would run out first, their ammunition or their strength. "A period of crisis was approaching," he scribbled weakly in his diary. "Meat is around but is proving extremely costly to acquire."

And there was something else that was bothering McKinlay, something deeply disturbing to think about, and yet he could not get it out of his mind. It had to do with Breddy. He kept flashing on the way Breddy had looked when they'd found him dead in the tent. The position of his arms, his hand. The location of the Mauser. It had all happened so fast, and they'd moved him so quickly.

On the evening of June 28, McKinlay brought another load of wood up to Breddy's grave. He went alone. He bent down and pulled the planks aside and lifted the blanket off the body. He studied him there, trying to remember him exactly as he'd been just moments after the fatal gunshot. He closed his eyes and pictured the scene as best he could. Then he returned the planks and added the wood he'd brought and went back down to his tent to jot some notes down in his diary. The image was coming clearer now, though it had been three days: "His right hand was not in such a formation as would hold a revolver," he wrote, shuddering at what it might mean. "His four fingers being bent slightly at the first joint and the thumb quite straight and hard against the first finger."

The next day, McKinlay took Hadley aside. Though it was troubling to bring up, he mentioned his misgivings about Breddy's death, the strange positioning of his hands. Hadley agreed that something felt wrong. If he'd shot himself with his right hand, why did Williamson pick up the gun from Breddy's left side? How did it get there? They agreed to ask Chafe, who'd been out hunting when it happened, to press Williamson for more details and see what his story was, since he was the first to find Breddy dead, the one who had called out to the others. Chafe could simply pass off his inquiry as wanting to know everything, since he had not been there.

On the last night of June, McKinlay, Hadley, and Chafe brought more wood, some tattered skins, and armfuls of moss up to Breddy's grave site.

Mist and fog hovered over the cape, and it was eerily quiet; even the crow-bills had stopped their incessant squawking. On top of the planks and driftwood branches they laid out the skins, then heaped moss over the skins and covered everything with piles of the frozen soil, tamping down the mound with their boots and the wooden makeshift shovel. In hushed tones, Chafe told them that he'd asked Williamson about the event, and Williamson had said that he couldn't recall where the pistol was, whether it had been in Breddy's hand or somewhere else. Hadley and McKinlay confirmed that Williamson had handed Hadley the gun, picking it off the floor from Breddy's left side. There was no doubt about that.

The three men agreed not to say anything to anyone else, but to keep a close eye on Williamson. Then they trundled wearily back down the hill to their tents. Neither McKinlay nor Hadley could sleep. Both retreated to their diaries, their thoughts tortured. "Our suspicions have been raised," wrote McKinlay, "by Williamson's strange conduct and by other circumstances, that Breddy did not die by his own hand—either suicide or accidental."

Hadley was even more explicit, beyond suspicion. In his diary he wrote his conclusion: "I think it's nothing but murder."

40
SALAD OIL AND
SCURVY GRASS

DENSE FOG CONSUMED CAPE WARING, CASTING A GLOOM OVER THE camp. Slow hunting and periods of heavy rains added to the dismal mood. Whenever the fog lifted, McKinlay and Hadley and Kuraluk would climb to low hills and scan seaward for seals. Warmer temperatures had moved some of the ice offshore, leaving large stretches of open water. Most of the seals they saw were far out on the ice, and to get them, they'd need a boat.

Hadley and McKinlay convinced Kuraluk to attempt building a kayak. Kuraluk was at first reluctant, and his reservations were reasonable. Hunting seals or walrus in a small, one-person kayak was dangerous. If you capsized offshore in that icy water, you'd drown in minutes. And Kuraluk well knew that he was the only one among them who had experience using a kayak, so it was his life that would be at risk. Kuraluk also did not appear nearly so concerned as the others about their lack of food, telling McKinlay he had "no fear of starving as long as there was blubber." McKinlay argued that he had no desire to exist solely on blubber, and after constant urging, Kuraluk finally agreed to build a kayak if they worked on it together.

Kuraluk found a couple of logs long enough to cut lengths for the frame, and they dragged these near the tents, where they could sit on a stump and work. For tools, all they had were their skinning knives, a snow knife, an ax, and a hatchet. Kuraluk used the hatchet blade as an adze, and with this he began roughing out the side rails and rib frames from the logs. While McKinlay helped, peeling and whittling and bending ribs and cutting lengths of sealskin for lashing the craft together, Hadley and Chafe kept hunting. But both the weather and the game were uncooperative.

Sometimes when ascending the hills to survey the ice conditions for seals or the remote chance of a ship, McKinlay and Hadley passed by Breddy's grave. So far it had remained unmolested by animals, but it was a constant reminder of one of the expedition's darkest hours. In the weeks following Breddy's death, neither of them had openly broached their suspicion about Williamson. Both McKinlay and Hadley, despite having recorded their fears and distrusts in their diaries, went about daily existence. Perhaps, in the emotion and trauma of the event, their minds had played tricks on them. Maybe what they'd seen (or thought they saw) in the tent was like the mirage of Borden Land, an illusion. The more McKinlay pondered it, the less likely it seemed that it was murder. For one thing, he could think of no clear motive for such a violent, unprovoked act. Certainly, Breddy and Williamson had argued in the past, even bitterly—and they'd almost come to blows. But, hell, they'd *all* argued at one time or another. At any rate, Williamson no longer had a gun, and other than begging Auntie for extra seal meat and blubber now and again, he wasn't bothering anyone. And Breddy had endured fits of depression aboard the *Karluk*, so it could have been suicide. Who knew how tormented he really was? As to the odd position of Breddy's hands and the location of the gun afterward, those details were troubling but inconclusive. It was no use creating tension over something they could not prove. Daily survival was difficult enough as it was. Better to let it go. McKinlay seemed to, writing of the event in his diary, "We would never know the answers. . . . Life went on."

As the ice broke apart and created open water in the bay, McKinlay and Hadley encouraged Kuraluk to work on the kayak as much as possible. The construction was a slow, painstaking process. Days of rain helped—the torrential squall made for dismal hunting conditions and provided Kuraluk with time to work. McKinlay was impressed by the man's skill: "He spent one of the wettest days working outside in the rain, putting the finishing touches to the framework, lashing all the separate pieces together with sealskin thongs." He carved and whittled a double-bladed paddle out of a washed-up plank of lumber, and two weeks after starting the task, they brought the frame inside out of the rain to dry. Auntie took measurements and cut lengths of sealskin and sewed these taut around the frame, and the boat was complete on July 18. Everyone was impressed. "When finished," wrote Chafe, "it looked as if it had been made by some expert boat builder, with modern tools and conveniences . . . instead of with only a hatchet and a knife."

He'd finished just in time, because as he readied to launch the kayak for its first hunt, the camp was once again out of food. As McKinlay put it, "the egg market had closed . . . and we were close to starvation level, reduced to chewing sealskin." They ate rancid seal blubber and even tails and flippers that had sat outside in the storage tin so long they were mealy and rotten. Auntie's reserve when the meat ran out was blubber dipped into a special oil she made.

McKinlay watched carefully and recorded the process for making what he called, with some irony, "salad oil": "The oil is made by cutting blubber into small pieces and putting it in a 'poke,' which is a sealskin cut in such a way that the skin is complete except for a hole at the neck and another at the tail." The blubber-filled poke was then left outside until the blubber fermented into a sour-tasting oil. Into this oil they dipped the chunks of blubber, making it slightly more palatable than straight blubber. The Eskimos relished it, but McKinlay and the others ate the oil-dipped blubber only out of desperate hunger.

When the rain finally stopped for a couple of days, they decided to move the tents a few hundred yards to the northern end of the beach, which was closer to more driftwood. During the move, McKinlay stumbled upon a plant that looked familiar to him, like sorrel he knew from his home in Scotland. He bent to check it out: it had small green leaves and little white flowers. He plucked a few of the leaves, put them in his mouth, and chewed, finding the flavor acidic but not unpleasant. He took a few handfuls back to the new campsite and showed it to the others. Hadley recognized it, having seen and even eaten it before, when he was living and trading at Point Barrow. He called it "scurvy grass" and said it got its name because mariners used to eat it to prevent scurvy. Everyone liked it, and McKinlay kept collecting handfuls along the shore, where it grew in little clusters. Auntie added bunches of it to her scant larder, using it as an herb or spice to flavor any food she cooked.

By late July, they were surviving on rancid blubber and oil; thin, weak blood soup from Auntie's final stash; seal flippers and tails; and the scurvy grass. They'd picked over the last of the crowbill and seagull carcasses, eating the necks, heads, feet, and other "nameless parts," as McKinlay put it. Chafe continued at Crowbill Point with the Mauser, but most of the birds in the big colonies had left the cliffs, and to get at the few that remained was too dangerous in his diminished state. His legs had become so weak that he could no longer leap over small leads or tidal cracks, and while out hunting, he'd had to use the sled as a bridge whenever he came to even small gaps of open water, crawling over it to the other side.

McKinlay kept up his daily ritual of climbing the hill behind camp, above Breddy's grave, and scanning to the east, out into the vast Arctic Ocean. On clear days, he could see the pressure ridges, that imposing ice range they'd fought their way through for weeks. Warmer temperatures and shifting ice were grinding the ridges down, crumbling them to pieces as the ice twisted and shattered beneath them. He could hear the distant rumbling as they disintegrated, and he hoped this movement presaged open seas and the arrival of a ship. But he knew in his heart that it was too soon. He thought of Munro and Maurer and Templeman at Rodger's Harbor and wondered how they were faring. Someone should try to get there to check on them, but he doubted anyone had the strength. He certainly didn't. They'd need more food before such an attempt. They needed more food soon, period, or it was over for them all. "We can stand a bit yet," he wrote, "but let us pray something will turn up before things get too bad."

And then, almost as if he'd willed it to happen, something did turn up: a distinct barking and bellowing, the lionlike roars of walrus* in the bay.

---

* To this day, Wrangel Island supports the world's largest population of Pacific walrus.

41

"DOING SOMETHING AT LAST"

CAPTAIN BARTLETT BOARDED THE *BEAR* ON JULY 13 IN NOME, ALASKA, as a guest of Captain Cochran. "It was a great relief," wrote Bartlett on finally steaming away, "to be really doing something at last. My thoughts were constantly on the castaways, and I wondered how things had been going with them since the middle of March." So far, there'd been no official word from Washington that the *Bear* should be dispatched and rerouted for the rescue mission, but Bartlett had convinced Cochran to allow him passage on the ship during her continued duties along the Siberian coast; should the hoped-for order come through, he'd already be on board.

Bartlett remained anxious, his face taut as he paced the decks of the *Bear*. He'd spent nearly a month in Nome as a guest of Jafet Lindeberg, president of the Pioneer Company and cofounder of Nome. The diversion had been good for Bartlett. He felt strong again, having gained back most of the forty pounds that had been drained from him during the arduous trek with Kataktovik. To pass the time waiting for the ice to clear, he'd accompanied Lindeberg on horseback during a couple of inspection trips. (Lindeberg had conceived of and created a forty-mile ditch that brought water from the mountains to his mining sluices, and in the short season between June and September, before the winter snows shut everything down, the ditch required inspection and maintenance.)

He'd spent the rest of the time between the Golden Gate Hotel, where he stayed and slept, and the Log Cabin Club—a meeting place that boasted a Japanese chef who prepared excellent, memorable dishes. "One dined as well there," said Bartlett, "as at any good hotel in San Francisco." The Log Cabin Club had a massive, rock-chimneyed fireplace, and patrons reclined in comfortable leather-backed chairs after dinner for lively political conversation as they smoked their pipes and cigars and drank tumblers of whiskey and brandy. Bartlett met a host of interesting people and compelling characters at the club, doctors and writers and captains of industry and hardened Alaskan sourdoughs, but all the while, his mind was on those he'd left at Wrangel Island.

Aboard the *Bear*, Bartlett had been invited to sleep in the captain's cabin and was given access to the chart room, where he spent much of his time. He chatted amiably with the crew and officers and learned a great deal from the chief navigating officer, Lieutenant Dempwolf, who was an expert in Alaskan and Siberian waters. Though a master mariner himself, Bartlett was impressed by Cochran's command, Lieutenant Dempwolf's exhaustive breadth of knowledge, and the entire officer corps, crew, and running of the *Bear*. One of their first stops was at Emma Town, where Bartlett disembarked to take care of some important business. He met with his kind host, Mr. Caraieff, who, along with Baron Kleist, had taken him to Emma Harbor. He paid him for his previous help and services, and left money for Mr. Caraieff's brother as well. Then he looked in on the dogs he'd left there. He'd intended to collect them but in the end decided to leave them, as they'd be able to do good work for Mr. Caraieff, and he had no present work for them.

Bartlett could hardly believe how different Emma Town appeared. When he was last here, in late April, everything had been covered in deep snow. Now the ground was bare, the skies cobalt blue, and he could see the high mountains rising up from the ragged, cliffy shoreline. And when he was last here, he'd arrived with Kataktovik after traveling over seven hundred miles—threadbare, sick, and in a kind of stupor. But his goal, then as now, was singular and focused: return to Wrangel Island.

Although the weather was glorious on this mid-July day, it appeared his goal would remain elusive. Reports were coming in from whalers and walrus hunters that ice in the region—and especially offshore—remained heavy and densely packed. By all accounts, it looked to be even worse than last year. The news was discouraging, but Bartlett remained optimistic, knowing how quickly fortunes could shift in the Arctic. There was another impediment, and that was the *Bear*'s busy itinerary. She had numerous stops to make at various communities on both sides of the Bering Strait: at reindeer stations, schools, tiny Native settlements they could only reach by lowering and sending smaller steam launches while the *Bear* sat at harbor. Bartlett knew that Cochran would drop everything the instant official orders came through from Washington, but in the meantime, it was an interminable, tedious, and taxing series of starts and stops. At every stop, he cast his gaze to the north, across the Long Strait, and when it was clear, he thought he could see the dark outline of Wrangel Island rising out of the sea. But he knew it might just be another Arctic mirage.

42

THE SEA SERPENT

KURALUK CREPT DOWN TO THE EDGE OF THE ICE FOOT AT CAPE Waring, quietly dragging the skin kayak behind him. He eased the boat into a small open lead, keeping his eyes always on the massive brown creatures lazing on a small ice floe a few hundred yards offshore. His heart pounded and his hands were clammy inside his mittens, but he grabbed the two-bladed paddle in one hand, his rifle in the other, and slid into the boat. Winds were light and favorable, and he could see an open lane skirting around the floe on which the pod of five enormous animals were sunning. If he took his time and didn't spook them, he might be able to paddle into position for a shot.

Kuraluk had made no secret of his terror of hunting walrus in a skin kayak. He'd told McKinlay and Hadley about it more than once, as soon as the massive creatures had announced themselves with their barking and roaring in the bay. His fears were not unfounded. McKinlay had glassed the animals with binoculars from a bluff, awed by their immense size. The full-grown adults measured up to twelve feet long and could weigh up to three thousand pounds, and though they appeared awkward and lumbering when up on the ice, they were surprisingly agile in the water.

It was their huge white ivory tusks—protruding two feet long straight out of their mouths like spears—that most concerned Kuraluk. Walrus used them to haul their colossal bodies up onto the ice, dig and forage for food, and defend themselves against predators—though given their great size, only polar bears, killer whales, and humans posed any threat to them.

Kuraluk knew that a tusk through the thin skin of the kayak would sink him in an instant. Or the powerful waves of a walrus swimming beneath him or sliding from the ice into the water would capsize him and he would drown. He also knew from experience that with their thick, tough skin and dense, almost impenetrable heads, they were extremely difficult to kill. And a wounded, angry walrus was the last thing he wanted. He'd seen them attack even after being shot numerous times. But he'd had no choice. The camp needed food, and he could not dishonor his family with cowardice. So, he'd gone alone down to the seashore, everyone's hopes for survival depending on his courage and skill.

Between the two tents at Cape Waring, they'd been surviving on seal blubber and scurvy grass for the last couple of weeks. Dejection and depression hung over the wide, flat sandspit. Even Auntie, normally composed in the direst of circumstances, was affected. For many nights she'd lain awake, terror-struck as she listened to the haunting cries of a sea serpent. The unearthly wails and moans came from beneath the sea ice and kept her awake, shaking with fear. McKinlay had asked what was wrong, and Hadley explained that the creature was part of her lore, a mythical underwater serpent with tusks and long, sharp teeth. It was believed to attack ships and boats, sinking them. The cries of the creature came like an omen to Auntie during the first few days that Kuraluk was out hunting in the kayak.

While they waited anxiously for Kuraluk to return, Auntie told everyone to collect all the bird wings in camp. Helen and Mugpi ran around excitedly, picking discarded crowbill and seagull wings from storage tins and plucking them clean down to the bone. With help from Chafe and Williamson, they managed to find fifty-two wings, and Auntie put them in a pot to boil into a bird-wing soup. "We were sitting around the fire anxiously waiting for the bird-wing soup to be ready," wrote Chafe, "as we hoped it would give us new life and strengthen us." The soup had been boiling for about an hour when Hadley, resting in camp after an unsuccessful hunt, called out, "Hey, boys! The Native's got a walrus."

Hadley waved the others over and gave each a turn with his binoculars. Sure enough, there was Kuraluk, paddling along slowly, towing what was clearly a small walrus behind the kayak. "We danced with joy," Chafe remembered of the moment. He went to the cook fire and set the bird bones aside. Auntie started fresh pots of water, and the others hustled down to the shoreline to meet Kuraluk. Soon he paddled up, beaming with pride. Though it was a young walrus, it weighed about seven hundred pounds and required all hands to haul it up a strip of grounded ice and onto shore, dragging it by its short tusks over the icy gravel bar. Kuraluk set to butchering it on the spot to avoid having to drag the heavy carcass any farther. He cut off the broad, oar-shaped front flippers, then the fan-shaped rear flippers. As Kuraluk sliced through the thick, brown, leathery skin, he paused to sharpen his skinning knife, remarking that it had taken five shots in the head to kill the animal.

Both camps ate very well that night. McKinlay described his first meal of walrus as "Excellent! Tasted like roast beef." He had said the same thing about his first bear meat, too, but was so hungry, apparently any large animal meat reminded him of roast beef. When everyone had gorged until they were full, Auntie treated them with a special "dessert" of boiled walrus skin and blubber. "Well boiled," reported McKinlay, "the inner lining resembled a jelly mold, about one-and-a-half inches thick, but it required prolonged chewing before it could be swallowed." Chafe was slightly more generous in his description of Auntie's offering: "The blubber is . . . of a gristly nature, and when boiled for two hours, is very much like cornstarch pudding." Auntie, Kuraluk, and the girls chewed happily, considering the skin and blubber a special treat.

Kuraluk took the kayak out daily through the end of July, even in two short but violent snowstorms, but he had no more success hunting walrus. It may have been that he'd intentionally shot a small youngster and was now avoiding tangling with the three-thousand-pound adults, and no one could blame him. Even so, the kayak proved a lifesaving addition to their hunting tools. During the last days of July, to everyone's joy, Kuraluk killed and secured three bearded seals, the largest about five hundred pounds. Again, as with the walrus, everyone went down to the shoreline and helped heave them out of the water and watched Kuraluk and Auntie skin and butcher them. McKinlay was impressed with the precision and time they took: "Great care was taken in the skinning of the ugruks, for it is their skins that are used in the making of umiaks as well as for boot soles." McKinlay understood that they might very well need an umiak— the skin boats could hold a dozen people—before they were through and could certainly use the tough bearded sealskin for boot soles; his own were riddled with holes.

Kuraluk and Auntie used every part of the large bearded seals, including the intestines, which provided the Scottish schoolteacher with a new culinary experience reminiscent—at least in terms of its containing offal—of his homeland's famed haggis. "The outer skin of the intestines is chopped up with blubber and served as a native delicacy. I thoroughly enjoyed it today; it suggested raw clams!" Kuraluk showed McKinlay the inner intestines, explaining that they could be used as window material in a hut, as well as for waterproof rain parkas.

During the first days of August, Kuraluk cut long strips of lean bearded seal meat and hung them to dry on wooden racks Hadley had built. "We were by now quietly preparing to face another winter," wrote McKinlay with resignation, "so that if a relief ship did not turn up, we would not be completely unprepared." Kuraluk had even located a suitable site for a winter hut they could construct from driftwood, near a little inland valley where he hoped they could secure polar bears and Arctic foxes. Hadley was less than sanguine about their prospects: "I think if we have to winter here that we shall be up against it," he wrote in his diary.

Unfortunately, the hunting successes and elation of having fresh meat proved short-lived. Both Kuraluk and Hadley managed to shoot a few more walrus, but the animals either escaped by swimming off, or sank before either man could get to them. With each passing day, more attention was paid to the condition of the ice and the behavior of the winds. McKinlay climbed to the promontory above Breddy's grave every day, a summit he'd named Storm Top, because from there he could get a good sense of the coming weather. He looked out, noting that "the edge of the pack was many miles off from our bay. . . . Our hopes were high that this wind would bring a ship." But Kuraluk returned later that day from high above the headland, where he'd been scouting, and he reported that the ice remained close to the land there all along the coast; the next day, strong winds blew from the north, completely filling the bay with ice once again and closing off any chance for a ship to land.

Both McKinlay and Hadley had become obsessed with the state of the sea, the behavior of the pack. Hadley returned from hunting empty-handed every day, and on his way back, he would scan the ice, the water, and the horizon for any sign of a ship. One day in early August, he reported that he thought he'd seen smoke from a steamship very far off the island, and there was a momentary buzz of excitement at camp, but most thought he'd probably imagined it, or just wanted it to be true. McKinlay quipped, "It may be that the wish is father to the thought."

The desire—which became more a need—to see a ship became so powerful that Chafe cut holes in the southeast-facing walls of the canvas tent so they could look out toward the sea at any time, night or day. Everyone knew that it wasn't here at Cape Waring, but rather farther south at Rodger's Harbor, that Bartlett intended to come, but there was no way of knowing what was going on down there, or even if Munro, Maurer, and Templeman were still alive to hail or receive a rescue ship. Surely Bartlett would continue up the coast. "That is now our only thought in our waking moments," McKinlay committed to his diary. "When will she come? Will she come? Was the Captain lost? Only time will give the answers. But God forbid that we should have to winter here; it is a hopeless proposition. Our chances will be slim."

One bright spot at Cape Waring was that both Clam and second engineer Williamson were improving physically. Their swollen limbs had improved considerably in the days of eating fresh walrus and bearded seal meat. What tensions had existed between the two tents had also mostly subsided. McKinlay decided it had been too long—over a month—since they'd had contact with those at Rodger's Harbor, so on August 6, he asked Chafe to travel with him there to check on them. He reckoned it was about twenty-five to thirty miles, depending on the route. They took along some of the dried bearded seal meat to eat along the way, and some for Munro, Maurer, and Templeman too.

McKinlay and Chafe bore south along the coast, ascending a high headland that afforded sweeping views seaward; they saw several miles of open water to the north, and a mile or so to the southeast, which was encouraging. They tromped over hilly, rocky ground that became slick and muddy where creeks came down from the high inland mountains. At Hooper's Cairn—about halfway to Rodger's Harbor—they saw heavy ice pack extending from the island's southern coast for miles. Thick mist enveloped them and they skirted inland for some miles, the soles of their skin boots tearing on sharp rocks. They pressed on until they came to a snowmelt river some twenty yards wide. The current was raging too strong to attempt a crossing, and they were forced to turn back. "We got back to camp early the next morning," wrote Chafe. "And almost barefooted. The soles were completely worn off our boots, and our feet were blistered, and so sore that we could not walk for several days."

For weeks after their return, the hunting yielded nothing. Hadley sat hour after hour at seal holes without success; Kuraluk paddled day after day in the bay, but walrus and seals eluded him. Ever industrious, Auntie and the girls started digging into the hard ground near camp to collect the roots of a long, fibrous plant. "It had to be boiled for a long time and required a great deal of chewing," McKinlay wrote, "but it prevented the violent muscular contractions of an empty stomach and deadened the sickening hunger pains." It tasted faintly of licorice. Auntie boiled these roots with scurvy grass and, as McKinlay recalled with disgust, "rotting scraps from our meat tin." Supplementing their diet in this way, Auntie was able to conserve their store of dried seal meat.

But the lack of food and the dull, unvaried days wore on everyone. The days were growing shorter, too, and the nights colder. In the afternoons, after yet another day of unsuccessful hunting, everyone would retire to the tents to rest, and wait, and think. "Think, think, think!" McKinlay recorded in his diary, "That is all we can do these days. All day long, and in our waking moments at night. The strain becomes more acute as the days pass. . . . We pray that it may end soon."

Two concurrent events temporarily broke the monotony. On the morning of August 18, Williamson declared that he was going to attempt to reach Rodger's Harbor alone; and Hadley's dog, Molly, disappeared. Williamson's departure came as a surprise, since he'd been sick and barely ambulatory from the moment they arrived on the island back in March, and as McKinlay put it, "had never walked a mile from camp." Now he intended to trek some sixty to seventy miles round trip, a journey that McKinlay and Chafe had recently failed to complete. But it was agreed that the colder temperatures may have eased the flow of the river that had stopped McKinlay and Chafe, so perhaps he might make it. It was worth a try to see how the others were faring down south.

Molly's disappearance troubled everyone. Hadley was very attached to her, as was Chafe—ever since she'd saved his life by dragging him for thirty miles over the ice back to Shore Camp. Recently, Hadley had tethered her to a stake because she was about to give birth to a litter of pups, and he wanted to be there when it happened to prevent her from possibly eating her puppies. She and the other three dogs that remained were all dangerously hungry. Hadley had hoped that if enough pups survived, they might be used as sled dogs the next spring to attempt reaching Siberia. But the same morning Williamson left, Hadley found her gone and the stake pulled out of the ground. Hadley's first thought was that Williamson had taken her. Ever since the mysterious shooting of Breddy, he'd harbored suspicions about Williamson. He recorded in his diary, "Williamson went to Rodger's Harbor this morning and he took . . . Molly with him."

Everyone looked for her all around the camp, calling her name and whistling for her, but for two days there was no sign of her. Late on the afternoon of August 20, McKinlay went up to Breddy's grave to retrieve a snow knife he remembered having left there. As he neared the grave, he thought he heard something over gusting wind—little cries and yelps.

Some of the logs they'd piled on the grave had been clawed loose at one end; there were animal markings and scratches in the ground, and strewn wood. McKinlay bent down cautiously and was astonished to see Molly there, having burrowed under the driftwood and skins, nursing a litter of eight puppies right next to Breddy's body. McKinlay called out for Hadley, who came quickly and threw a lead around Molly's neck. They collected the puppies—three looked fairly strong and alert, while five were so weak and listless it appeared doubtful they would survive—and McKinlay noticed something disturbing: Breddy's clothes were ripped open, the flesh of his corpse recently gnawed. "There were clear signs," McKinlay wrote of the macabre spectacle, "that she was bent on rearing her family from Breddy's body."

43

THE WORLD AT WAR

THE *BEAR* WAS IN KOTZEBUE SOUND ON AUGUST 4, 1914, SOUTH OF Point Hope, Alaska, when the first reports started coming in over the wireless. Captain Bartlett sat with Captain Cochran and the officers, listening with disbelief at the news they were hearing: "War had been declared between Germany and France and then between Germany and England," Bartlett recalled.* The news shocked everyone who heard the broadcast, though they felt strangely disconnected from events, being in such a remote place and unable to really process what this could mean for them in the days, weeks, and months ahead. The captains and officers talked it over—there seemed to be no question about the report's accuracy.

Lord Percy, still performing his ongoing waterfowl studies aboard the *Bear*, was particularly shaken by the news. As an officer in the British army, he was directly affected by the outbreak of war between England and Germany, and he requested to go ashore at the town of Kotzebue, Alaska, immediately. Bartlett wished his new friend well and worried about his fate.

On the same day that Bartlett and the others were learning of the commencement of the Great War, the Russian icebreaker *Vaigatch* was within ten miles of Wrangel Island. Along with its sister ship, the *Taimir*,

---

* The actual declarations were, of course, more complicated and nuanced than Bartlett's summation affords, and involved more countries on August 4, 1914, including Austria-Hungary, Serbia, Russia, and Belgium.

it had received the Canadian government's appeal, and both were en route to rescue the survivors of the *Karluk*. Unfortunately for the castaways, the Russian ships also received the news of war in Europe, and because Russia was involved, the vessels were ordered to return immediately to port in Anadyr and await instructions. The powerful icebreakers would almost certainly have forced their way the last ten miles, but they'd had no choice but to turn around and speed back to Russia to join the fray.

The *Bear* sailed north to Point Hope, where Bartlett was pleased to meet up with Kataktovik, who had been taken there from East Cape by Captain Pedersen in the *Herman*. Kataktovik looked well and had fully recovered his health and vigor. Bartlett thanked him again for his courage and tenacity during their long journey, and, true to his word, the captain paid Kataktovik the wages owed to him for his work as a member of the Canadian Arctic Expedition. Bartlett also gave him a set of new clothing, paid for by the Canadian government. Kataktovik expressed a desire to board the *Bear* and join the captain to help on the rescue mission, but as official orders had yet to come through, Captain Cochran said it would not be possible. As Bartlett bade his stalwart companion goodbye for the last time, he learned, to his great pleasure, that the young widower— whose wife had died not long before he boarded the *Karluk*—was to be married again. It was terrific news, and Bartlett hoped that Kataktovik would also soon be reunited with his infant daughter, whom he'd left with relatives before departing on the expedition.

And then, during the first week of August, Captain Cochran finally got word from the United States government that he could take the *Bear*, and Bartlett, to Wrangel Island. They steamed immediately toward Point Barrow but ran into dense sea ice en route, off Icy Cape, and their progress was slowed considerably.* "The ice through which we were making our toilsome way was not so heavy as it was closely packed," recorded Bartlett with some frustration. The wizened ice master wished he could be up in

---

* It was here at Icy Cape that Captain Cook, in 1778, was stopped by sea ice during his attempted route through the Arctic from the Pacific Ocean.

the crow's nest helping to navigate, but he was relegated to the role of a passenger and could only stand on the deck and watch their slow progress through the mosaic of thick pack ice. Sometimes leads opened, and Cochran sped for them. "It was great to see the good old *Bear* charging and recharging, twisting and turning," Bartlett wrote. "Heavy in the water she was able, with her great momentum, to smash off points and corners of the ice and make her way through it." But as the dense pack encroached from the north, Bartlett could not help remembering the *Karluk*'s great difficulties with the same pack almost exactly a year ago, and he feared that the window for getting to Wrangel Island was about to slam shut.

Accompanying the *Bear* through the maze of ice were two other ships. Bartlett inquired about them, considering whether one or both might potentially be enlisted to help in the rescue attempt. One was a Canadian schooner heavily loaded with supplies intended for the mounted police at Herschel Island. Bartlett watched it carefully as it moved through the water and observed that it was "not sheathed and had no stem plates, and was evidently not at all suited for ice work." The other ship, though, impressed Bartlett the moment he saw it. The *King and Winge*, a 110-foot walrus-hunter and trading schooner, had, to Bartlett's well-trained eye, "just the right ballast for bucking the ice; besides being small, she was short for her beam and was quick to answer the helm." He learned that the ship was brand-new—built earlier in 1914—and was managed by a Mr. Olaf Swenson, whose company, Hibbard-Swenson, Bartlett knew of.

The *Bear* wove and plowed through the tightening leads. At Wainwright Inlet—about one hundred miles from Point Barrow—Bartlett was frustrated when they stopped to help a four-masted schooner that had run aground. Using a heavy line, Cochran tried multiple times to pull her off, but the ship was too heavily loaded to budge. While thus engaged, said Bartlett, "The ice began to close in, and we had to turn round and steam south in a hurry." The delay took a couple of valuable days, but with skillful ice navigating, Cochran managed to reach Point Barrow on the evening of August 21. There, they would deliver mail and take on coal and water for the journey across the Arctic Ocean and the Chukchi Sea.

As Bartlett disembarked to stretch his legs on land, he could hardly believe who was there to greet him on the dock: it was Burt McConnell, Stefansson's secretary, who'd left the *Karluk* with Stefansson the year before, back in September of 1913.

But there was no sign of Stefansson.

44

"STARVATION TIN"

WILLIAMSON STAGGERED BACK INTO CAMP AT CAPE WARING EARLY on the morning of August 21. His eyes were wild, and he babbled incoherently, saying something about an owl. The others attended to him, giving him tea and adding wood to the fire to warm him. They wanted to know about the men at Rodger's Harbor, but Williamson was having trouble stringing intelligible sentences together. He kept saying he'd been lost, but that through the mist, "pale faces and waving arms beckoned me on."

Clearly the man was out of his mind. McKinlay asked whether he'd made it all the way down and Williamson nodded between gulps of hot tea, his hands trembling clenched hard around the mug. If true, this was remarkable. Only recently fit enough to move around, he'd walked a great distance, over hilly, crumbling, difficult terrain, in only three days. McKinlay was doubtful: "It just did not make sense that a man who had been inactive for so long should be capable of covering between sixty and seventy miles in that short period."

And yet, Williamson said he had done just that. As he began to revive from his strenuous journey, he said he'd been lost in a storm on the way back, but a snowy owl had led him here, hooting and flying ahead and doubling back for him, leading him through the mist and fog. "Ten times . . . he hooted . . . truly as if he were guiding me."

McKinlay eyed Williamson suspiciously, then looked at Hadley. Neither believed him and thought he must be crazed by fatigue and hunger.

Then Williamson reached into his bag and pulled out a .45 Colt revolver and thirty-six cartridges. They recognized the pistol as Templeman's. Hadley gave the man a quick look and barked, "You better not have any more accidents with guns . . . because I would not stand for any more."

So, it was true. Well, probably he'd imagined or hallucinated the owl. But somehow, miraculously, he had made it to Rodger's Harbor and back. The gun was proof. As Williamson regained his senses, he said he'd arrived there the morning after he left, after walking almost continuously. He'd found the camp when he spotted the Canadian ensign flying at half-mast. He said that the men had moved Mamen and Malloch and buried them properly and flown the flag above their grave to honor them. Williamson was making more sense now, giving more details. He said that the men had killed five seals long ago but were now surviving only on sealskin. He'd told them about Breddy's death, and how everyone was holding on at Cape Waring. Munro informed him that ice had been heavy all along the south coast and that he did not anticipate any chance for a ship until the end of the month. Williamson said he'd slept for twelve hours and then returned. There was nothing for him there, and little he could do for them. They had no food, but at least they were surviving.

McKinlay and the others took in the strange story, glad to know that they remained alive down there, and well enough to hail a ship per Captain Bartlett's instructions. During Williamson's absence, McKinlay and Hadley had moved Molly and the puppies away from Breddy's grave and covered the dead man properly once more, appalled at the grim spectacle of his waist and torso where Molly had chewed at the flesh. They'd kept three of the pups and drowned the five weakest, certain they would not survive anyway.

The members at Cape Waring were now eating a measly breakfast soup made from what McKinlay dubbed the "Starvation tin," followed each day by two other so-called meals: "Lunch—a cup of tea with a piece of walrus hide and raw blubber from the 'poke'; Supper—cooked roots with oil." McKinlay suggested—and everyone agreed—that they should eat two ounces of dried seal meat per person per day. Dipping into their winter store was drastic, but they had no choice if they were to live. By the end of August, it had been four weeks since Kuraluk had killed the three bearded seals, and since then, nothing. "Not a single living thing fell to our hunters" in a month, wrote McKinlay.

Kuraluk began stalking shorebirds and fledgling crowbills along the coastline and below the cliffs. He tried using a spear and a "throwing stick" he fashioned out of found materials on the beach; they were down to just eighty rounds of ammunition and must try to preserve it for the winter, in the hope that they might get a polar bear. The bullets could not be wasted on small birds any longer. Kuraluk hunted all day, but the birds were too small and elusive. One day when he returned empty-handed, he said he had an idea. He led McKinlay and Chafe over to a big snowdrift and they began digging, finally uncovering a net he remembered they'd brought from the *Karluk*.

They cleaned the net of snow and ice and followed Kuraluk up the shoreline. Kuraluk, putting his fingers to his lips to remind McKinlay and Chafe to be quiet, crept forward, waving the others on behind him. Between pans of ice in the bay there were small pools of open water, and the pools were filled with squawking crowbills, mostly juveniles. Taking opposite sides of the net, the men swung it in unison, heaving it out above the pool. The net unfurled, landing over scores of the birds, and they hauled it in, snagging thirty their first try. They spent much of the next day netting birds, bringing in 120. "The haul," wrote McKinlay, "was not to be compared to an ugruk, or a walrus, or a bear, but it was such an unexpected windfall, and all achieved without the expenditure of a single cartridge. We forgot for the time being that August had ended and hope of rescue had dwindled almost to vanishing point."

The crowbills were young and so small that it took a few to supplement one person's ration, so they did not last long. Wanting to do something to help, Chafe, Williamson, and Clam walked about five miles north to a place where Williamson had seen kelp washed up onshore. "This kelp must have been on the beach for years," wrote Chafe, "for it was all colors of the rainbow and half rotten." They collected armfuls of the briny, decomposing seaweed and took it back to camp, boiling it and eating it along with some juvenile crowbills. "We seemed to have reached a point where putrid food did not harm us," Chafe went on, "and it helped to fill our empty stomachs and satisfy that awful craving which we had for something to eat."

The dreadful proposition of wintering on Wrangel Island seemed certain now. All that could be done was to try to secure as much food as possible, to sew and repair winter clothing, and prepare for the move to the winter quarters site Kuraluk had found, which was about ten miles away. The move would be difficult in their emaciated condition, as would building the structure. But the place was less exposed to the elements than the barren coastline of Cape Waring; it was tucked into a little canyon protected from the wind, and Kuraluk was counting on bears and foxes moving through the narrow valley.

A storm blew in on the first of September, covering Cape Waring with snow. "It was snowing and blowing," wrote Chafe, "and the temperature was getting lower; and we had already begun to feel the cold sting of the Arctic winter." Kuraluk's family and Hadley had joined the expedition with proper Arctic clothing, but the others—the *Karluk* crew and scientists—were poorly clad from the beginning, thanks to Stefansson's poor planning. Auntie rarely ceased sewing coats and trousers and mukluks, but even with help from Mamen and McKinlay and a few others, she'd simply run out of time and materials to fit out everyone. Now they scoured the camp for any spare skins or woolens and assessed the state of their footwear; most had holes in the bottoms. "We had nothing but what we stood in," remarked Chafe, "and that was nearly worn out."

By now, everyone knew the gruesome toll frostbite could exact. Clam's amputated big toe was evidence enough. Auntie had secreted away a few of the ugruk skins for making boots, but they had nothing left for socks. While discussing the situation one evening, someone said, "The blanket that we buried with Breddy would come in handy for making socks." Chafe and Williamson went up the hill and partially exhumed Breddy: "On removing the blanket, we noticed that his boots were in good condition, and, knowing that someone would need a pair of boots before the winter was out, we removed them, too." To clean the blanket, they spread it out and covered it with snow and scuffed it with their mukluks, then hung it up to bleach out in the elements before using it for sewing socks.

It was getting so cold that the ground became too hard for Auntie and the girls to dig up any roots. The ducks had moved offshore to larger water ponds, so McKinlay and Hadley tried their luck trapping foxes, and managed to catch a young one, but it was small and provided so little meat that, as McKinlay put it, "It merely proved tantalizing." Still, they kept trying, hoping to get more, not just for the meat, but for the skins. McKinlay imagined wishfully that he might capture enough to make a fur jacket for the coming winter.

One afternoon, McKinlay saw Kuraluk down at the beach cutting away a long piece of whalebone from a skeleton that had washed up. When McKinlay asked him what he was doing, he said he was planning to use it to shoe the runners of a sled he would build during the winter, "for use on our long journey to Siberia in the spring."

They were living on hope now; it was just about all they had left.

45

"DAYS TO TRY
A MAN'S SOUL"

CAPTAIN BARTLETT WAS GLAD TO SEE BURT MCCONNELL AT POINT
Barrow. He'd last seen him nearly a year ago, striding away from the icebound *Karluk* with Stefansson on September 20, 1913. He was of course
relieved that Stefansson had managed to get McConnell and the other
members of the so-called "caribou hunting party" safely to land, but he
was incensed to learn the rest of the story: how Stefansson had reoutfitted
what he was calling "the New Northern Party," spending his time acquiring gear and dogs and ships and continuing with the expedition, with
what sounded like utter disregard for the *Karluk* and its crew and scientific
members. McConnell told Captain Bartlett he'd last seen Stefansson in
early April of 1914, fifty miles out on the ice north of the Alaskan coast,
embarking on a search for Crocker Land, or any new lands to be discovered in the Beaufort Sea. He had with him two Norwegian men—Storker
Storkerson and Ole Andreason, six dogs, a sled, twelve hundred pounds
of supplies and equipment, two rifles with about four hundred rounds of
ammunition, and food for thirty to forty days.

It was now late August, and no one had seen or heard from him since.

Well, good riddance, thought Bartlett. But he did not wish to expend
any further time or emotional energy on Stefansson, not now. He needed
to get back on the *Bear* and get to Wrangel Island. McConnell said he
had quit the Canadian Arctic Expedition in June and was on his way

to Nome. When he'd learned recently of the plight of the survivors, he independently petitioned the Canadian government to send a relief ship, but his request had been denied since they'd already enlisted the *Bear*. McConnell was a young and ambitious writer who knew a good story when he saw one. He figured if he could get involved with the rescue one way or another—whether it ended with triumph or tragedy—he wanted to be there to get the scoop. And as a former member of the expedition who personally knew those stranded, he felt duty bound to help if he could.

By August 23, the *Bear* was ready to depart for Wrangel Island. McConnell had received no invitation from Bartlett to come along—the *Bear* was not, after all, under Bartlett's command; he was only a passenger. But McConnell had an idea. While in port he'd learned that the *King and Winge* was headed back to Nome, and then was scheduled to head to the Siberian coast on a walrus-hunting trip. McConnell discovered that the *King and Winge* had on board two motion picture photographers from Los Angeles who were filming for the Sunset Motion Picture Company. Perhaps the captain would not mind having a journalist along, at least as far as Nome. McConnell managed to talk his way on board. Maybe he could convince the captain, or the owner of the ship, to join in the rescue, and if so, he'd have professional filmmakers there to document the historical event for posterity—and profit.

A strong north-northeast wind blew behind the *Bear* as she sailed, finally, across the Arctic Ocean toward Wrangel Island. "The harder it blew, the better I liked it," wrote Bartlett.

He was relieved to be headed there at long last, but he worried that either the weather or the ice—or both—might still thwart the rescue attempt: "It was getting late and before many weeks the ice might close in around the island and render it inaccessible to a ship." The distance from Point Barrow to Wrangel Island was considerable as well—a little over five hundred miles—so it was going to be a couple of days at best, and that was if things went perfectly. Bartlett had cause for nervousness since things in the Arctic rarely went perfectly. He worried not only about the survivors' food supply but about their mental state as well: "The longer the men were kept on the island the greater would be their suspense and the harder it would be to keep up their spirits."

After twenty-four hours of clear, fast sailing, they encountered the ice pack. The *Bear* bashed its way through large, loose ice and kept moving well until a thick haze settled over the seascape, turning to dense fog. "All the square sails were taken in," wrote Bartlett, "and we slowly steamed to the northwest." The engines were shut down and the *Bear* drifted southeast all night long. The next morning the fog lifted enough for them to fire the boilers and work toward the island again, ramming and parting small floes until after many hours they struck even larger, impenetrable ice. Bartlett stood on the deck, scanning the horizon, his face wet with vapor and sea spray. He saw long lines of dark V-shapes winging their way south, and he knew they must be close to the island—perhaps within just fifteen or twenty miles. Bartlett's pulse quickened as he thought about how near they were. But the fog descended again, diminishing their vision to less than a mile, until he could only hear the distant honks of geese.

All day they waited, shrouded in haze and fog. As darkness fell, Bartlett heard the deflating sound of the engines shutting down again, "and the ship was hove hull to and allowed to drift." For the next two days, they drifted slowly to the south-southeast, away from Wrangel Island. At 4:12 on the morning of August 27, Captain Cochran ordered the engines fired and said they must return to Nome for more coal. Bartlett felt sick with disappointment and regret. He knew in his heart that Captain Cochran was right—they'd used up most of the ninety tons of coal in the bunkers, and they needed enough to get to the island and, importantly, return. It would be too dangerous to run out of coal and be powerless out here. But even so, his heart sank as they steamed southeast: "The days that followed were days to try a man's soul," he said. "I spent such a wretched time as I had never in my life."

The *Bear* steamed first to Siberia, stopping at Cape Serdze. Bartlett hurried ashore and inquired there whether the Russian icebreakers had made it to Wrangel Island. No one had any definitive information. They continued to East Cape, where Bartlett learned, to his dismay, that on August 4 the *Vaigatch* had been within ten miles of the island but because of the outbreak of war, the ship had been immediately recalled for active duty. He could hardly believe it. First the *Vaigatch* so close, then the *Bear*. It was all too cruel. "I could only hope," said Bartlett, "that when we reached Nome, we should hear that some other ship had been to the island and taken the men off." Winter was closing in fast, and it was becoming clear that it would take more than one ship for a rescue—should anyone still be alive when they finally got there.

Bartlett stood at the foredeck of the *Bear* offshore of Nome, frustrated beyond words. They'd anchored on the evening of August 30, but high winds and heavy seas forced them to weigh anchor and put to sea to avoid damage, and now they were trying to land again to load enough coal for the next attempt. At last, on September 3—the first lull in many days— the *Bear* was able to land, and Bartlett went quickly ashore. He sought out Jafet Lindeberg, the mining man who'd hosted him for nearly a month earlier in the summer. Bartlett told Lindeberg how close two ships had come to Wrangel Island and expressed his despair at all the near misses and the closing of the season. Time was running out.

Lindeberg empathized with Bartlett's fears that the marooned party would be hard-pressed to survive another winter. He vowed to use his local power and reach—and his considerable coffers—to advantage. He promised to spend his own funds to outfit the SS *Corwin* with a captain, crew, and supplies and dispatch it immediately to attempt a rescue. Bartlett was moved by the offer, and hopeful, too, since the *Corwin* had been the last ship to land on Wrangel Island—albeit over thirty years before. Still, it was finally a stroke of good fortune.

Later in the afternoon, Bartlett went to find Olaf Swenson, who managed the *King and Winge*. He located him in a well-known Nome trading post frequented by seamen and miners and traders. Bartlett told Swenson how much he'd admired the little schooner when he saw it recently off Point Barrow. They talked for some time, and Swenson mentioned that he'd brought Burt McConnell on the *King and Winge* from Point Barrow, and McConnell had filled him in on the dire situation at hand. Bartlett asked Swenson, if he was anywhere in the vicinity during his walrus hunt, to investigate the shoreline to see whether there was anyone around Rodger's Harbor, and Swenson promised that he would make it part of his itinerary. It was a substantial favor, Bartlett knew. The trip from Nome to Wrangel Island was six hundred miles each way and would be costly. Still, Bartlett had to ask; his conscience demanded it, and it was a request he hoped that any seafarer would ask of him.

Bartlett hurried to the telegraph office and sent a telegram to Ottawa, alerting the authorities that there were now three ships—*Bear*, *King and Winge*, and *Corwin*—joined in the rescue effort. As he climbed back aboard the *Bear* on the afternoon of September 4, he prayed that all his efforts had not come too late.

46

CONFLUENCE

THE CASTAWAYS AT CAPE WARING HAD FULLY COMMITTED TO MOV-
ing camp. Kuraluk and Hadley told McKinlay and the others that there
appeared to be no prospects for large game in the immediate area, and the
river valley Kuraluk had located would be at least as good, and hopefully
better. There might be fish in the stream they could net, and perhaps bears
moving off the ice to their inland dens on the tundra plateau to the east
of the new campsite. Kuraluk said this would be their best chance at the
bears, because soon many would seek out dens to hibernate during the
coming freezing months. On clear days, thousands of ducks and geese
darkened the skies overhead, but they were heading south.

McKinlay and Kuraluk busied themselves making fox traps. They'd
seen a fair number of young foxes slinking around, and the juveniles were
less wary and more curious than the cagey adults and might therefore be
tricked more easily. Williamson was enticed by the foxes too. He went
out with Templeman's revolver and stalked the young foxes, one morning
blazing away at a pair of them and wasting thirteen cartridges in one flurry
of smoke and gunpower without hitting either of them, their snow-white
fur making them difficult targets against the recent snowfall. McKinlay
and Hadley just shook their heads in disgust, for he'd also scared off the
foxes they were trying to trap.

Auntie and Helen and Mugpi were down at the beach, jigging for tomcod. Auntie had spotted schools of these fish, which were about fifteen inches

long, swimming fast through shallow water in a tidal crack in the beach ice. She made a crude jig by bending a sewing pin and piercing it through one end of a long length of sinew. She and the girls would hover motionless at the edge of the tidal crack, lowering their jigs down into the water. When the fish swam by, they'd jerk hard upward, skewering the tomcod on the pin and yanking them out of the water and onto the beach ice. It was slow and tedious fishing, but they were getting a few, the first fish they'd caught since arriving on the island. As the fish provided new and different food—and were very tasty—it was worth the effort.

There wasn't much else to do but bundle up bedding skins and prepare for the move up the coast. Chafe and Clam spent their time "gathering up all the old bits of skin that lay around the camp," wrote Chafe. "We used them to patch and reinforce what little clothes we had, and even then, our clothes were not fit to protect us from the cold winds that seemed to penetrate to the bone."

Molly and her remaining three puppies were being allowed to sleep in one corner of Kuraluk's tent. Hadley and Kuraluk had disagreed about it, since on the first day inside, Molly had snatched a piece of cooked crowbill one of the girls was eating. Kuraluk was furious and wanted Molly and the pups taken back outside, but Hadley argued that the pups would freeze to death, and they might need them come spring. While this was going on, Mugpi was crying that the cat was gone, and McKinlay took a lantern and looked around the tent, checking all Nigeraurak's normal hiding places. After a time, he heard a scratching noise above, and high-pitched yowling. He could see a hole in the canvas roof, a narrow beam of light streaming through, and he went outside to investigate. There, perched high on the tent roof's ridgepole, sat Nigeraurak. Apparently, in her effort to get away from the unwelcome and hungry canines in the tent, she'd clawed a hole through the roof and leaped outside. Eventually, she came back in.

On September 4, while out scouting the ice, Hadley saw a large bearded seal surface in a hole not far offshore. He eased his way out on the ice, sometimes slithering along on his belly to mimic the behavior of another seal. By the time he got to the hole, the seal had ducked underwater again, but the prospect of obtaining large quarry—hundreds of pounds of meat—steeled Hadley's patience. He sat motionless except for his shivering for six long hours, but the ugruk never reappeared. Hadley was dejected, writing in his diary: "Ship don't show up very soon now I guess it's all up with us."

Captain Bartlett felt good as the *Bear* found open water through the Bering Strait. He stood at the bow, scanning the sea. He remained apprehensive but was calmer now that he had three ships engaged. And he had a hunch that Swenson, with the *King and Winge*—which had left Nome a day ahead of the *Bear*—"would go straight to the island, whether the *Bear* ever got there or not." For two days they had fair winds and ran well with all sails set until the early afternoon of September 6. As they rounded Russia's East Cape in the late afternoon, the winds shifted, hitting them dead ahead. Near dark, traveling once more under steam, they reached Cape Serdze, in the lower reaches of the Chukchi Sea. On they went, chugging slowly through the night. The next morning, Bartlett went to the helm to find the sea eerily smooth, "A thing which told us clearly that the ice was near." He was right. That evening they came to fields of ice, packed close and foreboding, glaring and magnificent and powerful. By Bartlett's reckoning, they were about 130 miles from Rodger's Harbor. Now, as always, everything depended on the behavior of the winds and ice. They would make their final push tomorrow. Wrote Bartlett, "We lay near the edge of the ice and waited for daylight."

The Yuit men on the deck of the *King and Winge* waved their arms excitedly, and some raised their rifles while others rushed to the side of the ship to lower the umiak. The fast and nimble *King and Winge* had reached the first ice floes about 150 miles south of Rodger's Harbor on September 5, 1914, a day ahead of Bartlett and the *Bear*. Many of the ice floes were black with walrus herds, the animals roaring warnings as the ship approached. Olaf Swenson went to the deck and told the fifteen Yuit hunters he'd hired on at East Cape the day before to put their rifles away; there would be no walrus hunting yet. They had another job to do first.

After his meeting with Bartlett in Nome, Swenson had directed the *King and Winge* to East Cape, where he acquired the men and the umiak not only for hunting walrus but also for getting ashore at Wrangel Island, should the ice prevent the ship from landing, as it had the *Bear*. If they were stopped short, the able, experienced hunters could reach the island with the umiak, which, as Swenson reasoned, "could be dragged over the ice . . . launched whenever we reached a patch of open water, pulled out again if we encountered another ice field, and the process repeated over and over again for a hundred miles if necessary."

Swenson had put his faith and his ship in the hands of the skillful and daring Captain A. P. Jochimsen, who wove the nimble craft deftly through the floes. He'd also agreed to allow Burt McConnell—at the man's persistent urgings—to come along. Beyond the woofing walrus herds, they encountered immense ice fields, larger and more densely woven floes webbed with narrow leads. Jochimsen threaded the ship through, chasing open water. For nearly one hundred miles they battled the ice, as Swenson recorded in his memoir: "The plucky little *King and Winge* had to dodge and turn in every direction, backing up and starting over again as she plowed her way through. Sometimes, at full speed ahead, she would literally climb up on an ice-floe, her prow sliding over the edge like a polar bear's paws, until she had broken it down with her own weight." Then Jochimsen pushed the 140-horsepower gasoline engine to its limit, bashing her steel-nosed bow into smaller floes and pulverizing them as he forged ahead.

At last, rising out of the vaporous white-blue ice fields, emerged Wrangel Island. It showed itself above the horizon, monolithic and volcanic looking, dun colored and ominous. But between its forbidding shores and the *King and Winge* remained an unforgiving expanse of ice, animated by winds and current—and powerful, like a living thing. All day long, creeping slowly into a strong southwest wind, they snaked through tightening leads, any one of which might clutch the ship in its grasp. Swenson and McConnell and the crew watched in reverent awe as they eased by great pressure ridges, jagged and threatening, thrust up all around them. Some of the ridges rose high above the ship's sixty-foot masts, the ice crumbling and precarious. The floes beneath the ridges smashed together, creating a grinding, churning rumble that was both deafening and chilling.

Captain Jochimsen ordered full steam, and by the morning of September 7, they got to within two miles of the island. He fired flares to alert anyone on shore of their arrival, then powered on through slush and chop, backing off the engine when they came to shore ice extending a half mile out into the strait. Captain Jochimsen shouted to the lookout in the crow's nest, who yelled back that he saw something on the beach. Captain Jochimsen and McConnell each scoured the shoreline with binoculars; it was blanketed with a recent dusting of snow. Then McConnell saw the scene clearly and confirmed it with the captain: "We could only see a dilapidated four-man tent, a flag-pole, and a cross." Captain Jochimsen blew the ship's whistle, the high-pitched wail piercing the sharp Arctic air, and they watched and waited anxiously for any signs of movement, any signs of life.

The *Karluk*'s fireman Fred Maurer sat upright on his wet and matted skin bed. His forehead touched the damp canvas interior of the tent where it slumped to one side, the tent pole leaning over from the wind. He'd fix it later if he had the strength. He brushed sleep from his eyes and listened, wondering what he'd heard outside. Was it the high-pitched howling of an Arctic fox? They'd been around camp in small numbers recently, and the six they'd killed about a week before had just kept them alive. They'd been down to sealskin and blubber for nearly a month before that. Walrus and seals had been thick in the waters and on the ice, but with no boat and little energy, there'd been no way to get them. They were too far out.

Maurer crawled to the south side of the tent and tried to look out through some tears in the canvas, but he saw nothing. He could hear the wheezy, shallow breathing of Munro and Templeman, and an occasional rheumy cough, which was encouraging. Neither had died in the night. But also, neither had awakened, so perhaps he was imagining the eerie sound.

He'd imagined plenty in his months stranded on these shores: steaming plates of food, pies and bread and desserts; his family back in Ohio, who never wanted him to go to the Arctic at all. Too many risks, they'd warned him. And in weak moments—of which there were more and more—he'd imagined death. It was easy enough to do, with the graves of Malloch and Mamen not far from the tent, marked by a rough driftwood cross. It was a daily reminder, death right at the doorstep.

The sound came again, louder and lower this time, more of a long, moaning wail. It was coming from the sea. It was no animal. He crawled for the tent door, parted the canvas, and once outside, stood up, his legs quavering, his eyes blinded by the midday glare off the ice. He blinked and shielded his eyes with his forearm. There, lying offshore just a few hundred yards, was a small two-masted vessel. He blinked a few more times and cleared his eyes with the back of a grimy hand to make sure. When he was certain, he summoned his voice, calling out to Munro and Templeman in a hoarse rasp: "The ship is here."

Captain Jochimsen and Olaf Swenson and Burt McConnell had watched carefully for many minutes as the ship's whistle sounded, but for a long time no one appeared, and they feared the worst. Then, after the third or fourth whistle blast, a man had crawled from the tent. "I shall never forget his actions," wrote McConnell. "He did not show any signs of joy. . . . The poor creature simply rose and stood rigidly beside the tent, gazing at us as if dazed." They watched from the ship as he turned back and went inside the tent, emerging a few moments later holding up a flag, which he ran up the flagpole to half-mast. With the position of the flag, and the cross in the ground, McConnell now knew that at least one person had died, and he began to assume the worst. Had all but this man perished? Where was everyone else?

Moments later, two other men came from the tent and stood by the other, all three staring out at the ship, transfixed in a kind of stupor. Jochimsen had worked the *King and Winge* to within two hundred yards of the shoreline, but he would go no closer for fear of running aground, and Swenson had his first mate lower the umiak. Swenson, McConnell, the two cameramen,* and a few of Swenson's hired Yuit men boarded the umiak and started paddling ashore. As they neared the beach, McConnell saw one of the men trotting down to the beach edge, sliding a rifle from its scabbard as he came. He looked crazed, and the Yuit men stopped paddling, afraid for their lives, but Swenson urged them on, and they landed and pulled the umiak up on the beach.

They met the man halfway between the tent and the umiak. He held the rifle in both hands but did not point it at them. McConnell recorded the encounter: "His shaggy, matted hair streamed down over his eyes in wild disorder. His grimy face was streaked and furrowed with lines and wrinkles. His clothes were in tatters, begrimed with seal oil, blood, and dirt. . . . His full, unkempt beard effectually hid the emaciation of his cheeks, but his sunken eyes told of suffering and want." McConnell stared at him, looking carefully at his eyes, and then he recognized him. It was the chief engineer, John Munro.

Munro looked at the rescuers and said, "I don't know who you are, but I'm mighty glad to see you all." McConnell stepped forward and introduced Munro to Mr. Olaf Swenson. It was only then that Munro seemed to recognize McConnell. He had not seen him for almost a year. He set down his rifle and embraced McConnell, thanking him for coming. Then, his voice raspy and strained, he fired a series of questions: "Did Captain Bartlett reach shore all right? How is he, and where is he? How did you get here, and where is Mr. Stefansson?"

By now Maurer and Templeman, who had been hanging back, approached, shuffling in their rags. It took a moment for McConnell to recognize them as well; both were so grimy and emaciated. They each looked to have lost thirty to forty pounds. Maurer was shaking and in tears, too overcome with emotion to speak. Templeman's eyes were wide and dilated, darting about, and "he seemed to be on the verge of a nervous breakdown."

---

* The two cameramen were Fred L. Granville and Charles Zalibra.

McConnell answered Munro's questions briefly. Clearly, these men needed food and warmth and medical aid. They'd best get them on the *King and Winge* as soon as possible. But he did tell them that Bartlett and Kataktovik had reached Siberia; Bartlett had made it to Alaska and organized a rescue. As for Stefansson, he was adrift on the ice somewhere north of Canada. But that wasn't important. They could discuss it all later.

McConnell then asked—haltingly, fearing the worst from the look of these men—about the others. Munro waved his hand toward the grave, saying that Malloch and Mamen had both died here during the spring. The others . . . It took Munro a minute to think about it. There were nine others camped at Cape Waring as of two weeks ago. Up the coast some thirty miles or so. In his delirious state, Munro neglected to mention—or forgot—that fireman Breddy had been there, too, but died recently by gunshot.

Swenson could hear the ice grating and shrieking in the strait, roiling before a strong southwest wind. He did not wish to linger long, worried that the *King and Winge* might be trapped inshore. McConnell walked to the tent and watched the three men collect their few belongings, observing the piteous conditions they'd endured: Empty pemmican tins were strewn about, one filled with congealed seal oil. Two pairs of worn-out mukluks hung drying on a snarl of driftwood root. Arctic fox carcasses—including the skulls—lay in a pile, picked clean to the bone.

Munro slid his rifle back in its case, remarking that they were down to twelve cartridges to get them through the winter. He ran the Canadian ensign down the flagpole and tucked it away. "You fellows came in the nick of time," he said. Swenson led the three survivors to the umiak, with Maurer clutching in his hands the Bible his mother had given to him before he left home. He looked back at where Malloch and Mamen lay buried, and thanked God for his own salvation. As he turned away, he vowed to understand, someday, the trials he'd undergone here.

McConnell entered the tattered, foul-smelling tent. The floor inside, covered with shredded animal skins, was wet and rank with the tang of urine and feces. Rips in the canvas walls allowed slats of light in. McConnell sat down and wrote a note for any ship that might come, explaining that they'd taken off three of the *Karluk* survivors. He tethered the note to the inside tent pole with a strip of sinew and then tied the door tight to prevent wind and drifting snow from destroying the note; then he joined the others at the umiak.

Standing on the gravelly beach, Munro and the others took a long, last look at Rodger's Harbor. The conical tent, the grave of their comrades with its cross, and the spindly flagpole all stood as reminders of the death and deprivation the three men had experienced on this desperate shore. After they'd climbed into the umiak and the Yuit men paddled toward the *King and Winge*, Munro turned to Swenson. "Do you have a doctor on board?" he asked. All three castaways were severely dehydrated and malnourished.

In fact, Swenson did not have a doctor on board. He'd brought along two professional cameramen, but no physician. Trying to lighten the mood, he answered, "You don't need a doctor. What you need is a cook, and we have a first-class one."

The cook on the *King and Winge* lived up to his billing, though Munro and Templeman and Maurer would have eaten practically anything. As Captain Jochimsen worked to maneuver the ship offshore into more open water, the rescued men were resuscitated with a hearty breakfast of soft-boiled eggs, toast, cereal, and quarts of coffee heaped with sugar and condensed milk.

Not long after finishing, Munro looked up from his empty plates and bowl. "Mr. Swenson, I want to ask a great favor of you," he said. "For several months I have been dreaming of eating a whole can of condensed milk with a spoon."

Swenson called for the cook, who rushed three cans and three spoons from the galley, and Munro, Maurer, and Templeman consumed the sweet, thick milk one spoonful at a time, as if they were eating ice cream. Afterward, they had their first baths in nearly eight months and were each handed a change of clothes from the ship's stores. They were offered more food and soon were eating large helpings of ham, eggs, fried potatoes, and

Cream of Wheat, onto which they poured more condensed milk. "There was nothing we wanted but we got," wrote Munro.

And then, after bumping and weaving through a mass of encroaching ice floes to reach open water, the *King and Winge* sped north toward Cape Waring.

47

"UMIAKPIK KUNNO!"

SUNRISE ILLUMINATED CAPE WARING IN BANDS OF GOLDEN LIGHT. McKinlay, Hadley, and Kuraluk were down at the tidal crack, jigging for tomcod with Auntie and the girls. The previous day they'd caught two dozen, and the fish were so delicious everyone now wanted them for breakfast. It was September 7, 1914, the agreed-upon day to move to the winter camp and start building the wooden shelter. They'd talked it over with the other tent, and all decided it was their best hope to survive the coming winter, which could bring temperatures as low as –70°F.

Everyone was feeling a little bit stronger this morning. In addition to the fresh tomcod, the previous day Kuraluk had killed and secured a very young seal, their first in a month. It was so small as to provide only one main meal for the two tents, but compared with the scraps and skins they'd been eating, it seemed like a banquet. "Unashamedly we gorged on seal meat and blood soup," McKinlay wrote.

After catching a dozen fish on their improvised sewing pin jigs, McKinlay, Hadley, and Kuraluk headed back to the tent to make final preparations for leaving Cape Waring. There was still much to do. McKinlay tinkered with a stove—one fabricated from an empty metal storage container—which they planned to use to heat the cabin they would build. Hadley spent a few hours making four new fox traps, and Kuraluk whittled arrows for his bow out of lengths of wood he'd dried for the purpose. He'd been trying to get foxes with his bow and arrow but was more successful at losing arrows than killing foxes.

When he finished the arrows, Kuraluk headed back outside. He'd found a long piece of driftwood that would make a perfect seal-hunting spear. McKinlay and Hadley kept working on their projects until a few minutes later, when they heard Kuraluk shouting.

"Umiakpik kunno!" he yelled. *"Umiakpik kunno!"*

McKinlay and Hadley looked at each other and dropped what they were doing. *"A ship," maybe?* Was that what he was yelling? They scrambled out of the tent to see what was going on. McKinlay raised his binoculars as he trotted down the beach. He came to a stop and tried to calm his breathing to keep the binoculars from bobbing up and down. As he brought them into focus, sure enough, there it was: "It was a ship beyond all doubt," wrote McKinlay. "She was on the edge of the bay ice about three miles off and seemed to be steaming along to the north."

The ship was moving along and did not appear to be stopping, and McKinlay felt a moment of panic mixed with dread. Perhaps it was not a relief ship, just a walrus-hunting schooner on a late-season run. Then McKinlay saw her hoist her sail, and his heart skipped. The ship was leaving. They yelled for Kuraluk to run out over the ice and try to head off the ship, and he sprinted away. McKinlay and Hadley leaped up and down, shouting and waving their arms. Hearing all the commotion, Chafe came out of his tent with his boots halfway on, and Clam and Williamson—who'd been out collecting firewood—came running at all the commotion. Seeing the ship, they, too, started shouting and jumping and waving.

Finally, fearing they had not been spotted, Hadley took out his revolver and fired a series of rounds into the air. McKinlay peered through the binoculars and held his breath until he saw the ship lower her sail and stop along the edge of the ice. To his utter relief, he watched as a group of men disembarked the schooner and started walking toward them across the ice.

During all the excitement, Auntie and the girls had returned with a few pounds of tomcod, and Auntie was just boiling the fish on the fire when the first of the rescuers came up the beach and arrived at the camp. Kuraluk was with them, having intercepted them on the ice. He kept touching the arms of one of the men, as if to confirm he was real. It was Burt McConnell. Next to him stood Olaf Swenson, and beyond, a handful of the Yuit walrus hunters and two men carrying cameras. The entire scene was surreal.

"We were in a daze," wrote McKinlay of the encounter. "It was so unreal, like a dream." All he could think of was that Captain Bartlett had indeed won through and they were saved. After handshakes and introductions, Swenson and McConnell peppered them with information. Captain Bartlett had gotten through and organized the rescue operation, engaging two Russian icebreakers, the revenue cutter *Bear*—which he was aboard—as well as the *Corwin* and Swenson's ship, *King and Winge*. Earlier in the morning, they'd picked up Munro, Maurer, and Templeman at Rodger's Harbor. All three were safely aboard *King and Winge*—well fed and doing fine. McConnell told them that Stefansson was somewhere out on the Arctic ice in Northern Canada, and that the world was at war. It was all an overwhelming blur of words and ideas, an onslaught of information. "Our heads were awhirl and not much of this registered with us," wrote McKinlay. All that mattered now, agreed Chafe, was that they "were saved from starving to death on that desolate island."

The cameramen asked permission to follow the survivors around and film them as they packed up their personal belongings. Chafe, still limping around on his bandaged foot, happily consented. "Now that we are safe, you can keep us here and take movies for a whole week," he joked. Mugpi and Helen showed off Nigeraurak and the three puppies, holding them up for the camera. As had been done at Rodger's Harbor, the tents were left standing, with notes affixed to the tent poles inside in case any of the other rescue ships should arrive. It did not take long to pack up what little they had left, but everyone bundled their personal effects with care: their notebooks, diaries, and letters to loved ones. Before leaving, the cameramen wanted a group photo. The nine survivors huddled together, looking much happier and more unified than they had been during the last desperate months. Now Swenson said it was time to go.

Despite assuring their rescuers that they could walk by themselves the two miles over the ice to the ship, each of the survivors was assisted—for cinematic drama—by two members of the *King and Winge* crew as the cameramen followed behind, their cameras whirring. McKinlay, using a driftwood stick as a crutch, walked beside Olaf Swenson, pointing to various landmarks along the coast and at the campsite: Crowbill Point, where he'd scaled the cliffs on ladders hunting murres and eggs; Storm Top, the bluff he and Hadley had ascended daily, searching for a ship; and Breddy's grave site, marked by a mound of piled driftwood and stones.

Hadley, smoking his first cigarette in months, walked with Molly and the puppies trotting alongside him. Kuraluk, Auntie, and the girls walked unassisted. Mugpi carried Nigeraurak in her arms. It was quite remarkable, and ironic, really. The little black-and-white cat had been smuggled aboard at Esquimalt—for good luck—just moments before the *Karluk's* departure, against Stefansson's wishes. He'd been convinced that a ship's cat would soon be eaten by the ravenous sled dogs. But here she was, having survived the crushing of the *Karluk*, the freezing months on the ice at Shipwreck Camp, the journey through the pressure ridges, the six long months on Wrangel Island. Maybe—as the remaining *Karluk* crewmen firmly believed—she'd brought the luck of the rescue.

By half past one in the afternoon, September 7, all twelve *Karluk* survivors were safely aboard the *King and Winge*. Before going inside for a meal, some of the members lingered on the deck and took a last look at their camp at Cape Waring. From two miles distant, the tents, pitched as they were on the wide, flat beach, looked like boulders that had rolled down from Wrangel Island's crumbling heights and come to rest there haphazardly. Drifts of snow blew across the headland, and the five-mile-long line of eastern cliffs loomed craggy and forbidding above the lagoon. A thin line of smoke rose from the driftwood fire they'd left burning; then, caught by the Arctic wind, the smoke swirled into the air, merged with the storm clouds amassing over Wrangel Island, and disappeared. The clouds closed in fast, and it started to snow, until everything—the cliffs, the gravel strand, the tents, the ice-filled bay—was awash in wintry white, frozen in time.

48

REUNITED

ABOARD THE *KING AND WINGE*, MCKINLAY AND THE OTHERS WERE reunited with Munro, Maurer, and Templeman. Everyone was glad to be together again, but for McKinlay, everything remained a blur, a haze of new voices and sensations: the smell of fresh coffee; the sweet, sharp burn of tobacco on his lips and in his lungs; the yeasty taste of bread slathered with savory melted butter. The men had fantasized for so long about all the different things they would eat if they survived, but something as simple as bread and butter tasted as delicious as any elaborate fare they'd imagined.

As McKinlay ate, chewing mechanically, "still in a dream," as he put it, words and chatter and information swirled around the galley. The officers and crew of the *King and Winge* hovered around, doting on and congratulating the survivors for their grit and tenacity. They said they had been following the rescue, riveted for months, ever since Captain Bartlett had made it safely ashore and sent news to the world. Someone reiterated that all the world—except the United States—was at war, but even this startling fact failed to register or matter: "The news made almost no impact on our reeling brains," wrote McKinlay. "The news of the war and everything else, it didn't mean a thing."

It was not so much that they did not care about the war. But six months of surviving day to day, thinking only about how to kill or capture their next meal, had rendered them primal, instinctual, and diminished their ability to process all but their most immediate needs of food and shelter. Except for Kuraluk and his family—who appeared in remarkably good shape—the others were gaunt with malnourishment, feeble, and sickly. Their circadian rhythms were so disrupted that few could sleep despite their exhaustion. "Sleep was impossible," wrote McKinlay of the first night aboard the *King and Winge*. "We lay on beds of skins spread on the deck. We got up again and drank coffee in the galley, where the coffee pot was kept continuously bubbling on the stove for our special benefit. We smoked and smoked. We lay down again, got up again. . . . My head was not my own."

At some point during the afternoon, McKinlay had a bath. He luxuriated in the warm water, trying to scrub away the months of grime and grease, though as the water darkened with his filth, he knew one bath would not suffice: "It would take many soakings," he joked. But he felt much better as he put on new clothing from the ship's "slop chest." It mattered little that the clothes did not fit perfectly; they were warm and clean and dry. That evening, on one of his forays to the deck, McKinlay stood at the rail, watching the ice cluster around the ship. "The ice had thickened up, but strangely enough the risk of being frozen in again never crossed my mind." He brought the clothes he'd worn the entire time on Wrangel Island with him, and the garments sat on deck next to him in a sodden pile.

He stood at the rail for a long time, smoking cigarette after cigarette. As he was about to go back in for more food and coffee, Ernest Chafe came on deck with a large pile of his own frayed and grubby skin coats and pants, all begrimed with blood and oil. McKinlay stood next to Chafe, and the two men tossed their old clothes overboard, then stared numbly as "the threadbare shirts and trousers hit the ice and the water and drifted away."

The *King and Winge* had anchored to an ice floe during the night but got away just after sunrise. Swenson ordered Captain Jochimsen to steam toward nearby Herald Island. It was unlikely—but remotely possible—that the vanished party had survived there. Bartlett had informed Swenson that the missing advance shore party—consisting of first mate Sandy Anderson, second mate Charles Barker, and seamen John Brady and Edmund

Golightly—was last seen out on the ice within a few miles of Herald Island. Swenson wished to search for them if he could, and they steamed east, bucking and twisting and jarring through the floes, but they soon came to heavy ice. They skirted the pack for many miles but found no open leads heading toward the island. Mindful of entrapment, Swenson determined they could get no closer, and he turned the ship south toward Nome.

The *Bear* ran at full speed, parting loose slurry ice as she drove north. Captain Bartlett stood in the chart room, anxiously monitoring their progress. By the charts, he reckoned they were within seventy-five miles of Wrangel Island. But beyond the port bow lay a wall of closely packed ice, and Bartlett dreaded the possibility of being stopped short once again. And then, straight off the bow, he saw the masts of a schooner running fast before the wind. Bartlett reached for a pair of binoculars, peered through them— and immediately recognized the *King and Winge*. His pulse quickened and his mind raced with different scenarios. "I hoped . . . she had been to the island, or she would hardly be coming back so soon. Then I began to fear that perhaps she had broken a propeller and was now taking advantage of the favoring wind to put for Bering Strait and Alaska."

Captain Bartlett watched as the *King and Winge* slowly approached and then eased up alongside. Bartlett could see a huddle of people on the foredeck, but he did not recognize anyone. He hurried to the rail to get a closer look. He stared and stared, trying to focus on faces, trying to conjure someone from his crew. "I looked sharply at the men on her deck," wrote Bartlett, "her own crew was fairly large, but soon I could pick out Munro and McKinlay and Chafe, and of course the Eskimo family, and I knew that our quest was over."

A whaleboat was lowered from the *Bear*, and Captain Bartlett boarded it and they rowed through slushy sea ice to the *King and Winge*. As he climbed onto the able schooner, he could see the deck bustling, and more familiar faces huddled around him, the figures reaching out to embrace him. "Hip hip hooray!" they were shouting in unison. "Hip hip hooray!" "We gave him three hearty cheers," wrote Chafe of their reunion, "for we knew that it was his hazardous trip to Siberia that had saved our lives . . . for us and our safety he would have braved any danger."

McKinlay was moved to tears on seeing his captain. "We shook hands as heartily as ever men did," he wrote. Then Bartlett asked him, "All of you here?"

McKinlay looked Bartlett straight in his eyes. His throat was tight, his voice thin with regret. "No," he reported. "Malloch and Mamen and Breddy died on the island." Bartlett bowed his head, acknowledging the painful loss. He'd get the details later, but the news stung him deeply. As much as he rejoiced in seeing the others alive, he could not help feeling a twinge of guilt and responsibility run through him at the loss of the men. "It was an especially sad and bitter blow," he wrote, "to learn that three of the men whom I had seen arrive at Wrangel Island had thus reached safety only to die."

After the short reunion, Captain Bartlett shook hands with Olaf Swenson and Captain Jochimsen, thanking them profusely—from his own heart, and on behalf of the Canadian government—for their courageous efforts and their success. Then he asked Swenson's permission to transfer the *Karluk* survivors to the *Bear*, where they could receive immediate medical attention by the ship's doctor. And after all, these people were members of the Canadian Arctic Expedition and thus under Captain Bartlett's charge. Also, Bartlett wished the *King and Winge* the freedom to continue its walrus-hunting expedition.* The arrangement was agreed

---

* The Seattle-based owners of the *King and Winge*—the Hibbard-Stewart Company (formerly Hibbard-Swenson)—later sent a $3,000 invoice to the Canadian government for using the ship to rescue the survivors on Wrangel Island (Auditor General Report, 1920). This added to Stefansson's ballooning expenses. The *King and Winge*, brand-new in 1914 at the time of the rescue, went on to have an illustrious career, becoming one of the most celebrated ships ever built in Seattle. It was present at the wreck of the ocean steamer *Princess Sophia* in 1918, one of the great tragedies in North American maritime history, with the loss of more than 350 passengers and crew. The nearby *King and Winge* attempted to help but was thwarted by dangerous sea conditions and in the end could only retrieve floating bodies and transport them to Juneau, Alaska. The *King and Winge* then saw duty as a rumrunner during Prohibition, as the Columbia Bar pilot boat, and as a crab-fishing vessel in Alaskan waters and the Bering Sea. The worthy ship saw over eighty years of duty, ultimately sinking in high waves in the Bering Sea on February 23, 1994, without loss of life.

upon, and within an hour all the *Karluk* party was aboard the *Bear*. Burt McConnell transferred along with them.

Captain Bartlett convinced Captain Cochran to try for Herald Island, to see if there might be signs of the missing parties. They steamed slowly through the darkness all night, arriving at an impenetrable ice barrier at eight o'clock on September 9. Bartlett calculated they were only twelve miles away, but the ice was too thick to enter, and Captain Cochran was forced to retreat, turning the *Bear* for Nome. Bartlett stared out into the abyss of ice, thinking about Sandy Anderson's party, and also Dr. Mackay's party; the doctor, together with seaman Morris and scientists Murray and Beuchat, had left Shipwreck Camp to go it alone. When last they'd been seen out on the ice, they appeared to have only days left to live. As the *Bear* bore south, Bartlett reflected:

"It was as certain as anything could be that both parties had long since perished," he wrote, "but it was very hard for me to give them up, men with whom I had spent so many months, men with the future still before them."

The survivors were thoroughly examined one at a time by the surgeon on the *Bear*, who also questioned them as to their diet over the last many months. Some members had blood in their urine, and though emaciated, a few—including McKinlay—presented with swollen limbs. McKinlay informed the doctor of the "mystery illness" that had most likely killed Malloch and Mamen, and the doctor suspected that it was "nephritis," a general term for inflammation of the kidneys. He believed it might very well have been caused by faulty pemmican, especially if the pemmican did not possess high enough fat content to balance out the protein.

None of them appeared to have suffered from scurvy, probably because of relatively regular consumption of fresh meat. Almost everyone, to the doctor's surprise, was in fair condition, especially given the deprivation they'd endured. Clam Williams would require further surgery on his foot, and Chafe needed observation for his lingering frostbite. Templeman, who'd been babbling in delirium at the time of his rescue, was sickest among them, and the doctor pronounced that he would certainly not have survived many more days of exposure and famine. Other than that, the rest looked as though they would recover without drastic medical intervention. Kuraluk's family had fared better than everyone else; even little Mugpi came through unscathed except for a scar on her chin where Nigeraurak had scratched her.

The *Bear* reached Nome harbor on September 13, 1914. As it anchored, an enormous crowd had assembled along the beach to greet the returning members of the *Karluk*. Captain Cochran had sent a wireless message from the *Bear* the night before, alerting authorities of their imminent arrival. "The news spread rapidly over the town," wrote Chafe, who was overwhelmed by the outpouring, "and when we arrived there, nearly every inhabitant of the place was on the beach waiting to receive us." The story of the concerted rescue effort organized by Captain Bartlett had become an international sensation too. Stories would quickly appear in *The New York Times*, which devoted a full page to the rescue story, alongside its reporting on the initial battles of World War I.

But a proper "heroes' welcome" would have to wait a few days, despite the enthusiastic throng lined up on the beach. Captain Bartlett, after consulting with the ship's doctor, did not want to send the members ashore in their weakened condition, with their compromised immune systems. "It seemed to me best," he reflected, "to keep the men on board the *Bear* for a day or two, for in their reduced state they would be more than usually susceptible to contagious diseases." The captain was right to err on the side of caution. He also could not bear the thought—and the dark irony—of any one of them falling victim "to some ailment of the civilization to which they had so longed to return."

As a concession, Captain Bartlett allowed several dignitaries to board, including the author and poet Esther Birdsall Darling; Jafet Lindeberg, who'd dispatched the *Corwin**; and the editor of the *Nome Daily Nugget*, who wanted a story. Bartlett called on McKinlay to recount the tale to the

---

* The *Corwin*, as Jafet Lindeberg had promised Captain Bartlett, sailed to help, reaching Wrangel Island one day after the survivors were rescued. The ship continued on, circling Herald Island but could see no sign of the missing members of the expedition. Returning home, the *Corwin* struck a reef off Cape Douglas, but was refloated with help from the *Bear*.

editor, and McKinlay did his best to summon his memory and give an overview of the events. "Whether we liked it or not," wrote McKinlay, "we were being treated as heroes." The editor's photographer took the survivors out on the deck and shot dozens of pictures of them. As they posed for the camera, some of the assembled onlookers on the beach waved up to them and cheered, and they waved back. Ernest Chafe, taking in the scene, was overcome by the vibrant brilliance of it all: the burst of colors, the tall trees and verdant grasses. "There was no snow anywhere around Nome; the landscape, as far as the eye could see, was green, and the hills were covered with luxuriant pasture. . . . After our stay on Wrangel Island, Nome was a sunny California to us. The icy north was far behind."

As they waited to disembark—they wouldn't be allowed off the ship for two days—the survivors told Captain Bartlett more details of their story and learned of his trials on the ice of Long Strait with Kataktovik, and of their Siberian sled journey. It was miraculous that any of them had lived to tell their stories. "We talked and talked unceasingly," wrote McKinlay, "with the sheer exhilaration of being alive. Yet all the time our happiness was shadowed by the memory of those we had left behind."

The fact that he was alive overwhelmed McKinlay. While still aboard the *Bear*, once he knew that he was safe and their ordeal finally over, he wrote a letter to his family in Scotland. He'd been thinking about his younger brother, whom he feared would soon be joining the fighting in Europe. Life was so fleeting, so hard fought, so precious, as McKinlay had seen firsthand. He would wait until they were reunited to tell them the whole story, but for now, he simply expressed his elation at having been saved from certain death: *The one thing I wish this letter to do is show you I am alive, and how much I am alive.*

He had come north with misgivings about his preparation. He'd had no idea of the tribulations that awaited him, no practical experience in the Arctic—only the knowledge he'd learned from books. He had joined the expedition as its magnetician and meteorologist, but once the *Karluk* was locked in ice, and after it sank, he had become something much greater: a dogsled driver, an igloo builder, an Arctic hunter and explorer, a skier, a leader of men. Captain Bartlett's most trusted man. He was transformed, but that would all take time to process and comprehend. For now, in this moment, he was simply alive:

Just think of it all of you—I am alive. And more than alive, I am living. None of you know what life is, nor will you ever know until you come as near losing it as we were. The escapes I had. Think of it again: I am alive, and not lying on the pitiless Arctic floes or buried beneath the unfriendly soil of Wrangel Island. Think again, and know that of six scientists aboard the Karluk, I alone remain . . . Think of it all and thank God that your son and brother has won through and will soon be among you to tell you a story the world has never heard . . . I tell you, it's a tale in a million!

49

BEYOND THE ICE

FOR MOST OF THE SURVIVORS, THE JOURNEY AND THE ORDEAL OF the *Karluk*'s last voyage was over. For some, it would never truly be over and would haunt them for the rest of their lives.

Kuraluk, Auntie, Helen, and Mugpi remained in Alaska, returning to their home near Point Barrow. Kuraluk's hunting and survival skills had kept them all alive right up to the day before their rescue. Auntie, too, served a critical role in many ways: her sewing abilities outfitted the men with essential Native fur clothing and skin boots, her experience and economy in cooking provided them with varied meals and extended their ever-diminishing rations, her positive attitude buoyed spirits when they were low, and her maternal instincts made her a natural caregiver. "There is not a man alive from that ill-fated expedition," wrote Ernest Chafe once he was safely home, "who does not remember that faithful Eskimo woman with gratitude. We looked upon her as a mother." Auntie had two more children, both boys, and she named one of them Bartlett to honor the intrepid Newfoundland captain.

Mugpi (later Ruth Makpii Ipalook) lived to be the last surviving member of the *Karluk* disaster. She married Fred Ipalook, and the couple had nine children (four died in infancy). In 2001, at the age of ninety, she received an award—presented jointly by the Canadian Polar Commission and the United States Arctic Research Commission—for her family's contributions to Arctic science. She died on June 2, 2008, at the Alaska Native Medical Center, at the age of ninety-seven.

John Hadley, who had lived alternately in igloos and tents with Kura-luk and his family while stranded on the ice and on Wrangel Island, lived for some time with them in Alaska before embarking on a year of travel. He left his trusted dog Molly with them while he was gone, then returned to get her before leaving Alaska to go to San Francisco, where he died in January 1919 during the Spanish flu pandemic.

William McKinlay became desperately ill on the *Bear*'s final leg back to Esquimalt, British Columbia. By the time they reached Unalaska, he was barely conscious—suffering from a high fever and debilitating headache—and Captain Bartlett and others carried him to the hospital. McKinlay's neck and face were swollen and blistered with raised, fiery red rashes. The doctor quickly diagnosed him with erysipelas, a severe bacterial skin infection. After three days of treatment and rest, he was released. Captain Bartlett greeted McKinlay as he came out of the hospital, joking about how hard the tough young Scot seemed to kill: "I guess they'll have to shoot you, boy!"

Indeed, he would be shot at soon enough. But first, he had to get home. The *Bear* anchored at Victoria, British Columbia, and McKinlay and the remaining Canadian Arctic Expedition members were taken by launch the short distance to Esquimalt, the location from which the *Karluk* had originally embarked back in June of 1913. A lifetime ago. All of them had changed, and indeed, the world had changed. "It was only when a patrol boat stopped our launch to make sure we were not German spies," McKinlay recalled, "that we realized there was a war on . . . we had to thread our way through Canadian and British cruisers, submarines and other vessels."

By the time he finally reached home, McKinlay learned that his younger brother had entered the fight and was serving somewhere in France. McKinlay was eager to join him, hoping to erase the horrible recurring memories of his experience in the Arctic. But first he had to recover physically before he'd be deemed fit for service, a process that took a year. While he recuperated, his mind cast back to those *Karluk* comrades who did not return, "To those we had left behind under the ice and snow and freezing Arctic waters—Malloch, Mamen, Breddy, Dr. Mackay, Murray, Beuchat, Morris, Barker, King (Golightly), Brady, and my dear friend Sandy Anderson."

McKinlay finally signed on in October 1915, serving as an officer in the Fifty-first Highland Division (the Gordon Highlanders) until 1917, when he was wounded and summarily discharged. His younger brother died in battle. But throughout the rest of McKinlay's life—which included falling in love, marrying, and teaching (a career that culminated in a headmaster position)—nothing would ever have so profound an impact on him as the Canadian Arctic Expedition. Though he tried to process it all and come to some kind of understanding, he would never forget what he'd witnessed and been a part of. "Not all the horrors of the Western Front," he wrote, "not the rubble of Arras, nor the hell of Ypres, nor all the mud of Flanders leading to Passchendale, could blot out the memories of that year in the Arctic."

So, instead of blotting the memories out, McKinlay wrote about them, publishing Karluk: *The Great Untold Story of Arctic Exploration* in 1976, when he was eighty-seven. (In 1990, the book was reissued under the title *The Last Voyage of the* Karluk.) For many years, he maintained a correspondence with Captain Bartlett, for whom he had profound respect. "There was for me only one real hero in the whole [*Karluk*] story—Bob Bartlett. Honest, fearless, reliable, loyal, everything a man should be." William Laird McKinlay died in Glasgow, Scotland, on May 9, 1983, at the age of ninety-four.

Ernest Chafe (messroom boy and assistant steward) spent four months in the hospital in Victoria, British Columbia, receiving treatment for his foot, unfortunately including further amputation. When he recovered, he received three months' "bonus pay" from the Canadian government and was formally discharged from the expedition.

Hugh "Clam" Williams (seaman) also required further medical treatment in Victoria, British Columbia. He needed subsequent operations on his severely frostbitten foot and was not released until January of 1915. He served at sea during the war, and though his ship was struck by a torpedo, he survived, returning home to Wales, where he eventually married and had three children. He died in 1937.

Robert Williamson (second engineer) served in both World War I and World War II with the Royal Canadian Navy, but throughout his life he had to address the claims made by John Hadley that he had murdered

George Breddy. Responding to inquiries about it, Williamson was defensive and adamant that the charges were spurious, possibly driven by Hadley's paranoia: "Hadley's account of the death of Breddy," he wrote, "is another one of his hallucinations & absolutely untrue." Williamson never published his own full account of his experiences on the expedition, but he did publish a short piece called "The Cry of the Owl" in the *Daily Colonist* in 1959, which told of his visit to see John Munro and Robert Templeman at Rodger's Harbor in August 1913. In the piece, he described being guided back to Cape Waring with the aid of a snowy owl showing him the way. He died in 1975, in Victoria, British Columbia, at the age of ninety-seven.

Very little is known about the post-*Karluk* lives of two of the men rescued at Rodger's Harbor. Robert "Bob" Templeman (cook and steward) remained true to his word to Bjarne Mamen and returned Mamen's diary to his family in Norway. Templeman emigrated to Australia, and not much else is known about him after that. John Munro (chief engineer), who shared the tent with Templeman at Rodger's Harbor, worked for a time with the Canadian Department of Marine and Fisheries, then eventually moved to California and got married.

Fred Maurer (fireman) returned to his home in New Philadelphia, Ohio. Before leaving Alaska, he arranged to have Nigeraurak, the ship's cat, sent to his home, where it lived with his family until 1926. Nigeraurak produced numerous litters of kittens, some of which Maurer gave as presents to members of the Canadian Arctic Expedition. As for Maurer, for a few years after his rescue—urged by and with assistance from Vilhjalmur Stefansson—he made some money on a lecture tour (Chautauqua circuit) speaking about his Arctic experiences. He also continued a relationship and correspondence with Stefansson, and in 1921, having only recently been married, Fred Maurer left on an expedition returning to Wrangel Island. The decision to revisit the place where he'd experienced such misery and death is hard to comprehend, though perhaps his youth—and Stefansson's persuasion—played roles.

For most of the year, Stefansson had been planning an expedition in which he intended to colonize Wrangel Island, after which he would form an exploration company for tourism there, and the commercial raising of reindeer. He also believed the island could serve as an airstrip for future trans-Arctic aviation and as a meteorological and radio base. Stefansson, failing to garner enough support from the Canadian government for his plans, instead secretly organized an expedition himself with an outfit he called the Stefansson Arctic Exploration Company. The company raised enough money to send four men to the island—including Fred Maurer— and one woman. Stefansson did not go.

The expedition proved to be another disaster. One of the men died of scurvy. Fred Maurer and the two other men attempted to cross the Long Strait as Bartlett had done with Kataktovik, leaving Wrangel Island on January 28, 1923. None were ever seen again. The woman, a tough and industrious Inupiat named Ada Blackjack,* was the lone survivor. She had been recruited to sew fur clothing for the expedition members. Once the others had perished, she trapped foxes, hunted seals, and caught fish, and she managed to survive by herself until she was rescued on August 20, 1923.

Though Stefansson never set foot on Wrangel Island himself, he bore responsibility, directly and indirectly, for the deaths of the eleven *Karluk* members, and the four who were part of his colonization scheme.†

---

* The woman's remarkable ordeal is recounted in an excellent 2003 book by Jennifer Niven titled *Ada Blackjack: A True Story of Survival in the Arctic*.
† Two other men, Captain Peter Bernard and Charles Thomsen, died on the ice in 1916 as part of the Canadian Arctic Expedition while serving Stefansson and his continued northern exploration. Another man, named Andre Norem, who served as cook on the *Mary Sachs* for the Southern Party of the Canadian Arctic Expedition, suffered depression and shot himself in the head on April 17, 1914. Captain Daniel Blue, engineer of the Southern Party's *Alaska*, died of scurvy and pneumonia during the winter of 1915. Thus, all told sixteen members died during the CAE.

50

BARTLETT VERSUS STEFANSSON

CAPTAIN BOB BARTLETT'S HEROIC EFFORTS TO RESCUE THE MA-
rooned *Karluk* survivors made him an international hero. He was already in an elite echelon of polar explorers, having received in 1909
the rare Hubbard Medal, the National Geographic Society's highest
honor. Peary and Amundsen, respectively, received the award in the
two years prior, and Sir Ernest Shackleton in the year after, so Bartlett
indeed ranked among the Olympians of polar exploration.* But despite
the accolades of the global—and particularly the American—press, the
loss of the eleven members of the expedition would weigh on him until his last days. He would never be able to push completely from his
mind the thought of Mamen and Malloch dying inside the fetid tent
at Rodger's Harbor, the macabre circumstances of Breddy's shooting,
or the grim imaginings of first mate Sandy Anderson's party starving

---

* Bartlett received the third Hubbard Medal, awarded for distinction in exploration, discovery, and research—and not limited to polar explorers. Later recipients include aviator Charles
Lindbergh, astronauts John Glenn and Neil Armstrong, and zoologist Jane Goodall.

to death on the lonely, frozen shores of Herald Island.* He called the events connected to the *Karluk* "the most tragic and ill-fated . . . in my whole career."

Not long after Bartlett's return home, these hauntings surfaced when an Admiralty commission charged with investigating the deaths associated with the *Karluk* disaster faulted him for getting the ship stuck in the ice in the first place. He was also censured for allowing Dr. Alistair Forbes Mackay and his party to leave the ship. The commission drew dubious conclusions in key respects. As to getting the *Karluk* stuck, Bartlett was at the time trying to appease Stefansson, then the expedition's leader. Stefansson would later admit that the decision to steam away from land and head out into the ice was his alone, even going so far as to take full responsibility: "I was in command," he wrote of the fateful choice, "and the decision and responsibility had to be mine. I decided for . . . the bolder course. I chose the wrong alternative. . . . Events were to prove this decision my most serious error of the whole expedition."

As to the charge of allowing Dr. Mackay's departure, the commission wrongly overlooked several critical facts. For one thing, although Bartlett was the ship's captain—and by virtue of Stefansson's abandonment of the ship, the expedition's leader de facto—he was not formally in charge of the scientists. No official papers or orders were ever generated that in any way dictated his control over their actions. There was no military com-

---

* Both Captain Bartlett and Vilhjalmur Stefansson would eventually learn the grim fate of first mate Sandy Anderson's party. In 1924, Captain Louis Lane, aboard the *Herman*, went ashore on Herald Island at a gravel beach on its northwestern shore. The captain and his men discovered the partial skeletal remains of four men, along with numerous artifacts, including tent poles and cloth, snow goggles, pocket and hunting knives, a pocket compass, and a watch. Significantly, they also found a rusted short-barreled rifle with the initials BM carved into the stock. The rifle, it was later confirmed, had belonged to Burt McConnell, who'd left it on the *Karluk* when he departed the ship with Stefansson on the caribou-hunting fiasco. Captain Lane collected and conveyed the bodily remains and artifacts to the Canadian government, and they were thoroughly examined. It was concluded that the remains were those of Sandy Anderson, Charles Barker, John Brady, and Edmund Lawrence Golightly. In a strange twist to the story, some of the artifacts and remains, including a jawbone, were auctioned on eBay in 1999 and purchased by author Jennifer Niven, who wrote of the *Karluk* disaster in her excellent book *The Ice Master* (2000). Details of the discovery from the *Daily Colonist*, October 14, 1924.

mand structure enabling him to order them to do anything. Stefansson had left him in a nearly impossible predicament, complicated of course by Dr. Mackay's and the others' eventual desire to seek out land on their own. Bartlett had done his best to persuade them to stay with the rest of the group, but Dr. Mackay and Murray's overconfidence, deriving from their experience in Antarctica with Shackleton, convinced them to go it alone, hauling sleds without the use of dogs. Other than have them write a letter absolving Bartlett of responsibility for their actions, there was little else that could be done. He certainly wasn't about to hold them at gunpoint or try to imprison them at Shipwreck Camp. It's absurd to think he could have kept them there against their will.

Fortunately for Captain Bartlett, public opinion held much more sway than did a single obscure commission report, and his reputation withstood any criticisms and would continue to enlarge over the next few decades as he led dozens of subsequent Arctic expeditions, served in the United States Army and Navy during World War I, and during World War II worked for the US military,* resupplying bases in Canada and Greenland. As captain of his own schooner, the *Effie M. Morrissey*, Bartlett made scientific and exploratory voyages to remote parts of Greenland and the Canadian Arctic. These expeditions, supported by the Smithsonian Institution, the American Museum of Natural History, and the New York Botanical Garden, conducted important atmospheric, oceanographic, and archeological research, all of which was remarkable considering Bartlett had left school in his teens and possessed little formal scientific or academic education.

Vilhjalmur Stefansson finally reappeared from his northern ice journeys in 1918, having failed to participate in the rescue of the *Karluk* survivors and having conveniently missed the entirety of the First World War while out exploring. He'd planned to continue his explorations, but he contracted typhoid fever, which progressed to pneumonia, forcing his return to Fort

---

* Though born in Newfoundland, Bartlett had become an American citizen by 1913 when he joined the Canadian Arctic Expedition.

Yukon, Alaska, for treatment. He'd been gone and essentially out of touch with the rest of the world—except for a few periods of brief contact with his Canadian Arctic Expedition and correspondence with the Canadian government—since September of 1913. After three months of convalescence, Stefansson returned alone—by riverboat, ship, and finally rail—to Ottawa to report to the Canadian government, and then continued to New York. But for his brief and whirlwind fundraising and organizing stint in 1912, he had been in the Arctic almost continuously for twelve years. When he left the Arctic in 1918—for the last time, as it turned out—he also left behind his Inupiat wife, Fanny, and his son, Alex. He never saw them again.

When Stefansson resurfaced, he had some explaining to do. Like Bartlett, he was also blamed for his role in the *Karluk* disaster. But he did not have to answer for his culpability immediately, because the Canadian government did not conduct any inquiry on Stefansson and the loss of the *Karluk* at that time, allowing Stefansson to focus instead on the positives, on all that he had, in his eyes, accomplished. Now thirty-nine years old, Stefansson had returned as a world-famous explorer, and both he and the Canadian government reveled in what Stefansson and the Canadian Arctic Expedition had achieved, which was significant. It mattered little, apparently, that the ultimate cost of the expedition (not counting the loss of sixteen human lives) came to a staggering $600,000, ten times his original estimate and the equivalent of over $10,000,000 today.

Stefansson and his repurposed Northern Party discovered five previously unknown islands in the North American Arctic, claiming them for Canada and naming them: Brock, Meighen, Lougheed, and Borden (named for Canada's prime minister, it later proved to be two islands). In the Beaufort Sea, Stefansson established the outermost fringes of the continental shelf, thus ruling out the existence of a continent north of Alaska, and proving that Crocker Land, for which he and others had been searching, did not exist. He planted flags on numerous previously unknown High Arctic islands, claiming them for Canada. These discoveries were lauded by the international media, by fellow explorers (including General Adolphus Greely and Admiral Peary), and by the scientific community and its loftiest dignitaries. The Royal Geographic Society awarded him the coveted Gold Medal in 1921 "for his distinguished services in the exploration of the Arctic Ocean."

Stefansson wasted no time parlaying his fame into fortune, becoming a professional speaker and racking up appearance fees of up to $2,000 a week (over $30,000 in today's dollars). When not on the lecture circuit, he devoted his attention to writing his popular book *The Friendly Arctic*, which was published in late 1921 and quickly became a *New York Times* bestseller, with broad acclaim and wide US distribution. The title itself alludes to one of the central themes of the wide-ranging, often meandering 784-page tome: rather than a dangerous death trap, the Arctic was really a benign place, and small, well-outfitted groups, adopting the practices of the region's Native peoples, could live off the ice and land for extended periods of time, perhaps even indefinitely. The book also gave Stefansson's account of the fate of the *Karluk*, which raised many eyebrows because he wasn't present for most of its members' trials, having himself deserted the ship.

But the book's commercial and critical successes were countered in equal measure by intense, even virulent reactions from numerous fronts, including the Canadian government, a host of noted Arctic and Antarctic explorers, and members of the Canadian Arctic Expedition itself. The book made serious charges of conspiracy and even mutiny among members of the Southern Party (Stefansson had already profited from some of these sensational stories by means of his lectures), charges that set off a firestorm of claims and counterclaims, particularly by Dr. Rudolph Anderson, who'd ably headed up the Southern Party after Stefansson left on his ice journeys.

To Anderson, the book was filled with outright lies, libelous claims, and sections that were so far removed from the truth that they read like fiction. On the publication of *The Friendly Arctic*, he called Stefansson "a liar and an imposter." Anderson went on to assert, through press releases and interviews, that as expedition leader, Stefansson bore sole blame for the *Karluk* disaster, since he had procured an unsuitable ship and later irresponsibly abandoned it, and these mistakes resulted in the loss of human lives.

Roald Amundsen, at the time one of the most famous explorers in the world, said of the book, "Of all the fantastic rot I have ever heard, this comes close to the top." Amundsen eviscerated Stefansson's *Friendly Arctic* (in the press on its release, and later, in his own autobiography published the following year) as reckless, calling the promotion of the Arctic as a "friendly" place a gross misrepresentation liable to send inexperienced adventurers or thrill seekers to their deaths. Amundsen conceded that a highly skilled and experienced explorer and expert marksman—if he had incredibly favorable weather and high game populations—"might for a very short time 'live off the country.'" Then he cautioned, "But I would not try it myself. I would consider it sheer suicide."

Amundsen also scoffed at Stefansson's Blond Eskimo theory, one of the most enticing promotional tools Stefansson had originally used to attract funding for the Canadian Arctic Expedition. Amundsen, whose opinions were widely respected, called the Blond Eskimo theory essentially a hoax that was "a far-fetched idea that should be taken with many grains of salt." He countered with what he considered a perfectly obvious explanation: "the natural intermingling of races" during a few hundred years of exploration in the region by the British and Scandinavians. As far as he was concerned, on this subject, anyway, Stefansson had discovered nothing new, and had used the entire dubious conceit to draw media attention and raise money for exploring.

At least publicly, Captain Bartlett had little to say about Stefansson's controversial and bestselling book, even though it chronicled portions of the trip during which Stefansson was not present. "I kept my mouth shut . . . and made no comment," wrote Bartlett in a letter to McKinlay after the book came out. But privately he was outraged by the book's numerous misrepresentations and inaccuracies, particularly those that cast Bartlett in a negative light or directly questioned his leadership and decisions. One claim was particularly damning and stung Bartlett, angering him deeply. In recapping the trials after the *Karluk* sank, Stefansson made this observation: "The only thing that surprised me was that the men should have been left on Wrangel Island. It appeared to me that they should have walked ashore at the same time that Captain Bartlett did. . . . A hundred miles over ordinary arctic sea ice is not far to walk." Not having been there himself, Stefansson was speaking out of complete ignorance. Bartlett had just led the party from Shipwreck Camp on the arduous three-week trek, hacking their way through mountains of pressure ridges, and many of the members were suffering from fatigue, frostbite, malnourishment, and were in no shape to embark on another hundred-mile trip. And the "ordinary arctic sea ice" Stefansson describes nonchalantly nearly took the lives of Bartlett and Kataktovik more than once.

And then there was the matter of the suspicious appendix Stefansson included at the end of *The Friendly Arctic*. He reproduced an account of "The Story of the *Karluk*," as told to him by John Hadley, who of course *was* there for the entire ordeal. Hadley had died by the time the book was published. Hadley's "version" of events is in many places critical of Captain Bartlett and highly favorable of Stefansson, which appears a convenient way for Stefansson to disparage Bartlett through Hadley, thereby avoiding calling him out himself. Hadley's story was written in 1918 at Herald Island, where Hadley spent some time after returning from Wrangel Island. Stefansson apparently encouraged Hadley to write his version of the events and had the document in hand for several years after Hadley's death in 1919, before publishing it himself in 1921. There is ample evidence that Stefansson altered the text for his own purposes. For one thing, the style of Hadley's actual diary is terse, cryptic, riddled with misspellings, and devoid of any sustained narrative. William McKinlay had this to say on reading both Hadley's diary and his story in the appendix of Stefansson's book: "I am of the opinion that the author was not Hadley but Stefansson."

Despite the outright lies and a host of criticisms Hadley (via Stefansson) made concerning the captain's leadership and decision-making, Bartlett kept mum, at least so far as the press was concerned. Perhaps it was because in other parts of the book, Stefansson generally praised Bartlett.

"When Bartlett took charge of the *Karluk*," Stefansson wrote, "I found him everything that Peary had said. With the reputation he brought with him and his efficiency in managing the affairs of the ship, he won the admiration and confidence of everybody." And on the controversial decision to take the *Karluk* away from land and out into the ice—the decision for which Bartlett endured censure by the Admiralty commission—Stefansson did take responsibility, at least in print.

Privately, and among close friends and colleagues in the exploration community, Bartlett seethed for decades, developing a deep and enduring hatred of Stefansson. He personally blamed him for the disaster, believing that his lack of organization and leadership had cost numerous lives. Abandoning the *Karluk* was, in the captain's mind, totally unforgivable. When *The Friendly Arctic* came out, Bartlett wrote to McKinlay about his reaction: "I was so damned mad that I went over to the Harvard Club where Stefansson was staying; fortunately for me he was not in. Had we met I believe that I could have killed him." Bartlett held Stefansson in such low regard that he even threatened to start a petition to have him expelled from the prestigious Explorers Club, though he never formally followed up on it. Later, he heard that Stefansson had been spreading rumors that Bartlett should be sent to jail for losing the *Karluk*. Livid, Bartlett confided to McKinlay: "My day will come if I ever get him alone. I will beat him to within an inch of his life."

The intensity of Bartlett's ire was undoubtedly fueled by alcohol. Although he claimed in his books to be a teetotaler, during the 1920s, precipitated by Admiral Peary's death on February 20, 1920, Captain Bartlett descended into alcoholism. Prohibition had just been enacted, but Bartlett was industrious enough to obtain whiskey from a Manhattan bootlegger, and he took his bottles to his room in the Murray Hill Hotel and drank alone. When he went out to visit with fellow explorers, he was often already drunk: "He made a well-oiled fool of himself more than once in the Explorers Club and elsewhere," writes biographer Maura Hanrahan.

Bartlett and Stefansson did encounter each other in 1922, at a Washington Club tea service following the unveiling of the Peary Monument at Arlington National Cemetery. Given Bartlett's booze-fueled bravado, the meeting was surprisingly anticlimactic. According to Bartlett, out of respect for the decorum of the event, he intentionally avoided Stefansson, but afterward Stefansson approached him, saying, "Why, Bartlett, didn't you see me?" Bartlett cut him off right there, barking under his breath, "No, nor do I want to see you," and he abruptly took his leave.

In the end, Captain Robert Abram Bartlett, ice pilot and master mariner, remains the hero of the *Karluk* saga, and Vilhjalmur Stefansson its villain. The two factors that contribute most to this perception are these: Bartlett's courageous journey with Kataktovik over the ice of Long Strait and across northern Siberia; and Stefansson's desertion of his flagship (for which going caribou hunting was an unsatisfactory excuse) and his failure to do anything to rescue possible survivors. Such diametrically opposed reactions to the same disaster say much about each man's character.

From the start, Stefansson made poor decisions, one after another. The expedition was doomed before it began because of Stefansson's hurried, even frenetic organization. He cobbled together ships, equipment, crew, and scientific staff in just a few hectic months in late 1912 and early 1913. The vessel he chose as flagship, the *Karluk*, was egregiously ill suited for the Arctic tasks required of it, and when he purchased the steamship, its condition was abysmal. Worse yet, Stefansson allowed the expedition to depart Alaska for Herschel Island with the wrong men and equipment aboard the wrong ships, and he unforgivably failed to properly outfit the expedition members with Arctic clothing. Hiring the seamstress Kiruk (Auntie) was a good idea, but it happened at the last possible moment. Had he been responsible, he would have procured many, many more complete sets of winter fur and skin garments. In the end, Auntie—assisted by the unskilled men—was forced to be sewing garments even after the *Karluk* was crushed and they were surviving on the ice at Shipwreck Camp. She was still sewing clothes long after they were stranded on Wrangel Island. Stefansson's poor planning and shoddy organization were colossal, inexcusable blunders.

It's inarguable that Stefansson was brilliant, driven, ambitious and charismatic. But he was also a narcissist who craved the spotlight. In the field he was best suited for life on the ice with very small teams that included Indigenous inhabitants. As an organizer of an international expedition the size, scope, and logistical complexity of the Canadian Arctic Expedition (CAE)—with multiple ships; dozens of men; tons of food, gear, and scientific equipment—he proved an abject failure. He was too self-consumed, too vain to be an effective leader. Even after the *Karluk* had departed Esquimalt, British Columbia, in June of 1913 and his expedition was officially under way, Stefansson was dictating and editing *My Life with the Eskimo* with his personal secretary and an editorial assistant! His attentions were scattered, and his inattention to the CAE cost lives.

Captain Bartlett, on the other hand—though also ambitious—proved time and again to be a skilled and selfless leader able to contend with shipwreck, perilous life camped on moving ice, and the organization and orchestration of a harrowing trek across treacherous sea ice to the safety of Wrangel Island. Once there, he rightly chose not to take a large group of famished, ill, and frostbitten people across the Long Strait to Siberia with insufficient food stores. That trip, given the condition of various members, would certainly have resulted in death to some if not all of them. Instead, he risked his own life, embarking with Kataktovik on a heroic journey of more than seven hundred miles to get news of the survivors to the world. Had he not succeeded, all the members left on Wrangel Island probably would have died. Then, after alerting the Canadian government to the plight of those marooned, Bartlett spent tireless, anxious months organizing a rescue mission for the survivors, all while Stefansson was out exploring, having long since put the fate of the *Karluk* and its complement out of his mind. Stefansson—as he always did—simply moved on.

It is fair to say that Bartlett's only true love was the sea. He never married—in fact, there is no record of any significant romantic relationship. He just never seemed entirely content on land, always bored and restless, always planning for his next adventure. He had become, like many who ventured to the frozen north, a pagophile—a creature most suited to life on sea ice. "It's all right when you're out exploring," he said in his 1928 memoir. "You get used to rotten meat, frozen fingers, lice, and dirt. The hard times come when you get back." He did not elaborate on the statement, but one senses that he was lonely and out of place on land, even when hobnobbing with other great men and famous adventurers at the Explorers Club. The camaraderie developed on a ship, bonding with men through shared hardships and life-or-death perils, could not be replicated back in civilization, where life was too easy.

Perhaps, also, his unease grew from a kind of imposter syndrome, for although he was eventually bestowed an honorary master's degree from Bowdoin College in 1920 (Admiral Peary's alma mater), Bartlett's formal education was pursued not in the classrooms of the prestigious colleges and universities attended by many of his contemporaries but at sea. The captain's decades of contributions to polar exploration were significant enough for him to be awarded (in addition to the Hubbard Medal) the American Geographical Society's Charles P. Daly Medal (1925) and the Peary Polar Expedition Medal.

Of the two men, Bartlett was the first to die, contracting pneumonia in late April of 1946. He lingered for a few days in a New York hospital and was said to be cheerful in his final hours before he lost consciousness. Unfortunately, poor weather conditions prevented any family members from making the trip from Newfoundland to his bedside in time, and he died alone on April 28, 1946, at the age of seventy. But in memory, he was anything but alone. A few days after his death, seven hundred people attended memorial services in his honor at Methodist Christ Church in Manhattan. A delegation representing the Explorers Club attended, as did Matthew Henson, who had gone on toward the North Pole in 1909 while Bartlett, following Peary's orders, dutifully returned to the *Roosevelt*.

Many newspaper editors were present, as were decorated military men with whom Bartlett had served. There were representatives from the American Museum of Natural History, the Brooklyn Museum, and a contingent of admiring Newfoundlanders then living in New York. All pressed in close to hear Bartlett memorialized, with the Reverend Dr. Henry

Darlington—a dear old friend—paying tribute, saying "the world needs especially today the things for which Captain Bartlett stood: reliability and sturdiness of character, devotion to his friends and family and the ability to carry through a job once started, no matter how difficult."

Somewhere in the audience, his head bowed in at least the semblance of deference, was Vilhjalmur Stefansson, who had also come to pay his respects.

Stefansson would live another sixteen years, succumbing to a stroke at the age of eighty-two at his home in Hanover, New Hampshire, in 1962. Evelyn Stefansson, his wife of twenty years, was at his side. The *New York Times* heralded Stefansson "among the last of the Dog-Team explorers," and his ambitious if disastrous Canadian Arctic Expedition effectively— and significantly—concluded the Heroic Age of Discovery. During his lifetime, the remarkable if self-centered Stefansson had seamlessly transitioned from explorer to lecturer to popular author to academic scholar. He wrote twenty-five books and published some four hundred articles in his lifetime, many about the Far North and its people, encompassing a wide range of subjects, including anthropology, linguistics, medicine, and ethnology. He correctly predicted travel to the North Pole by airplane and by submarine. In 1953, he sold his vast and comprehensive Arctic library to Dartmouth College, where it remains housed today. His early explorations in the Arctic, and his subsequent writings about them, ultimately won him the everlasting fame he seemed to desire and even need. Chameleonlike from childhood to the end, he once said, with prescient self-awareness, "I am what I want to be."

Despite everything Vilhjalmur Stefansson achieved, he remains inextricably linked to Captain Bob Bartlett and the doomed *Karluk*, the ship that brought them together, defined their characters, and now rests somewhere at the bottom of the Arctic Ocean.

ACKNOWLEDGMENTS

Numerous shout-outs are necessary here. I wrote this book at a strange and challenging time in history, during the most devastating global pandemic since the Spanish flu, the Great Influenza epidemic of 1918 (which, interestingly, occurred in the years just following the period this story covers). Lockdowns, quarantines, and Russia's war on Ukraine prohibited some research travel, including a scheduled trip to Wrangel Island in the summer of 2021, but there were some unexpected silver linings.

I became a grandfather for the first time just a few months into the pandemic, and my grandson, Luke, was born in a hospital about one hundred yards from the downtown Moscow, Idaho, office where I wrote *Empire of Ice and Stone*. Because my daughter and her husband were living here in our town at the time, I was able to see Luke nearly every day for the first year of his life, and those times, those breaks from the research and writing, were bonding experiences I will never forget. The stroller perambulations, the playdates at the parks and playgrounds, the dog park jaunts—all were special and stress-relieving. Thank you, Logan and Chris and Luke, for all that love and joy during my deskbound toil. And Logan, who is a therapist, was always there—is always there—when I just need to talk things through. Love you, Bunners.

I offer the same love and gratitude to my wife, Camie; son, Hunter; and Abigail Dow. Being around family for much of the process was essential in maintaining a reasonable work-life balance (or trying to at least). Family meals, game nights, and outdoor outings all contributed to my ability to finish this book. Love you all so much. To Hunter, a young man of letters:

it has been fulfilling to collaborate on these literary journeys and to share and discuss ideas.

My agent Scott Waxman has been a champion, an ally, and a friend for over twenty years. I deeply appreciate his enthusiasm and belief in my projects and the fact that he has stuck with me through both good and lean times and helped me navigate the whims, fluctuations, and challenges within the publishing industry. He's a consummate pro and I'm lucky to call him both my agent and my friend. One of Scott's superpowers is connecting people and helping foster relationships, and this book is a result of that skill in at least two ways. Scott originally introduced me to Marc Resnick, senior editor at St. Martin's Press, with whom I've now worked on two books. Like Scott, Marc is a great guy, a consummate professional, and a superb teammate. I hope and believe that Marc and I will be working together on many more books, for as long as I have the brain cells and stamina to write them. Thanks, Marc, for your wisdom, your industry knowledge, and your trust in my intuition.

At St. Martin's Press, the entire team does terrific, professional work. Thanks to marketing manager Sara Beth Haring, Rebecca Lang, assistant director of publicity, and Lily Cronig, editorial assistant. And kudos to freelance copy editor extraordinaire Eliani Torres.

Scott Waxman also connected me with agent Susan Canavan, who joined Waxman Literary Agency in 2019 after an illustrious career as senior executive editor at Houghton Mifflin Harcourt. Susan has been terrific to work with, conspiring with me on future book ideas, thinking of me for coauthoring partnerships, and generally being an awesome sounding board. She negotiated the deal with St. Martin's Press on *Empire of Ice and Stone*, and I appreciate her deep understanding of storytelling, strong narrative, and the vicissitudes of the publishing landscape.

Numerous individuals and institutions were immensely helpful with my research. Their jobs were made even more difficult since many of the libraries and archives both in the United States and abroad were either closed or had limited staffing and hours during the crunch time of my research. Lynsey Halliday at the National Library of Scotland was tireless and patient with me (to a fault!), searching for and providing me with documents relating to the expedition through the library's significant holdings compiled by and related to William Laird McKinlay. Thanks, Lynsey, for your heroic efforts. I can't thank you enough.

Many thanks to Scout Noffke, reference and administrative specialist at the Rauner Special Collections Library, Dartmouth College. Scout's expertise and searching efficiency were so helpful, especially in locating expedition member diaries in the archives when I could no longer see straight, much less search straight.

The entire staff at the Library and Archives Canada in Ottawa deserves my thanks and praise. The staff members provided thorough and ongoing assistance, navigating the many databases connected to the Canadian Arctic Expedition, and I greatly appreciate their resourcefulness.

Bowdoin College and the Peary-Macmillan Arctic Museum and Arctic Studies Center helped me immensely. I offer particular thanks to Genny LeMoine, Curator/Registrar, who gracefully handled my near-constant pestering.

Thanks also to the good folks at the Maritime Museum of British Columbia, in Victoria.

As always, many thanks to the ongoing support of the Washington State University College of Arts and Sciences (along with the Department of English), which has supported my research and writing for many years. For *Empire of Ice and Stone*, a departmental 2021 Summer Research Fellowship provided me with funding for the maps in the book. That reminds me—I've used master mapmaker Jeff Ward on numerous projects, and he's fast, detailed, and easy to work with. Jeff, you're the best in the business!

In the early phases of researching *Empire of Ice and Stone*, I discovered that a scholar named Matthew Shupe, who incidentally comes from my town (his father coincidentally delivered both my children!), was one of the leaders of the amazing MOSAiC project. The MOSAiC project (Multidisciplinary drifting Observatory for the Study of Arctic Climate) 2019–20 was the most ambitious scientific undertaking in the Arctic in history. It intentionally got the icebreaker RV *Polarstern* trapped in ice;

then some one hundred scientists remained on board for an entire year following the ship's drift in the first year-round expedition into the central Arctic, exploring the Arctic climate system. Because the drift of the *Polarstern* would mirror those of Nansen, De Long, and Bartlett, I wanted to learn as much as I could about polar drift and Arctic currents and gyres. A researcher at CIRES, the University of Colorado, and NOAA, Shupe was co-leader and co-coordinator of the MOSAiC project, yet amazingly, despite his incredibly busy schedule, he answered my questions by phone and email. Thanks, Matthew. I remain awed by your work and indebted to you.

To the esteemed and honorable barrister Tim "Sneaky" Gresback—thanks for providing me with a place to land and work. It's been a tremendously productive space, and I appreciate your generosity and fine spirit. You have my vote!

John Larkin has been my first reader on nearly all my books, providing timely edits, notes, and humor exactly when I need them most. His maritime knowledge was indispensable in *Empire of Ice and Stone*, just as it was for *Labyrinth of Ice*. He's always there with the right nautical terminology and has a great eye and ear for story. John, I have one word for you: PORCH!

Thanks, love, and ongoing appreciation for my Free Range Writers: Kim Barnes, Collin Hughes, Lisa Norris, and Jane Varley. It was wonderful reconvening during summer 2021 after a year hiatus because of the pandemic. Hope we can keep it rolling for another decade or three, by which time we're going to need ramps and pulleys and porters for Kim's coolers.

My siblings—Lisa, Lance, and Lex Levy—offer emotional support and love always and forever. Time for a family reunion?

A NOTE ON THE TEXT AND SOURCES

I came across the story of the Canadian Arctic Expedition while doing research for my book *Labyrinth of Ice: The Triumphant and Tragic Greely Polar Expedition*. I must admit I was a little surprised not to have heard of it before. I had long been fascinated by Arctic exploration and discovery ever since visiting Greenland in 2003, and had read widely on the subject, which is rich in thrilling adventure, feats of endurance, desperation, and tragedy. The story of the *Karluk* disaster enthralled me as an epic survival and rescue narrative, but mostly I was drawn to the two men—Captain Robert "Bob" Bartlett and Vilhjalmur Stefansson—who seemed to be the protagonist and antagonist of the remarkable events that followed. Or perhaps they were dual protagonists or dueling protagonists. At any rate, I needed to find out.

Much has been written about the Canadian Arctic Expedition, at the time in countless national and international newspapers, and in the decades that followed by some of the survivors themselves and by journalists and writers trying to piece together the complex sequence of events surrounding the expedition. I wished to tell the story in my own way, focusing on the heroism, sacrifice, and fateful decisions of the central figures involved. Fortunately, the literature on Arctic exploration, and especially on the region and period this story covers, is voluminous. For readers wishing to discover much more, relevant selected works are listed below and in the bibliography that follows—works that have been cited, quoted directly, or consulted as valuable references in the writing of *Empire of Ice and Stone*.

Fortunately, numerous members of the Canadian Arctic Expedition kept journals and diaries of their experiences, and these were essential in re-creating the story. Foremost among these—because it is the most comprehensive (and I think best written) is the diary of William Laird McKinlay, available at the National Library of Scotland. At nearly three hundred pages, McKinlay's diary is incredibly thorough and detailed, including daily weather, temperature, estimated locations, the movements and actions of key expedition members, delightful descriptions of the sea, ice, and land, and his many observations—in real time—about all the participants. Honest, vulnerable—and often sarcastic and humorous even while facing the specter of looming death—McKinlay dedicated time each day (except when incapacitated by illness) to his diary, which spans June 18, 1913, to October 25, 1914, and is written in remarkably legible handwriting, especially considering the difficult circumstances and conditions he was sometimes in. I relied on it heavily, cross-checking his recollections and observations with his later published book *The Last Voyage of the* Karluk: *A Survivor's Memoir of Arctic Disaster*.

The diary of Bjarne Mamen spans the period of June 17, 1913, to May 22, 1914, and was also essential. It is available through the Library and Archives Canada, and has by great fortune been translated into English, typed, and digitized. Mamen was nearly as detailed as McKinlay, and he provided as well numerous insights and observations about the moods, personalities, and characteristics of the participants, both on board the *Karluk* and at Shipwreck Camp and Wrangel Island. Mamen bares his soul on the page, and we learn a great deal about his and others' dreams, fears, sufferings, and triumphs.

The diary of Robert Abram Bartlett spans the time frame of September 11, 1913, to February 23, 1914, and is available through the Peary-MacMillan Arctic Museum at Bowdoin College, Brunswick, Maine. Bartlett is cryptic, terse, and factual in his diary, providing very little editorializing. By good fortune, his diary can (and should) be read alongside two of his published works: *The Last Voyage of the* Karluk: *Flagship of Vilhjalmur Stefansson's Canadian Arctic Expedition of 1913–16* and *The Log of Bob Bartlett.*

Other firsthand diaries I consulted were those of the following expedition members:

John Hadley. I obtained his diary as typed, digitized transcripts via the William Laird McKinlay Papers at the National Library of Scotland. The diary covers the dates March 12, 1914 (upon landing on Wrangel Island), to September 7, 1914 (the day of his rescue). Hadley's reports are brief and concise, but he provides detail and insight into the months stranded on Wrangel Island. He never hedges or pulls punches in his personal opinions of other members. As with some of the other diaries, his is best read as a companion to his later account, "The Story of the *Karluk*," which appeared in Stefansson's 1921 work *The Friendly Arctic.*

John Munro. Munro began his diary at Icy Spit, Wrangel Island, on March 17, 1914, recording events there up to September 1914 and the time of the rescue. The diary provides insights into the events that occurred at Rodger's Harbor on the island's southeast shore. His diary was also obtained from the National Library of Scotland.

Ernest Chafe. Not exactly a diary but a closely related overview, Ernest Chafe's unpublished manuscript "The Voyage of the *Karluk* and Its Tragic Ending" chronicles his version of the entire expedition. At eighty pages long, it is quite thorough and written in narrative form. I obtained the digitized manuscript through the Maritime Museum of British Columbia. A shorter version of Chafe's recollections was published in the *Geographical Journal* in May 1918.

Burt McConnell's diary (September 19, 1913–April 7, 1914) includes McConnell's account of his time from leaving the *Karluk* with Stefansson and Stefansson's subsequent activities and whereabouts during the winter of 1913 and spring of 1914. It proved a valuable resource.

Two of the most important works contributing to my reconstruction of the events are the aforementioned books by Bartlett and Stefansson. Bartlett's *The Last Voyage of the* Karluk is essential reading because he was the ship's captain and as such provides a unique perspective, one based on his significant previous experience as trusted captain under Robert Peary. The book offers plenty of insights into his thoughts and decisions, and revelations about his personality, but of course, one must bear in mind that he is conscious of crafting a particular self-image in his narrative, one of relative nonchalance even when in the most perilous predicaments. Most important, Bartlett offers the only existing first-person written account of the trip with Kataktovik from Wrangel Island back to Alaska via the Long Strait and overland across Siberia—a journey of more than seven hundred miles. Stefansson's *The Friendly Arctic* provides his version of events up until the time he departed the *Karluk* on September 20, 1913, and is useful in understanding, insofar as he explains them (albeit peppered with highly debatable and even dubious accounts), his subsequent decisions and movements.

A few essential sources deserve special mention. In 2000, author Jennifer Niven published *The Ice Master: The Doomed 1913 Voyage of the* Karluk. Niven's excellent book—and the heavy lifting she did with her research over twenty years ago—tackles the expedition month by month, providing a meticulous chronological time line of the expedition. Particularly useful was her exhaustive research following up the lives, whereabouts, and subsequent movements of the survivors. I am indebted to this fine scholar and writer.

It was a great stroke of luck when I stumbled upon the book *Travelling Passions: The Hidden Life of Vilhjalmur Stefansson* by Gísli Pálsson. Pálsson's book was the only work I encountered that revealed and discussed in detail the existence of Stefansson's secret family: his Inupiat wife, Pannigabluk (Fanny), and their son, Alex Stefansson. Stefansson himself never publicly (as far as I know) acknowledged them as his wife and child, and Pálsson's thorough, scholarly digging unearthed a great deal of fascinating information about them and about what happened to them during the remainder of their lives after Stefansson left the Arctic.

Undoubtedly, the most complete single volume of research yet published on the subject is Stuart Jenness's *Stefansson, Dr. Anderson and the Canadian Arctic Expedition 1913–1918: A Story of Exploration, Science and*

Sovereignty. Stuart Jenness, a Canadian geologist, is the son of Diamond Jenness, a member of the Canadian Arctic Expedition's Southern Party and one of the men who left the *Karluk* with Stefansson. Stuart Jenness was deeply and personally connected to the story, and he also became friends with William McKinlay, who encouraged Jenness to write his work "to set the record straight." Jenness's scholarly work is the most complete book in existence in terms of recording the entire Canadian Arctic Expedition from its origins to its end, and as such provides the most accurate historical account of the contributions of the Southern Party and of Stefansson's movements after departing the *Karluk*. Stuart Jenness's decades of research were instrumental in my understanding of the expedition, its objectives, and its outcomes.

Finally, I gained much valuable insight into Captain Bob Bartlett through the book *Unchained Man: The Arctic Life and Times of Robert Abram Bartlett* by Maura Hanrahan. Hanrahan, an associate professor at the University of Lethbridge in Alberta, Canada, does a splendid job of placing Bartlett in the context of his times and demythologizing him to better understand him today. Hanrahan points out quite rightly that Bartlett was part of an ongoing process of "heroic masculine image-making," which is true and of which, I must admit, I am also a perpetrator. Hanrahan also provides lesser-known facts about Bartlett's life in the decades after his return from the expedition. Most perceptive and fascinating are Hanrahan's analysis of the lifesaving importance of the Indigenous peoples to the expedition—particularly Kataktovik, Kiruk (Auntie), and Kuraluk—but also of the vital role Indigenous people played in Arctic exploration generally, an often unsung and unreported role that should not be overlooked. In *Empire of Ice and Stone*, I have certainly endeavored to highlight their crucial, often lifesaving contributions as well.

For those who enjoy slogging through exhaustive governmental reports and expedition journals (as, I do), the warehouses for such materials are the Reports of the Canadian Arctic Expedition, 1913–18, which include those of both the Northern and Southern Parties, now housed in the Library and Archives Canada in Ottawa.

The bibliography that follows offers more detail as regards these works and represents much of the other material I consulted and sourced while writing *Empire of Ice and Stone*. There should be something intriguing for either the Arctic aficionado or the armchair explorer.

DOCUMENT COLLECTIONS AND SELECTED BIBLIOGRAPHY

DOCUMENT COLLECTIONS

Explorers Club, New York

Canadian Museum of History, Gatineau, Quebec

    Canadian Arctic Expedition

Canadian Museum of Nature

George J. Mitchell Department of Special Collections and Archives, Bowdoin College Library, Brunswick, Maine

    Robert Abram Bartlett Papers

Geological Survey of Canada, Ottawa

Library and Archives Canada, Ottawa

    Canadian Arctic Expedition—Stefansson Arctic Expedition

Library of Congress, Washington, DC

    Canadian Arctic Expedition

Maritime Museum of British Columbia, Victoria, British Columbia

National Library of Scotland, Edinburgh, Scotland

    William Laird McKinlay Papers

    Peary-Macmillan Arctic Museum and Arctic Studies Center, Brunswick, Maine

Rauner Special Collections, Dartmouth College Library, Hanover, New Hampshire

    The Stefansson Collection on Polar Exploration, Robert Abram Bartlett Papers

    Reports of the Canadian Arctic Expedition, 1913–1918

HISTORICAL NEWSPAPER RESOURCES

America's Historical Newspapers. Readex: A Division of NewsBank. https://www
.readex.com/products/americas-historical-newspapers

California Digital Newspaper Collection. https://cdnc.ucr.edu

TimesMachine. *The New York Times.* https://timesmachine.nytimes.com/browser

Washington State Library and Archives ILLiad/Interlibrary Loans

BOOKS AND OFFICIAL REPORTS

Alexander, Caroline. *The* Endurance: *Shackleton's Legendary Antarctic Expedition.* New York: Knopf, 1998.

Amundsen, Roald. *My Life as an Explorer.* Garden City, NY: Doubleday, 1927.

———. *The Northwest Passage: Being the Record of a Voyage of Exploration of the Ship "Gjøa," 1903–1907.* New York: E. P. Dutton, 1908.

———. *The South Pole: An Account of the Norwegian Antarctic Expedition in the "Fram," 1910–1912.* Translated by A. G. Chater. 2 vols. London: John Murray, 1912.

Ashlee, Jette Elsebeth. *An Arctic Epic of Family and Fortune: The Theories of Vilhjalmur Stefansson and Their Influence in Practice on Storker Storkerson and His Family.* Philadelphia: self-published, Xlibris, 2008.

Astrup, Eivind. *With Peary Near the Pole.* Translated by H. J. Bull. London: C. Arthur Pearson, 1898.

Bartlett, Robert A., and Ralph T. Hale. *The Last Voyage of the* Karluk: *Flagship of Vilhjalmur Stefansson's Canadian Arctic Expedition of 1913–16.* Boston: Small, Maynard, 1916.

Bartlett, Robert A. *The Log of Bob Bartlett: The True Story of Forty Years of Seafaring and Exploration.* New York: G. P. Putnam's Sons, 1928.

Beatie, Owen, and John Geiger. *Frozen in Time: The Fate of the Franklin Expedition.* New York: MJF Books, 2004.

Bown, Stephen R. *The Company: The Rise and Fall of the Hudson's Bay Empire.* Toronto: Doubleday Canada, 2020.

———. *Island of the Blue Foxes: Disaster and Triumph on the World's Greatest Scientific Expedition.* New York: Da Capo, 2017.

———. *The Last Viking: The Life of Roald Amundsen.* New York: Da Capo, 2012.

Breton, Pierre. *The Arctic Grail: The Quest for the Northwest Passage and the North Pole, 1818–1909.* New York: Viking, 1988.

Brower, Charles. *Fifty Years Below Zero: A Lifetime of Adventure in the Far North.* Anchorage: University of Alaska Press, 1994.

Canada. Parliament. Sessional Papers, 1920. Paper no. 1. *Report of the Auditor General for the Year Ended March 31, 1919.* Ottawa: King's Printer, 1920.

Cross, L. D. *The Luck of the* Karluk: *Shipwrecked in the Arctic.* Victoria, BC: Heritage House, 2015.

Diubaldo, Richard J. *Stefansson and the Canadian Arctic.* Montreal: McGill-Queen's University Press, 1978.

Dolan, Erik Jay. *Leviathan: The History of Whaling in America.* New York: W. W. Norton, 2007.

Gertner, Jon. *The Ice at the End of the World: An Epic Journey into Greenland's Buried Past and Our Perilous Future.* New York: Random House, 2019.

Green, Fitzhugh. *Bob Bartlett: Master Mariner.* New York: G. P. Putnam's Sons, 1929.

Feeney, Robert F. *Polar Journeys: The Role of Food and Nutrition in Early Exploration.* Fairbanks: University of Alaska Press, 1997.

Fleming, Fergus. *Ninety Degrees North: The Quest for the North Pole.* London: Grove, 2001.

Francis, D. *Discovery of the North: The Exploration of Canada's Arctic.* Edmonton, AB: Hurtig Publishers, 1986.

Hanson, Earl Parker. *Stefansson, Prophet of the North.* New York: Harper & Brothers, 1941.

Henderson, Bruce. *True North: Peary, Cook, and the Race to the Pole.* New York: W. W. Norton, 2005.

Henson, Matthew. *A Journey for the Ages: Matthew Henson and Robert Peary's Historic North Pole Expedition.* New York: Skyhorse, 2016.

Herbert, Wally. *Noose of Laurels: The Race to the North Pole.* New York: Macmillan, 1989.

Herman, Arthur. *The Viking Heart: How Scandinavians Conquered the World.* New York: Mariner Books, 2021.

Hunt, William. *Stef: A Biography of Vilhjalmur Stefansson, Canadian Explorer.* Vancouver: University of British Columbia Press, 1986.

Jenness, Stuart E. *The Making of an Explorer: George Hubert Wilkins and the Canadian Arctic Expedition, 1913–1916.* Montreal: McGill-Queen's University Press, 2004.

———. *Stefansson, Dr. Anderson and the Canadian Arctic Expedition, 1913–1918: A Story of Exploration, Science and Sovereignty.* Quebec: CMCC, 2011.

Johnson, Charles W. *Ice Ship. The Epic Voyages of the Polar Adventurer* Fram. New York: ForeEdge, 2014.

Jones, H. G. "Christian Klengenberg and the Opening of Trade with the Copper Inuit." *Etudes/Inuit/Studies* 20, no. 2 (1996): 101–8, Association Inuksiutiit Katimajiit.

Jones, Huw-Lewis. *Imagining the Arctic: Heroism, Spectacle and Polar Exploration.* London: I. B. Tauris, 2017.

Kaplan, Susan, and Genivieve LeMoine. *Peary's Arctic Quest: Untold Stories from Robert E. Peary's North Pole Expeditions.* Maine: Down East Books, 2019.

Lansing, Alfred. *Endurance: Shackleton's Incredible Voyage.* New York: Basic Books, 2014.

Larson, Edward J. *To the Edges of the Earth: 1909, the Race for the Poles, and the Climax of the Age of Exploration.* New York: William Morrow, 2018.

Levy, Buddy. *Labyrinth of Ice: The Triumphant and Tragic Greely Polar Expedition.* New York: St. Martin's, 2019.

Lopez, Barry. *Arctic Dreams: Imagination and Desire in a Northern Landscape.* New York: Bantam, 1986.

MacFarlane, Barney. "The Scot Who Was Left Out in the Cold." *Scottish Field* (March 6, 2020).

McCurdy, H. W. *Marine History of the Pacific Northwest.* Seattle: Superior, 1966.

McGoogan, Ken. *Dead Reckoning: The Untold Story of the Northwest Passage.* Canada: Patrick Crean Editions, 2017.

Fatal Passage: The Story of John Rae, the Arctic Hero Time Forgot. New York: Carroll & Graf, 2002.

McGuire, Ian. *The North Water.* New York: Henry Holt, 2016.

McKinlay, William Laird. *The Last Voyage of the* Karluk. New York: St. Martin's Griffin, 1999.

Muir, John. *The Cruise of the* Corwin: *Journal of the Arctic Expedition in Search of De Long and the* Jeannette. New York: Houghton Mifflin, 2000.

Nansen, Fridtjof. *The First Crossing of Greenland.* Edinburgh: Birlinn, 2002.

———. *Farthest North: The Epic Adventure of a Visionary Explorer.* New York: Skyhorse, 2008.

Neil, Christopher. *Unikkaaqtauat: An Introduction to Myths and Legends.* Canada: Inhabit Media, 2011.

Niven, Jennifer. *Ada Blackjack: A True Story of Survival in the Arctic.* New York: Hyperion, 2003.

———. *The Ice Master: The Doomed 1913 Voyage of the* Karluk. New York: Hyperion, 2000.

Peary, Robert E. *Secrets of Polar Travel.* New York: Century, 1917.

———. *The North Pole.* New York: Frederick A. Stokes, 1910.

Pálsson, Gísli. *Travelling Passions: The Hidden Life of Vilhjalmur Stefansson.* Translated by Keneva Kunz. Hanover: Dartmouth College Press, 2005.

Pitzer, Andrea. *Icebound: Shipwrecked at the Edge of the World.* New York: Scribner, 2021.

Philbrick, Nathaniel. *Sea of Glory: America's Voyage of Discovery, The U.S. Exploring Expedition, 1838–1842.* New York: Viking, 2003.

Putnam, George Palmer. *Mariner of the North: The Life of Captain Bob Bartlett.* New York: Duell, Sloan & Pearce, 1947.

Roberts, David. *Alone on the Ice: The Greatest Survival Story in the History of Exploration.* New York: W. W. Norton, 2013.

Rytkheu, Yuri. *A Dream in Polar Fog.* Translated by Ilona Yazhbin Chavasse. Brooklyn: Archipelago Books, 2005.

Sancton, Julian. *Madhouse at the End of the Earth: The* Belgica's *Journey into the Dark Antarctic Night.* New York: Crown, 2021.

Sarnoff, Paul. *Ice Pilot Bob Bartlett.* New York: Julian Messner, 1966.

Sides, Hampton. *In the Kingdom of Ice: The Grand and Terrible Polar Voyage of the USS* Jeannette. New York: Anchor, 2015.

Steckley, John. *White Lies About the Inuit*. Toronto: University of Toronto Press, 2007.

Stefansson, Vilhjalmur. *My Life with the Eskimo*. New York: Macmillan, 1913.

———. *The Friendly Arctic*. New York: Macmillan, 1921.

———. *Hunters of the Great North*. New York. Harcourt Brace, 1922.

Streever, Bill. *Cold: Adventures in the World's Frozen Places*. New York: Little, Brown, 2009.

Swenson, Olaf. *Northwest of the World: Forty Years Trading and Hunting in Northern Siberia*. New York: Dodd, Mead, 1944.

Walters, Eric. *Trapped in Ice*. New York: Penguin, 1997.

Watson, Paul. *Ice Ghosts: The Epic Hunt for the Lost Franklin Expedition*. New York: W. W. Norton, 2017.

Webb, Melody. *Chronicles of a Cold, Cold War: The Paperwork Battle for Wrangel Island*. Occasional Paper no. 28. Anthropology and Historic Preservation, Cooperative Park Studies Unit. Fairbanks: University of Alaska, 1981.

Williams, Glyn. *Arctic Labyrinth: The Quest for the Northwest Passage*. Berkeley: University of California Press, 2009.

ARTICLES

American Geographical Society. "Loss of the *Karluk* and Escape of the Expedition to Wrangell Island." *Bulletin of the American Geographical Society* 46, no. 7 (1914): 520–23.

Anichtchenko, Evgenia. "Open Skin Boats of the Aleutians, Kodiak Island, and Prince William Sound." *Études/Inuit/Studies* 36, no. 1 (2012): 157–81.

Bartlett, Robert. "Peary's Extended Exploration of Arctic Lands Culminating in the Attainment of the North Pole." *Proceedings of the American Philosophical Society*, 82, no. 5 (June 29, 1940): 935–47.

Beach, Stanley Yale. "A Canadian Arctic Expedition." *Scientific American* 108, no. 11 (March 15, 1913): 240.

Cavell, Janice. "Vilhjalmur Stefansson, Robert Bartlett, and the *Karluk* Disaster: A Reassessment." *Journal of the Hakluyt Society* (April 2018): 1–22.

Chafe, Ernest F. "The Voyage of the *Karluk* and Its Tragic Ending." *Geographical Journal* 51, no. 5 (May 1918): 307–16.

Dawson, Peter C. "Seeing Like an Inuit Family: The Relationship Between House Form and Culture in Northern Canada." *Études/Inuit/Studies* 30, no. 2 (2006): 113–35.

Diubaldo, Richard J. "Wrangling Over Wrangel Island." *Canadian Historical Review* 48, no. 3 (September 1967): 201–26.

Giddings, Jr., J. L. "Driftwood and Problems of Arctic Sea Currents." *Proceedings of the American Philosophical Society* 96, no. 2 (April 21, 1952): 129–42.

Harper, Kenn. "Ruth Makpii Ipalook: 1911–2008." *Nunatsiaq News* (July 18, 2008).

Holme, John G. "Stefansson in the Arctic." *Scientific American* 120, no. 23 (June 7, 1919): 603, 615–16.

Humble, Kate. "*Karluk*: Victoria's Ill-Fated Arctic Expedition." *Victoria News* (February 27, 2015).

Jenness, Diamond. "Origin of the Copper Eskimos and Their Copper Culture." *Geographical Review* 13, no. 4 (October 1923): 540–51.

———. "The 'Blond' Eskimos." *American Anthropologist* 23, no. 3 (July–September 1921): 257–267.

Levere, Trevor H. "Vilhjalmur Stefansson, the Continental Shelf, and a New Arctic Continent." *The British Journal for the History of Science* 21 (1988): 233–47.

"Loss of the *Karluk* and Escape of the Expedition to Wrangell Island." *Bulletin of the American Geographical Society*. Vol. 46, No 7 (1914): 520-523.

McConnell, Burt. "The Rescue of the *Karluk* Survivors." *Harper's Magazine* (February 1915): 349–60.

Noice, H. H. "Further Discussion of the 'Blond' Eskimo." *American Anthropologist* 24, no. 2 (April–June, 1922): 228–32.

Philonoë. "At Large and At Small: The Arctic Hedonist." *The American Scholar* 72, no. 1 (Winter 2003): 7–13.

Richling, Barnett. "Henri Beuchat, 1878–1914." *Arctic* 66, no. 1 (March 2013): 117–19.

Siber, Kate. "The Inuit Woman Who Survived the Arctic Alone." *Outside*, January 18, 2018.

Sides, Hampton. "Tracing the Steps of Lost Explorers in Miserable, Beautiful Siberia." *Outside*, July 8, 2014.

Solomon, Susan. "To the Ends of the Earth: The Heroic Age of Polar Exploration." *Scientific American*, January 17, 2013.

Spinden, Herbert J. "Stefansson's New Found Land." *Scientific American* 113, no. 14 (October 2, 1915): 289, 306–7.

Stefansson, Vilhjalmur. "Letter from Mr. Stefansson." *Geographical Journal* 52, no. 4 (October 1918): 248–55.

———. "Living Off the Country as a Method of Arctic Exploration." *Geographical Review* 7, no. 5 (May 1919): 291–310.

———. "Stefansson's Expedition." *Bulletin of the American Geographical Society* 46, no. 3 (1914): 184–91.

———. "The Canadian Arctic Expedition." *Geographical Journal* 42, no. 1 (July 1913): 49–53.

Stewart, Hugh. "Robert Bartlett: 1875–1946." *Arctic* 39, no. 2 (June 1986): 188–89.

Webb, Melody. "Arctic Saga: Vilhjalmur Stefansson's Attempt to Colonize Wrangel Island." *Pacific Historical Review* 61, no. 2 (May 1992): 215–39.

White, Gavin. "Obituary: William Laird McKinlay, 1889–1983." *Arctic* 36, no. 3 (September 1983): 309–10.

Williamson, Robert. "The Cry of the Owl." *Daily Colonist* (March 8, 1959): 5.

"Wrangel Island." *Geographical Journal* 62, no. 6 (December 1923).

Znamenski, Andrei A. "Vague Sense of Belonging to the Russian Empire: The Reindeer Chukchi's Status in Nineteenth Century Northeastern Siberia." *Arctic Anthropology* 36, no. 1/2 (1999): 19–36

FILMS

Aaron, Wil and Deb Proc, dirs. *Icebound: The Final Voyage of the* Karluk (2004).

Canadian Museum of Civilization. *Expedition: Arctic—Geographic Discoveries* (2011).

Higgins, Jenny, dir. *Bob Bartlett: Arctic Adventurer*. Newfoundland and Labrador Heritage Website, 2017.

Radford, Tom, and Peter Raymont, dirs. *Arctic Dreamer: The Lonely Quest of Vilhjalmur Stefansson*. Toronto: National Film Board of Canada, White Pine Pictures, 2003.

WEB RESOURCES

Alaska Native Language Center. https://www.uaf.edu/anlc/languages/inupiaq.php.

Canadian Museum of History. "Northern People, Northern Knowledge: The Story of the Canadian Arctic Expedition, 1913–1918." https://www.historymuseum.ca/cmc/exhibitions/hist/cae/indexe.html.

Everyculture.com "Chukchi," Countries and Their Cultures. https://www.everyculture.com/wc/Norway-to-Russia/Chukchi.html.

MOSAiC: The Largest Polar Expedition in History. https://mosaic-expedition.org.

Heritage: Newfoundland and Labrador. https://www.heritage.nf.ca.

Maritime Museum of British Columbia. https://mmbc.bc.ca.

National Snow and Ice Data Center: Arctic Phenomena. https://nsidc.org/cryosphere/arctic-meteorology/phenomena.html.

Newfoundland/Labrador, Canada. Brigus and Cupids. https://www.newfoundlandlabrador.com/top-destinations/brigus-and-cupids.

The Newfoundland and Labrador Heritage Website. https://www.heritage.nf.ca.

Siberian Wonders! "The Chukchi People of the Chukchi Sea" (web blog), May 2011, http://siberianwonders.com/2011/05/chukchi-people-chukchi-sea-chukotka-nation-of-reindeer-herders-whale-hunters-chukotka-far-east-russia/.

INDEX